W9-AEY-901

2 PETER, JUDE

VOLUME 37C

THE ANCHOR BIBLE is a fresh approach to the world's greatest classic. Its object is to make the Bible accessible to the modern reader; its method is to arrive at the meaning of biblical literature through exact translation and extended exposition, and to reconstruct the ancient setting of the biblical story, as well as the circumstances of its transcription and the characteristics of its transcribers.

THE ANCHOR BIBLE is a project of international and interfaith scope. Protestant, Catholic, and Jewish scholars from many countries contribute individual volumes. The project is not sponsored by any ecclesiastical organization and is not intended to reflect any particular theological doctrine. Prepared under our joint supervision, THE ANCHOR BIBLE is an effort to make available all the significant historical and linguistic knowledge which bears on the interpretation of the biblical record.

THE ANCHOR BIBLE is aimed at the general reader with no special formal training in biblical studies; yet, it is written with the most exacting standards of scholarship, reflecting the highest technical accomplishment.

This project marks the beginning of a new era of cooperation among scholars in biblical research, thus forming a common body of knowledge to be shared by all.

William Foxwell Albright
David Noel Freedman
GENERAL EDITORS

THE ANCHOR BIBLE

2 PETER, JUDE

♦

A New Translation
with
Introduction and Commentary

JEROME H. NEYREY

VOLUME 37 C

THE ANCHOR BIBLE
Doubleday
New York London Toronto Sydney Auckland

THE ANCHOR BIBLE
PUBLISHED BY DOUBLEDAY
a division of Bantam Doubleday Dell Publishing Group, Inc.
1540 Broadway, New York, New York 10036.

Library of Congress Cataloging-in-Publication Data

Bible. N.T. Peter, 2nd. English. Neyrey. 1993.
2 Peter, Jude : a new translation with introduction and commentary / Jerome H. Neyrey.
p. cm.—(The Anchor Bible ; 37C)
Includes bibliographical references and indexes.
1. Bible. N.T. Peter, 2nd—Commentaries. 2. Bible. N.T. Jude—Commentaries. I. Neyrey, Jerome H., 1940– . II. Bible. N.T. Jude. English. Neyrey. 1993. III. Title. IV. Title: 2nd Peter, Jude. V. Series: Bible. English. Anchor Bible. 1964 ; v. 37C.
BS192.2.A1 1964.G3 vol. 37C
[BS2793]
220.7'7 s—dc20
[227'.93077] 92-21142
CIP

ISBN 0-385-41362-9

Printed in the United States of America
November 1993

First Edition

10 9 8 7 6 5 4 3 2 1

Contents

◆

ABBREVIATIONS

◆

AnB	Anchor Bible
AnBib	Analecta Biblica
ANRW	*Aufstieg und Niedergang der Römischen Welt*
APOT	R. H. Charles, *The Apocrypha and Pseudepigrapha of the Old Testament*
AUSS	*Andrews University Seminary Studies*
BAG	Walter Bauer, W. F. Arndt, F. W. Gingrich, *Greek-English Lexicon of the New Testament*, 2d ed., Chicago: University of Chicago Press, 1979
BDF	F. Blass, A. Debrunner, and R. W. Funk, *Greek Grammar of the New Testament*
BHT	Beiträge zur historischen Theologie
Bib	*Biblica*
BibT	*The Bible Today*
BSac	*Bibliotheca Sacra*
BSOAS	*Bulletin of the School of Oriental and African Studies*
BTB	*Biblical Theology Bulletin*
BVC	*Bible et vie chrétienne*
BZ	*Biblische Zeitschrift*
BZNW	*Beihefte zur die Zeitschrift für neutestamentliche Wissenschaft*
CBQ	*Catholic Biblical Quarterly*
ConBNT	Coniectanea biblica, New Testament
CQ	*Classical Quarterly*
CTJ	*Calvin Theological Journal*
EBib	Etudes biblique
EvQ	*Evangelical Quarterly*
Exp	*Expositor*
ExpT	*Expository Times*
FRLANT	Forschungen zur Religion und Literatur des Alten und Neuen Testaments
GCS	Griechische christliche Schriftsteller

GRBS	*Greek, Roman and Byzantine Studies*
HKNT	Handkommentar zum Neuen Testament
HNT	Handbuch zum Neuen Testament
HR	*History of Religion*
HTKNT	Herders theologischer Kommentar zum Neuen Testament
HTR	*Harvard Theological Review*
HUCA	*Hebrew Union College Annual*
IDB	G. A. Buttrick (ed.), *Interpreters Dictionary of the Bible*
IDBSup	Supplementary volume to *IDB*
IESS	*International Encyclopedia of the Social Sciences*
JBL	*Journal of Biblical Literature*
J.E.	*Jewish Encyclopedia*
JETS	*Journal of the Evangelical Theological Society*
JSJ	*Journal for the Study of Judaism*
JSNT	*Journal for the Study of the New Testament*
JTS	*Journal of Theological Studies*
LSJ	Henry Liddell, Robert Scott, and Henry Jones, A *Greek-English Lexicon*
MeyerK	H. A. W. Meyer, Kritisch-exegetischer Kommentar über das Neue Testament
M-M	James Moulton and George Milligan, *The Vocabulary of the Greek Testament*
MNTC	Moffatt New Testament Commentary
MSGVK	Mitteilungen der schlesischen Gesellschaft für Volkskunde
NCB	New Century Bible
NedTTs	*Nederlands theologisch Tijdschrift*
Neot	*Neotestamentica*
NJBC	*The New Jerome Biblical Commentary*
NorTT	*Norsk Teologisk Tidsskrift*
NovT	*Novum Testamentum*
NovTSup	Novum Testamentum, Supplements
NT Apoc.	Edgar Hennecke and Wilhelm Schneemelcher, *New Testament Apocrypha*
NTD	Das Neue Testament Deutsch
NTS	*New Testament Studies*
OTP	James H. Charlesworth (ed.), *The Old Testament Pseudepigrapha*
RAC	*Reallexikon für Antike und Christentum*
RB	*Revue Biblique*
REJ	*Revue des études juives*
ResQ	*Restoration Quarterly*
RHR	*Revue de l'histoire des religions*

RivB	*Rivista Biblica*
RNT	Regensburger Neues Testament
RSR	*Recherches de science religieuse*
RSRev	*Religious Studies Review*
RTP	*Revue de Théologie et Philosophie*
SBLASP	*Society of Biblical Literature Abstracts and Seminar Papers*
SBLDS	Society of Biblical Literature Dissertation Series
SBLSBS	Society of Biblical Literature Sources for Biblical Study
SBLSCS	Society of Biblical Literature Septuagint and Cognate Studies
SC	Sources chrétiennes
Scr	*Scripture*
SNTSMS	Society for New Testament Studies Monograph Series
SPB	Studia postbiblica
ST	*Studia Theologica*
Str-B	H. Strack and P. Billerbeck, *Kommentar zum Neuen Testament*
SVF	*Stoicorum Veterum Fragmenta*
TAPA	*Transactions and Proceedings of the American Philological Association*
TDNT	*Theological Dictionary of the New Testament*
THKNT	Theologischer Handkommentar zum Neuen Testament
TLZ	*Theologische Literaturzeitung*
TQ	*Theologische Quartalschrift*
TRu	*Theologische Rundschau*
TS	*Theological Studies*
TynB	*Tyndale Bulletin*
TZ	*Theologische Zeitschrift*
VC	*Virgiliae christianae*
VT	*Vetus Testamentum*
WTJ	*Westminster Theological Journal*
WUNT	Wissenschaftliche Untersuchungen zum Neuen Testament
ZNW	*Zeitschrift für die Neutestamentliche Wissenschaft*
ZTK	*Zeitschrift für Theologie und Kirche*

2 PETER, JUDE

General Introduction

♦

A. Perspective of This Commentary

Every generation sees the publication of fresh commentary series which update conventional wisdom or advance the prevailing scholarly perspectives. In recent years this has meant a rich offering of new volumes on Jude and 2 Peter, some of which are outstanding and distinguished works (e.g., J. N. D. Kelly, *The Epistles of Peter and of Jude* [London: Adam and Charles Black, 1969]; Richard Bauckham, *Jude, 2 Peter* [Waco, TX: Word Books, 1983]). All of these recent volumes are written from the prevailing scholarly approach, the historical-critical method, which attempts to locate and describe a specific document in terms of comparison with other documents. In this perspective, texts are interpreted by noting the parallels in language or perspective with other known writings. Thus shades of meaning, literary forms, topoi, and the like can be delineated. The precise place of a given document in the history of early Christianity is carefully examined and established. But in time, only so many parallels can be noted, most of which have previously been cited in other commentaries. Bauckham's recent commentary on Jude and 2 Peter has greatly illumined these documents with a generous display of comparable materials.

Yet commentaries continue to be written because new scholars see different things in the old documents and allege new comparisons. The perspective of this commentary differs from previous ones in several distinctive ways. From research on the document, I conclude that the author of 2 Peter, for example, can be shown to engage his opponents on a quite specific issue, the justification of God's judgment, which we will call "theodicy" in the course of the investigation. This topic was commonly discussed in antiquity, by both Greeks and Jews alike. We will show that Epicureans held a certain view about the Deity which precluded all notion of divine judgment. Their complex argument in time became reduced to a convenient topos attacking any notion of divine judgment. In response, others considered their viewpoint heretical and responded with a typical argument, which also was reduced to an apologetic topos. This new perspective on the conflict in 2 Peter will lead us to read it in a fresh light; it will warrant evaluation according to a different set of comparative materials both from the Greco-Roman world and from Jewish sources.

In recent years, NT scholarship has been vitalized by a new interest in the literary techniques of writing, reading, and rhetoric (e.g., D. F. Watson, *Invention, Arrangement and Style* [SBLDS 104. Atlanta: Scholars Press, 1988]). Considerable new light is shed on Jude and 2 Peter when one notes the many literary forms that comprise them or when one studies the shape of the rhetorical argument.

This commentary respects the traditional wisdom on 2 Peter, although it will argue that new historical parallels in the area of arguments about "theodicy" should shape our perception of the background of the conflict in the document. It will also give considerable attention to literary issues: epistolography, form criticism, literary analysis, and rhetoric.

B. A New Scholarly Perspective

But this commentary employs a new and perhaps unfamiliar method for reading these documents, namely, the use of the social sciences for interpretation of ancient documents. In the past decades many scholars have increasingly become interested in the social description of the early Christians, mainly a historical quest. Still other scholars have attempted to develop native reading scenarios to facilitate people from a modern, postindustrial, and strictly urban culture being able to grasp the point of view and social dynamics of an ancient, agrarian, and largely peasant culture. The reader's shift from modernity to antiquity is much more than a bridge of time. Compared to the cultural and social patterns of the ancient people described in biblical texts, those of typical American and European readers have radically changed. This means that modern readers would normally have acute difficulty in understanding the worldview, social dynamics, and cultural perspective of authors writing in a totally different and strange culture. There ought to be a culture shock that all visitors receive who visit the Middle East for the first time. Dorothy correctly tells Toto that they are no longer in Kansas.

For example, it is never enough for modern interpreters to translate terms like "father," "mother," and "family" from biblical texts into English words and think that they understand what these terms meant to the ancient authors. The modern nuclear family and its changing roles of male and female parents are not at all what were spoken about when ancient authors described a different kind of family, with different understandings of what were the appropriate rights and duties of male and female parents. To know that we need to know more about the gender division of society prevalent in antiquity, the values that motivated people then (honor and shame), the importance of the institution of kinship, and the economic life of a social group which did not work in factories, punch time clocks, or work in cities at all. All of this is to say that the social sciences can offer fresh and compelling reading scenarios about the social world of the ancient authors which greatly complement standard exegesis. These perspectives are essential to an adequate interpretation of a document, not just its historical location or description.

This commentary uses a specific number of social science models or perspectives to interpret Jude and 2 Peter. We do not consider these perspectives intrusive into the interpretative process, but rather friendly and compatible templates which help us to see what would otherwise escape notice. The perspectives developed in this volume, moreover, are solidly rooted in cross-cultural anthropology as well as more historically oriented studies of Greek, Roman, and Jewish literatures. In other words, they have been tested and refined so that they are suitable lenses for perceiving a social and cultural world quite different from our own.

Some attempt will be made both in the introductions to Jude and 2 Peter and in the various notes to indicate more about how the ancients viewed the world differently from us. For example, the prevailing cultural importance given to the past and tradition can profitably be explained by recourse to models for studying just such variations in cultural values.

Five distinctive social science models are presented in this introduction to give readers some familiarity with them before they appear in the commentary part of this volume. The following are sketches of five cultural perspectives needed for appreciating the symbolic and social world of a people not only separated from us by two thousand years but also by a radically different culture. They are offered as useful and necessary lenses through which to see what would not be perceived without special cultural sensitivity.

C. Honor (and Shame): Pivotal Values

"A prophet has no honor in his own country" (John 4:44). Paul describes how even Christians seek "glory and honor and immortality" (Rom 2:7), which quest God is quick to reward with "glory and honor and peace" (Rom 2:10). Males in the eastern Mediterranean constantly attended to their own honor and that of their village or group. They were highly sensitive to their own reputation, worth, fame, respect, and status as well as that of those around them. Indeed, "honor" might be considered the pivotal value of the Mediterranean world

(Malina, *New Testament World*, 25–27). How important it is to be thought well of by one's neighbors (1 Tim 3:7).

Honor is either ascribed to individuals or achieved by them. Ascribed honor is like inherited wealth: one has it by birth or adoption from a person with the power and status to bestow it. Primarily, honor derives from one's clan, family, and father. Sons have the same social position as their fathers, whether senators or fishermen or artisans ("All should honor the Son even as they honor the Father," John 5:23). Honor accrues to one's family name, and all family members share in it when it is publicly acknowledged and respected. Some individuals may have honor assigned to them by a sovereign: Caesar honored Pontius Pilate by ascribing to him the status of governor of Judea; Jesus honored Peter by appointing him an apostle, even the rock of his church (Matt 16:18). God ascribed honor to Jesus when God raised him from his shameful death, seated him at his right hand, and made him Lord (Acts 2:34–36). Ascribed honor, especially that which comes with blood and family, is a group matter; when one member is honored, all are honored; but when one is shamed, the group shares this loss.

Acquired honor comes to an individual in virtue of some achievement or benefaction. The centurion who built the synagogue in a Galilean village is acclaimed "worthy!" by the locals (Luke 7:4–5). Similarly, warriors such as David acquire honor by slaying their Goliaths; athletes and poets win laurels and so honor for success in contests (2 Tim 4:7–8). The elites especially acquire honor by activities appropriate to their social status.

F. W. Danker collected numerous public inscriptions of honor paid to benefactors (*Benefactor* [Clayton Publishing House, 1982]). The following example illustrates many of the aspects of ascribed and achieved honor just described. A certain Quintus Python enjoys ascribed honor from the Roman emperor (*flamen* or priest, superintendent, envoy, etc.), but also achieved honor from his impressive benefaction to his native city. He is honored by having this inscription engraved in the city's center for all to read, and so he enjoys a most favorable reputation and is publicly praised by all.

> In honor of their benefactor, Quintus Popillius Python, flamen of the Caesars for life, and superintendent of the contests of the Macedonian League; who served as envoy of his native city Beroia to God Nerva and succeeded in securing for it the sole right to be entitled "Keeper of the Temple of the Caesars," along with the rank of metropolis; who during his office as flamen paid the poll tax for the entire province, constructed roads at his own expense, announced and sponsored theatrical and athletic contests that ranked with the Actian, with a talent in prize money, and which included combats of all kinds of local and foreign wild animals, as well as gladiatorial combats; who sold grain below cost

> and brought down the price in times of need; who, during his entire term as flamen, at every public assembly treated the province to distributions; who publicly offered his generous services to those in charge of gymnastic training and privately proved himself a kindly citizen—in honor of him this dedication was made by the Tribe of Peukaste [Danker, *Benefactor*, 75–76].

The vast majority of the nonelites, however, seem to have competed with their social peers in villages and cities for scraps of honor and respect in the endless challenge-riposte games that characterize their lives (Malina and Neyrey, "Honor and Shame in Luke-Acts," 49–52). It is part of the peasant perception of the ancients that all things existed in limited supply ("limited good"). There was only so much land, so much water, so much wealth, even a limited amount of honor. If someone is perceived as gaining wealth or honor, this means that someone is losing (G. M. Foster, "The Image of Limited Good," *Peasant Society: A Reader* [J. Potter, M. Diaz, G. Foster, eds.; Boston: Little, Brown, and Co., 1967], 300–23). Hence, people are acutely sensitive to any claim to precedence by another or to any challenge, either to their own reputation and honor or to that of their patron or family. Males are required to be highly public figures in village marketplaces and city squares; they engage in face-to-face social interaction constantly. They are, then, highly sensitive to whether they are receiving the respect due them or whether someone else is claiming more than he should. If one gains, someone else must necessarily lose. Their life, then, is highly agonistic and is played out in a "zero sum" game of competition for scarce resources.

The typical form of the honor-shame game contains four elements: (1) claim to honor or precedence, (2) challenge, (3) riposte to challenge, and (4) public verdict. Jesus' actions in the marketplaces and synagogues of Galilee repeatedly illustrate the full nature of this pattern. He does an action or says a word which presumes a certain power or status; thus he makes a *claim*. Because of the public nature of his actions, others consider his claims excessive or wrong: they *challenge* his claims with hard questions or murmuring or accusations. Once challenged, Jesus must respond or lose face. Hence, he always gives a strong *riposte* to those who challenge him. Finally, the crowds who witness the entire exchange voice their *verdict* about the contest, indicating who was shamed and who achieved honor. A classic example of this challenge-riposte contest may be found in Luke 13:10–17. Jesus *claims* authority and power by his healing of the infirm woman (13:12–13). His claim is immediately *challenged* by those whose reputation will diminish by the new honor garnered by this new prophet. The ruler of the synagogue becomes indignant and tarnishes the moral quality of Jesus' actions (13:14). Thus challenged, Jesus *responds* with name-calling ("Hypocrites!") and hard questions (13:15–16), silencing his critics. Since all such honor games are played in public, the crowds *determine the winner* and apportion honor and shame accordingly. "All his adversaries were put to shame" (13:17a), but Jesus himself gained honor when "the people rejoiced at the glorious things done by him" (13:17b). But the key to this interaction is the public nature of the dispute and the public acknowledgment or denial of respect. Any other claim would be "empty," "boastful," or "vainglorious," unless acknowledged.

What does honor look like? Since honor is acquired from one's clan or family, it resides in the name of the clan or father. Simon Peter, who is the son of Jonah, shares the name and trade of his father (Matt 16:17). Honor, moreover, is linked to one's birth order; first sons enjoy more status and honor in the family than other sons and certainly more than daughters (i.e., "firstborn," Exod 13:2). Individuals might symbolize their honorable status to others by the clothes they wear, the foods they consume, the animals they ride, and so forth. Kings wear crowns, but even observant Jews might claim a certain honor by wearing phylacteries, marks of their total devotion to Torah (Matt 23:5). Honor is associated with certain bodily parts. It resides primarily in the head and face; crowns are set on anointed heads and so localize honor. Some faces are so honorable that slaves or courtiers bow profoundly and avoid looking at them. Conversely, a blow to the head or face immediately bespeaks dishonor.

Honor is a precarious commodity, quickly threatened and easily lost. When a male is challenged and bested in any number of public ways, he may lose his reputation and be considered less worthy than before. He experiences "shame." He might be physically affronted (Acts 23:2), verbally abused (Matt 5:22; Luke 12:20), ignored, or in a variety of ways diminished in regard to what popularly constitutes manliness (Luke 13:17). When an elite sends emissaries to others and they are either ignored, maltreated, or shamed (Matt 21:34–37), the sender loses face and thus honor. Failure to answer difficult questions entails a certain shame. Yet since life is an endless game of seeking honor, there must needs be losers; "shame" is an ever-present reality, appearing in a variety of shapes, and greatly to be feared.

When we read documents such as Jude and 2 Peter, we must be sensitive to the pervasive presence of terms and actions that belong to the honor-shame game of social interaction being played. The letter-senders signal their honor in the way they present themselves (i.e., their status or roles) and by their family connections. They claim ascribed honor, both from God and Jesus, which should be a stable source of their authority vis-à-vis their addressees. They act as agents of very honorable persons, both God and the Lord Jesus; and so they are highly sensitive to any slight given to God or Jesus ("they deny the Master"). They constantly honor their patrons with doxologies, but more typically they remember and remind others of the respect and honor due God and Jesus. Since God and Jesus are the great benefactors of the group, failure to "remember" their words or deeds betokens shame. The two authors constantly speak of the many ways in which God and Jesus assert their honor, in particular by acting in power to judge those who disregard their laws, deny their powers, or fail to honor their patrons by exemplary behavior. The very documents are tangible examples of the letter-senders' riposte to actual or perceived challenges to the honor system of the early church. The apology for the tradition or the defense of God's judgment or the response to slurs and scoffing all should be seen in terms of a riposte to perceived shame and insult.

BIBLIOGRAPHY

Daube, David, "Disgrace," *The New Testament and Rabbinic Judaism* (New York: Arno Press, 1973), 301–24.

Fisher, N. R. E., "Hybris and Dishonour," *Greece and Rome* 23 (1976): 177–93.

Gilmore, David D., *Honor and Shame and the Unity of the Mediterranean* (American Anthropological Association special publication #22. Washington: American Anthropological Association, 1987).

Klose, F., "Altrömische Wertbegriffe (*honos* und *dignitas*)," *Neue Jahrbücher für Antike und deutsche Bildung* 1 (1938): 268–78.

Malina, Bruce J., *The New Testament World: Insights from Cultural Anthropology* (Atlanta: John Knox Press, 1981).

Malina, Bruce, and Neyrey, Jerome, "Honor and Shame in Luke-Acts: Pivotal Values of the Mediterranean World," *The World of Luke-Acts. Models for Interpretation* (Peabody, MA: Stephen Hendrickson, Inc., 1991), 25–65.

Marshall, Peter, "A Metaphor of Social Shame: *Thriambeuein* in 2 Cor. 2:14," *NT* 25 (1983): 303–17.

Moxnes, Halvor, "Honour and Righteousness in Romans," *JSNT* 32 (1988): 61–77.

Peristiani, J. G. (ed.), *Honour and Shame: The Values of Mediterranean Society* (Chicago: University of Chicago Press, 1966).

Pitt-Rivers, Julian, "Honor," *IESS* 6.503–10.

Stansbury, Harry Adams, *Corinthian Honor, Corinthian Conflict: A Social History of Early Roman Corinth and Its Pauline Community* (unpublished dissertation: University of California—Irvine, 1990).

D. Patron and Client Relationships

Gospel readers are familiar with the story of the Roman centurion who asks Jesus to cure his slave (Luke 7:1–10). He sent the village elders to Jesus to plead his cause. They acknowledge that he is "worthy" of Jesus' favor, because "he loves our nation, and he built us our synagogue" (7:5). The centurion himself confesses that he has many under his authority, and by a word he summons or dismisses them (7:8). Jesus finally cures his slave. This story is a perfect illustration of patron-client relationships, and from it we can learn quickly and clearly what these relationships are and how they work.

The centurion originally acts as the "patron" of the village: he has access to resources which he puts at the disposal of the villagers, who then become his clients. He acts as their benefactor-patron by building their synagogue; and in turn they owe him a debt of both honor and loyalty. These clients begin to pay back that debt by asking Jesus to become a patron to the centurion by curing his slave. By his cure, Jesus acts as a benefactor, and so the centurion is then in his debt and owes him honor and loyalty in turn. He partially pays that debt in the story when he praises the power of Jesus' word (7:7–8). Thus resources are exchanged when needed: the centurion builds a synagogue; Jesus cures his slave; Jesus in turn receives great public honor. In short, wealth, honor, and influence are distributed in limited ways in specific situations (B. J. Malina, *Christian Origins and Cultural Anthropology* [Atlanta: John Knox, 1986], 76–84). The centurion, who began the story as a patron to the villagers, asks to become Jesus' client. And the elders of the village, who begin the story as clients of the centurion, become mediators of patronage between Jesus and the centurion. Jesus always remains a type of patron and benefactor (Moxnes, "Patron-Client Relations," 252–53).

This specific form of social relations occurred in a wide variety of ways in diverse institutions in antiquity. But from this classic example, we try to learn more about the general dynamic of patron-client relationships.

> Patronage is a model or analytical construct which the social scientist applies in order to understand and explain a range of apparently different social relationships: father-son, God-man, saint-devotee, godfather-godchild, lord-vassal, landlord-tenant, politician-voter, professor-assistant, and so forth. All these different sets of social relationships can thus be considered from one particular point of view which may render them comprehensible [A. Blok, "Variations in Patronage," *Sociologische Gids* 16 (1969): 366].

Patron-client relationships cover a full range of exchanges from private to public life. They might describe (1) the protection, financial or legal assistance which politicians afforded their clients; (2) the enduring bonds and obligations between former slave owners and their emancipated slaves (Momigliano, "Cliens," 252); (3) the power and benefit which local elites extend to villagers; or (4) the administration of the empire by the Roman emperor (Momigliano, "Patronus," 791).

The ancient world called certain persons "benefactors" (Luke 22:25), a formal title usually reserved for elites. Records of their name and benefaction were typically inscribed in public places like the agora or temples, as in the case of Quintus Python quoted above (Danker, *Benefactor*, 30–44). Yet even when the formal title "benefactor" was not used, people who acted as "saviors" and who bestowed power or wealth or assistance would be acknowledged as patrons to those to whom such help was given (Acts 10:38). Althought "client" and "patron" are legal terms, in the public realm their harder edges were masked with more ingratiating terms such as "friend" and "savior."

What is common in all of these relationships is some sort of exchange. "Self-sufficiency" was the ideal (A. W. H. Adkins, " 'Friendship' and 'Self-Sufficiency' in Homer and Aristotle," *CQ* 13 [1963]: 30–43). Yet people always find themselves in some need; and typically, someone else has what is needed. Except in family circles where altruism is the rule, nothing is ever simply given or bestowed without some consideration of reciprocity. Thus a sort of calculus takes place. Those in need request assistance from a person able to help; but the giver will want something in exchange and the receiver will thus incur some debt. In general the benefactor patron will bestow wealth, influence, or power; and the recipient client will incur a debt of loyalty and an obligation to honor the patron publicly. To the ancients, this was a fair exchange, for honor is a commodity more precious than gold.

When we consider parts of Jude and 2 Peter in the light of patron-client relationships, we will attend first and foremost to the way God and Jesus are described in their relationships to the addressees. They may occasionally be labeled "savior," which implies a larger pattern of benefaction and patronage to the members of the churches of Jude and 2 Peter. The authors of both documents present themselves as agents of these heavenly patrons, that is, as mediators and brokers of their benefactor patrons. Thus they are the designated defenders of their patrons' claims and honor. They will tend to interpret any attack on themselves as a repudiation of their heavenly patrons, and so respond vigorously to all real or perceived slights. Finally, this model suggests that we search for what response is expected of the clients or addressees in virtue of their status as clients of such noble patrons. They are expected to reciprocate to their patrons loyalty, honor, "faith," "acknowledgment," and the like (Mott, "The Power of Giving and Receiving," 63–64).

BIBLIOGRAPHY

Boissevain, Jeremy, *Friends of Friends: Networks, Manipulators and Coalitions* (New York: St. Martin's, 1974).

Danker, F. W., "Jesus—Benefactor of the World," *Proclamation Commentaries: Luke* (Philadelphia: Fortress Press, 1976), 6–17.

———, *Benefactor: Epigraphic Study of a Graeco-Roman and New Testament Semantic Field* (St. Louis: Clayton Publishing House, 1982).

Eisenstadt, S. N., and Roniger, L., *Patrons, Clients and Friends: Interpersonal Relations and the Structure of Trust in Society* (Cambridge: Cambridge University, 1984).

Elliott, John H., "Patronage and Clientism in the Social World of Early Christianity," *Forum* 3.4 (1987): 39–48.

Gellner, E., and Waterbury, J., *Patrons and Clients in Mediterranean Societies* (London: Duckworth, 1977).

Lull, D. J., "The Servant-Benefactor as a Model of Greatness (Luke 22:24–30)," *NovT* 28 (1986): 289–305.

Malina, Bruce J., "Patron and Client: The Analogy Behind Synoptic Theology," *Forum* 4.1 (1988): 2–32.

Momigliano, Arnaldo, "Cliens" and "Patronus," *The Oxford Classical Dictionary* (Oxford: Clarendon Press, 1970), 252 and 791.

Mott, Stephen Charles, "The Power of Giving and Receiving: Reciprocity in Hellenistic Benevolence," *Current Issues in Biblical and Patristic Interpretation* (Gerald F. Hawthorne, ed.; Grand Rapids, MI: W. B. Eerdmans, 1975), 60–72.

Moxnes, Halvor, *The Economy of the Kingdom: Social Conflict and Economic Relations in Luke's Gospel* (Philadelphia: Fortress Press, 1988).

———, "Patron-Client Relations and the New Community in Luke-Acts," *The Social World of Luke-Acts: Models for Interpretation* (Peabody, MA: Stephen Hendrickson, Inc., 1991), 241–68.

Nock, Arthur D., "*Soter* and *Euergetes*," *Essays on Religion and the Ancient World* (Cambridge: Harvard University Press, 1972), 2.724–35.

Saller, R. P., *Personal Patronage Under the Early Empire* (Cambridge: Cambridge University, 1982).

Schmidt, S. W., Scott, J. C., Landé, C., and Guasti, L., eds., *Friends, Followers and Factions: A Reader in Political Clientelism* (Berkeley: University of California Press, 1977).

E. Purity and Pollution: The Symbolic Universe of the Ancients

Ancient Jews and Greeks alike thought of the universe and all in it as a *kosmos*, an organized and structured whole. This general sense of order and appropriate classification is what is meant by "purity" on a general, abstract level. Individuals are socialized from birth to know the appropriate code of what is "in place" or "out of place" (see Barré, " 'Fear of God' and the World of Wisdom," 41–43). Paul reminds the Corinthians of just such a sense of social ordering when he remarks: "God has arranged the organs in the body, each one of them, as he chose" (1 Cor 12:18). Something is "pure" or "clean" when it is in accord with the social expectation of order and propriety; conversely, things are "polluted" or "unclean" when they violate the common assumptions of the way the world is structured. Thus we may not necessarily find the terms "pure" or "polluted" in a document to discern that there is a strong sense of order. All attempts to classify, to hierarchize, to draw boundary lines and the like indicate a strong sense of "purity" or order.

Yet it may be, as in the case of Jewish and Christian documents, that we find a wide range of terms which specifically speak of "pure" and "polluted."

Semantic Word Field on Clean and Unclean

A. *Terms for "Purity":*

1. clean, to cleanse, cleanness *(katharos, katharizō, katharismos):* Luke 2:22; 5:12; 11:41; Acts 10:15; 15:9; Rom 14:20; 2 Cor 7:1
2. sweep *(saroō):* Luke 11:25//Matt 12:44
3. pure, to purify, purity *(hagnos, hagnizō, hagnotes):* Acts 21:24, 26; 24:18; 2 Cor 6:6; 7:11; 11:2, 3; Phil 4:8
4. holy, to make holy, holiness *(hagios, hagiazō, hagiotēs, hagiasmos):*
   hagios: Rom 1:7; 12:1, 13; 1 Cor 1:2; 3:17; 6:19; 16:1, 20; 2 Cor 1:1; 13:12; Phil 1:1; 4:21, 22; 1 Thess 3:13; 5:26, 27
   hagiazō: Rom 15:16; 1 Cor 1:2; 6:11; 7:14; 1 Thess 5:23
   hagiotēs: 2 Cor 1:12; Heb 12:10
   hagiasmos: Rom 6:19, 22; 1 Cor 1:30; 1 Thess 4:3, 4, 7
5. innocent *(akeraios):* Matt 10:16; Rom 16:19; Phil 2:5
6. spotless *(amiantos):* Heb 7:26; 13:4; Jas 1:27; 1 Pet 1:4
7. unstained *(aspilos):* Jas 1:27; 1 Pet 1:19; 2 Pet 3:14
8. blameless *(amōmos):* Eph 1:4; 5:27; Phil 2:15; 1 Pet 1:19
9. blameless *(anegklētos):* 1 Cor 1:8; Col 1:22; 1 Tim 3:10; Titus 1:6–7
10. faultless *(anepilēmptos):* 1 Tim 3:2; 5:7; 6:14
11. innocent *(amemtōs):* Phil 2:1; 3:6; 1 Thess 2:10; 3:13; 5:23
12. innocent *(athōos):* Matt 27:4, 24
13. innocent *(akakos):* Rom 16:18; Heb 7:26
14. incorrupted *(aphthartos):* 1 Cor 15:52; 1 Pet 1:4, 23

B. *Terms for "Pollution":*

1. defilement, to defile *(miasmos, miainō, miasma):* John 18:28; Titus 1:15; 2 Pet 2:10, 20
2. defilement, to defile *(molusmos, molunō):* 1 Cor 8:7; 2 Cor 7:1; Rev 3:4
3. unclean (*akathartos, akatharsia*):
   akathartos: 1 Cor 7:14; 2 Cor 6:17; Eph 5:5
   akatharsia: Rom 1:24; 6:19; 2 Cor 12:21; Gal 5:19; 1 Thess 2:3; 4:7
4. spot *(spilos, spiloō):* Eph 5:27; 2 Pet 2:13; Jas 3:6; Jude 23
5. stain *(momos):* 2 Pet 2:13
6. common, profane *(koinos, koinoō):* Acts 10:14–15,28; 11:8–9; 21:28; Rom 14:14
7. defilement *(halisgēma):* Acts 15:20
8. corruption *(phthora):* 1 Cor 15:42, 50; 2 Pet 1:4; 2:12, 19

The God of Jews and Christians is a "holy" God: "Be ye holy as I am holy" (Lev 11:44–45; 1 Pet 1:16). And this God demands "holiness" of those called into relationship with God: "This is the will of God, your sanctification" (1 Thess 4:3). "God has not called us for uncleanness but in holiness" (1 Thess 4:7). This shared perception informs both Jude and 2 Peter. As abstract as it may sound, group members are socialized to know in considerable detail what is clean or unclean, what is virtue or vice, what is praiseworthy or blameworthy. Since "holiness" means "separated," a strong boundary line is drawn which separates insiders from outsiders, light from dark, good from bad, etc. Hence, both Jude and 2 Peter can convincingly demand of loyal disciples that they be spotless, stainless, blameless, and free from all corruption, that is, completely separated from evil.

Purity or spotlessness pertains both to the doctrine professed by the group and to the way the body is regulated. One important aspect of "purity" is the sense of wholeness implied: what is whole, total, and complete is worthy of consideration by God. Only "whole" or unblemished animals may be offered on God's altar; only those who enjoy bodily wholeness may offer them (Lev 21:16–21; 1 Q Sa 2:3–10; Josephus, *Ant.* 14.366). When extended to the group's doctrine, the whole tradition handed on must be confessed in its totality. Thus attempts to ignore or contradict elements of it risk polluting it and bringing uncleanness on those who do this.

A physical body is pure when it is controlled and governed just as the social body is. After all, it is the microcosm of the macrocosm; and the rules that classify and order the social body are replicated in appropriate rules for the physical body. In particular this means control of the bodily orifices: mouth, ears, eyes, and genitals. Great care is taken (i.e., "self-control") concerning what enters and leaves these orifices. Only holy things should enter a holy body, not lust through the eyes or gluttonous foods through the mouth or deceitful slogans through the ears. Sexual control goes without saying. Pollution stalks the body in the name of "desire" *(epithymia)* and "pleasure" *(hēdonē)*.

This type of perception takes on moral imperatives. "Purity" is a prerequisite for standing in God's holy persence. But it is a state easily threatened and corrupted. Indeed, "pollution" is regularly compared in NT documents either with leaven (1 Cor 5:6–8) or gangrene (2 Tim 2:17). Such corruption is life-threatening; even a pinch will corrupt the whole batch of flour or the entire body if left unchecked. Hence the labeling of something "unclean" or "polluted" serves to marshal intolerance toward it, with the attendant urgency to expel or excommunicate it before it can harm the rest of the whole. One bad apple does indeed spoil the whole bushel.

When we examine Jude and 2 Peter we should first be attentive to the various terms for "pure" and "polluted" in them. The semantic word field noted above should easily assist us in this. Second, we will attend to the sense of social and cosmic order in each document. This will entail gaining a sense of the social ranking of all the persons in the document, beginning with God and Jesus, including the author, and then attending to the group and its author's opponents. Third, we cannot but notice that certain actions are praised and others blamed, usually virtues and vices. Finally, we should pay particular attention to the way the physical body is discussed: what evil things are said to be the practices and doctrines of the various opponents, as well as what good things are urged on loyal disciples. All dualistic language in the documents can serve as a convenient way into the world of perceptions.

BIBLIOGRAPHY

Barré, Michael, " 'Fear of God' and the World of Wisdom," *BTB* 11 (1981): 41–43.

Buchanan, George W., "The Role of Purity in the Structure of the Essene Sect," *ResQ* 4 (1963): 397–406.

Douglas, Mary, *Purity and Danger* (London: Routledge and Kegan Paul, 1966).

———, "Pollution," *IESS* 12.336–42.

Eilberg-Schwartz, Howard, "Creation and Classification in Judaism: From Priestly to Rabbinic Concepts," *HR* 26 (1987): 357–81.

Malina, Bruce, *The New Testament World: Insights from Cultural Anthropology* (Atlanta: John Knox Press, 1981), 122–50.

Neusner, Jacob, *The Idea of Purity in Ancient Judaism* (Leiden: E. J. Brill, 1973).

———, "History and Purity in First-Century Judaism," *HR* 18 (1978): 1–17.

Newton, Michael, *The Concept of Purity at Qumran and in the Letters of Paul* (SNTSMS 53. Cambridge: Cambridge University Press, 1985).
Neyrey, Jerome H. "The Idea of Purity in Mark," *Semeia* 35 (1986): 91–128.
———, "A Symbolic Approach to Mark 7," *Forum* 4.3 (1988): 63–92.
———, "Unclean, Common, Polluted and Taboo," *Forum* 4.4 (1988): 72–82.
———, *Paul, in Other Words: A Cultural Reading of His Letters* (Louisville, KY: Westminster/John Knox Press, 1990).
———, "The Symbolic Universe of Luke-Acts: 'They Turn the World Upside Down,' " *The Social World of Luke-Acts: Models for Interpretation* (Peabody, MA: Stephen Hendrickson, 1991) 271–304.
Parker, R., *Miasma Pollution and Purification in Early Greek Religion* (Oxford: Clarendon Press, 1983).
Soler, Jean, "The Dietary Prohibitions of the Hebrews," *New York Review of Books* (June 14, 1979): 24–30. Reprinted in Robert Forster and Orest Ranum (eds.), *Food and Drink in History* (Baltimore: Johns Hopkins University Press, 1979), 126–38.

F. The Physical Body

Noted anthropologist Marcel Mauss remarked that every bodily action carries the imprint of learning ("Techniques of the Body," *Economy and Society* 2 [1973]: 70–88). Bodily actions are learned behavior, that is, how one uses one's body is governed by rules and norms from the social system into which one is socialized. We noted above the concern that NT authors have for a rather complex and complete system of classification and ordering. At this point we are refining that perspective to extend explicitly to the way the human body is perceived and controlled.

The viewpoint here is that developed by Mary Douglas. She argues for a replication of values and structures between the social and the physical body. The physical body is but a microcosm of the social body, the macrocosm:

> The social body constrains the way the physical body is perceived. The physical experience of the body, always modified by the social categories through which it is known, sustains a particular view of society. There is a continual exchange of meanings between the two kinds of bodily experience so that each reinforces the categories of the other [*Natural Symbols*, 65].

This means that we should expect that the physical body is perceived in the same structural categories in which the social body is perceived. Just as the social body has external boundaries, margins/exits and entrances, and internal structure, so too the physical body. The converse is also true:

> The body is a model which can stand for any bounded system. Its boundaries can represent any boundaries which are threatened or precarious. The body is a complex structure. The function of its different parts and their relation afford a source of symbols for other complex structures [Douglas, *Purity and Danger,* 115].

What we have learned about "purity systems" we can apply to the social perception of the physical body. Thus we attend to three dimensions: (1) structure (head/feet, eyes/hands, i.e. bodily hierarchy of parts); (2) boundaries (skin or clothing); (3) entrances or exits (bodily orifices such as eyes, ears, mouth, genitals).

Applying this perspective to 2 Peter, we note first of all that there are no references to the body's overall structure. The author never speaks about the "head," although he clearly indicates that the eyes of certain people see for the whole group (1:16–17) just as the mouth of official speakers speaks for all. Depending on what is seen and heard, the feet of others are stable and walk correctly on the right way. The converse is equally true: an evil mouth can control the feet of some so as to cause them to stumble and fall.

Some mention is made of bodily surfaces. The author announces that he will put off his bodily tent (1:13–14). This would leave him naked, a shameful state; but he expects to put on appropriate new clothing in the new heavens. He pays attention to the bodily surface when he speaks about "purification" for sins (1:9), which seems to refer to some washing rite such as baptism. Like other Jews and Christians in antiquity, he is concerned with the purity of the skin or bodily surface. Hence, he labors to be "spotless" (3:14), while criticizing "blots and blemishes" (2:13). He likens apostate disciples to pigs returning to wallow in mire after being washed.

The author gives most of his attention to bodily orifices. We note that in the beginning of the letter, he called for "self-control" (*egkrateia*), that is, control and governance of the body. This specifically means the virtuous guarding of the ears, eyes, mouth, and genitals.

Ears: Certain things should be heard and taken to heart, namely, the promises and prophecies spoken by God and the exhortations of the author. The author celebrates that his ears heard holy and true words from God at Jesus' transfiguration (1:17–18). But other things should not be listened to, such as the false teachings of the opponents (2:1–2) or their scoffings (3:3–4). How much Lot suffered in "sound and sight" in the company of the Sodomites (2:9).

Eyes: The author claims to be an eyewitness (1:16–17), and so his eyes see holy things. He urges the group to use its eyes correctly and attend to the lamp of prophecy and to look for the Morning Star (1:19). Conversely, other eyes are unguarded and full of evil. Those who do not remember the traditions of the group have defective eyes ("blind, shortsighted," 1:9). The eyes of the opponents are "filled with adulteries" (2:14).

Mouth: The author has only negative things to say about the uncontrolled mouths of his opponents. He criticizes them for what comes out of them (false speech) and what goes into them (food). First, he accuses them of bad mouths when he identifies them as "false teachers" who teach doctrines of destruction (2:1); they are scoffers, whose mocking speech degrades the group's prophetic tradition (3:3–4); they and others "defame" *(blasphemeō)* many sacred things (2:10, 12); their mouths are filled with empty boasts (2:18). He notes that their eating is not the holy consumption of foods at the group's feasts, but "dissipation" (2:13). And lapsed disciples are like dogs returning to eat vomit (2:22), a universally unclean substance. In contrast, the proper use of the mouth is the loyal "acknowledgment" of the Lord (1:3–4; 2:20–21), not his denial. The author's own mouth is controlled to speak only the truth about the group's tradition.

Genitals: The author accuses his opponents of total lack of control of their genital orifice. They themselves are full of adulteries (2:14) and they entice others to debauchery (2:2, 18) and desires of the flesh (2:18).

The author himself, then, exhibits a controlled physical body. He urges and practices "self-control." His control replicates the strong sense of purity which he has concerning the social body of the group. In contrast, he portrays his opponents as lacking totally in bodily control; and those who follow their teaching also exhibit weak and dangerous lack of control. As we noted above, the opponents are perceived as radically unclean, and thus polluting the holy group. This is visualized by the total lack of control over their bodily orifices.

BIBLIOGRAPHY

Barkan, Leonard, *Nature's Work of Art: The Human Body as Image of the World* (New Haven, CT: Yale University Press, 1975).

Benthall, J., and Polhemus, T. (eds.), *The Body as Medium of Expression* (New York: Dutton, 1975).

Blacking, John (ed.), *The Anthropology of the Body* (ASA Monograph 15. New York: Academic Press, 1977).

Douglas, Mary, *Purity and Danger* (Routledge and Kegan Paul, 1966).

———, *Natural Symbols* (New York: Pantheon, 1982).

Gager, John G., "Body-Symbols and Social Reality: Resurrection, Incarnation and Asceticism in Early Christianity," *Religion* 12 (1982): 345–64.

Mauss, Marcel, "Techniques of the Body," *Economy and Society* 2 (1973): 70–88.

Neyrey, Jerome H., "Body Language in 1 Corinthians: The Use of Anthropological Models for Understanding Paul and His Opponents," *Semeia* 35 (1986): 129–70.

———, "A Symbolic Approach to Mark 7," *Forum* 4.3 (1988): 63–92.

———, *Paul, in Other Words: A Cultural Reading of His Letters* (Louisville, KY: Westminster/John Knox Press, 1990) 102–46.

Pilch, John, "Biblical Leprosy and Body Symbolism," *BTB* 11 (1981): 108–13.

Polhemus, T., *The Body Reader: Social Aspects of the Human Body* (New York: Pantheon, 1978).

Scheflen, Albert and Alice, *Body Language and the Social Order: Communication as Behavioral Control* (Englewood Cliffs, NJ: Princeton-Hall, 1972).

Ullendorf, E., "The Bawdy Bible," *BSOAS* 42 (1979): 426–56.

G. Group-Oriented Person, Not Modern Individualist

Anthropologist Clifford Geertz remarked that the modern concept of an autonomous individual as an ideal of personhood is "a rather peculiar idea within the context of the world's cultures" ("From the Native's Point of View," 225). In the ancient world, while individuals abound, individualism as we know it today was both rare and deviant. For people characteristically understood other people in terms of their embeddedness in social relations, not in terms of their uniqueness or autonomy. They knew themselves and were readily known in terms of their belonging to some recognized group.

For example, when Saul is first introduced to the reader, he is described in terms of his family and clan: "There was a man of Benjamin whose name was Kish, the son of Abiel, son of Zeror, son of Becorath, son of Aphiah, a Benjaminite, a man of wealth; and he had a son whose name was Saul" (1 Sam 9:1–2). Since it is expected that sons are "chips off the old block," to know their fathers and their fathers' fathers is to know them. Thus Simon Peter is the "son of Jonah" (Matt 16:17) and James and John are "sons of Zebedee" (Matt 4:21); like their fathers, they too are fishermen. Although we do not know the name of Paul's father, he describes himself in terms of his father's clan: "of the people of Israel, of the tribe of Benjamin, a Hebrew born of Hebrews" (Phil 3:5). Sons, of course, were ranked; so firstborn sons enjoyed a role and status higher than other sons; all sons ranked higher than daughters. Thus birth order and gender were essential elements in the identity of individuals in terms of their belonging to a particular family.

People likewise were known in terms of their place of origin: Paul of Tarsus

(Acts 22:3), Jesus of Nazareth (John 18:5), Barnabas of Cyprus (Acts 4:36). This presumes some stereotypical knowledge about the place of origin which attaches to the individual born there. For example, Nazareth is an impossible place from which the Messiah can come (John 1:46). Yet Tarsus is "no mean city," and so a worthy place from which an honorable person like Paul sprang (Acts 21:39). Crete, however, produces shameful people: "Cretans are always liars, evil beasts, lazy gluttons" (Titus 1:12). It is important for the modern reader, then, to strive to learn what sort of stereotype was attached to a given village, city or region.

As well as family or place of origin, people were known in terms of group of origin. Paul, for example, regularly maintains that he was a Pharisee (Phil 3: 5–6), which means that he was zealous for the law. Likewise, people were known in terms of their trade, for status and honor was attached to these and to know them was to know the worth of an individual. Simon is a tanner (Acts 9:43); Andrew and Peter, fishermen (Matt 4:18); Jesus, a carpenter (Mark 6:3); Paul, a worker in leather (Acts 18:3). As in the case of place of origin, such identifications presume stereotypical knowledge of the kind of person in antiquity who was a laborer, a scribe, or a king.

Indeed, individuals were quickly and readily socialized to know their identity in terms of family, place, trade, and the like. A vast body of folklore and proverbial wisdom provided individual members with the social expectations of the group in which they were embedded. Thus individuals grew up knowing the social expectations of males or females, of firstborn and last-born males. They were socialized early on to gender expectations, to what was honorable and shameful, and to what was pure or polluted according to the group to which they belonged. Hence, ancient people, when they spoke of "conscience," understood this in terms of its root meaning: knowledge shared with others (Latin: *cum scientia;* Greek: *syn-eidesis*). Their "conscience" was formed by the public and explicit expectations of others (1 Cor 10:27–29). Hence, public praise or censure was an ongoing part of the constant socialization of individuals to the norms and expectations of the group. We call this kind of person "group-oriented," as opposed to the modern notion of "individual."

Group-oriented persons are socialized, moreover, to subordinate personal desires, ambitions, and wishes to the goals of the family or group. The prodigal son broke this rule by asking for a division of his father's property so that he could indulge himself (Luke 15:12–13). The son neither honored his father nor cast his lot with the welfare of the family. Josephus states the matter as clearly as possible: group-oriented persons put family and fellowship above individualistic desires:

> Our sacrifices are not occasions for drunken self-indulgence—such practices are abhorrent to God—but for sobriety. At these sacrifices prayers for the welfare of the community must take precedence of those

> for ourselves; for we are born for fellowship, and he who sets its claims above his private interests is specially acceptable to God [*Apion* 2.195–96].

Moreover, group-oriented persons are acutely sensitive to the family's or group's traditions. Education is basically the process of learning the proverbs and aphorisms which indicate social expectations and behavior. All are subject to this sort of socialization, and so all experience themselves in some sort of continued relationship with others, as the following observation by Plutarch indicates:

> The nurse rules the infant, the teacher the boy, the gymnasiarch the youth, his admirer the young man who, when he comes of age, is ruled by law and his commanding general. No one is his own master, no one is unrestricted [*Dialogue on Love* 754D].

When we turn to Jude and 2 Peter, these notions will be important for understanding the range of social relationships described there. God and Jesus have shown benefaction to the church and given the members a "holy rule" to follow. They are socialized to know the stories, exhortations, and myths about God, Jesus, and their own relationship to their heavenly patrons. Thus knowledge of and loyalty to the traditions of the elders are paramount values in these documents. The opponents in both documents are deviants who disregard the group's tenets and patterns of behavior and act independently in ways that are individualistic. One might accurately describe these documents as continued socialization of the addressees in the social and cultural norms espoused by the disciples of Jesus.

BIBLIOGRAPHY

Duby, Georges, and Braunstein, Philippe, "The Emergence of the Individual," *A History of Private Life: II. Revelations of the Medieval World* (Georges Duby, ed.; Cambridge: Belknap Press, 1988), 507–630.

Evans, Elizabeth, "Physiognomics in the Ancient World," *TAPA* n.s. 59 (1969): 51–58.

Geertz, Clifford, " 'From the Native's Point of View': On the Nature of Anthropological Understanding," *Meaning and Anthropology* (Kenneth H. Basso and Henry A. Selby, eds.; Albuquerque: University of New Mexico Press, 1976) 221–37.

Gill, Christopher, "The Character-Personality Distinction," *Characterization and Individuality in Greek Literature* (Christopher Pelling, ed.; Oxford: Clarendon Press, 1990), 1–31.

Halliwell, Stephen, "Traditional Greek Conceptions of Character," *Characterization and Individuality in Greek Literature* (Christopher Pelling, ed.; Oxford: Clarendon Press, 1990), 32–59.

Harding, John, "Stereotypes," *IESS* 15.259–62.

Hui, C. Harry, and Triandis, Harry C., "Individualism-Collectivism—a Study of Cross-Cultural Researchers," *Journal of Cross-Cultural Psychology* 17 (1986): 225–48.

Malina, Bruce, J., "The Individual and the Community—Personality in the Social World of Early Christianity" *BTB* 9 (1979): 126–38.

———, *New Testament World. Insights from Cultural Anthropology* (Atlanta: John Knox Press, 1981), 51–70.

———, "Dealing with Biblical (Mediterranean) Characters: A Guide for U.S. Consumers," *BTB* 19 (1989): 127–41.

Malina, Bruce, and Neyrey, Jerome, "First-Century Personality: Dyadic, Not Individualistic," *The Social World of Luke-Acts. Models for Interpretation* (Peabody, MA: Stephen Hendrickson, Inc., 1991), 67–96.

Pelling, Christopher, "Childhood and Personality in Greek Biography," *Characterization and Individuality in Greek Literature* (Oxford: Clarendon Press, 1990), 213–44.

Sattler, W. M., "Conceptions of *Ethos* in Ancient Rhetoric," *Speech Monographs* 14 (1957): 55–65.

JUDE
TRANSLATION AND OUTLINE

♦

I. Letter Opening: Address and Greeting (Jude 1–2)
1. Jude, servant of Jesus Christ and brother of James, to those beloved of God the Father and called and kept by Jesus Christ. 2. May mercy and peace and love be multiplied in you.

II. Letter Occasion: Insinuation of Deviants (Jude 3–4)
3. Beloved, while making haste to correspond with you about our common salvation, I found it necessary to write and exhort you to contend for the faith delivered once and for all to the saints. 4. For certain men have crept in, who ages ago were proscribed for judgment. Godless men, they turn away from God's favor to debauchery and deny our only Master and Lord Jesus Christ.

III. Crimes Judged: Three Old Testament Examples (Jude 5–7)
5. Once you knew all about this, yet I want to remind you that although Jesus saved a people from the land of Egypt, he afterward destroyed those who were unfaithful. 6. And angels, who did not keep to their own position but left their proper abode, he is keeping with everlasting chains in darkness for the judgment of the great day. 7. Similarly, Sodom and Gomorrah and the villages around them likewise committed fornication and went after other flesh; they are set as examples, suffering a punishment of eternal fire.

IV. Triple Crimes and Their Judgment (Jude 8–9)
8. But in like manner, these dreamers defile the flesh, flout authority, and insult the glorious ones. 9. But Michael the archangel, when he argued with the devil and disputed over the body of Moses, did not himself dare bring a judgment against insult, but he said: "The Lord will rebuke you."

V. Triple Example of Deviants Judged (Jude 10–13)
10. But these men insult whatever they do not know; by nature they understand like animals without reason, and are destroyed in this. 11. Woe to these who have gone the way of Cain, and abandoned themselves for gain to the deceit of Balaam, and are destroyed in the rebellion of Korah. 12. These men are stains on your fellowship meals; they feast fearlessly with you and pasture only themselves. They are rainless clouds borne by the wind, fruitless trees in autumn, doubly dead and uprooted. 13. They are wild waves of the sea who cast foam over their shames, wandering stars for whom the gloomy darkness is forever kept.

VI. Prediction of Future Judgment (Jude 14–16)
14. Enoch, the seventh from Adam, prophesied about these, saying, "Behold, the Lord is coming with his tens of thousands of holy ones, 15. to pass judgment on all and to convict all the ungodly of both the godless deeds they godlessly did and the defiant words these godless sinners spoke against him." 16. These men are disgruntled murmurers who go the way of passion. Their mouths speak inflatedly and they show partiality for gain.

VII. Comparison and Contrast: Faithless Deviants and Faithful Disciples (Jude 17–23)
17. But you, beloved, remember what the apostles of our Lord Jesus Christ foretold, 18. how they told you: "At the final time, scoffers will come who go the way of godless desires. 19. These men, who create division, are physical and have no Spirit." 20. But you, beloved, build yourselves up by the most sacred faithfulness, praying in the Holy Spirit. 21. Keep yourselves in the love of God and await the mercy of our Lord Jesus Christ unto eternal life. 22. On the one hand, snatch some from the fire. 23. On the other, have mercy with fear on those who dispute. Hate even the garment stained by the flesh.

VIII. Letter Closing: Doxology (Jude 24–25)
24. To the One who can guard you from stumbling and make you stand before his glory without blemish and in joy, 25. to the only God who saves us through Jesus Christ our Lord be glory, majesty, might, and authority, before all ages, now and forever. Amen.

Jude: Introduction

♦

1. Literary Structure

Like most New Testament documents, Jude formally appears as a letter, although epistolary conventions pertain basically to its opening and closing. Within this framework the document contains a remarkably clear structure, which may have much to do with persistent oral techniques.

- 1–2 Letter Opening + Blessing
- 3 Exhortation to *agapētoi* for faithfulness
- 4–16 Letter Body: Exposure of *asebeis . . . houtoi* "Crimes and Punishment"
  - 4 Triple charges
  - 5–7 Triple paradigms of punishment
  - 8 Triple charges
  - 9 Prediction of punishment
  - 10 Charge and punishment
  - 11 Triple paradigms of punished sinners
  - 12–13 Multiple metaphors of charges
  - 14–16 Prediction of punishment
- 17–23 Exhortation to *agapētoi* for faithfulness, love, mercy "Warnings and Exhortation"
  - 17–19 Prediction of godless people
  - 20–23 Exhortations to the faithful
- 24–25 Letter Closing + Doxology

The letter begins and ends with affirmation of divine benefaction to the addressees. In a document where God's honor is challenged and slighted, these elements of praise should not be taken for granted. Guided by Jude's use of catchwords, we note how the document first urges the addressees, who are called "beloved," to faithfulness toward God (v 3) and then returns to the same theme (vv 20–23). He juxtaposes their positive behavior to the extended polemic against certain scoffers and opponents (vv 4–16). This "comparison" *(synkrisis)* is a common rhetorical element of the literature of praise and blame (C. Forbes, "Comparison, Self-Praise and Irony: Paul's Boasting and the Conventions of Hellenistic Rhetoric," *NTS* 32 [1986]: 2–8). The letter, then, begins and ends with the affirmation of God's honor; its core contains alternating exhortation, warning, and exhortation, which contrasts virtue with vice.

The bulk of the letter (vv 4–16) deals with the crisis provoking the letter, namely, an invasion of the holy church by godless scoffers. There are hints of a chiastic structure in this particular part of the document:

A. v 4a Opponents proscribed *(progegrammenoi)*
  B. v 4b Opponents labeled as godless *(asebeis)*
    C. v 6 Those judged kept in darkness *(hypo zophon tetērēken)*
    C′. v 13 Those judged kept in darkness *(ho zophos tetērētai)*
  B′. vv 15–16 Opponents labeled as godless *(asebeis)*
A′. v 17 Opponents pretold *(proeirēmenōn)*

At the very least, readers should appreciate that this brief document is carefully crafted, with a skill and intent that commands attention and respect.

Jude does not simply describe "those" people, but charges and convicts them of evil. This he does by an alternating pattern of "crime and punishment." As we shall see, Jude characteristically states his case in triplets. In the case of the opponents, they are charged with three crimes (vv 4, 8). In an honor-shame world, crimes must be punished; hence after establishing the charges, Jude cites triple examples of sinners punished for such crimes (vv 5–7, 11). In two key spots, he cites two texts in which the judgment of the Lord is formally proclaimed against all such sinners (vv 9, 14–16). Thus Jude acts as a prosecutor who conducts a prophetic lawsuit against evildoers, charging them with crimes, proclaiming the consistent norm of judgment, and announcing a sure judgment of punishment.

The present structural exposition is grounded in Jude's pervasive use of oral techniques such as catchwords and triplets. Scholars have long noted the use of linkwords or catchwords in regard to gospel materials (C. H. Lohr, "Oral Technique in the Gospel of Matthew," *CBQ* 23 [1961]: 422–23), and the same technique has a bearing on Jude's structure. Some of the linkwords appear in the letter's beginning and ending. The addresses, who are "beloved" of God (v 1), are addressed as such in v 3 and later in vv 17 and 20. A prayer for God's "mercy" (v 2) becomes part of their hope in v 21 and their exhortation in vv 22–23. "Salvation" is both a present benefaction (v 3) and God's future gift (v 25). They are exhorted to contend for "the faith" (v 3) and build themselves up in faithfulness (v 20). The addressees are the "saints" (v 3) who must build themselves up in "sacred" faithfulness and by prayer in the "holy" Spirit (v 21). "Only" describes the Lord Jesus who is shamed (v 4) and God who is honored (v 25). Thus the presentation of key terms in the letter's beginning serves to accent the positive themes and issues which are resumed at the letter's ending, the rhetorical power residing in the *inclusio* or repetition of them (Lohr, 408–9).

Certain words, moreover, link the exhortation to the faithful as well as the polemic against the opponents. For example, the addressees are "kept" in God's favor (v 1). But those who do not "keep" their proper place will be "kept" in disfavor (v 6, 13). Yet the saints are then exhorted to "keep" themselves in God's favor (v 21).

If "link words" bind sections of a document together, the repetition of "key words" within certain sections gives them unity and coherence (J. Magne, "Répétitions de mots et exégèse dans quelques psaumes et le *Pater*," *Bib* 39 [1958]: 177–97). It is evident especially in the section of the letter where the opponents are described that the repetition of key words holds together the various pieces of the author's criticism. They are the "godless" (vv 4, 15, 18), who "go" deviant ways (11, 16, 18). The opponents are described negatively as "these" folk (8, 10, 12, 16, 19), whose characteristic is "deceit" (11, 13). Their end is destruction (5, 11).

The literary structure urged above must be viewed in light of another study of Jude's structure presented by a student of classical rhetoric. Watson (*Invention, Arrangement, and Style*, 40–77) presented a detailed examination, which can only be summarized and modified here; but it deserves attention now for the light it sheds on the logic of Jude.

The letter begins with an *exordium* (vv 1–3), which traditionally lays out the rhetor's hortatory intention, the topics to be discussed, and a request for a hearing (Cicero, *Part.* 27.97). As Watson noted, Jude renders the audience friendly by acknowledgment of its status and by prayer for its future; he establishes his own ethos as worthy of a serious hearing; and he introduces topics which will shortly be developed in the *probatio*. Jude exhorts his audience to give him a hearing because a crisis has arisen (v 3).

In the *narratio* (v 4), Jude explains why attention must be paid. He states his case (Cicero, *Part.* 9.31–32) that subversives have crept in who threaten the group because of their godlessness. At this point, Jude asks his audience to form a judgment about the case he presents them; they should be persuaded of the malice of the opponents and be convinced of their prescribed punishment.

Then follows the *probatio*, where "proof" is offered and the rhetor's case is made. Four types of "proofs" function in vv 5–16: (a) attacks on the ethos of the opponents (i.e., charges); (b) examples from the past (crimes are always punished); (c) comparison between past crimes punished and present accusations; and (d) legal precedent or legal warrant for judgment. The following list labels the various proofs according to their proper rhetorical character:

v 4	attack on ethos: charges made
vv 5–7	examples from the past: crimes are always punished
v 8	comparison: those charged are like past evildoers
v 9	legal/judicial precedent: "The Lord will rebuke"
v 10	attack on ethos: more charges made
v 11	examples from the past: crimes are punished
vv 12–13	attack on ethos: still more charges
vv 14–16	legal/judicial precedent: the Lord will judge

Thus Jude presents various "proofs" to convince his addressees of the evil of the opponents, and so to shun them.

Then comes the *peroratio*, the end and conclusion of the presentation; it generally contains a repetition of the argument as well as *indignatio* (ill will against the opponents) and *conquestio* (pity and sympathy; Cicero, *Inv. Rhet.* 1.52.98). Jude repeats his charges against the opponents in vv 17–19, arousing negative pathos or ill will toward them. Part of his technique is the appeal to the opinion of distinguished others (the apostles) in an oracle that such godless people would come (Quintilian, *Inst.* 5.11.36 & 42). Alternately he elicits goodwill for himself and his cause in vv 20–23 with exhortations to virtue and faithfulness. Thus he balances blame (vv 17–19) with praise (vv 20–23, 24–25), or, as the rhetorical structure indicates, *indignatio* with *conquestio*.

Watson, while urging us to consider Jude in terms of deliberative rhetoric, carefully notes how this document exhibits many of the conventions of a genuine letter (White, "Ancient Greek Letters," 85–105; R. W. Funk, *Language, Hermeneutic, and Word of God* [New York: Harper and Row, 1966], 250–75). Thus the rather rigid rhetorical rules are adapted and modified in light of the epistolary character of Jude. Those epistolary elements are:

1–2	Epistolary opening: sender, addressees, benediction
3–4	Body opening: principal occasion for the letter, cast in form of a petition
5–16	Body of the letter

17–23 Body closing:
introduced by disclosure formula

24–25 Epistolary doxology

The literary structure defined by epistolary conventions and repeated phrases and words squares well with the formal sense of rhetorical argument as outlined by Watson. The author is clearly arguing a strong case, which in virtue of its stress on crime and punishment seems to evoke more a sense of forensic than deliberative rhetoric as Watson suggested. It contrasts virtue with vice, praise with blame, honor with shame, and *conquestio* with *indignatio*. The respect for epistolary convention as well as the conformity to rhetorical practice indicates that the document was crafted by a skilled scribe and was intended to have a decided and powerful social effect, however stereotyped the polemic seems to us today.

2. Vocabulary and Style

Origen said of Jude that it was a small letter, "but filled with a vigorous vocabulary" (*Comment. in Mt.* 10.17; GCS 10.22). His vocabulary pool contains fifteen words not found elsewhere in the New Testament: *apodiorizein* (v 19); *aptaistos* (v 24); *goggystēs* (v 16); *deigma* (v 7); *ekporneuein* (v 7); *epagōnizesthai* (v 3); *epaphrizein* (v 13); *mempsimoiros* (v 16); *pareisdyein* (v 4); *planētēs* (v 13); *spilas* (v 12); *hypechein* (v 7); *phthinopōrinos* (v 12); *physikōs* (v 16). Three other words, found only in 2 Peter, are dependent upon Jude: *empaiktēs* (v 18), *syneuōcheisthai* (v 12), and *hyperogkos* (v 16). Of these, only four can be found in some Greek translation of the Old Testament. Another twenty-two words in Jude are only rarely found in the New Testament. This suggests that Jude was educated in a literary environment which contained considerably more than Hebrew and Christian Scriptures. In the following commentary, frequent note will be made of Hellenistic linguistic parallels to Jude's vocabulary.

Commentators regularly note the presence of Semitisms in Jude, for example, *ek gēs Aigyptou* (v 5); *ouai autois* (v 11); *en tēi hodōi tou Kain eporeuthēsan* (v 11; see Chaine, *Les Epîtres Catholiques*, 275–77). They also call attention to good Greek idioms (*spoudēn poiesthai*, v 7; *dikēn hypechein*, v 7) and poetic Greek phrases (*hypo zophon*, v 6; *kymata agria*, v 13) and the use of Greek particles (*men . . . de . . . de*, vv 8, 10, 22–23). Bauckham (*Jude, 2 Peter*, 6) describes Jude's vocabulary as varied, effectively chosen, appropriate, and literary.

First Mayor (*The Epistle of St. Jude and the Second Epistle of St. Peter*, lvi) and then Charles ("Jude's Use of Pseudepigraphical Source-Material," 132 #5, and "Literary Artifice in the Epistle of Jude," 122–23) noted the occurrence of triplets in Jude, which are evidence of a concern for coherence and texture in the discourse:

v 1	identification of the addressees: "beloved . . . called . . . kept"
v 2	benediction: "mercy and peace and love be multiplied"
v 4	identification of the opponents: "proscribed . . . turn away . . . deny"
vv 5–7	precedents of sinners judged: Israel in wilderness, angels, Sodom
v 8	identification of the opponents: "defile . . . flout . . . insult"
v 11	woe to three sinners judged: Cain, Balaam, Korah "gone the way of . . . abandoned themselves . . . destroyed"
v 12	metaphors of vanity "rainless clouds . . . fruitless trees . . . doubly dead"
v 14	the judgment of the Lord "coming . . . pass judgment . . . convict"
v 16	identification of the opponents: "disgruntled . . . murmurers . . . go the way of passion"
v 19	vices of the opponents: "create division . . . physical . . . have no Spirit"
vv 20–21	virtues of the faithful: "build yourselves up . . . praying . . . await"
vv 22–23	on dealing with the opponents: "on the one hand . . . on the other" "snatch . . . have mercy . . . hate"
v 25	honorable attributes of God: "glory, majesty, might, and authority"
v 25	duration of God's honor: "before all ages, now and forever"

The triplets, which Watson (*Invention, Arrangement, and Style*, 42) describes as "amplification by accumulation," are no mere ornaments, for they form a cadence of expectation which is satisfied regularly. And as Dobschütz has shown

("Zwei- und Dreigliedrige Formeln," *JBL* 50 [1931]: 118–32), triplets are a common feature in Hebrew and Christian Scriptures. Thus they serve as a regular rhythm which is found in all parts of the letter, beginning and ending, exhortation and comparison.

Watson (*Invention, Arrangement, and Style,* 50–77), moreover, identifies numerous instances of Jude's embellishment of his argument according to rhetorical techniques urged in the handbooks. In addition, we call attention to the elegant anaphora built around the repeating term, "These . . ." (vv 8, 10, 12, 16, 19). In the discussion of literary structure above, we called attention to the *inclusio* linking the letter opening and its closing through repeated key terms. And there seems to be a form of chiasm in the arrangement of the polemic against the opponents in vv 5–16. The stylistic sophistication of the letter again indicates that the author is well educated, suggesting a scribal background. As Chaine (*Les Epîtres catholiques,* 274) noted, "The style, like its vocabulary, shows that the author was good at Greek and a good Greek as well."

3. Place, Date, Author

Scholars have tended to argue that Jude was written in either Palestine/Syria or Alexandria. J. J. Gunther revived the Alexandrian hypothesis ("The Alexandrian Epistle of Jude," *NTS* 30 [1984]: 549–62), urging the following points: (1) Jude's strong Jewish strain and its knowledge of *1 Enoch* and *Testament of Moses* are satisfied in Alexandria, as well as his fine Hellenistic style; (2) miscellaneous items, such as homiletic references, rocks in a harbor, and scant rain, accord with Alexandria; (3) numerous affinities with the *Preaching of Peter* and the Gospel of John suggest an Egyptian site; (4) Jude's opponents can possibly be identified as Carpocratians. Although there is no compelling reason for Alexandria, Gunther offers telling arguments why a Palestinian or Syrian provenance is improbable. Jude was listed among the disputed writings by Eusebius (*H.E.* 2.23.25; 3.25.3); it was not until the sixth century that Philoxenus brought Jude into the Syriac canon.

Yet J. N. D. Kelly (*The Epistles of Peter and of Jude,* 233–34) and more recently R. Bauckham (*Jude and the Relatives of Jesus,* 181–211) have urged a Palestinian origin. Some evidence is extrinsic, namely, that James, Jude, and the relatives of Jesus were popular figures in that part of the Mediterranean. Other evidence points to a pesher-type exegesis practiced by Jude, which suggests close ties with Palestine. As persuasive as this argument is, it is by no means clear or settled that Jude contains such a pattern of exegesis as Bauckham describes. H. Koester (*History and Literature of Early Christianity* [Philadelphia:

Fortress, 1982], II.246–47) argues for Syria on the basis of the extrinsic reason that the *Gospel of Thomas*, a document which was written in Syria in the first century, was addressed to Judas Didymus Thomas.

Yet as inconclusive as these arguments are, they help to shape the issue. Wherever Jude was composed, it must be an area where both Jewish lore and esoteric literature were accessible, as well as where classical Greek rhetoric was taught and appreciated. Jude was written by someone with a strong scribal background. It must have been composed in a city sufficiently close to where 2 Peter was written, for the author of the latter document knew and used the former. This makes Rome an unlikely prospect. Antioch or Alexandria remain likely places, with the latter the more probable site if only because Jude was known and commented on by Alexandrians such as Clement.

The date of Jude remains a mystery, with scholars suggesting a date as early as the late apostolic age (50–60 CE) and as late as the mid–second century. Since there are no data in the document for a probable date, arguments depend on a variety of interpretations of its contents: (1) if authentically from Jude, the brother of James, then it must be quite early; (2) if it reflects "early catholicism," then 100 CE is a reasonable date; (3) if written to combat gnosticism, then a much later date is warranted. Some items in the document remain suggestive of an early-second-century date: (1) the sophistication of the Greek, (2) the remark in v 17 about the prophecy of the apostles, suggesting that it belongs to the past, (3) controversy over leadership. Yet none of this yields hard data for a firm decision. Suffice it to note that the date will be pegged to one's assessment of the opponents whom Jude combats.

The discussion of the identity of the author divides over whether the letter is authentic or pseudonymous. Even if pseudonymous, the author claims to be Jude, the brother of James. Scholars tend to identify the claimant more precisely as Judas, one of the brothers of the Lord (Mark 6:3; Matt 13:55; Eusebius, *H.E.* 3.19.1; see R. Bauckham, *Jude and the Relatives of Jesus*, 5–32). Other possible Judes include: (1) "Judas of James" (Luke 6:16, Acts 1:13), but common usage demands that we read this as "son of," not "brother of" James; (2) "Judas Thomas" (Eusebius, *H.E.* 1.13.11; *Gos. Thom.* Prologue), but this does not explain why Jude is "brother of James," a seemingly more prominent person; (3) "Judas Barsabbas" (Acts 15:22, 27, 32); or (4) "Jude, third bishop of Jerusalem" (*Apos. Const.* 7.46).

It is argued that the letter must be authentic because Jude is an obscure figure in the early church and no honor or authority accrues from claiming the identity of a nobody. Yet there is evidence that Jude was the subject of considerable legendary development. For example, Hegesippus tells about Jude's grandsons brought before Domitian because they were of the family of David and related to Christ himself (Eusebius, *H.E.* 3.19.1–20.7). In the *Acts of Paul*, "the blessed Judas, the brother of the Lord," took Paul into a great church in

Damascus after his enlightenment (*NT Apoc.* 2.388). And Julius Africanus tells how relatives of Jesus went about expounding the gospel genealogy about Jesus, which honored them as well (Eusebius, *H.E.* 1.7.14). Thus it seems facile to consider Jude, mentioned both in the gospels and in later historical and/or legendary narratives, as unknown or insignificant. Therefore, if one Christian document can be said to come from James, brother of the Lord, Jude, also a blood relative of Jesus and a figure of history and legend, is a likely candidate for author of a pseudonymous composition.

Arguments for and against authenticity, moreover, tend to depend on scholarly assessments of the dating of the document and its contents. Against authenticity, moreover, one should note the fine quality of Greek and the highly literate scribal authority of the author. These are unlikely achievements of Jesus' blood relatives, who, like him, were landless artisans living in peasant villages. Thus there is scant data for taking a firm position as to date, place, and author. Until fresh evidence or new ways of framing the question are introduced, we can only surmise historical judgments in this regard.

4. Jude's Opponents

We can only speculate what teaching or doctrines the opponents of Jude spoke to his church. Whenever Jude speaks about them, he negatively labels them in such a way as to present them as thoroughly evil and corrupting of the holy church (R. J. Karris, "The Background and Significance of the Polemic of the Pastoral Epistles," *JBL* 92 [1973]: 549–64). Moreover, we have only Jude's perception of them, and not their own materials; and it may well be that Jude tailors their remarks into a commonplace, just as Josephus organized various remarks about the Jewish parties of his time so that they could be recognized as Pythagoreans, Stoics, and Epicureans (*B.J.* 2.119–66; *Ant.* 13.171–73; 18.11–22).

Given all these cautions, can we know anything about the doctrine of Jude's opponents? Let us examine a scenario which scholars call "overly realized eschatology." Because Jude states that his opponents are within the group of disciples, they cannot be formally hostile to the one true God or to Jesus the Savior. But Jude may perceive them as being heterodox in such a way that could be perceived as hostile to certain aspects of the tradition. (1) For example, they "deny our only master and lord" (v 4), not because they reject the lordship of Jesus, but inasmuch as they confess that the resurrection has already occurred, they cannot imagine that the saints will be judged. Hence, "denial of the Lord" might be perceived as the rejection of future judgment of the saints. Jude, of course, confesses that Jesus judges all, even those previously saved (v 5); he quotes an obscure authority to the effect, "The Lord will rebuke you" (v 9). (2) They "insult the glorious ones" (v 8) who might well be the angels who accompany Jesus at his parousia and who gather all to judgment. The contest between Michael and the devil over Moses' body implies that angels have some role in regard to the rewards or punishments of those who come to judgment after death. Rejecting future judgment, the opponents likewise deny this role to God's agents. Yet Jude quotes *1 Enoch* to the effect that "the Lord is coming with his tens of thousands of holy ones to pass judgment on all and to convict all the ungodly" (vv 14–15). (3) Jude denies them the Holy Spirit, which presumably they claimed. This Spirit, if the opponents truly possessed it, might well be interpreted by them to mean that they are beyond the world of flesh and that they enjoy freedom from laws which control the flesh. Hence, when Jude accuses them of debauchery (v 4) and defilement of the flesh (v 8), he challenges their view of the body as "indifferent." When he accuses them of being "animals" (v 10) and "physical" (v 19), he denies their claims to be beyond the body, and so, laws and customs that govern it. (4) The opponents "flout authority" (v 8) and insult and revile (v 15) figures of status within the hierarchical world of the church (heavenly and earthly). This might be an expression of a special spiritual status of freedom from law as well as victory over evil spirits, Death included. Jude affirms the sovereignty of the Lord (vv 5–7, 9, 14–15) and of those appointed by the Lord (v 8). Paul appears to have configured remarks by some at Corinth in this way (see D. W. Kuck, *Judgment and Community Conflict* [NovTSup 66. Leiden: E. J. Brill, 1992], 16–25). Moreover 2 Tim 2:17–18 claims that Hymenaeus and Philetus are proclaiming that "the resurrection is already past."

This reconstruction may suggest more about how Jude perceives his rivals than about what they actually said themselves, which at any rate is not accessible to us. He may have imagined the end to which this or that remark would lead, conflating them and labeling them as we have suggested. The above scenario, while it accounts for many remarks about the opponents and relates them according to a particular logic, enjoys little proof. It remains, at best, a possible scenario.

5. The Social Location of the Author

A new and potentially valuable question can be asked which is developed out of the sociology of knowledge and sociorhetorical criticism. V. Robbins ("The Social Location of the Implied Author of Luke-Acts," *The Social World of Luke-Acts* [J. H. Neyrey, ed.; Peabody, MA: Hendrickson, 1991], 305–30) developed a model for gleaning information about an author from a careful reading of a document. He lists nine arenas of the possible social system in which authors are found and seeks to learn not just about the social location of the authors, but also the wider social context in which they work. Not all of the nine arenas are appropriate to so modest a document as Jude, but we employ those which are useful as new lenses for examining this text.

(a) Previous Events. He refers to the "past," but this is a common cultural bias in his world which values what is old over what is new and seeks solutions to present problems by appeal to tradition. He notes an earlier delivery of the Christian belief system given once for all (v 3), which should suffice as the group's basic belief system. He cites as examples, moreover, past figures who were punished (vv 5–7) or who embodied vices to be avoided (v 11). He cites as exhortation for present behavior past literary works which confirm judgment against challenging and evil people (vv 9, 14–15). Finally he quotes a prophecy delivered in the recent past that scoffers would come (vv 17–18). His references to past events suggest that (1) his audience was supposed to be fully instructed once for all in the past, and any novelty must be classified as deviant; (2) hortatory examples from legend and history have a bearing on the present; (3) ancient writings continue to influence present behavior. The thrust of this has to do with moral exhortation rather than history, for past events are expected to continue to have bearing on the present as behavioral controls.

In two places Jude refers to certain past events which help to position him in terms of the history of his relationship with his addressees. When he writes about "the faith delivered once and for all to the saints" (v 3), he does not appear to have been the founder of the church now addressed. Paul was very emphatic about his role as founding father of his churches (e.g., 1 Cor 3:6, 10; 4:15; Rom 15:20–21; 2 Cor 11:2); church tradition, moreover, speaks of the apostles as foundation stones of the new edifice (Eph 2:20; Rev 21:14). Jude does not claim such role and consequent status, which would certainly aid him in his defense of his ascribed authority. He is, moreover, absent, hence he writes a letter; it is his wont, moreover, to write to this group ("make haste to correspond with you about our common salvation," v 3a). He appears to be a second-generation member of the group, not its founder. On the contrary, he positions himself as their reminder of past indoctrination.

Furthermore, when he urges the church to remember "what the apostles foretold" (v 17), this suggests that he does not consider himself an apostle. Bauckham has vigorously argued that v 17 need not indicate a late date for the author (*Jude, 2 Peter,* 103–4), but all the more striking is the fact that Jude makes no claim to have founded this group nor is he the primary purveyor of Jesus and church traditions to them. That has all been done earlier by someone else. Hence, Jude refers to past events in the history of his addressees in such a way that he suggests certain things about his social location. He implies that he is a more recent member of the group, a second-generation member, but one of noteworthy status. Yet he is not the founder, the apostle who first gathered them. The group itself enjoys a noble past, in which they were fully instructed; Jude styles himself as the reminder of what they once knew.

(b) Natural Environment. Although Jude mentions "Egypt" (v 5), it represents a place of legend and history and does not suggest that he or his audience lived there. When speaking about "Sodom, Gomorrah, and the villages around them" (v 7), the author reflects accurate knowledge about the relationship of cities to satellite villages. The Hebrew text speaks about Sodom, Gomorrah, and "the valley" they occupy (Gen. 19:28, 29), but not the rather technical description of "villages around them." R. Rohrbaugh ("The Pre-Industrial City in Luke-Acts," *The Social World of Luke-Acts* [J. H. Neyrey, ed.; Peabody, MA: Hendrickson, 1991], 126–27, 31–33) notes how 1 Macc 5:56 speaks about "Hebron and its villages" and Mark 8:27 speaks about "the villages around Caesarea Philippi." The author, who is presumably a city dweller, knows that cities have a reciprocal relationship to a specific group of surrounding villages. When the author describes the opponents in metaphors in vv 12–13, he seemingly alludes to air (clouds), earth (trees), water (waves), and sky (stars). Whether he depends on *1 Enoch* 2.1.–5.4 (Bauckham, *Jude and the Relatives of Jesus*, 191–92) or whether this is a more Greek allusion to the four elements (air = clouds; earth = trees; water = waves; fire = stars), there is no particular knowledge of geography noted which describes the author's particular experience or location. Thus the author accurately knows about cities and surrounding villages, but other places are known from legend and history.

(c) Population Structure. Although *agapētoi* (vv 3, 20) may refer to both females and males, all of the other persons in the document are males. Jude is brother to James, servant to Jesus; the opponents appear to be males, both because the examples of males who are punished (vv 5–7, 11) apply to them and because they are accused of characteristic male behavior, such as sexual aggressiveness (vv 4, [6,7], 16, 18) and honor challenges (vv 4, 8, 16). Male authorities are noted (Enoch, v 14; apostles, v 17); because they are doing male actions (i.e., public quarreling). Michael and Satan are presumably males (v 9); Enoch's descent is through the male Adam (v 14); and the Lord Jesus Christ is male and does male things. The dominant actions of the persons in the letter can be described as male behavior: public speech, honor challenges, law-court disputes, sexual prowess. The author appears to be male as well, in virtue of his scribal sophistication. His scribal background suggests that he and his audience are city dwellers, not peasants in villages. But nothing in the document suggests whether they are elite or nonelite.

(d) Technology. If technology is knowledge for practical ends, the main illustrations of this have to do with speech and writing. The author can write good Greek; he has access to other writings, two esoteric books which were not exactly household items (*T. Moses*, v 9; *1 Enoch*, vv 14–15). Presumably he writes on papyrus. The world expressed in Jude is one of writing and school traditions.

(e) Socialization and Personality. The author exhibits a scribal background because of (1) his ability to write letters; (2) his good Greek vocabulary and style; (3) his knowledge of lore and tradition; (4) his access to esoteric writings; (5) his rhetorical excellence. This suggests a nonelite status for the author, presumably that of an urban retainer class. Such people are readily found as the retainers of elites, either as slaves or freedmen. Jude writes on his own behalf, thereby acknowledging an honor challenge from opponents who contest his role and status in the group. It is often suggested that Jude quotes esoteric writings because his opponents do. But at least he knows these writings and employs them with rhetorical effect.

(f) Culture. This refers to artistic, literary, historical, and aesthetic competencies. The author appears to have good scribal competencies. Evidently he has literary training, for he can read a variety of documents, those pertaining to his tradition and those outside it. A writer of good Greek, he is classically educated and expresses himself in fine rhetorical style. He knows a variety of literary forms, e.g., letters, woe oracles, doxologies, etc.; he knows biblical examples in a haggadic manner, not simply from reading the scriptural text. This indicates some form of school tradition. He is part of a system of teachers and literary resources.

The provenance of his lore and literature are distinctly Jewish. A full catalog of citations of, echoes of, and allusions to Jewish materials is not possible here, but the following give a strong sense of what Jude knows (see Wolthuis, "Jude and Jewish Traditions," 21–39). Full documentation on where these parallels or affinities are found in Jewish literature is found in the commentary *ad loc*, and is not repeated here.

Jewish Traditions Known by Jude

(1) Biblical examples from Genesis (vv 5–7)
(2) Allusion to *Testament of Moses* (v 9)
(3) Angels as "glorious ones" (v 8)
(4) Reference to Cain, Balaam, Korah (v 11)
(5) Enoch, seventh from Adam (v 14)
(6) Citation of *1 Enoch* (vv 14–15); Bauckham (*Jude, 2 Peter*, 94–96) argues that Jude translated *1 Enoch* from the Aramaic and (*Jude and*

the Relatives of Jesus, 211–16) presents a lengthy list of possible uses of *1 Enoch* in Jude

(7) Flattery/partiality condemned (v 16)

(8) Possible citations from LXX (Chaine, *Les Epîtres Catholiques*, 277)

(9) Semitisms (Bauckham, *Jude, 2 Peter*, 6)

(10) Knowledge of Hebrew (Bauckham, "Jude: An Account of Research," 3793–94)

What is cogent here is that when arguments are made or precedents cited, they come from Jewish traditions. These apparently are considered by Jude as his best authorities in a culture which valued tradition. Moreover, two esoteric writings are used, one merely alluded to (*Testament of Moses*, v 9) and one cited explicitly (*1 Enoch*, vv 14–15). If they are used because they both clearly state that the Lord will judge, there are more mainstream documents which express this. Hence Jude may be said to favor use of unusual materials, either because his opponents use them or because they enhance his status.

Jude's knowledge of and citation of Christian materials demands attention. The following is a partial list of affinities with Christian writings (see Cantinat, *Les Epîtres de Saint Jacques et de Saint Jude*, 270–76). They hardly indicate literary dependence, but are more in the nature of commonplaces and general traditions shared.

(1) Jude as "servant" (Rom 1:1; 1:10; Phil 1:1; James 1:1)

(2) addressees called "beloved" (Rom 1:7; 1 Cor 4:14; 1 John 3:2)

(3) epistolary benediction (Roman 1:7; 1 Tim 1:2; 2 Tim 1:2)

(4) faith delivered (1 Cor 11:2; 15:1–3)

(5) contend for faith (1 Tim 1:18)

(6) changing grace to vice (Gal 5:13; Rom 6:15)

(7) Exodus generation as example (1 Cor 10:6–13)

(8) authority spurned (Titus 1:16)

(9) apostolic predictions of crises (Acts 20:29–30)

(10) triad: faith, love, hope (1 Thess 1:3; 5:8; 1 Cor 13:13)

(11) build up (1 Cor 8:1; 10:23; 14:4, 17; Gal 2:18)

(12) divisions (1 Cor 1:11; 3:3)

(13) unblemished (Eph 1:4; Col 1:22; 1 Thess 3:13)

(14) epistolary doxology (Rom 16:25–27; Eph 3:20)

Jude's vocabulary contains many unique and rare words, and does not cite explicitly either gospel traditions or Pauline letters. This may be evidence of a scribal attempt to upgrade less felicitous language or of a mere oral acquaintance with Christian traditions. But the lack of specific links with Christian documents and the strong preference for Jewish materials is noteworthy.

(g) Foreign Affairs. There are no allusions to Rome and its officials or to Jerusalem and its temple elite. Jude reflects a strictly in-house view of the Christian world and its distinctive sense of role, power, and status: the only true God (v 25), Jesus the Christ, who is Master and Lord (vv 4, 25), apostles (v 17), relatives of the Lord (v 1), and prophets (v 14–15). God is described in the fashion of a great Patron-Benefactor, which is probably visible to the author from the example of local urban dignitaries. At least he knows of this common and important form of social relations.

(h) Belief Systems and Ideology. Jude claims to represent the common and consistent traditions of the early disciples of Jesus. We are more interested here in sketching the contours of his symbolic or cultural universe, rather than simply indicating with historical precision Jude's knowledge of this or that tradition. Our investigation of his shared symbolic universe draws upon the interpretative categories suggested by Mary Douglas as lenses for viewing and organizing the various elements of the symbolic universe of Jude (see *Purity and Danger* and *Natural Symbols*).

(1) *Purity and pollution.* Jude describes a world which classifies every person, place, and thing according to the shared social and moral norms of his tradition. He labels his addressees as saints and beloved of God (vv 1, 3); he exhorts them to remain such (vv 20–21). In contrast, the opponents are classified broadly as "godless" (vv 4, 15, 18), as animals (v 11), and as rebellious scoffers (v 16). We should note the extensive set of dualistic expressions in Jude which function to classify his addressees and his opponents:

Addressees	*Opponents/Scoffers*
(a) holy/holiness (vv 3, 20, 24)	(a) godlessness (vv 4, 15, 18)
(b) await mercy (vv 2, 21, 22–23)	(b) await judgment (vv 4, 6, 9, 15)
(c) in fear (v 23)	(c) fearlessness (v12)

Addressees	*Opponents/Scoffers*
(d) unblemished (v 24)	(d) defiled/stained (vv 8, 12, 23)
(e) pray in the Spirit (v 20)	(e) do not have the Spirit (v 19)
(f) build up (v 20)	(f) divide (v 19)
(g) stand before God (v 24)	(g) stumble —
(h) are saved (v 25)	(h) are destroyed (vv 5, 11)
(i) honor God (vv 24–25)	(i) challenge God (vv 4, 17)

There is, then, a clear classification system: saints are faithful to the tradition; the opponents are not. There appears to be a blurring of classification within the group, as the godless have made inroads into the group membership and claim some as their followers (vv 22–23).

This classification extends to places as well, for there is a place for everyone and everyone in his place. The addressees are properly placed in the traditional group, but they must contend for it (v 3) and build it up (v 20); thus they are "kept" in the right place (vv 2, 21) and will consequently enter a new and appropriate place (v 24). But others are clearly "out of place": the opponents have crept in where they do not belong (v 4). Worse, they seem to be characterized by having no fixed place, indicating a rootlessness which is deviance: clouds drifting and trees uprooted (v 12), waves blown about and wandering stars (v 13). Angels (v 6) are mentioned who left their proper place, thus causing pollution, for which they are kept in a new place, which is one of punishment for such evil.

This extends to the roles of persons in the document, which are clearly described and thus exactly classified. God enjoys supreme authority as "the only God," who deserves honor and glory (vv 24–25). Jesus is "the only Master and Lord" (v 4). Both of these figures are responsible for the moral order of the universe, especially Jesus, who will act as judge and "rebuke" the wicked (v 8) and "convict all the ungodly" (v 14). Angels (vv 9, 14–15) serve as Jesus' agents and messengers. Jude is Jesus' "servant" (v 1) and so acts with exact authority as his agent. Conversely, the opponents are described as contesting this classification: they "deny our only Master" (v 4) and despise authority (v 8). They are presented as rebels, contesting traditional teachings and authority (vv 8, 11, 16).

In addition to these abstract notions of what is "in place" or "out of place,"

Jude explicitly uses the language of purity and pollution. The addressees are saints ("called," "kept" by God, v 1), "beloved" of God (v 2); they should pray with God's *Holy* Spirit (v 20); and so enter "without blemish" into the presence of the holy God (v 24). In contrast, the opponents are corrupt and polluted: they pervert grace (v 4), engage in sexual impurity (vv 4, 7, 12), and defile the flesh (v 8); they are blemishes (v 12). Jude, then, perceives the whole world as exactly classified in terms of good/evil, pure/polluted, and in place/out of place. Part of his rhetorical strategy is to affirm this classification system.

(2) *Characteristic rituals*. If the world were truly orderly, then Jude's traditional classification system would hold. But the situation is one of breached boundaries and threatened perimeters. Hence, Jude, like most New Testament letters, serves as the occasion to identify a deceptive threat, an incipient corruption, a wall breached. It mobilizes attention and energy to the perimeter for defensive action. Although Jude does not demand the expulsion of the opponents, by labeling them as "godless," he situates them as "out of place." And by twice indicating the Lord will judge (vv 9, 14–15), he indicates the boundaries will finally be restored by the Lord and the threat removed.

(3) *Sin*. Evil and sin are perceived as a form of corruption, such as "leaven" (Matt 16:6, 12) or "gangrene" (2 Tim 2:16). Jude does not use such images, but he perceives the evil scoffers in this way. If left unchecked, the holy group would be corrupted and destroyed. Moreover, faced with such an imminent pollution, the appropriate response is a form of intolerance, which itself indicates a perception of evil as a form of death-dealing pollution.

(4) *Physical body*. The physical body, which is a microcosm of the social body, is perceived as normed and regulated by a set of rules comparable to the social rules which regulate its performance. Bodies must be holy and pure; hence, the saints must "keep" themselves in the practice of virtue: faithfulness, love, and hope (vv 20–21). This means holy activity, such as prayer in the Spirit (v 20). Conversely, the opponents exhibit loose body control: they are accused of sexual deviance, that is, failure to govern passions. Besides lack of control of the genital orifice, their mouths too lack control, for they contest authority (v 8), flatter and grumble (v 16); they are said to "blaspheme" often (vv 8, 15). They are like animals, who totally lack control.

(5) *Suffering and misfortune*. Why is there evil in the world? whence comes the suffering we endure? It was characteristic of ancient Jews and Christians to explain the presence of suffering and misfortune in terms of a personalized agent: "Who did this to me?" For example, God sent plagues on Egypt, as well as sickness and illness upon Israel for David's sin (2 Sam 21:1–6). Yet the agent

of evil might just as well be God's servant Satan, who caused Job great suffering and misfortune, or God's enemy, the devil, who is the agent of sin and death in the world. For example, disease and illness were thought to be caused by an evil personal power, the "Moon" (Matt 4:25; 17:15) or Satan (Luke 13:16). Jesus treats storms of wind the same as an evil spirit which he expels: he "rebukes" the wind and "commands" it (Mark 3:39); and the wind and storm obey him. In another vein, Jesus' disciples asked why a certain man was born blind, "Rabbi, who sinned, this man or his parents, that he was born blind?" (John 9:2).

Despite Jude's desire that everything remain in its place, he senses great threat to this ordered cosmos. He knows of the devil, a wicked figure who disparaged Moses, one of God's saints (v 9). Presumably this functions as one instance of a larger scenario in which Satan or some evil figure attacks God's holy ones. This macrocosmic attack of evil is replicated in the microcosm on earth where scoffers are attacking and seducing the holy church of God (vv 4, 12, 16, 18). In short, Jude perceives a world under siege: goodness is threatened by godlessness, God-given authority is challenged by interlopers.

Given the choice of personal agents of suffering and misfortune, the evil which they inflict might be justly or unjustly deserved. In certain times, popular wisdom perceived the world as a *kosmos*, that is, an orderly and rational world where the rules of God and society were well known and where God acted as a just judge. Hence, suffering would be perceived in terms of some crime-punishment schema. "As you sow, so shall you reap" (Gal 6:7). The common *lex talionis* applies here: an eye for an eye, a tooth for a tooth. Yet suffering, as in the case of Job and others, clearly is not explained by this moral pattern. In many such cases the world is *not* perceived as a *kosmos* of order and fairness; evil agents, such as Satan, hostile angelic powers, and the like, attack good people and make war on them (e.g., Luke 4:1–13; 22:31). Thus the prophets of old, John the Baptizer, Jesus and his disciples are all attacked by evil powers. Their suffering is unjust; their misfortune is a personal assault.

Jude's world resembles the orderly *kosmos* of God's clear laws, firm control, and just judgment. Indeed, the document's most persistent theme is the just punishment by God of past and present sinners for crimes clearly proscribed. God's just judgment means that God "keeps" safe the righteous (v 1) and "keeps" the wicked for judgment (v 6). Jude's addressees are told to keep themselves spotless and stainless, and so to await the mercy of Christ on the judgment day (vv 21, 24).

Yet because of the polemical nature of the document, Jude articulates more carefully God's judgment of the wicked, both past and present. Although the generation that escaped Egypt experienced God's mercy, they subsequently sinned and received a just judgment (v 5). Indeed all three biblical examples in vv 5–7 testify to God's punishment of the wicked. Jude twice quotes from Jewish writings to the effect that "the Lord will rebuke you" (v 9) or that "the Lord is coming with his tens of thousands of holy ones, to pass judgment on all and to convict all the ungodly" (vv 14–15). He cites woes against those who go the way of traditional sinners such as Cain, Balaam, and Korah (v 11); like them, they too will meet a terrible judgment. Thus Jude frequently speaks of God punishing or condemning the ungodly (vv 4, 5–7, 8, 10, 12–13, 14–16, 17–29). In this document, suffering and misfortune are indeed caused by a personal agent. But in Jude's moral world, that agent is the just God who rewards the faithful and requites the godless.

What, then, does this tell us about the social location of the implied author? This male writer appears to be a person trained as a scribe who practices his craft with considerable sophistication. He is an urban retainer, a nonelite member of his city. He may be a slave or freedman, but there is no way of knowing this. He is definitely Jewish, a fact clearly demonstrated by his almost exclusive use of Jewish canonical and extracanonical lore and literature as well as Jewish benedictions and doxologies. His symbolic world shares the same value orientations characteristic of Jews in antiquity (honor and shame; purity systems). He claims and defends a particular role and status within the group. Within the Christian group, he positions himself as the guardian of tradition, and so, of orthodoxy. Hence, he is no mere member of the group, but enjoys a particular status because of his blood ties to James and to Jesus. His entire focus is intramural, namely, the Christian group and more specifically, a dispute over leadership within it. It is difficult to distinguish the claims of the implied author, if the letter is pseudonymous, from the claims of the real author, if authentic. If pseudonymous, then the author knows how to present his document within that literary and social tradition.

BIBLIOGRAPHY

R. Bauckham, *Jude, 2 Peter* (Waco, TX: Word Books, 1983).

———, "The Letter to Jude: An Account of Research," *ANRW* II.2.25.5 (1988): 3791–3826. Reprinted as ch. 3 in *Jude and the Relatives of Jesus in the Early Church*, 134–78.

———, *Jude and the Relatives of Jesus in the Early Church* (Edinburgh: T. & T. Clark, 1990).

Cantinat, J., *Les Epîtres de Saint Jacques et de Saint Jude* (Paris: Gabalda, 1973).

Chaine, Joseph, *Les Epîtres Catholiques* (Paris: Gabalda, 1939).

Charles, J. Daryl, "Jude's Use of Pseudepigraphical Source-Material as Part of a Literary Strategy," *NTS* 37 (1991): 130–45.

———, "Literary Artifice in the Epistle of Jude," *ZNW* 82 (1991): 106–24.

Douglas, Mary, *Purity and Danger: An Analysis of the Concepts of Pollution and Taboo* (London: Routledge and Kegan Paul, 1966).

———, *Natural Symbols: Explorations in Cosmology* (New York: Pantheon Books, 1982).

Dunnett, W. M., "The Hermeneutics of Jude and 2 Peter: The Use of Ancient Jewish Traditions," *JETS* 31 (1988): 287–92.

Eybers, I. H., "Aspects of the Background of the Letter of Jude," *Neot* 9 (1975): 113–23.

Gunther, John J., "The Alexandrian Epistle of Jude," *NTS* 30 (1984): 549–62.

Heilgenthal, R., "Der Judasbrief: Aspekte der Forschung in den letzten Jahrzehnten," *TRu* 51 (1986): 117–29.

Isenberg, Sheldon, and Owen, Dennis E., "Bodies, Natural and Contrived: The Work of Mary Douglas," *RSRev* 3 (1977): 1–17.

Joubert, S. J., "Language, Ideology and the Social Context of the Letter of Jude," *Neot* 24 (1990): 335–49.

Rowston, Douglas J., "The Most Neglected Book in the New Testament," *NTS* 21 (1975): 554–63.

Sellin, G., "Die Häretiker des Judasbriefes," *ZNW* 77 (1986): 206–25.

Watson, Duane F., *Invention, Arrangement, and Style: Rhetorical Criticism of Jude and 2 Peter* (SBLDS 104. Atlanta: Scholars Press, 1986), 34–79.

White, John L., "Ancient Greek Letters," *Greco-Roman Literature and the New Testament* (D. E. Aune, ed.; SBLSBS 21. Atlanta: Scholars Press, 1988) 85–105.

Wolthuis, T. R., "Jude and Jewish Traditions," *CTJ* 22 (1987): 21–41.

———, "Jude and Rhetoricism: A Dialogue on the Rhetorical Nature of the Epistle of Jude," *CTJ* 24 (1989): 126–34.

I.
Letter Opening: Address and Greeting (Jude 1–2)

♦

1. Jude, servant of Jesus Christ and brother of James, to those beloved of God the Father and called and kept by Jesus Christ. 2. May mercy and peace and love be multiplied in you.

Letter Genre

Except for four "gospels" and the Acts of the Apostles, New Testament documents tend to be "letters," either actual letters sent to particular churches or communications written in a letter form. The New Testament contains (1) seven undisputed Pauline letters as well as 2 Thess, Eph, Col, 1–2 Tim and Titus; (2) two Petrine letters; (3) one letter from James; (4) three Johannine letters; and (5) seven letters to the churches of Asia Minor. Besides the letters Paul carried to the synagogue in Damascus (9:2; 22:5), Acts records the text of a letter from the Jerusalem church to Antioch, Syria, and Cilicia (15:23–26) and from the Roman centurion to Felix (23:26–30). Early Christian literature includes Ignatius' seven letters, as well as letters from Clement, Polycarp, and Barnabas. Whether real letters or documents written in letter form, the New Testament overwhelmingly selected the epistolary genre as the form of its communication.

Typical New Testament letters contain the following formal elements (Doty, *Letters in Primitive Christianity*, 27–43):

(1) Opening (sender, addressees, greeting)
(2) Thanksgiving or Blessing
(3) Body

(4) Parenesis

(5) Closing (doxology, greetings)

In contrast, Jude contains only an epistolary opening and closing, as does the letter cited in Acts 15:23–26. Jude 3–23 can be said to constitute the body of the letter. In terms of letter type, Jude should be classified as a "parenetic" letter; for at the beginning of the document the author states his exhortatory purpose: "I found it necessary to write and *exhort* you to contend for the faith" (v 3; see S. K. Stowers, *Letter Writing in Greco-Roman Antiquity* [Philadelphia: Westminster, 1986], 94–106). Although Jude exhorts his addressees to fight, this is hardly a petitionary letter as Bauckham has described it (*Jude, 2 Peter*, 28), for no specific thing is requested; on petitionary letters, see T. Y. Mullins, "Petition as a Literary Form," *NovT* 5 (1962): 46–54.

LETTER OPENING

Sender. The author identifies himself as "Jude, servant of Jesus Christ and brother of James." He is not an apostle himself, but knows of this elite circle (v 17); rather he is "servant." Although we tend today to idealize Christian leadership in terms of service, not hierarchy or power, the label of "servant" identifies special agents of God who were either kings, patriarchs, or prophets: Abraham, Isaac, and Jacob (Exod 32:13; Deut 9:27), Moses (Deut 34:5; 1 Kgs 8:53; Josephus, *Ant.* 5.39), Samuel (1 Sam 3:9–10), David (1 Sam 17:32; 2 Sam 3:18), Ahijah (1 Kgs 15:29). Courtiers at Saul's court call themselves "servants" (1 Sam 18:5, 30); Ahaz addresses the king of Assyria as his "servant" (2 Kgs 16:7). Disciples of Jesus with leadership roles likewise describe themselves with this honorific label: Paul (Rom 1:1; Gal 1:10; Phil 1:1; Titus 1:1), James (1:1), and Peter (2 Pet 1:1). All of these figures are "servants of God," trusted members of the circle that surrounds the sheik, pharaoh, the king, or God. As officials in the household of God they have specific rights and duties (see J. N. Collins, *Diakonia: Re-interpreting the Ancient Sources* [Oxford: Oxford University Press, 1990], 92–95).

The sender claims to be "brother of James." While both "Jude" and "James" are common names in ancient Judea, the implied author presumes that his addressees will recognize this "James" and this "Jude." Modern readers unfortunately lack ready clues as to the sure identity of these two persons which would have come from the locale where the document was read, the members of the group addressed, and other defining elements of its situation in life. Thus we must speculate as to the probability of their identity. Scholars have traditionally identified this James as "James, the brother of the Lord." Mark's list of the four brothers of Jesus includes "Jude" or "Judas" (6:3; see Matt 13:55). Early Christian literature records numerous notices of the brothers of the Lord, which suggests both interest in them and their importance in the circle of the early disciples. Bauckham (*Jude, 2 Peter*, 24) notes that after the death of James, son of Zebedee, only one early Christian leader was known simply as "James" (Acts 12:17; 15:13; 21:18; 1 Cor 15:7; Gal 2:9, 12). Moreover, only one pair of brothers called Jude and James is known in the New Testament (Mark 6:3). Thus, although we lack the data for exactly identifying James and Jude, the material just noted makes it probable that the implied author expects his addressees to recognize him as the brother of James, who was himself the brother of the Lord.

Then why not claim the higher honor of being "brother of the Lord"? Why settle for "brother of James"? Although we can only speculate about the precise rhetorical strategy involved here, it would not have been a mean thing to be kin of a prominent figure like James. We have general evidence that the kinsmen of Jesus enjoyed special honor and status in the early church. Eusebius, for example, records that some of these kinsmen seemed indeed to traffic in this association:

> They themselves, either remembering the names or otherwise deriving them from copies, gloried in the preservation of the memory of their good birth; among these were those mentioned above, called *desposyni*, because of their relation to the family of the Saviour, and from the Jewish villages of Nazareth and Cochaba they traversed the rest of the land and expounded the preceding genealogy of their descent ([*H.E.* 1.7.14]).

There is another story from the early church that Jude's own grandsons were politically suspect because of their kinship ties with Jesus, who was himself of the house of David.

> There still survived of the family of the Lord grandsons of Jude, who was said to have been his brother according to the flesh, and they were delated as being of the family of David . . . But when they were released they were the leaders of the churches, both for their testimony and for their relation to the Lord ([*H.E.* 3.20.1 & 6]).

Honor and status, then, clearly come from kinship with important people. We surmise that James, the brother of the Lord, was a person of prominence, and so kinship with him would mean special honor and status as well. Bauckham (*Jude, 2 Peter*, 24–25) suggests that it would be incongruous for the sender to identify himself both as "servant of Jesus Christ" and "brother of the Lord." And so, status is claimed by being Jesus' servant, whereas honor is claimed by kinship with the prominent figure James.

Addressees. Unlike the practice in other New Testament letters, the addressees are not identified. Either specific individuals might be addressed (i.e,. Philemon, Timothy, Titus), particular churches (i.e., Corinth, Philippi), or general regions (i.e., Galatia, Asia Minor, the diaspora; see N. A. Dahl, "The Particularity of the Pauline Epistles as a Problem in the Ancient Church," *Neotestamentica et Patristica* [NovTSup 6. Leiden: E. J. Brill, 1962], 261–71). But Jude writes "to those beloved of God." We should not think of this as a "catholic" letter written about general topics to a general audience, such as Ephesians, although the author speaks about the "faith handed on once for all" (v 3). The author treats specific issues, although we find no clues to the specific churches or regions addressed. From remarks about opponents seeking gain and profit (vv 11, 16), we find ourselves in the world of nonelites, that is, artisans and peasants who made up 90 percent of the population of the ancient world. The mention of flattery (v 16), moreover, suggests the social phenomenon of patrons and clients and the use of flattery for gaining economic or honorable advantages. The author himself is Jewish, and there is nothing in his remarks to suggest that he is addressing other than people of Jewish background.

Greetings. Typical Hellenistic letters open with a simple "Greetings!" (e.g., Acts 15:23; 23:26). New Testament letters typically wish the recipients "grace and peace from God our Father and the Lord Jesus Christ" (Rom 1:7; 1 Cor 1:3; etc.). Although a triple greeting ("grace, mercy, and peace") is found in 1–2 Tim, Jude's wish of "mercy, peace, and love" is distinctive, as is the simple wish that the recipients "be filled" (see 1 Pet 1:2; Polycarp, *Phil.*). The letter opening, although distinctive, falls well within the formulas of New Testament letters. The triple benefaction from God is the first of the many triplets which characterize Jude's style (J. D. Charles, "Jude's Use of Pseudepigraphical Source-Material as Part of a Literary Strategy," *NTS* 37 [1991]: 132).

In terms of the letter's structure, the greeting in v 2 is balanced with v 21 where the recipients are exhorted to "keep . . . in the *love* of God and await the *mercy* of our Lord." The stereotypical formula in v 2, moreover, may contain hints of themes to be developed in the document: (1) as they have received mercy, they should have mercy on others (vv 22–23); (2) the peace they enjoy is disturbed by those causing division (v 19), who speak defiant words (vv 4, 15); (3) love and being beloved pertain to kinship identity in the group and loyalty to it (vv 1, 12, 21), in contrast to the selfishness of certain scoffers (vv 4, 12).

Honor All Around

Honor is the value, reputation, or worth of persons both in the eyes of those who claim it and those who acknowledge it. In establishing his credentials to be a legitimate authority, the author claims an honorable rank and status on two counts. First, he is "servant" of Jesus Christ, a label which identifies him as an official agent of the household of the Lord, a steward or majordomo. Then in claiming blood relationship to James, he shares in the honorable status of that "pillar of the church" (Gal 2:9; Bauckham, *Jude and the Relatives of Jesus*, 14–15). J. N. D. Kelly observed that it is natural enough to mention a man's father, but why his brother (*The Epistles of Peter and of Jude* [London: Adam and Charles Black, 1969], 242)? Yet brothers are presented precisely as pairs (Peter and Andrew; James and John) and the lesser is identified in relation to the more prominent brother, a cultural phenomenon rooted not just in the Bible (Gen 10:21; Exod 4:14; Josh 15:17; 1 Sam 14:3) but in the general ancient culture. A younger sibling, whose birth ranks him lower than his older brother, claims honor by blood ties with his richer, stronger, or more influential brother.

If Jude is the brother of James, is he not then "brother of the Lord" as James was (Gal 1:19)? Honor resides in blood, especially the clan and family of Jesus (see D. J. Rowston, "The Most Neglected Book in the New Testament," *NTS* 21 [1975]: 559). Despite the polemic against family ties in the gospels (Matt 12:46–50; Luke 9:57–61; John 1:12–13), kinship relationship with Jesus continued to be a source of honor and status in the early church. James, the brother of the Lord, became a leader in the Jerusalem church (Acts 12:17; 15:13–21; see 1 Cor 15:7); this person is presumably the author of the Letter of James (1:1). As noted in the "Introduction to Jude # 3," Eusebius records early witnesses to the fact that some relatives of Jesus traveled about proclaiming the family genealogy, in which Jesus and they are attested as members of the house of David (*H.E.* 1.7.14). Eusebius also quotes Hegesippus' report that Jude's grandsons testified before the emperor Domitian about their Davidic lineage (*H.E.* 3.19.1–20.7). In virtue of this type of ascribed authority, Jude writes a letter which he expects will command respect.

In assessing the ways that persons claim authority or honorable roles and status, anthropologists indicate that authority may be either ascribed or achieved. Ascribed authority is like inherited wealth: it comes to individuals independently of their achievements. For example, sons born to the king enjoy ascribed roles and status as royal heirs; governors and procurators are appointed by Caesar or the Roman senate; to those born of pure Levitical lines priesthood is ascribed. Jude claims ascribed authority by virtue of kinship with James, a known and respected figure in the early Church. If Jude is likewise a "brother of the Lord" (Mark 6:3; Matt 13:55), his authority resides likewise in blood relationship to the Lord, that is, ascribed or inherited honor. And since Jesus is descended from David, Jude is ascribed the same honor from the ancient royal ancestor.

In the New Testament, the ascribed authority of apostles and church founders is generally expressed in formulas such as: (1) specific commissions, e.g., Peter's designation as "rock" (Matt 16:17–19) or the apostles' selection and commissioning (Matt 10:2–4); (2) comments about being "set aside from one's mother's womb," e.g., Paul (Gal 1:15–17; Rom 1:1; K. O. Sandnes, *Paul—One of the Prophets?* [Tübingen: J. C. B. Mohr, 1991], 48–65); and (3) statements that one has been "called" (1 Cor 1:1) or that "grace was given me" (1 Cor 3:10). When Jude describes himself as "servant" of Jesus Christ, this should be understood as a recognized form of ascribed authority (see 1 Peter 1:1). Thus Jude enjoys status and authority because of kinship with James (and the Lord) and because of a specific commission as "servant."

Jude's honor rests on the better type of authority, ascribed not achieved. Achieved authority comes in virtue of performance and achievement, such as a warrior's success in combat (1 Sam 17:50–51; 18:7), victory in games (1 Cor 9:24–27), benefaction (Luke 7:5), and charismatic behavior (1 Cor 14:18). It seems likely that Jude's opponents claim achieved authority, thus challenging the ascribed role and status of a person with more traditional credentials for group leadership.

His addressees are described as honorable people. They are the recipients of great benefactions by God, for they are "beloved" (i.e., fictive kinship members of God's family), "called," and "kept." God has deemed them worthy of this benefaction, and so they take honor from being the worthy clients of a worthy patron. By beginning with this record of benefaction, the author positions himself to remind them of the debt of honor and faithfulness owed their heavenly patron, unlike the scoffers who despise authority and deny the sovereignty of the Lord, and thus shame their patron.

Oddly, there are no honorific labels ascribed either to Jesus or to God in the letter opening, which is not the case in other New Testament letters. Yet as the document continues, the surpassing honor of the Lord Jesus (v 4) and the excellence of God (vv 24–25) will be highlighted.

NOTES

Jude/Judas. We translate the same Greek name *Ioudas* both as "Judas" and "Jude." It was evidently a common Jewish name, for we know of many Judes/ Judases:

1. Judas Iscariot (Matt 10:4)
2. the apostle Judas, son of James (Luke 6:16; Acts 1:13)
3. Judas, a brother of the Lord (Mark 6:3; Matt 13:55)
4. Judas, an associate of Paul and Barnabas (Acts 15:22)
5. Judas, the fifteenth bishop of Jerusalem (Eusebius, *H.E.* 4.5.3)
6. Didymus Judas Thomas, the implied author of the *Gospel of Thomas*

By describing himself as "brother of James," he seems to expect his addressees to identify him as a "brother of the Lord," in accord with the traditions cited in Mark 6:3 and Matt 13:55. All of this retains some element of conjecture on our part. Modern readers, however, may at least confidently identify this Jude as a Jew, who cites two noncanonical Jewish writings (*Testament of Moses* and *1 Enoch*) and alludes frequently to exemplary figures from the Pentateuch. His letter salutation is likewise distinctively Jewish, as is the letter's final doxology.

Some traditions from eastern Syria near Edessa identify a certain Jude with the apostle Thomas, also known as Judas Thomas, the implied author of the *Gospel of Thomas*. Eusebius records a Syriac letter speaking of a certain Judas Thomas: "After the ascension of Jesus, Judas, who is also Thomas, sent Thaddaeus to him as an apostle" (*H.E.* 1.13.11). Since Thomas is a twin ("Didymus," John 14:22), he would presumably be Jesus' twin brother (H. Koester, "*GNOMAI DIAPHOROI*," *HTR* 58 [1965]: 297). But this tradition is late and quite local. Moreover, the sender of this letter does not identify himself as "brother of the Lord," twin or other, but as "brother of James."

JAMES

Mark 6:3 records that Jesus has four brothers (James, Joses, Judas, and Simon) and an undisclosed number of sisters (see Matt 13:55). Although John 7:3–5 and Mark 3:31 indicate that Jesus' brothers did not believe in him, Acts and Paul's letters indicate that James, at least, became a disciple and a high-ranking person in the early church. Luke records that after the death of a certain James (son of Zebedee), another James becomes prominent, who is James the brother of the Lord (see Acts 12:17 and 15:14). In the lists of Jerusalem's bishops, he is regularly listed first (Eusebius *H.E.* 4.5.3–4; 5.12.1–2). This is the "James the brother of the Lord" whom Paul visited in Jerusalem (Gal 1:19) and of whom Paul testifies that the Lord appeared to him (1 Cor 15:7). He is sometimes called "James the Less" for his shortness, but also "James the Just" for his piety: "The charge of the church passed to James the brother of the Lord . . . called the 'Just' by all men from the Lord's time to ours, since many were called James, but he was holy from his mother's womb" (Eusebius, *H.E.* 2.23.4–7). He is credited with authorizing the mission to the Gentiles, and thus became Paul's patron. And he is the alleged author of the Epistle to James. Ananus the high priest had James arrested and executed: "He convened the Sanhedrin and brought before them a man named James, the brother of Jesus who is called Christ . . . and delivered them up to be stoned" (Josephus, *Ant.* 20.200; Eusebius, *H.E.* 2.23.22).

CALLED

Bauckham shows that Jude evokes the general ideology in Isaiah LXX of Israel as called, loved, and kept (*Jude, 2 Peter*, 25). More specifically, Isa 42:6

speaks of the servant: "I have called . . . I will hold . . . I will strengthen" and Isa 48:15, "I have spoken . . . I have called . . . I have led him . . . I will prosper his ways." In such formulas, great honor is bestowed by a heavenly patron on his clients. Similarly, Paul speaks of the disciples of Jesus as "called to be saints" (Rom 1:6–7; 1 Cor 1:2), whereas Heb 9:15 speaks of them as called to be heirs. We note that ancient peoples depend upon invitations to join and share and act, although their association is generally described as "voluntary." They are expected to be self-sufficient and owe no one anything; it would be an honor challenge to offer oneself or volunteer for anything. This language, then, identifies them as group-oriented people who enjoy ascribed honor from a great benefactor.

BIBLIOGRAPHY

Bauckham, Richard, *Jude, 2 Peter* (Waco, TX: Word Books, 1983).

———, *Jude and the Relatives of Jesus in the Early Church* (Edinburgh: T. & T. Clark, 1990).

Berger, Klaus, "Apostelbrief und apostolische Rede," ZNW 65 (1974): 191–201.

Doty, William G., *Letters in Primitive Christianity* (Philadelphia: Fortress Press, 1973), 21–47.

White, John L., *Light from Ancient Letters* (Philadelphia: Fortress Press, 1986), 189–220.

II.
Letter Occasion: Insinuation of Deviants (Jude 3–4)

♦

3. Beloved, while making haste to correspond with you about our common salvation, I found it necessary to write and exhort you to contend for the faith delivered once and for all to the saints. 4. For certain men have crept in, who ages ago were proscribed for judgment. Godless men, they turn away from God's favor to debauchery and deny our only Master and Lord Jesus Christ.

Fictive Occasion of the Document: Challenge and Riposte

Jude's remark about correspondence and writing suggests some separation between the author and the addressees. Were he present there would be no need to write. Jude's posture is that of an official of the group, who not only looks to its general welfare ("about our common salvation"), but shepherds it in time of crisis ("certain men have crept in"). One might read v 4 as a statement about either traveling prophets who arrive with novel doctrines which threaten the group's purity or rivals to Jude for leadership of the group, especially if he is absent, which is suggested by the fact that a letter is sent (see G. Karlsson, "Formelhaftes in Paulusbriefes," *Eranos* 54 [1956]: 138–41). In other words, the issue sounds "dogmatic," but it might just as well be "sociological." Although the bulk of the document will catalog the vices of these rivals, it contains as well a strong defense of the author's honor, i.e., his role and status. He is the official "servant" of Jesus' household; he is kin to James (and Jesus). He is steward of "our common salvation," and reminds the group of its prophetic heritage. He guards them against the pollutions of false teachers, how they preach heterodoxy and cause divisions. He defends the honor of Jesus, as well as the honorable status of authorized persons in the group (v 8).

The document may profitably be examined as the author's riposte to an honor challenge. The world of Jude and indeed the first-century Mediterranean is rightly described as highly agonistic. On the level of peasants and artisans there was an ongoing social game of push and shove, of honor claimed and honor challenged. Jude claims a certain honor by virtue of blood relations with James (and Jesus); his official status is that of "servant" of Jesus. But "certain men" are obviously challenging this status. This letter constitutes the author's riposte, a defense both of the honor of Jesus which is slighted (vv 4, 8) and of the honor ascribed to Jude which is challenged. The very generality of his attack on these interlopers dissuades us from trying to identify their specific ideology (F. Wisse, "The Epistle of Jude in the History of Heresiology," *Essays on the Nag Hammadi Texts in Honor of Alexander Boehlig* [Martin Krause, ed.; Leiden: E. J. Brill, 1972], 133–43), and suggests that we can profitably read it sociologically as riposte to challenges to Jude's role and status.

These rivals are "godless" men, who spurn the divine benefaction ("they turn away from the favor of God to debauchery"), thus shaming their patron. They also shame Jesus, denying "our only Master and Lord" (v 4). Hence Jude presents them first and foremost as people who challenge honor, the honor of the group's heavenly patrons and that of the earthly agent of those patrons. Although Jude writes his own riposte, he cleverly notes that the true riposte comes from God: "ages ago they were proscribed for judgment" (v 4). And indeed vv 5–15 contain an extended record of how God has always given a divine riposte to rebellious and defiant people. The author speaks now as God's agent, who issues the first riposte, which consists of a reminder of how "the Lord will rebuke you" (v 9). The fact that we still have this document and revere it as the work of Jude suggests that the public verdict in this contest between rival authorities went in favor of Jude.

PURITY AND POLLUTION

As we noted in the introduction, "purity" and "pollution" are general abstract terms which define what conforms or violates specific values and norms of a given group. Hence, we do not simply look for terms such as "pure" or "corrupt," but what is praised and blamed. Often this material is presented in terms of dualistic expressions. Jude presents himself as the shepherd of things pure: he writes of "our common salvation"; he acknowledges threats to "the faith delivered once and for all"; he knows of "God's favor" and he acknowledges "our only Master and Lord Jesus Christ"—all of this is "pure." But he knows too of "pollution," which he sees threatening the group's purity: certain men have insinuated themselves into the holy group, implying that they are like corrupting leaven or gangrene.

Purity and pollution have to do with the proper use of entrances and exits. What enters must be scrutinized to determine whether it belongs within. In this case, the defiling opponents have "crept in," a term which implies illicit entry with harmful results. Verbs such as this with a prefix of *par-eis* connote what is "illegal, secret or unobserved" (W. Michaelis, "Pareisagō," *TDNT* 7.824). Philo described the unalloyed state of the soul while yet "no infirmity, disease or evil affection intruded itself into it" (*Opif.* 150; see Polybius 1.18.3). One is reminded of the thief who breaks into the house at night (Matt 24:43) or the false shepherd who climbs into the sheepfold by a way other than the gate (John 10:1; see Barn 2:10; 4:9; 2 Pet 2:1; Gal 2:4). Pollution, then, is threatened by the entrance of deviants who subvert the pure tradition of the group: they are out of place.

They have, moreover, "turned away from God's favor to debauchery," that is, profaned what is holy; and they prefer what is unclean to what is pure. Their denial of "our only Master and Lord" indicates that they are truly outside the circle of God's "holy ones" (i.e., "saints"). Thus dualisms such as are listed below serve as moral indicators of the purity or correctness of Jude and the pollution or error of his rivals:

faith delivered once and for all	vs	scoffers of tradition
contend for faith	vs	turn away from faith
servant of Jesus	vs	those who crept in
saints	vs	sinners
God-fearing	vs	godless
confess the Lord	vs	deny the Lord
favor of God	vs	debauchery

We have only Jude's labeling of the situation, and we do not know how his rivals would describe it. But then success in the game of establishing one's own labels in a conflict situation is a key part of the strategy of success (B. J. Malina and J. H. Neyrey, *Calling Jesus Names* [Sonoma, CA: Polebridge Press, 1988], 35–38).

Cultural Notions of Time: Delivering the Past

Like other ethnic groups in the ancient world, Jews looked to the past for guidance or solutions to current problems (J. Pilch, "Sickness and Healing in

Luke-Acts," *The Social World of Luke-Acts* [Peabody, MA: Hendrickson, 1991], 183–89). The Romans spoke of the *mos maiorum*, namely, their ancestral customs, and the Jews of their "tradition." Being group-oriented persons, they look to the group and the group's past traditions (Rom 6:17). We find a formula in Jewish and Christian writings which describes how contemporary teachers "hand on" what they "received." Paul, speaking as a good Pharisee, prefaces his remarks on both Eucharist and Resurrection by noting that "I deliver to you what I received" (1 Cor 11:23; 15:3), thus indicating his personal subordination to the tradition and his affirmation of the past. We find references to "the tradition" of the elders in the gospels (Mark 7:3, 5, 13), the letters of Paul (Phil 4:9; 1 Thess 2:13), and contemporary Jewish writers (Philo, *Sp. Leg.* 4.149–50; Josephus, *Ant.* 13.297 & 408; *m. Aboth* 1, 2; Str-B 3.444; B. Gerhardsson, *Memory and Manuscript* [Lund: E. W. K. Gleerup, 1961], 288–323; James McDonald, *Kergyma and Didache* [SNTSMS 37. Cambridge, Cambridge University Press, 1980], 101–25). Thus Jude's remark about "faith handed on once and for all" indicates a typical appeal to the past by group-oriented people in a specifically Jewish mode of expression. Hence, he positively appeals to the cultural value given to things past and also negatively positions his rivals as those who either reject past traditions (see Acts 6:14) or introduce new doctrines.

NOTES

OUR COMMON SALVATION

The New Testament regularly speaks of God's "salvation," meaning a general benefaction of God (Luke 1:69; Acts 7:25; Rom 1:16). Reading this in context, we can contrast the believers' "salvation" (v 24) with the judgment and destruction of the opponents (vv 4, 5, 11). God who has saved from slavery (v 5) will save from corruption (v 25). Salvation then denotes freedom (v 5), the gift of the Spirit (v 20), God's favor (v 4), and purity (v 24). Jude's mention of "our common salvation" suggests the correct religious ideology and the right way of walking. In the ancient language about benefaction, the benefactor is frequently called "Savior" as well (see A. D. Nock, "*Soter* and *Euergetes*," *Essays on Religion and the Ancient World* [Z. Steward, ed.; Cambridge: Harvard University Press, 1972], 720–35).

CONTEND

This metaphor can refer to (a) military combat (John 18:36; 2 Tim 2:4; see "putting on armor" in preparation for combat for the faith in 1 Thess 5:8; Eph 6:10–13) or (b) sporting contests (1 Cor 9:24–25; 2 Tim 2:5; see V. C. Pfitzner, *Paul and the Agon Motif* [Supp NovT 16; Leiden: E. J. Brill, 1967]). Contending for the faith (1 Tim 6:12; 2 Tim 4:7) may be viewed in two complementary ways.

Paul regularly commented on the conflicts within and without the church which surrounded his service of the gospel (Phil 1:30; 1 Thess 2:2). Yet combat is best understood here in terms of honor and shame. For where Jude defends Jesus' claims and prerogatives, there appear to be prior challenges to them. For example, Plutarch notes that Cleanthes "championed" a certain Stoic doctrine, thus asserting a claim and provoking challenges (*Comm. Not.* 1075D). And so Jude and Cleanthes, having made claims, must give a riposte to challenges and contend for their claims. Similar arguments on behalf of beliefs held or virtue sought can be found in Philo (*Post.* 13; *Virt.* 142; *Aet.* 70) and in Hellenistic philosophical writings (see J. T. Fitzgerald, *Cracks in an Earthen Vessel* [SBLDS 99. Atlanta: Scholars Press, 1988], 87–90).

Second, this may be viewed in terms of purity and pollution. When boundaries are threatened, one sounds the alarm, posts guards, and seeks to identify, neutralize, and expel the threatening pollution. Hence, the group is put on guard to secure the boundary ("faith delivered once for all") against polluting scoffers, who have "crept in."

FAITH . . . ONCE AND FOR ALL

According to the proponents of the label "early catholicism," expressions such as "faith delivered once and for all" denote a lapse from the dynamic notion of faith in Paul. They consider specification of religious belief into formulas as somehow degenerative. Yet the use of such labels is misleading, for Paul often spoke of "faith" as the specific content of his preaching of the gospel (Rom 10:8; Gal 1:23) and as the confession of his churches (1 Cor 16:13; Gal 6:10). As evidenced by Phil 3, Gal 1–3, and 2 Cor 10–12, Paul contrasted right and wrong belief; for example, he distinguished "law" from "faith" (Gal 3:23, 25). 2 Peter apparently interpreted "faith" as way of life or "command of God" (2:21). The phrase "once and for all" reminds us of the injunction neither to add nor to omit anything from certain revelations (Deut 4:2; Rev 22:18–19).

PROSCRIBED

Whereas other New Testament writers use this verb positively in terms of a prediction (Rom 15:4) or description of blessing (Gal 3:1), G. Schrenk ("Prographō," *TDNT* 1.771) cites Polybius 32.5.12 in which the term refers to the ancient proscription lists of people marked for death. The substantive noun *programma* is the technical term for "edict" or "decree" (Josephus, *Ant* 10.254; 12:145), in this case the judicial decree of God. In a letter where God's authority and sovereignty are challenged, Jude considers it important to affirm that God has ever been in charge of affairs, and so suffers no loss of honor.

TURN AWAY FROM

This verb *(metatithēmi)* often has the meaning of changing loyalties, such as "going over to the other side" (Polybius 5.111.8 and 24.9.6; Diodorus of

Sicily 11.4.6). Yet it describes apostasy from ancestral traditions (2 Macc 7:24; Gal 1:6) or from party ideology (e.g., a certain Dionysius is called "the Renegade" for abandoning Stoic doctrine: Diog. Laert. 7.37 & 166). In both cases it denotes a failure of faithfulness and shame to one's party or family (see Gal 2:21).

DENY OUR . . . LORD

Paul regularly urged the followers of Jesus to confess him as Lord (Rom 10:9; 1 Cor 12:3; Phil 2:11). Here we deal with "denial," the antonym of confession (Mayor, *The Epistles of St. Jude*, 72); certain people "deny our Master and Lord." Normally "master" (*despotēs*) refers either to the head of the household, who has absolute rights over his family and slaves (2 Tim 2:21; Titus 2:9; 1 Pet 2:18), or to a ruler with sovereign power, such as the Roman emperors. It was used of Greek deities and the Hebrew God, especially in terms of God's absolute sovereignty and omnipotence (Josh 5:14; Wis 6:7; Job 5:8). Both the Greek Xenophon and the Jew Josephus remark on the reservation of the term "master" for the Deity: "To no human creature do you pay homage as master *(despotēn)*, but to the gods alone" (*An.* 3.2.13; see Josephus, *B.J.* 7.418–19). It is striking, then, that Jesus begins to be acclaimed by a term reserved for the most powerful earthly and heavenly rulers (K. Rengstorf, "Despotēs," *TDNT* 2.44–47).

In the honor/shame culture of antiquity, honor must be shown a "master," either the head of the household or the sovereign. Honor shown an earthly master redounds to the honor of the heavenly master: "Let all who are under the yoke of slavery regard their masters as worthy of all honor, so that the name of God and the teaching may not be defamed" (1 Tim 6:1). Shame, then, accompanies the denial of a master's power and sovereignty. This is aptly illustrated by the treatment of David's messengers sent to Hanum, the son of Nahash. Instead of receiving them honorably, the king of the Ammonites shaved off half their beards and cut their clothes in half, sending them home naked below the waist (2 Sam 10:4). David was thus publicly insulted by the treatment accorded his messengers. The story in 2 Sam 10 records David's honorable avenging of this insult to his messengers. Josephus records, moreover, that many Jews faced torture rather than acclaim the Roman emperor as "master": "Under every form of torture and laceration of body, devised for the sole object of making them acknowledge Caesar as master *(despotēn)*, not one submitted" (*B.J.* 7.417). In this case, they honored God as sole Master; for to acknowledge Caesar would compromise the exclusive honor of God.

If the scoffers in Jude are members of the church, they cannot be denying Jesus as Peter did (Mark 14:68, 70) or like certain Jerusalem Jews (Acts 3:13–14). If it is a theological situation imagined, their "denial" may be a rejection of some aspect of his honorable role and status, as the Exodus Jews denied Moses' authority (Acts 7:35). 2 Peter interprets this very phrase in terms of denial of

Jesus' authority and power to judge, namely, a denial of theodicy. The precise nature of the denial here seems impossible to specify, for Jude may simply interpret this "denial" as an honor challenge to those who claim to be Jesus' "servants" or agents. Jesus is denied when his agents are rejected, just as the king is shamed when his messengers are maltreated (Matt 22:5–7; Mark 12:2–9). Or it could just as well be his polemical and even exaggerated interpretation of their behavior. We find many references to faith being denied because of evil deeds or failure to act according to Jesus' tradition (1 Tim 5:8; 2 Tim 3:5; Titus 1:16; see *2 Clem* 17:7; *1 Enoch* 38:2; 45:2; 48:10). Whether theoretical or behavioral, such "denial" and shame will in turn be met with denial or judgment by Jesus (Matt 10:33; 2 Tim 2:12; see Mark 8:39). Culturally, all of this should be filtered through the lens of honor and shame. Ideally, group-oriented persons will honor or profess loyalty to their patrons and benefactors, while denying themselves (Luke 9:23). Living lives worthy of their calling, they will thereby confess the sovereignty of their master and his teaching. Denying their master either in confession or behavior, they shame him. Indeed any shaming of one's lord and master may be interpreted as denial.

BIBLIOGRAPHY

Bauckham, Richard, *Jude and the Relatives of Jesus in the Early Church* (Edinburgh: T. & T. Clark, 1990), 302–7.

Grundmann, Walter, "Zum Glaubensverständnis des Judasbriefes," *Der Brief des Judas und der zweite Brief des Petrus* (Berlin: Evangelische Verlagsanstalt, 1974), 26–27.

Hiebert, D. E., "Selected Studies from Jude. Part 1: An Exposition of Jude 3–4," *BSac* 142 (1985): 142–51.

Maier, Freidrich, "Zur Erklärung des Judasbriefes (Jud 5)," *BZ* 2 (1904): 383–91.

III. CRIMES JUDGED: THREE OLD TESTAMENT EXAMPLES (JUDE 5–7)

♦

5. Once you knew all about this, yet I want to remind you that although Jesus saved a people from the land of Egypt, he afterward destroyed those who were unfaithful. 6. And angels, who did not keep to their own position but left their proper abode, he is keeping with everlasting chains in darkness for the judgment of the great day. 7. Similarly, Sodom and Gomorrah and the villages around them likewise committed fornication and went after other flesh; they are set as examples, suffering a punishment of eternal fire.

EPISTOLARY CONVENTIONS

John White (*The Form and Function of the Body of the Greek Letter* [SBLDS 2. Missoula, MT: University of Montana Press, 1972], 11–15) lists a number of "disclosure formulas" which, among other such conventions, tend to introduce the body of a letter. Yet we would read v 3 as the signal of the letter's body (a "grief or anxiety expression," White, 20–21), and interpret v 5 as a more general disclosure formula such as is commonly found in the Pauline letters. "I do not wish you to be ignorant . . ." is a common formula introducing a wide variety of topics, which may or may not be central to the body of a letter (Rom 1:13; 11:25; 1 Cor 10:1; 12:1; 1 Thess 4:13). Only in Phil 1:12 do we find a more positive introduction, "I want you to know . . ." The basic topic of the letter, the insinuation of rival teachers, has already been noted in v 3; here a general disclosure formula "reminds" the recipients of examples of similar godless people who have been judged and punished. The predicted judgment mentioned in v 4 is grounded in these examples.

We best appreciate the politeness of the disclosure formula by seeing it in terms of honor and shame. Unless the author wanted to shame them and publicly call attention to their ignorance (Gal 3:1), he would courteously indicate that they already know the tradition and that his remark is but a humble reminder of that. When 2 Peter reinterprets Jude's remarks, he will give them a polemical edge, comparing true disciples who remember and so follow the tradition with false disciples who willfully forget what they knew (3:1–2, 5, 8). Those who know and remember, then, will continue to be socialized as group-oriented people, whose conscience is formed by Scripture and tradition.

HONOR DEFENDED

As we noted in regard to Jude 4, the scoffers challenge the honor of the "only Master and Lord." Honor challenges must be met, and so Jude narrates a series of three biblical examples of judgment in which the sovereignty of God is defended. The Exodus generation which rose up in rebellion (see Korah in Jude 11), the angels who stepped out of their assigned role and status, and Sodom and Gomorrah serve as "examples" of divine judgment. For the challenge of benefaction scorned, the Exodus generation is destroyed; for failing to "keep" their place, the angels are "kept" for judgment; and for immorality, Sodom and Gomorrah suffer the punishment of eternal fire. Readers will find more elaborate comments on these examples in terms of honor challenge-riposte dynamics in the comments on 2 Peter 2:3–10.

BACKGROUND OF THE EXAMPLES

In these three examples Jude draws on a common tradition in ancient Jewish literature. K. Berger ("Hartherzigkeit und Gottes Gesetz, die Vorgeschichte des anti-jüdischen Vorwurfs in Mc 10.5," *ZNW* 61 [1970]: 27–36) and J. Schlosser ("Les jours de Noé et de Lot: A propos de Luc, XVII, 26–30," *RB* 80 [1973]: 26–34) identify a common tradition found in Sir 16:7–10; CD 2:17–3:12; *T. Naph.* 3:4–5; 3 Macc 2:4–7; *m. San.* 10.3; 2 Peter 2:4–9; and Jude 5–7. In varying ways, each document cites a list of examples from the Pentateuch, always in the same order in which they occur in the Scriptures, but differing in function (Bauckham, *Jude, 2 Peter*, 46). The Damascus Document and *T. Naphtali* both warn against straying from the tradition, whereas 3 Macc cites these examples against those who profane the temple; the Mishnah simply lists those "who will have no share in the world to come." Jude is not dependent on any one of these documents, but reflects the common tradition which he redacts for his own purposes.

The examples speak to two groups in Jude's church. All of them apply to those who deny the Master, but especially the angels and Sodom and Gomorrah. The angels who ambitiously step "out of place" suggest the scoffers who are in the wrong place (they have crept in) and seek a new place (they challenge Jude's authority). Sodom and Gomorrah are the leading figures in the scene of debauchery envisioned, as are the scoffers who trade divine favor for debauchery (v 4), stain the flesh (v 8), and become stains on the church (v 12); their going "after other flesh" might be interpreted as spiritual seduction of the saints of this church. But the examples also warn the addressees of Jude. The example of the Exodus generation reminds his audience of the need for faithfulness and loyalty to their heavenly patrons, to which Jude exhorts them in vv 20 and 24. The faith may be delivered once for all, but the faithful must be loyal. Sodom and Gomorrah as well as "the villages around them" were destroyed, suggesting not just the scoffers but the group from which they drew their support, namely, Jude's church.

When 2 Peter interpreted this passage, he revised it in terms of the historical order of the examples and the specific argument they make. But what of Jude's order and his purpose? Are the examples haphazard or deficient? The leading example of the Exodus generation might well be considered a commonplace in the New Testament (see 1 Cor 10:6–13; W. A. Meeks, " 'And Rose Up to Play': Midrash and Paraenesis in 1 Corinthians 10:1–22," *JSNT* 16 [1982]: 64–78). It speaks to the general problem of apostasy (Heb 5:11–6:8; see H. W. Attridge, *Hebrews* [Philadelphia: Fortress, 1989], 168–69) and urges faithfulness. As noted above, it is sufficiently general to speak both to Jude's church and to the scoffers. But the next two examples correspond to the charges made in v 4. The angels who ambitiously left their place resemble those who deny the sovereignty of the only Master and Lord; Sodom's fornication and search for other flesh resembles the debauchery it exchanged for God's favor. Both the angels and Sodom are requited for their challenge according to a strict *lex talionis:* they did not keep, so the Master keeps them; they burned with lust and so are burned with an eternal fire. The examples, then, are more specific to Jude's description of his opponents than 2 Peter's use of them as general examples of God's reward and punishment. Jude's examples echo distinctively Jewish materials, whereas those in 2 Peter are phrased to appeal to Greek myths as well as Jewish Scriptures.

POLLUTION: OUT OF PLACE

We noted in the general introduction that "purity" is a general label for things that are "in place" according to the group's classification system; conversely, "pollution" refers to what is "out of place." The angels are described as "*not* keeping" to their divinely assigned place, thus challenging God's honor and authority (see Klijn, "Jude 5 to 7," 243). They lose their status as holy beings who stand in the presence of the holy God, and so are kept in another place suitable to polluted creatures, namely, darkness and chains. Likewise, Sodom and Gomorrah violate the biblical purity code by going after "other flesh," and so become polluted. Kashrut laws, which prohibit the mixing of things (Deut 22:9–11), emphatically insist on the separation of the sexes; men may not dress like women and vice versa (22:5). Yet in terms of sexual commerce, men may not have intercourse either with animals or men (Lev 18:22; 20:13), but only with women. Hence, Sodom and Gomorrah cause pollution by crossing the lines of acceptable sexual partners. Paul reflects the same pollution code in Rom 1:26–37, where he labels this pollution as "shameful" *(atimia)*.

NOTES

ONCE YOU KNEW ALL ABOUT THIS

At stake here is the position and meaning of "once" *(hapax)*. Some scholars argue that it should be read in the subordinate clause in the sense that Jesus "once" saved but "later" destroyed (Wikgren, "Some Problems in Jude 5," 147–48). But others argue that it modifies the knowledge that the addressees have received (Osburn, "The Text of Jude 5," 108–10; B. Metzger, *A Textual Commentary on the Greek New Testament* [New York: UBS, 1971], 726). The addressees' knowledge of the whole tradition given once for all accords with the author's constant defense of it.

JESUS AND EXODUS

Jude 5 contains a textual *crux interpretum* (Wikgren, "Some Problems in Jude 5," 148; Metzger, *A Textual Commentary on the Greek New Testament*, 725–26). Many weighty witnesses read "Jesus," whereas others read "Lord," with an important variant in P 72, "Christ God." Critics tend to prefer "Lord," primarily because a strong argument can be mounted that it could produce the other readings, whereas "Jesus" seems unable to yield the variants. "Lord" *(kyrios)*, if it were originally abbreviated as *KC*, might yield the transcriptional oversight of "Jesus" or *IC*. "Lord," moreover, is an ambiguous term, which might refer to God or to Jesus. It is possible to imagine how the uncertainty of this term might lead a scribe to specify the person as "Jesus"; and this desire for clarity might account for the more unusual reading "Christ God."

Yet a case can be made for reading "Jesus" here. It enjoys a weightier and more frequent textual attestation than the alternative readings; and it is the more difficult reading, with a presumption in its favor for this very reason. Although Metzger's committee (*A Textual Commentary on the Greek New Testament*, 726) considers this reading "difficult . . . to the point of impossibility," the reading of "Jesus" is hardly as theologically awkward as some claim. There is an early stream of Jewish-Christian christology which saw Jesus active and operative in events described in the Old Testament. First, Paul reflects a very early Christian reading of an Exodus tradition where Christ was present and active in that Old Testament event (1 Cor 10:4; possibly also in Heb 11:26–28). In several places, the Fourth Gospel states that Abraham, Jacob, and Isaiah saw Jesus (8:56; 12:41; see J. H. Neyrey, "The Jacob Allusions in John 1:51," *CBQ* 44 [1982]: 587–89). Such a christology is found in Jewish-Christian circles, as witnessed by the Pharisee Paul, the Fourth Gospel, and Justin *Dial.* 113; 120.3. Inasmuch as the scoffers "deny our only master and lord Jesus Christ." "Jesus" should give a riposte to this honor challenge. It must be admitted that if the original reading was "Lord," the author could still have understood this figure as Jesus, in accord with the Jewish-Christian stream of christology noted here.

AFTERWARD

The Greek term *ek deuterou*, although it could mean "second" in a sequence (Wikgren, "Some Problems in Jude 5," 147; see Titus 3:10), refers to a later action by Israel's Savior. Jude alludes to no biblical incident, but inasmuch as Paul in his typology of the Exodus generation cites Exod 32:4, 6 in 1 Cor 10:6–13, that is as good an allusion as any.

UNFAITHFUL

When Jude urged the church to fight for the "faith delivered once and for all" (v 3), he urged loyalty to a certain confession or gospel. But here his reference to those who "do not believe" reflects the more common understanding of *pistis* as loyalty or faithfulness. They fail in faithfulness to their heavenly patron.

CHAINS AND DARKNESS

In addition to the citation of *1 Enoch* in Jude 14–15, the account of the angels in v 6 contains many allusions to the treatment of the Watchers in Enoch. Although parallels can be found in many apocalyptic writings, Bauckham (*Jude, 2 Peter*, 52–53) notes parallels from *1 Enoch* to five phrases in v 6: (1) "abandon their home" = *1 Enoch* 12:4; 15:3; (2) "judgment of the great day" = *1 Enoch* 10:12; 22:11; 84:4; (3) "gloom" = *1 Enoch* 10:4–6; (4) "chains" = *1 Enoch* 13:1; 14:5; 56:1–4; (5) "kept" = 2 *Enoch* 7:2.

BIBLIOGRAPHY

Bauckham, Richard, *Jude and the Relatives of Jesus in the Early Church* (Edinburgh: T. & T. Clark, 1990), 307–12.

Black, Matthew, "Critical and Exegetical Notes on Three New Testament Texts. Hebrews xi.11, Jude 5, James i.27," *Apophoreta: Festschrift für Ernst Haenchen* (Walter Eltester, ed.; BZNW 30. Berlin: Alfred Töpelmann, 1964), 39–45.

Delcor, M., "Le mythe de la chute des anges et de l'origine des géants comme explication du mal dans le monde dans l'apocalyptique juive. Histoire des traditions," *RHR* 190 (1976): 3–53.

Dubarle, A. M., "Le péché des anges dans l'épître de Jude," *Memorial J. Chaine* (Lyons: Facultés Catholiques, 1950), 145–48.

Fossum, J., "Kyrios Jesus as the Angel of the Lord in Jude 5–7," *NTS* 33 (1987): 226–43.

Kellett, E. E., "Note on Jude 5," *ExpT* 15 (1903–4): 381.

Klijn, A. K. J., "Jude 5 to 7," *The New Testament Age: Essays in Honor of Bo Reicke* (William C. Weinrich, ed.; Macon, GA: Mercer University Press, 1984), I.237–44.

Maier, Freidrich, "Zur Erklärung des Judasbriefes (Jud 5)," *BZ* 2 (1904): 391–97.

Osburn, C. D., "The Text of Jude 5," *Bib* 62 (1981): 107–15.

Wikgren, A., "Some Problems in Jude 5," *Studies in the History and Text of the New Testament in Honor of Kenneth Willis Clark* (B. L. Daniels and M. Jack Suggs, eds.; Salt Lake City: University of Utah Press, 1967), 147–52.

IV.
Triple Crimes and Their Judgment (Jude 8–9)

♦

8. But in like manner, these dreamers defile the flesh, flout authority, and insult the glorious ones. 9. But Michael the archangel, when he argued with the devil and disputed over the body of Moses, did not himself dare bring a judgment against insult, but he said: "The Lord will rebuke you."

Structure of the Argument

Jude 4 should be considered as a topic sentence, in which the author charges those who have crept into the holy church with two vices: sexual impurity and challenges to authority. These charges serve as his riposte to their challenge, a riposte which is given support in two ways. First he notes biblical examples of how Jesus defended his honor by judging those who both challenged authority (v 6) and engaged in sexual impurity (vv 5, 7). But Jude brings the defense of Jesus' honor into the present by repeating his charge from v 4 here and by a fresh proclamation of heavenly judgment.

Although new terminology is used in v 8, it contains the same charges made in v 4. Instead of charging the scoffers with "debauchery," he accuses them of defiling the flesh; instead of noting how they "deny our only Master and Lord," he tells how they "flout authority, and insult the glorious ones." As the sins are the same, so is the heavenly riposte; in the past Jesus punished such (vv 5–7), as he will again in the future (v 9). Thus the "prediction of judgment" in v 4 is given specific notice in Michael's proclamation in v 9 that "the Lord will rebuke you."

The balance between vv 5–7 and 8–9 can be noticed in other ways. The conjunction linking the two indicates an intended parallelism: as in the past, so "in like manner" with the present (and future). The "only Master and Lord" (v 4) is "the Lord" who will rebuke (v 9). Contrasting with the angels who rebelled against divine authority are both the "glorious ones" who are shamed and Michael, who does not presume any authority but defers to the Lord.

MICHAEL AND THE DEVIL

The source of Jude's scene of conflict is not extant, although ancient commentators such as Clement of Alexandria identify it as stemming from the *Assumption of Moses*: "Hic confirmat assumptionem Moysi. Michael autem hic dicitur, qui per propinquum nobis angelum altercabatur cum diabolo" (GCS 3.207; see Origen, *De Princ.* 3.2.1). The substance of Michael's remark to the devil derives from Zech 3:2. More important, however, is the general tradition about angels and contests, which is reflected in Jude 9. Michael in particular enjoyed the role of Israel's patron and defender (Dan 12:1; 1 QM 17:6–8; Rev 12:7); and many writings tell of a contest between God's angels and Beliar or his angels (Zech 3:1; CD 5:17–18; *T. Asher* 6:4–6; 1 QS 3:18–25; Hermas, *Mand.* 6.2.1). Bauckham (*Jude, 2 Peter*, 65–76) collected a detailed list of ancient legends about Moses' death, whereas Berger ("Der Streit," 1–18) gathered texts illustrative of angelic judgment scenes. There is no doubt that Jude is drawing on distinctively Jewish lore at this point.

Ancient lists of noncanonical books often contain reference to both a *Testament of Moses* and an *Assumption of Moses* (J. Priest, *OTP* 2.924–25), presumably two different documents. R. H. Charles argued that the two works were conflated and the whole came to be known as the *Assumption of Moses* (*The Assumption of Moses*, xlv–1; *APOT* 2.407–8). In a recent study, Bauckham (*Jude and the Relatives of Jesus*, 238–70) analyzed a host of fragments and excerpts from catenae which seem to deal with the battle over Moses' body. He posits two distinct traditions which are embodied in two distinct works, the *Testament of Moses* and the *Assumption of Moses*. In the former, Sammaʾel contends that Moses' body should not receive an honorable burial because Moses committed murder (Exod 2:12–14). In the latter work, the devil, as a type of Demiurge, demands Moses' material body. Bauckham maintains that both works contain Michael's response to the devil, "The Lord will rebuke you." According to his reconstruction, Jude 9 would appear to derive from the *Testament of Moses* primarily because of the remark about the devil's slander (*blasphēmias*). Bauckham has offered a plausible way to distinguish and separate the conflated traditions of Moses' death, which offers a reasonable historical answer to the source of Jude 9. Yet because our extant texts of this ancient work are all fragmentary, no conclusive judgment can be made at this time about the precise contents of either the *Testament of Moses* or the *Assumption of Moses*.

The context into which Jude inserts this scene has much to say about how Jude understood and used it. If Jude 8 contains a slate of crimes, v 9 records their eventual punishment; or if v 8 is the challenge to the Lord's orderly system, Jude 9 is the formal riposte. Indeed there are many links between vv 8 and 9 that help us discern the author's point: (1) although the "glorious ones" are insulted (v 8), the archangel Michael acts out his role in v 9; (2) although "authority" is flouted in v 8, the Kyrios exercises it in v 9; (3) "insults" (*blasphēmousin*, v 8) are eventually avenged (*krisin blasphēmias*, v 9). Hence, Jude seems uninterested in the state of Moses' soul at death, but rather focuses both on Michael's "not daring" and especially on the Lord's eventual judgment.

Although in some cases "daring" reflects the classical virtue of courage, we can best understand it here in cultural terms. From the perspective of honor and shame, those who challenge Jesus "dare" to do so; and when Jesus has given adequate riposte, they "do *not* dare" to challenge him anymore (Matt 22:46; Mark 12:34; Acts 5:13; 7:32). Those who "dare" are perceived as stepping beyond group norms and so making honor claims or challenges (1 Cor 6:1; 2 Cor 10:12; 11:21). From the perspective of purity systems, Michael "does *not* dare" to overstep the role and authority ascribed to him, in contrast to other angels who did not keep to their place (v 6). Michael, then, serves as a foil to Jude's opponents: they challenge the honor of the Lord and his agents and they step "out of place" by virtue of their claim to role and status.

If Michael's role does not consist in judgment, that role belongs to the Lord. Hence, the heavenly agent defers to his Master's honor when he proclaims, "The Lord will rebuke you," the same Lord who was "denied" according to v 4. Honor challenged requires a defense. The judgment predicted in v 9 probably echoes the "proscribed" judgment announced in v 4, for Michael's words derive from Zech 3:2.

Since dualistic contrasts constitute much of Jude's perception, Michael versus the devil might well serve as a cipher for Jude himself versus his opponents. Hence, he would be implying their association with the devil and accusing them of sorcery (B. J. Malina and J. H. Neyrey, *Calling Jesus Names* [Sonoma, CA: Polebridge Press, 1988], 3–4); such accusations, whether implied or expressed, are important weapons of social control in situations of intense rivalry.

If there is any substance to my arguments that Jude perceives a general attack on authority (and judgment) by his opponents, the choice of this specific legend serves an apologetic purpose. We suggested that Jude's understanding of the insulting of "the glorious ones" had to do with challenging their role in the Lord's judgment, either as recorders of good and bad deeds, gatherers of the flock for judgment, weighers of souls, or so forth. Berger's collection of materials on the role of angels concerning the souls of the dead confirms this. The scenario in Jude 9 affirms some specific role of both Michael and the devil over the dead Moses in regard to judgment; that role is not the judgment itself, which is reserved for "the Lord." Hence, Michael's remark serves to confirm the traditional roles which Jude perceives as threatened, either those of the Lord, the angels, or Jude himself.

NOTES

DREAMERS

In Jewish and Christian Scriptures, God reveals true things in dreams (e.g., Gen 40:5–15; Judg 7:13; Matt 1:20; 2:12–13). Sometimes dreams serve as credentials for the dreamer (Num 12:6). Jacob is a celebrated dreamer who receives visions of God in his dreams (see Philo, *Somn.* 2.3, 133); Joseph too was a "dreamer" (Gen 37:5–10) and an interpreter of dreams (Gen 40:9–19; 41:1–36). Yet here we should understand "dreamer" as a negative label, such as Joseph's brothers used to criticize him (Gen 37:19; Philo, *Somn.* 2.105, 111, 135). Philo occasionally associates dreams with honor claims and vainglory (*Somn.* 2.105), which suggests a plausible interpretation that Jude's "dreamers" claimed honor or knowledge or legitimation because of their access to heavenly secrets (see G. Sellin, "Die Häretiker des Judasbriefes," ZNW 77 [1986]: 216). Jude denies that his rivals have God's spirit (v 19), and so their dreaming is false; hence their dreaming, if understood as a claim of credentials or authority based on achievement, is challenged and honor denied them.

But does Jude imply that they offered their dreams as a rival revelation (Bauckham, *Jude, 2 Peter*, 56)? Does this suggest anything about their teaching? Philo contrasts dreamers with practitioners of virtue who are awake (*Somn.* 2.105), just as Paul contrasts the sober with the drunk and those awake with those who sleep (1 Thess 5:5–7). Hence, Jude may be making a simple dualistic statement contrasting himself and the authority of the tradition with new claims of authority. It is tempting to see these dreamers as dreaming of false security, that is, as denying the final judgment of Jesus (1 Thess 5:3; Jer 27:9; Zech 10:3; Josephus, *Ap.* 1.207, 211). This is how 2 Peter interpreted his false teachers. But nothing in Jude supports this suggestion. Like other false dreamers, they should be expelled from the group (Deut 13:5).

DEFILE THE FLESH

As we noted in the general introduction, "defilement" belongs to the semantic word field about "purity and pollution." The connotations of this term are worth noting, so a brief excursus into the ways that Philo, a Jew sympathetic to the elaborate purity concerns of his nation, understands "defilement" can inform our appreciation of Jude's use of the term. "Defilement" can function as a dualistic term which contrasts good and evil, whole and diseased, and pure and polluted (*Cher.* 16; *Post.* 75; *Sp. Leg.* 1.257). Philo especially links it with fornication and sexual impurity (*Leg. All.* 3.148; *Jos.* 45; *Sp. Leg.* 1.206, 281); correspondingly, Philo associated faithfulness with purity and adultery with defilement (*Leg. All.* 3.150). He views vice and evil as defilement, which tragically contaminates all in contact with it (*Immut.* 133; *Agr.* 175; *Fuga* 115; *Sp. Leg.* 1.112; *Praem.* 68); he likens it to a disease or plague (*Sp. Leg.*3.51). Since defilement threatens all with contamination, it must be expelled (*Mos.* 2.158), purged (*Sp. Leg.* 3.89; see Josephus, *B.J.* 4.323), or punished (*Mos* 1.303; *Sp. Leg.* 3.42, 121).

When Jude labels his opponents as those who "defile the flesh," he too links defilement with sexual impurity; this contrasts the "saints" of his church, who must be "without blemish" (v 24), with those sinners who are stains (vv 12, 23). The saints must be faithful, whereas those who cause defilement challenge the tradition. Yet Jude also appreciates how such a contamination will corrupt the holy group, and so by identifying it, he urges that it be purged from the group and that the Lord expel it by punishment. This powerful label, then, legitimates intolerance and censure of those so labeled. To wield such a label is an act of power, just as the priest exercises great power by declaring something "unclean" and so excludes it (Philo, *Sob.* 49).

FLOUT AUTHORITY

This could be interpreted he regard to (1) human authorities in the church; (2) angels (Eph 1:21; Col 1:21); (3) God or the Christ (*Herm. Sim.* 5.6.1). Already the opponents have denied the only Lord and Master Jesus Christ (v 4), and shortly they will be accused of insulting angels (v 8). Yet the *Didache* gives evidence for reading this phrase as a reference to human authorities. The author prescribes honor to the man who speaks the words of God, for where God's authority is, there is God: "My child, thou shalt remember him who speaks the word of God to thee, and thou shalt honour him as the Lord, for where the Lord's nature [*kyriotēs*] is spoken of, there is he present" (*Did.* 4.1). Similarly, Paul remarked, "Whoever disregards [*athetōn*] this, disregards [*athetei*] not man but God" (1 Thess 4:8); thus rejecting earthly authority is also denying heavenly authority. If one is willing to see elements of an honor challenge to Jude in the document, then this remark makes excellent sense as his perception that all authority, that of Jesus, the angels, and especially of Jude, is challenged by these scoffers.

Yet the verb used *(atheteō)* connotes "breaking faith with" (1 Tim 5:12; Diodorus of Sicily 21.20; Polybius 9.36.10; 11.29.3). Jude associates these people with rebels such as Korah (v 11); more important, he accuses them of making divisions in the group (v 19). Thus Jude envisions a situation similar to

1 Cor 1:11–13, where as a result of rivalry, the authority of one person is promoted while that of another is challenged. Again, Jude senses at every turn an honor challenge, actual or implied.

GLORIOUS ONES

It is tempting to interpret this as a reference to the illustrious members of the church of Jude; after all, he notes that his opponents "flout authority" and evidently disparage his own position. God too is "glorious," and the opponents turn away from God's favor, thus denying glory and honor to God (v 4). But it probably refers to angels of the court of the God of glory (1QH 10:8; 2 *Enoch* 22:7, 10; Philo, *Spec. Leg.* 1.45; Heb 9:5). Sellin ("Die Häretiker des Judasbriefes," 215) suggests that *doxai* be considered as one of the species of angels such as are mentioned in Eph 1:20 and Col 1:16.

INSULT

They "insult" *(blasphēmousin)* them, that is, challenge their role and status. Although we think of "blasphemy" as dishonoring God, Philo uses the word for evil speech in general, such as reviling, insulting, slandering, or defaming speech (*Migr.* 115; *Dec.* 86; *Sp. Leg.* 4.197; *Flac.* 33, 35). As noted in the introduction to Jude, the opponents may be perceived as espousing an overly realized eschatology in which all judgment, including a role for the angels, is rejected; hence, the "insult" challenges their honor, just as the denial of the only Lord and Master challenges Jesus' judgmental role. In two places, Philo narrates "insults" against heavenly figures; first, commenting on the tower of Babel (Gen 11:6), he remarks that its builders insulted God's angels (*Conf.* 154), probably indicating the extent of their hubris by denigrating the power of heaven. Then he observes how some insult the sun, moon, and stars, demanding that the honor shown to those heavenly bodies be shown to them on earth (*Somn.* 2.131–32). Josephus uses this verb explicitly in situations of honor and shame (*Ant.* 4.215); he notes how various people "insult" (*blasphēmein*) authority figures: King Agrippa (*B.J.* 2.406, 637; *Life* 407); Tiberius (*B.J.* 2.493); Caesar (*B.J.* 5.393, 458); and the procurator Cumanus (*Ant.* 20.110), as well as ancient kings such as Abimelech (*Ant.* 5.242), David (*Ant.* 7.265, 388) and Joram (*Ant.* 9.118). On one occasion the people insult both God and king (*Ant.* 8.358–59).

JUDGMENT AGAINST INSULT

The genitive here is described in BDF #178 as the "genitive with verbs of accusing." The clearest parallel is found in Acts 19:40, where a certain Alexander remarked to the crowd that it was in danger of being "charged with rioting" *(egkaleisthai staseōs)*. Here the sense is that a judgment is rendered against insults from the devil.

REBUKE

H. C. Kee ("The Terminology of Mark's Exorcism Stories," *NTS* 14 (1968): 232–46) argued that *epitimaō* should be rendered as a "technical term for the commanding word by which evil powers are brought under submission," as in an exorcism. That accurate insight does not apply here, where notions of challenge and riposte indicate that "rebuke" of audacity is indicated.

BIBLIOGRAPHY

Bauckham, Richard J., *Jude, 2 Peter* (Waco, TX: Word, Inc., 1983).

———, *Jude and the Relatives of Jesus in the Early Church* (Edinburgh: T. & T. Clark, 1990), 235–80.

Berger, Klaus, "Der Streit des guten and des bösen Engels um die Seele: Beobachtungen zu 4QAmr b und Judas 9," *JSJ* 4 (1973): 1–18.

Charles, R. H., *The Assumption of Moses* (London: A. & C. Black, 1897).

Daniel, C., "La mention des Esséniens dans le texte grec de l'épître de St. Jude," *Museon* 81 (1968): 503–21.

Denis, A.-M., *Fragmenta Pseudepigraphorum Quae Supersunt Graeca* (Leiden: E. J. Brill, 1970), 63–67.

Kaacker, K., and Schäfer, P., "Nachbiblische Traditionen vom Tod des Mose," *Josephus-Studien: Untersuchungen zu Josephus, dem antiken Judentum und dem Neuen Testament* (O. Betz, K. Haacker, M. Hengel, eds.; Göttingen: Vandenhoeck and Ruprecht, 1974), 147–74.

Loewenstamm, S. E., "The Death of Moses," *Studies on the Testament of Abraham* (G. W. E. Nickelsburg, ed.; SBLSCS 6. Missoula, MT: Scholars Press, 1976), 185–217.

Milik, J. T., "4Q Visions de ʿAmram et une Citation d'Origène," *RB* 79 (1972): 77–97.

Priest, J., "Testament of Moses," *The Old Testament Pseudepigrapha* (Garden City, NY: Doubleday and Co., 1983), 1.919–34.

Sellin, G., "Die Häretiker des Judasbriefes," ZNW 77 (1986): 212–18.

Sickenberger, J., "Engels- oder Teufelslästerer im Judasbriefe (8–10) und im 2. Petrusbriefe (2, 10–12)?" *MSGVK* 13–14 (1911–12): 621–39.

V.
Triple Example of Deviants Judged (Jude 10–13)

♦

10. But these men insult whatever they do not know; by nature they understand
like animals without reason, and are destroyed in this. 11. Woe to these who
have gone the way of Cain, and abandoned themselves for gain to the deceit of
Balaam, and are destroyed in the rebellion of Korah. 12. These men are stains
on your fellowship meals; they feast fearlessly with you and pasture only
themselves. They are rainless clouds borne by the wind, fruitless trees in autumn,
doubly dead and uprooted. 13. They are wild waves of the sea who cast foam
over their shames, wandering stars for whom the gloomy darkness is forever kept.

Rhetoric and Form

Six times Jude refers to his opponents by the disparaging pronoun, "these":

v 8 "In like manner, *these* dreamers . . ."

v 10 "But *these* men . . ."

v 11 "Woe to *these* who have . . ."

v 12 "*These* men are . . ."

v 16 "*These* men are . . ."

v 19 "*These* men, who create division . . ."

Some interpret this pattern in terms of secrets revealed: (1) often in apocalyptic literature an interpretation of secrets is announced in this way: "*This* is the interpretation of the matter . . ." (Dan 5:25–26; see Zech 1:10, 19–20; Rev 7:14;

11:4; (2) in the Qumran pesharim, historical correlatives from cryptic texts are revealed: "*This* is the house which . . ." (4 Q Flor 1:2; see E. E. Ellis, *Prophecy and Hermeneutics in Early Christianity: New Testament Essays* [WUNT 18. Tübingen: J. C. B. Mohr, 1978], 225). Despite the renewed urgings of Bauckham and the impressive parallels which he cites (*Jude and the Relatives of Jesus,* 201–6), the repetition of "These . . ." does not formally function in an exposition of a text. Jude's repeated use of "These . . ." has less to do with revelation of secrets and more with a rhetorical catalog of the evils of his opponents. Moreover, in terms of rhetoric, it seems better to understand this repetition as a classical anaphora, a figure of speech in which similar items are linked through the repetition of an initial phrase or word (H. Lausberg, *Handbuch der literarischen Rhetorik* [2d ed.; Munich: Max Heuber, 1973], 318–20). George Kennedy (*New Testament Interpretation Through Rhetorical Criticism* [Chapel Hill, NC: University of North Carolina Press, 1984], 51) identified the repetitive structure of the "beatitudes" in Matt 5:3–12 as an anaphora.

Jude 11, however, is cast in the form of a woe oracle, which is found in Jewish prophetic and wisdom literature (E. Gerstenberger, "Woe-Oracles," *JBL* 81 [1962]: 249–63; G. Nickelsburg, "The Apocalyptic Message of 1 Enoch 92–105," *CBQ* 39 [1977]: 309–28) and Jewish-Christian literature (Matt 11:21; 23:13–23; Luke 6:24; Rev 8:13; 18:10; D. E. Garland, *The Interpretation of Matthew* 23 [NovTSup 52. Leiden: E. J. Brill, 1979], 72–80). This is the most dramatic use of biblical materials, combining the woe-oracle form with the example of three legendary sinners punished.

Cain, Balaam, Korah as Stereotypes

Paralleling the example of three punished sinners in vv 5–7 is the curse of those who imitate the three legendary sinners in v 11. Why these three? Given the stereotypical nature of examples in the ancient world, we should examine how the portrait of each reflects traditional vices and how this is utilized by Jude in his negative labeling of his opponents.

By the first century, the biblical story of Cain (Gen 4:1–16) became allegorized so that it became a stereotype of certain vices and heresies. Cain is best known as the man who hated his brother and slew him (*T. Benj.* 7:5), and so became the archetype of jealousy and envy (*1 Clem* 4:7). Philo interprets his name ("Possession" [*Cher.* 52; *Sac.* 2; Josephus, *Ant.* 1:52–53]) to mean that Cain incarnates possession or avarice (*Cher.* 64–66; *Det.* 103; Josephus, *Ant.* 1:53). As regards heresy, Philo and certain targums to Gen 4:8 label Cain an "atheist" (*Det.* 103, 119; *Post.* 42) and "godless" person (*Det.* 50; *Post.* 12, 38). Because Cain's offering was not accepted, nor does Genesis indicate why, Cain is portrayed as denying a just universe. Hence, he denies that God judges, that there is postmortem existence and rewards and punishments then (P. Grelot, "Les Targums du Pentateuch—Etude comparative d'après Genese IV.3–16," *Semitica* 9 [1959]: 59–88). Thus, Philo calls him "self-loved" or self-seeking (*Sac.* 3, 52; *Det.* 32, 68; *Post* 21). But Cain's secrets are uncovered by God (*Jub* 4:6; Josephus, *Ant.* 1.55), and he is cursed by God (*Jub* 4:5; Philo, *Post.* 12; Josephus, *Ant.* 1.57). This portrait, admittedly a stereotype, fits Jude's opponents in many ways: (1) they too seek possessions and profit (v 16); (2) like Cain, they are godless (vv 4, 16); (3) they deny the Lord (v 4), presumably spurning judgment after death; (4) he perceives them as hostile to his position (v 8); and (5) like Cain, they are accursed ("woe," v 11).

Balaam's biblical portrait served as the basis for other stereotypical vices. His greed was legendary (Philo, *Mos.* 1.266–68; Josephus, *Ant.* 4.118; Ps-Philo, *B.A.* 18.7). He counseled Balak to seduce Israel to sexual immorality (Philo, *Mos.* 1.295–99; Josephus, *Ant.* 4.129, 156; Ps-Philo, *B.A.* 18.13), and as a result to lead them to apostasy (Josephus, *Ant.* 4.130, 139; *Pirqe R. El.* 47; Rev 2:14). Balaam was curiously confronted by God's angel (Philo, *Cher.* 35; *Immut.* 181; *Mos.* 1.274; Josephus, *Ant.* 4.108–10) and rebuked by his donkey (*Ant.* 4.109). This stereotype also fits Jude's opponents: (1) they too seek profit and gain (vv 11, 16); (2) they commit debauchery and lead others to the same (vv 4, 16, 18–19); (3) Jude fears that they will cause apostasy from the truth (vv 3, 11).

Korah typifies ambition, envy, and challenge to established authority (*I Clem* 51.1–4). Interpreting Num 16:1–35, Philo explains that Korah sought to displace those to whom the priesthood was ascribed (*Praem.* 75; *Fuga* 145). Josephus portrays him as ambitious for leadership on the basis of equal or superior birth, wealth, age, etc. (*Ant.* 4.14–34). The tradition in *Sifre Num.* 117 contrasts honor ascribed by God to Aaron with honor claimed by Korah. Sirach labels Korah's action as envy (45:18). Some targums describe Korah as causing a schism in his rivalry for honor and status (*Tg. Neof.* Num 16:1; *Tg. Ps.-J.* Num 26:9). This stereotype fits Jude's view of his opponents: (1) they deny the authority of the Lord (v 4) and of other authorities (v 8); (2) they too cause divisions (v 19); and (3) Jude is conscious of their challenge to his own ascribed status. Jude's opponents, then, are labeled as envious, ambitious challengers to God's ascribed authority.

First-century sources about these three figures indicate that they are stereotypes of honor challenge, avarice, and godlessness. More important, however, all three were judged and met with a just punishment. Cain was cursed by God (Gen 4:11–12), whereas Balaam was slain (Num 31:8), and Korah was swallowed up (Num 16:30–33). The Mishnah says of them that they have no share in the world to come (*Sanh.* 10.2; *Aboth* 5.19; see *T. Sota* 4.19). The typical vices noted in v 11 are echoed in other descriptions of them in the letter (vv 4, 6–7, 16), and their punishment serves as one more example of God's defense of divine honor and that of his earthly servants.

Cultural Significance of the Evils Exposed

As important as it is to describe the historical background of Cain, Balaam, and Korah, we need also to know the cultural significance of their crimes. *Honor and shame:* Jude perceives his opponents as challenging not only his authority (v 8) but that of Jesus as well (v 4); he labels their remarks or posturing as "insulting" (v 10); he likens their behavior to the honor-seeking of Korah (v 11); and he notices that they hide their "shames" under disguises (v 13). By exposing these shameful deeds, he acts to discredit them in the eyes of the group. *Non-group-oriented persons:* he sees them breaking out of roles and statuses ascribed by God, as Korah did; they act individualistically, seeking their own advancement and gain, as did Balaam; they pasture themselves at others' expense (v 12). In accusing them of "pasturing only themselves," Jude echoes the stereotype of corrupt leaders who increased their well-being at the expense of the group (Ezek 34:2, 8; Isa 56:11; John 10:12–13). *Purity and pollution:* not only does Jude call them "stains," he accuses them of being "out of place" by walking on the path of Cain (v 11) and by uprootedness, wandering like stars and drifting like clouds (vv 12–13). As a result of their being "out of place," they are compared with trees uprooted, evoking the traditional notion of divine judgment (Prov 2:22; Jer 1:10). Thus the opponents are seen as deviants according to the cultural codes of Jude: challenging legitimate honor, trespassing on the roles and statuses ascribed, and polluting all they touch.

NOTES

STAINS

The Greek word *spilades* means "rock" (LSJ, 1628), which Bauckham (*Jude, 2 Peter*, 85) translates as "reef"; the metaphor then indicates that the faith of some people has been "shipwrecked" on rocks such as these heretics (1 Tim 1:19; Barn 3:6) or that they are the stones of scandal which cause people to stumble and fall (Isa 8:14–15; Matt 16:23; Rom 9:32–33). Traditionally this term has been rendered as "stain" (*spilas* = rock; *spilos* = stain), a difficult reading, but one which fits Jude's style and content. Whallon ("Should We Keep . . . *hoi* in Jude 12?" 158) argues that the reference is to an imperfection in a precious stone; instead of the notoriously difficult *apatais*, he offers the reading of *achatais*, i.e., "agate." "Stain" would be another linkword with the "garment *stained*" (v 23). Jude's first interpreter, 2 Peter 2:13, read it as "stain," as did early commentators such as Didymus and Hesychius. Jude, moreover, regularly presents his opponents as polluted, either because of sexual immorality or the deviance of mobility. Finally, it is hard to see how "rock" or "reef" applies to the group's fellowship meals, whereas pollution of a meal is a common perception. A. D. Knox ("*SPILADES*," *JTS* 14 [1913]: 547–49) read the term as an adjective with "wind" understood, thus suggesting a "foul wind" which stirs up dirt and debris (see Isa 57:20).

FELLOWSHIP MEALS

The bulk of the manuscripts read *agapais*, whereas some read *apatais*, which is found in 2 Peter 2:13. While Whallon ("Should We Keep . . . *hoi* in Jude 12?" 157) challenged both readings with his suggestion that the original text read *achatais*, he cites a study of G. D. Kilpatrick concerning one meaning of *apatē* as "meal" ("*Apatē* as Love-Feast in the New Testament," *Parola e Spirito: Studi in Onore di Settimio Cipriani* [Brescia: 1982], i.157–62). Although we do not know how frequently the early Christians met, evidence suggests that when they did meet it was on the occasion of a meal, when the Eucharist was shared (1 Cor 11:23–32).

GONE . . . ABANDONED . . . DESTROYED

The three figures and the three verbs which describe them are but another example of the triplets which characterize the style of the author. Boobyer ("The Verbs in Jude 11," 47) interprets the verbs in v 11 more directly in terms of punishment: "They *go to death* in the path of Cain; they are themselves *cast away* in the error of Balaam; and they *perish* in the insubordination of Korah." Rhetorically, however, each clause in v 11 begins with a noun which is the crime illustrated by each of the legendary sinners ("the way" of Cain; "the deceit" of Balaam; "the rebellion" of Korah); the verbs "going" and "abandoning" are part of the commission of the crime, whereas "perish" refers to the retribution for the crimes (see v 5). The woe oracle itself is enough indictment for the evils listed.

BIBLIOGRAPHY

Boobyer, G. H., "The Verbs in Jude 11," *NTS* 5 (1958): 45–47.

Charles, J. Daryl, "'Those' and 'These': The Use of the Old Testament in the Epistle of Jude," *JSNT* 38 (1990): 109–24.

Hiebert, D. E., "Selected Studies from Jude. Part 2: An Exposition of Jude 12–16," *BSac* 142 (1985): 238–44.

Magass, W., "Semiotik einer Ketzerpolemik am Beispeil von Judas 12f," *Linguistica Biblica* 19 (1972): 36–47.

Merkelbach, R., "Zwei Beiträge zum Neuen Testament," *Rheinisches Museum für Philologie* 134 (1991): 346–49.

Oleson, J. P., "An Echo of Hesiod's *Theogony* vv 190–2 in Jude 13," *NTS* 25 (1979): 492–503.

Sellin, G., "Die Häretiker des Judasbriefes," *ZNW* 77 (1986): 222–24.

Vermes, Geza, "The Story of Balaam—The Scriptural Origin of Haggadah," *Scripture and Tradition in Judaism: Haggadic Studies* (SPB 4. Leiden: E. J. Brill, 1961), 127–77.

———, "The Targumic Versions of Gen 4:3–16," *Post-Biblical Jewish Studies* (Leiden: E. J. Brill, 1975), 92–126.

Whallon, William, "Should We Keep, Omit, or Alter the *hoi* in Jude 12?" *NTS* 34 (1988): 56–59.

VI.
Prediction of Future Judgment (Jude 14–16)

◆

14. Enoch, the seventh from Adam, prophesied about these, saying, "Behold, the Lord is coming with his tens of thousands of holy ones, 15. to pass judgment on all and to convict all the ungodly of both the godless deeds they godlessly did and the defiant words these godless sinners spoke against him." 16. These men are disgruntled murmurers who go the way of passion. Their mouths speak inflatedly and they show partiality for gain.

Honor, Challenged and Defended

Enoch's prophecy functions as a riposte to the honor challenge of Jude's opponents. He describes "these men" as "murmurers," "disgruntled," inflated speakers; their words are "defiant." As "murmurers," they remind us of the revolt by the client people of Israel against their heavenly Patron (Exod 16–17); "murmurers" similarly challenged God's agents or brokers, both Moses (Num 14:2) and Aaron (Num 17:10). Murmuring, then, shames both the patron and his agents. "Disgruntled" *(mempsimoiroi)* describes people who constantly complain about their lot, and thus refuse to accept God's ascription of honor and status to them (Theophrastus, *Characters* 17.1; Plutarch, *De Ira* 461B; *Tran.* 469A; Philo, *Mos.* 1.181). The term "inflatedly" *(hyperogkos)* can be read positively when honor claims conform to the expectations about certain persons of the ancient world; for example, when God's thoughts are said to be vast (Philo, *Leg. All.* 3.82) or when kings act in a grand manner (Philo, *Mos.* 1.306; *Sp. Leg.* 3.18; *Somn.* 2.211). But it also describes the arrogance of claiming undeserved honor (Philo, *Sp. Leg.* 2.21), excess (*Mos.* 1.306), and challenge (Philo, *Leg. All.* 3.18; *Conf.* 17). Jude also accuses them of speaking "hard" (*schlērous*) words against God, either words which contradict God's words (John 6:60) or words which reject compromise (Diodorus of Sicily 14.105.2) or harsh words (Gen 21:11; 42:7). In short, he sketches "These men" as ambitious, honor-seeking, challenging persons.

What did they say? As we have noted, their actual remarks are difficult to extract from the generalized polemics of Jude. But he has accused them in v 4 of shaming their patron, they "deny our only Master and Lord"; he describes them in v 8 as claiming undeserved honor by flouting authority and reviling "the glorious ones." Hence, their speech is "godless" in that it challenges both the sovereignty of God, even to judge sinners, and the roles and statuses of those whom God has appointed to leadership positions in the group.

No honor challenge can be allowed to go without a riposte. Michael, a favorite agent of God, delivers a divine riposte to an honor challenge by predicting that "the Lord will rebuke you," whereas here Enoch, the first of the prophets and one who shares God's presence, delivers another riposte with a prediction, "The Lord is coming . . . to pass judgment . . ." The coming riposte is only predicted by heavenly agents such as archangels and prophets; it belongs to God, whose honor is challenged, to defend his challenged honor.

Sinning with the Mouth

Jude criticizes his opponents for many vices, but he levels his most emphatic censure for their sins of the mouth. From a social science perspective, we know that when the social organization is strongly organized and classified, this sense of order and propriety tends to be replicated in the control of the physical body. In particular, when social entrances and exits are controlled, there tends to be corresponding control given to the control of the exits and entrances of the physical body, namely, the eyes, ears, mouth, and genitals. We have noted repeatedly how Jude concerns himself with his opponents who have breached social boundaries ("certain men have crept in," v 4); they threaten to pollute the social body ("they turn to debauchery," v 4; they are "stains," v 12). They are folk truly "out of control," like wind-blown clouds, uprooted trees, and wild waves (v 13). According to Jude, then, they threaten the social boundaries and internal structure of the holy and orderly group. Correspondingly, Jude calls attention to their lack of bodily control, especially the polluting speech that creeps from their mouths. Social unrest is replicated in lack of bodily control.

For example, he notes that they deny the Lord (v 4), speaking disparaging words from a mouth that should be controlled so as to confess loyalty. They "flout authority, and insult the glorious ones" (v 8), again failing to exercise control over the mouth. We hear of arguments and disputes (v 9), which mirror their contentiousness. And here Jude elaborates on their lack of bodily control when he condemns them as those who speak "defiant words" against the Lord (v 15), who are "disgruntled murmurers" whose mouths speak inflated words of flattery (v 16). The speech from their uncontrolled mouths threatens the social order of Jude's group. Lack of control in the physical body, then, replicates disorder in the social body.

This anthropological perspective, which is commonly found in the New Testament, can be illustrated aptly in James. The author there indicates the paramount importance of control of the mouth when he states that "a perfect person" is one who "makes no mistake in what is said" (3:1). This perfection consists in order and control; and so as a bridle guides the horse and a rudder steers a ship, so the mouth controls the body (3:2). Thus order and control on the social level are replicated in control of a bodily member, especially the mouth. The issue is seen in moral perspective, for it is cast in terms of purity and pollution. A restless tongue is a "poison" to the whole body (3:8); it is a small fire which can ignite the whole forest (3:5–6). Yet the tongue is an uncontrollable member, a restless evil (3:8), and remains ever a threatening pollution to the physical and social body. James both prescribes certain speech and proscribes other. Correct speech is blessing God, but proscribed speech is cursing other human beings (3:9). He then identifies this evil speech in terms of "jealousy, selfish ambition and boasting" (3:14, 16), indicating how polluting speech from an uncontrolled bodily orifice corrupts the social body as well. Similar parenetic discussions of the control of the tongue are found in both Jewish literature (Prov 16:26–28; Pss 58:3–5; 120:2–3; Sir 14:1; 19:4–17) and Hellenistic philosophy (Philo, *Det.* 23, 44, 173–76; *Sp. Leg.* 1.53; Plutarch, *De Garrulitate*).

Jude, then, reflects not only a common polemic against ambitious and destabilizing speech, but also the underlying cultural assumptions about the value of social control and its replication in bodily control. Inasmuch as Jude's rivals speak flattering words, contest traditional doctrine, and threaten the place of traditional authority roles, he perceives their lack of oral control as a direct threat to the wholeness and holiness of the social body as he knows it. Pollution on the bodily level implies a threat to the health of the social body.

JUDE AND 1 ENOCH

Scholars agree that Jude cites *1 Enoch* in vv 14–15. We possess an Aramaic version of Enoch (4QEn 1:1:15–17), a Greek version, a Latin version (Pseudo-Cyprian, *Ad Novatianum* 16), and an Ethiopic one. Perhaps the most important fact is that *1 Enoch* was known by this Christian author and considered an eminently valid prophetic authority, which indicates the importance of that document and its circulation apart from the sectarians of Qumran (see *Barn.* 16:5; Tertullian, *De Idol.* 15.6; Clement of Alexandria, *Ecl. Proph.* 3). Debates over its canonicity come much later than the time of Jude (Tertullian, *De Cultu Fem.* 1.3; Jerome, *De Vir. Ill.* 4; *Apostolic Constitutions*, 6.16.3), who cites a portion of it which appears quite orthodox. The brief selection from *1 Enoch* agrees with the citation from the *Testament of Moses* quoted in Jude 9. Both speak of the Lord coming to judge, namely, to give a riposte to those who challenge the honor and authority of God:

v 8 "the Lord will rebuke you"
v 14–15 "the Lord is coming . . . to convict all the ungodly."

The tradition of the coming heavenly judgment, then, is firmly attested always, everywhere, and by all (*semper, ubique, ab omnibus*). Ancient Jewish prophets (Moses and Enoch) as well as current Christian ones all agree on this.

Although scholars agree that Jude cites *1 Enoch*, it is still a matter of discussion whether he reads from the Aramaic (Osburn, "The Christological Use of I Enoch I.9," 338–40; Bauckham, *Jude, 2 Peter*, 94–96) or Greek version (Kelly, *The Epistles of Peter and of Jude*, 276). Scholars note six points at which Jude diverges from the Greek text:

(a) "Behold" (*idou*); found here, but not in 4QEn or Greek;
(b) "he is coming" (*ēlthen*); the aorist represents a Semitic prophetic perfect, whereas the Greek and Ethiopic versions have the present tense;
(c) "the Lord"; this reference to the Lord Jesus is found only in Jude's version;
(d) "with his tens of thousands of holy ones"; Jude agrees with the shorter Ethiopic and Aramaic versions here against the longer, more complex Greek version;
(e) "to convict all the ungodly"; Jude presents a shorter version here, stressing only that the Lord will "pass judgment on" and "convict," whereas other versions add "and destroy";
(f) "all the defiant words these ungodly sinners spoke against him"; Jude stresses reviling speech which the Lord will requite, whereas the Greek text remarks on the Lord's judgment of generic evil deeds and words.

1 Enoch 1:9	*Jude 15*
peri pantōn tōn ergōn hōn ēsebēsan	*peri pantōn tōn sklērōn hōn elalēsan*

. . . on account of
all the deeds
they did against him

. . . on account of
all the defiant words
they said against him

NOTES

ENOCH, THE SEVENTH FROM ADAM

In a contest over authoritative prophetic speech, Enoch serves as an incontestable authority. In Jude's world where antiquity and ancestry were highly valued, Enoch is very old and so very honorable. According to the genealogy in Gen 5:3–20, if we include Adam, Enoch is the seventh generation after Adam (see *1 Enoch* 60:8; 93:3; *Jub* 7:39). In two recent studies J. M. Sasson has shown that special or important persons were conventionally placed seventh in genealogical lists ("A Genealogical 'Convention' in Biblical Chronology," ZAW 90 [1978]: 171–85; "Generation, Seventh," *IDBSup* 354–56). He was said to "walk with God," who finally took him to the heavenly court (Gen 5:24); hence, he became in certain strands of literature a prophet who mediated secret wisdom to his brethren still on earth. Jude indicates this honorable status when he notes that "Enoch prophesied." Moreover, Enoch is quoted as saying a traditional word about the heavenly judgment of sinners and godless teachers, and so his ancient word supports Jude's remarks about the judgment of the wicked, in particular, his opponents. Jude, then, celebrates Enoch's honorable pedigree and in doing so borrows respectability from the ancient and honorable seer. Thus he gains confirmation for his own teaching. He specifically indicates that Enoch spoke against these very rivals who disturb his group. In this he gives flesh to his earlier remark in v 4 that "certain men have crept in, who ages ago were proscribed for judgment."

PAROUSIA

The prediction from Enoch states that "the Lord is coming." The actual Greek verb *(ēlthen)* is an aorist, but is to be interpreted as a "Semitic prophetic perfect" Black, M., "The Christological Use of the Old Testament in the New Testament," *NTS* 18 [1971]:10–11; Osburn, "The Christological Use of I Enoch I.9," *NTS* 23 [1977]: 336–37).

TENS OF THOUSANDS OF HOLY ONES

Traditional Jewish scenarios depict the great parousia of God like the state visit of a monarch, whose honor and status are expressed by the number and bearing of his attendants and courtiers (Deut 33:2; Zech 14:5). Hence, myriads of heavenly, powerful, glorious angels attend the great God, who is often depicted as a warrior in triumphant procession (VanderKam, "The Theophany of Enoch I 3b–7, 9," 148–50). When the coming of Jesus came to be described, the honorable trappings of a monarch's parousia were transferred from God to him (Mark 8:38; Matt 25:31–33; 2 Thess 1:7). But the scenario here is more of a great assize than a warrior's progress, for the myriads of angels will separate the good from the wicked. Jude stresses that this parousia is "to pass judgment" and "convict" the wicked.

SHOW PARTIALITY

Behind this phrase lies the respectful oriental custom whereby clients turn their faces away from a patron or bow profoundly with face to the ground. The patron then "lifts the face" of the client, a phenomenon expressed by the Hebrew *nś' pnym* and the Greek *lambanein/thaumazein/gignōkein prosōpon* (E. Lohse, "Prosōpolēmpsia," *TDNT* 6.779–80). The Scriptures record praise for God, who does not show partiality (Deut 10:17; 2 Chron 19:7; Sir 35:12–13) but blame for those who do show partiality and take bribes (Deut 16:19; Job 13:10; Ps 81:1–4; Prov 18:5). Jude's opponents, then, are shamed for this easily recognized vice.

Yet we should not take this expression literally, imagining that Jude's rivals act as judges in the group (e.g., 1 Cor 6:1–6). Rather they are described as forming a faction by means of flattery ("their mouths speak inflatedly"). Moreover, they are described as contesting traditional authority, both the Lord's judgment (v 4) and that of the group's leaders (v 8). Bauckham (*Jude, 2 Peter*, 99–100) credits Jude's opponents with preaching an easy gospel, devoid of laws and punishment. Jude perceives them engaged in forming a circle by some sort of reciprocity: they flatter and encourage some, who give them honor and respect in return. The term *ōpheleia* simply means "gain" and not bribery (which in Greek is *diaphthora, dōrodokia*). The opponents gain advantage, i.e., respect, status, or honor. Yet it is a commonplace in polemical literature to accuse people of flattery for profit or of accommodating their words for money. It was a cultural sin for patronage or benefaction to be paid for in cash (A. R. Hands, *Charities and Social Aid in Greece and Rome* [London: Thames and Hudson, 1968], 33).

BIBLIOGRAPHY

Bassler, Jouette, *Divine Impartiality: Paul and a Theological Axiom* (SBLDS 59. Chico, CA: Scholars Press, 1982).

Bauckham, Richard J., "A Note on a Problem in the Greek Version of 1 Enoch i.9," *JTS* 32 (1981): 136–38.

Black, Matthew, "The Maranatha Invocation and Jude 14, 15 (I Enoch I:9)," *Christ and Spirit in the New Testament: Studies in Honour of Charles Francis Digby Moule* (B. Lindars and S. S. Smalley, eds.; Cambridge: Cambridge University Press, 1973), 189–96.

Hiebert, D. E., "Selected Studies from Jude. Part 2: An Exposition of Jude 12–16," *BSac* 142 (1985): 245–49.
Osburn, Carroll D., "The Christological Use of I Enoch I.9 in Jude 14–15," *NTS* 23 (1977): 334–41.
VanderKam, James, "The Theophany of Enoch I 3b–7, 9," *VT* 23 (1973): 129–50.

VII.
Comparison and Contrast: Faithless Deviants and Faithful Disciples (Jude 17–23)

♦

17. But you, beloved, remember what the apostles of our Lord Jesus Christ
foretold, 18. how they told you: "At the final time, scoffers will come who go
the way of godless desires. 19. These men, who create division, are physical
and have no Spirit." 20. But you, beloved, build yourselves up by the most
sacred faithfulness, praying in the Holy Spirit. 21. Keep yourselves in the love
of God and await the mercy of our Lord Jesus Christ unto eternal life. 22. On
the one hand, snatch some from the fire. 23. On the other, have mercy with
fear on those who dispute. Hate even the garment stained by the flesh.

Structure and Argument

In terms of the larger structure of the document, we apparently have an inclusion here with vv 3–4. The recipients were addressed in v 3 as "beloved," just as they are again in v 17. The author "reminded" them in v 5, just as he commands in v 17 that they "remember." The judgment of those who crept in was predicted in v 4, just as warning of them was "foretold" according to v 17. Just as he exhorted them in v 3 "to contend for the faith," he urges them in v 20 "to build yourselves up by the most sacred faithfulness."

This part of the letter is adversative to what has preceded. Beginning with "But . . . ," it juxtaposes the "beloved" with the "godless" mentioned above.

The adversative quality of the argument becomes clearer when we notice the dualistic presentation of the scoffers and the addressees:

Scoffers	*Addressees*
1. "scoffers," who reject the tradition	1. "rememberers," who are faithful to what they were told
2. they create "division," tearing down the group	2. they "build themselves up," in unity of faith
3. they go "the way of godless desires"	3. their way is "the most sacred faithfulness"
4. they are "physical"	4. they "hate even the garment stained by the flesh"
5. they "have no Spirit"	5. they "pray in the Holy Spirit"
6. they are "proscribed for judgment"	6. they "await the mercy of our Lord Jesus Christ"

Thus, as one sows, so one reaps. The scoffers, who are labeled as brutish animals who cause chaos, meet an appropriate end. The addressees, who are spiritual and abide in unity, know the mercy of heaven.

These final verses addressed to the faithful of the church function as an exhortation for the correctness of one of the two ways contrasted. The scoffers are identified with a brief vice list: "godless desires . . . create division . . . physical . . . have no Spirit" (vv 18–19), whereas the addressees are identified with a list of the classic three virtues: "faithfulness . . . love . . . await the mercy [hope]." Thus they are holy and pure, in contrast to the stained and corrupt opponents.

P 72 and the Text of Jude 22–23

The discovery of P 72 has challenged the traditional reading of the text of Jude 22–23, and for reasons that follow it has been adopted for this commentary. The UBS and Nestle texts present a three-member text, which basically reads:

And convince some, who doubt;
save some, by snatching them out of the fire;
on some have mercy with fear.

But P 72 records a two-member text of greater compression:

Snatch some from the fire,
and have mercy with fear on those who waver.

Commentators offer three reasons for preferring the briefer reading from P 72: (1) the antiquity of the reading and the widespread ancient witnesses to it, (2) its suitability to Jude, and (3) its explaining of other longer readings as adaptations or expansions of it.

First and foremost, the reading is found in the ancient Bodmer Papyrus VII; and it is supported by Clement of Alexandria (*Strom.* 6.8.65), early Latin versions, Jerome (*Ezek* 18), and Coptic and Syriac witnesses. The longer text is supported by Sinaiticus (Osburn, "The Text of Jude 22–23," 139–40, 142). Hence, the briefer text draws support from widespread early witnesses, and for this reason deserves respect. This briefer version, moreover, can better explain how other subsequent readings came about. Commentators point out that *eleeite* ("have mercy") in the original text was changed to *elegchete* ("convince"), especially as the participle *diakrinomenous* could be translated either as "those doubting" or "those disputing." If read as "doubt," then "mercy" seems the appropriate strategy; if "dispute," then "convince" fits better. Birdsall ("The Text of Jude," 395–97) argues that even when "mercy" is read, the original verb is *eleeite*, not *eleate*, for the mutation of verbs ending in *eō* only gradually came to be written with *aō* at a time later than this text. Finally, the arguments from style tend to be quite subjective and less cogent. Yet the issue is far from settled, as Sakae Kubo has mounted a strong case for the three-division text ("Jude 22–23: Two-division Form or Three?" 248–53).

Purity Versus Pollution/ Whole Versus Divided

In contrasting the ideal church members with the scoffers, Jude employs several important terms from the value world of purity and pollution.

(a) **Whole/Divided.** In an orderly world, where there is a place for everything and everything in its place, the act of separating and dividing contributes to the order of things, and so denotes "purity," i.e., something is pure because it is in its proper place. Hence, God's creative act divided and separated: (a) wet/dry, (b) night/day, (c) land/sea/air animals (Gen 1). God, moreover, separated Israel from the nations and so distinguished what is holy from that which is unclean (Exod 26:33; Lev 20:24). The tribes of Israel enjoy internal division into ranks and roles, which are part of the order of things (Josh 11:23; 1 Chron 24:1; 2 Chron 35:5; Neh 11:36). But the division in Jude 19 denotes pollution, for it is not a God-given allotment of proper place, but a violation of God's gathering of a whole people. The divisions caused by the scoffers attack the wholeness of the unit, and so cause blemish and uncleanness. One aspect of the general notion of "purity" reflects the equation of holiness with wholeness. A body which is defective in some way lacks wholeness and so is unclean; in the case of animals, such blemished beasts may not be offered to God. In the case of a marriage, what God has joined should not be split (Mark 10:9). When comparing the church to a physical body, Paul declared that factions and divisions blemish the purity of the body, resulting in a serious lack of wholeness (1 Cor 3:3; Rom 16:17). The scoffers, by creating factions in the church and dividing the group, cause the holy people of God to be blemished. Their division attacks its wholeness and so is a form of pollution (see J. H. Neyrey, *Paul, in Other Words* [Louisville: Westminster/John Knox Press, 1990], 112–14, 138–39).

(b) Spiritual/Physical. Recent scholars urge us not to interpret this contrast as gnostic terminology; nor do they see Jude dependent upon Paul for it (1 Cor 2:14; 15:44–46; B. Pearson, *The Pneumatikos-Psychikos Terminology*, 7–14). Although the origins of such a contrast may be located in speculation on the two types of humanity created in Gen 1:26–27 and 2:7a (R. Horsley, "Pneumatikos vs. Psychikos Distinctions," 277–80), Jude seems to refer to people in the group who are either unclean (*psychikoi*) or clean (*pneumatikoi*). Jude's opponents have been described in v 10 as those who "understand like animals." Moreover, according to v 8 they defile the flesh, and in vv 16 and 18 they follow the way of godless desires. Thus either the transformation which baptism should have marked, whereby they cross from death to life, from flesh to spirit, and from sin to grace, did not occur or they lapsed from that grace (see 2 Peter 2:22). They are, then, unclean and even polluting to a group which has indeed found its proper place through the gift of God's Spirit. Thus a correct cultural reading of Jude 19 should include the labeling of the opponents as "unclean" and "polluting" for the injury to the unified body which they cause and for their own lack of holiness in the holy circle of Jesus' disciples.

(c) Holy/Godless. As is well known, Jews in the first century expressed the abstract value of "purity" in terms of holiness. Of Israel's God we read, "Be ye holy as I am holy" (Lev 11:44–45; 1 Peter 1:16); and God's holiness consisted in separation from all sin, uncleanness, and corruption. The disciples honor God by building themselves up in faithfulness which is "most sacred," i.e., total loyalty to the holy Lord. They enjoy holiness because God empowers them by the "holy Spirit" to engage in holy activity, namely, "praying." If they "keep themselves in the love of God" and "await the mercy of our Lord," they act blamelessly, and so demonstrate their holiness. Thus they prove to be "the saints" (v 3) who are holy because of the wholeness of their life for God. In contrast, the opponents are "godless," a label which the author affixed to them four times in vv 15–16. As we have seen, they deny the Lord, flout authority, understand like animals, and walk in the way of passion. Thus they cannot be said to be holy and spotless; they are not separated from uncleanness. They are, moreover, totally "out of place" in the holy church of God.

(d) **Without Blemish/Stained.** The term "stain" (*spiloō*) conveys to both Greeks (Dionysius of Halicarnassus, *Ant.* 4.24.6) as well as Jews (*T. Asher* 2:7; Wis 15:4; Isa 63:3; Zech 3:3; Josephus, *B.J.* 1.82; *Ant.* 13.314) the sense of pollution which disqualifies one for the presence or service of the holy God. It is but one of the many terms in the semantic word field denoting the sense of "purity" that we are describing (J. H. Neyrey, *The Social World of Luke-Acts* [Peabody, MA: Hendrickson Publishers, 1991], 275–76). The opponents are "stained" at least because of their walking in "the way of passion" (vv 16, 18). Jude's faithful flock, on the other hand, is exhorted to be "without blemish" on the day of the Lord (v 24), a common expression in Christian exhortation (1 Cor 1:8; Phil 2:15; Col 1:22; 1 Thess 3:13).

(e) **Love/Hate.** These dualistic terms can describe either God's favor ("Jacob he loved; Esau he hated," Rom 9:13/Mal 1:2–3) or the two ways ("you love righteousness and hate iniquity," Heb 1:9/Ps 45:7; Rom 12:9). Ordinarily the disciples of Jesus are hated (Matt 10:22; 24:9; Luke 6:22; John 15:18–19; 1 John 3:13), but occasionally they too are told to hate "father and mother" for Jesus' sake (Luke 14:26) or to hate their own lives (John 12:25). Thus love and hate function as boundary markers, indicating where one stands in regard to God's righteousness or Jesus' discipleship. Jude exhorts his addressees to keep "in the love of God" (i.e., doctrinal and ethical purity) but also to "hate even the garment stained by the flesh." They themselves are "beloved" of God (vv 1, 3, 17, 20) and so should love what God loves and hate what God hates.

Two Types of Persons

When Jude compares and contrasts the scoffers with loyal disciples, he praises those who are group-oriented and blames those who act individualistically. Group-oriented persons internalize the norms and values of the group and seek to satisfy the expectations of those who are arbiters of honor and shame. Thus Jude exhorts them, and in so doing resocializes them to the expectations of true discipleship. His exhortation, moreover, is but a reminder of the tradition, the group's social conscience (v 17). He exhorts them to build themselves up in "love," which in this context seems to be understood as loyalty to the heavenly Patron whose benefaction enriches them. Thus they are to maintain their status as loyal clients of their heavenly Benefactor, and so act according to the will and pleasure of that Patron. Likewise they are to practice "faithfulness," that is, continued attention and loyalty to their Patron and his expectations. By awaiting mercy, they are exhorted to act in accord with the shared conscience of what is correct moral behavior, and thus prepare themselves to receive the praise of their Patron. Conversely, the opponents are hardly group-oriented, and seem to act quite individualistically. They scoff at the traditions held sacred by the group (v 18), and act immorally in ways that show contempt for the social conscience to which loyal disciples are schooled. In short, Jude praises those who maintain their group-oriented loyalty, but blames those who act independently.

NOTES

APOSTLES

Does Jude modestly exclude himself from the original apostles, or might this imply that the letter was written long after the death of the apostles (see 2 Peter 3:2)? The use of the term "apostles" reflects several traditions: (a) apostles were called the foundation stones of early churches (Eph 2:20; Rev 21:14), and so the author may accurately exclude himself as such a founder; (b) both Paul (1 Tim 4:1; 2 Tim 3:1–5; Acts 20:29) and Peter (2 Peter 3:1–4) predict that false teachers would come into the churches after their death. Hence, the author minimally reflects the sense of authority given to the churches' founders and the pervasive concern that later churches hold to the apostolic traditions.

PHYSICAL (PSYCHIKOI)

Although the term literally means "pertaining to the soul or life" (BAG, 894), it is best understood as the antithesis of "spiritual." Jude 19 specifically identifies these *psychikoi* as people who do not have God's Spirit. And so a correct interpretation of it seems to be "physical" (opponents) vs "spiritual" (saints). See 1 Cor 2:14; 15:44–46; Jas 3:15.

BUILD YOURSELVES UP

Paul describes the disciples of Jesus as a building, of which Paul himself is the wise master builder; the apostle threatens those who build upon his foundation (1 Cor 3:10–13). This "building" is traditionally a temple, "a spiritual house" where the disciples function as a holy priesthood and offer spiritual sacrifices to God (1 Peter 2:5; see Eph 2:20). Jude thinks along the same lines, as he encourages the loyal flock to be faithful to God and to pray in the Spirit. Thus virtue builds up, whereas vice tears down.

FAITHFULNESS

Commentators generally translate *pistis* here as a reference to the correct doctrine of the church, which parallels the advice in v 3 to "contend for the faith delivered once and for all." Yet "faithfulness" is a valid but related alternative translation. The author exhorts the church in vv 20–23 to practice certain virtues, the first of which seem to be the traditional triad of "faith," "love," and "hope" ("await the mercy of our Lord"). The three verbs "build," "keep," and "await" all denote constancy and fidelity. And in the context, the loyalty of the disciples is contrasted with the infidelity of the scoffers.

PRAYING IN THE HOLY SPIRIT

Since the author claims that his opponents do *not* have the Spirit, his group correspondingly does have it and prays in it. This simple antithesis contains both a denial and a claim of authenticity. Here, Jude presents the scoffers as rejecting the sacred tradition, implying that they claimed legitimation through inspiration of the Spirit. It is, of course, part of the tradition that the Spirit inspired people both to speak in new ways (Matt 22:43) and to act in different ways (Luke 4:1; Acts 19:21), thus legitimating new and different speech and behavior. And so the Spirit could stand for radical freedom (2 Cor 3:17). But other strands of the tradition present the Spirit as the agent of insight into previous statements of Jesus (John 14:26, 15:26; 16:14), and so supporting them. By urging faithfulness in vv 20–21, Jude seems to envision "praying in the Spirit" as an act supportive of the tradition. In this he resembles 1 Cor 12:3, where Paul described true charismatic speech as the affirmation of authority, not freedom: "Jesus is Lord." Similarly, the true Spirit inspires the faithful in 1 John to confess the orthodox formula (4:2). Thus because of its context, "praying in the Spirit" has to do with honoring God, not denying the Lord, and with acclaiming authority, not flouting it. For a typology of the Spirit in terms of freedom and tradition, see J. H. Neyrey, *An Ideology of Revolt* (Philadelphia: Fortress, 1988), 176–85. It may even be tied with the prayer "Maranatha!" (see M. Black, "The Maranatha Invocation and Jude 14, 15 (1 Enoch I:9)," *Christ and Spirit in the New Testament* [B. Lindars and S. Smalley, eds.; Cambridge: Cambridge University Press, 1973], 189–96). Correct speech would then be another antithesis between the faithful and the scoffers, who in vv 15–16 speak defiantly, murmur, and flatter.

KEEP YOURSELVES IN THE LOVE OF GOD

This remark parallels what Jude said at the beginning of the document:

v 1	v 21
to those *beloved* of God	in the *love* of God
and *kept* by Jesus Christ	*keep* yourselves

Scholars concerned with moral exhortation in the Scriptures often note that the "imperative" tends to follow the "indicative." God's favor is the preceding ground upon which moral commands rest. The gift of God's favor (v 1) becomes the basis for the command to honor God for the benefaction of divine favor (v 21).

"Keeping" has definite spatial denotations; in terms of a model of purity, since there should be a "place for everything and everything in its place," "keeping" oneself in the right place or relationship expresses a state of purity or spotlessness. The angels in v 6 did not keep their proper place (holiness in the heavenly realm) and so were kept in a lower place where unclean persons are imprisoned. "Keeping" has to do with fellowship with the correct social group (John 15:9), following group norms (Jas 1:27), or maintaining right relationships (1 John 4:16).

The right place is the "love" of God. Although Jude's followers are to "hate" corruption, they are to keep in "love." Love has to do with God's election of them as a holy people (see "called," v 1) and with covenant response (Deut 7:12–14). Hence, "keeping in love" suggests the public posture of loyalty, constancy, and honor. As the patron has bestowed grace and favor, so the clients respond with loyalty and faithfulness, which is what Jude urged in v 20.

AWAIT THE MERCY OF OUR LORD JESUS

The letter began with a prayer that "mercy, peace, and love" be "multiplied" (v 2). Yet the mercy awaited here seems quite different. "Mercy" in v 2 denotes *hesed* or the covenant election and kindness of God (R. Bultmann, "Eleos," *TDNT* 2.479). Jude prays that the group abide and grow in this past grace. But the "mercy" which they now await in the future pertains to the judgment of the Lord Jesus, who will rebuke the wicked (v 9) and "pass judgment on all" (v 14). Hence those waiting for the master to return (Luke 12:36) watch and pray, and live blamelessly so as to stand on the day of judgment.

Such a posture of awaiting mercy is rooted in the biblical tradition about God's definitive parousia to set right the evils of the world (2 Macc 2:7). Hence saints and righteous people are described as those who "await" God's action: Joseph of Arimathea awaited the kingdom of God (Mark 15:43); Simeon and Anna waited for the consolation of Israel and the redemption of Jerusalem (Luke 2:25, 38).

What is unusual is that Jude describes Jesus as the dispenser of mercy, not God. Normally the Lord God is acclaimed as merciful and has mercy (see 1 Peter 1:3), but here Jesus the Judge shows mercy to sinners (2 Tim 1:18; Titus 2:13). This accords with certain streams of New Testament traditions in which Jesus comes to judge (Matt 25:31–33; Mark 8:38).

SNATCH SOME FROM THE FIRE

Jude surely does not refer here to the scoffers; all along he has marked them for judgment and destruction (vv 4, 9, 13, 14–15). He may refer to those influenced by them who can be persuaded of the truth and remain in communion with the group. In terms of the model of purity, the scoffers are outside the boundary of the group and the mercy of God; by denying the Lord, flouting authority, and leading impure lives, they position themselves in the darkness and sin from which the saints have fled. Christians do not pray for such (1 John 5:16–17; Heb 6:4–8), for they are "unclean." But others seem to straddle the boundary, and while dangerous because of their fence-sitting, they may still be made clean and brought back within. Hence, we learn of a widespread tradition of praying for, rebuking, and correcting erring members who are not totally unclean in the perception of the holy group (Matt 18:15–17; Gal 6:1; 2 Thess 3:15; 1 Tim 5:20; Titus 3:10; Jas 5:19–20). The "fire" described belongs to the conventional imagery of hell or the place of judgment (see v 7; Mark 9:43–48). John the Baptizer described the coming judgment as the separation of the wheat from the chaff; the wheat was gathered into the barn, while the chaff was burned outside (Matt 3:12).

GARMENT STAINED BY THE FLESH

Baptismal parenesis exhorted new disciples to "put off your old nature . . . corrupt through deceitful lusts" and to "put on the new nature, created after the likeness of God in true righteousness and holiness" (Eph 4:22, 24). This might be expressed in terms of leaving "the flesh" and its passions so as to "live in the spirit like God" (1 Peter 4:1, 6). The radical crossing from death to life and from darkness to light which is symbolized in the Christian initiation rites is probably the correct scenario behind this language in Jude. We know that some later Christians put off the outer garment of skin and put on a new garment of linen (Jerome, *Ep. Fabiola* 19; J. Z. Smith, "Garments of Shame," *HR* 5 [1965], 224–33); they were exhorted to keep the new garment of grace unstained (Rev 3:4). Thus although they are exhorted to snatch some and have mercy on others, they must "hate" the former way of life in the flesh, with its vices and passions. With this impurity there can be no compromise.

BIBLIOGRAPHY

Bieder, W., "Judas 22f.: *Hous de eate en phobōi,*" *TZ* 6 (1950): 75–77.

Birdsall, J. Neville, "The Text of Jude in P 72," *JTS* 14 (1963): 394–99.

Hiebert, D. E., "Selected Studies from Jude. Part 3: An Exposition of Jude 17–23," *BSac* 142 (1985): 355–66.

Horsley, Richard A., "Pneumatikos vs. Psychikos Distinctions of Spiritual Status Among the Corinthians," *HTR* 69 (1976): 269–88.

Kubo, Sakae, "Jude 22–23: Two-division Form or Three?" *New Testament Text Criticism. Its Significance for Exegesis* (E. J. Epp and G. D. Fee, eds.; Oxford: Clarendon Press, 1981), 239–53.
Osburn, Carroll D., "The Text of Jude 22–23," ZNW 63 (1972): 139–44.
Pearson, Birger A., *The Pneumatikos-Psychikos Terminology in 1 Corinthians* (SBLDS 12. Missoula, MT: Scholars Press, 1973).
Ross, J. M., "Church Discipline in Jude 22–23," *ExpT* 100 (1989): 297–98.

VIII.
Letter Closing: Doxology (Jude 24–25)

◆

24. To the One who can guard you from stumbling and make you stand before his glory without blemish and in joy. 25. to the only God who saves us through Jesus Christ our Lord be glory, majesty, might, and authority, before all ages, now and forever. Amen.

Formal Considerations

This doxology functions as the formal letter closing. Typical New Testament letters conclude with a benediction in which the sender calls down upon the addressees generalized heavenly favor ("grace be upon you," 1 Cor 16:23; "grace . . . love . . . fellowship," 2 Cor 13:14; "peace," 1 Peter 5:14). In form this resembles the benediction which generally begins the letter. Benedictions, then, tend to begin and end early Christian letters.

In place of the typical benediction, however, Jude pronounces a doxology. In Christian letters doxologies tend to occur at irregular points within a document (Rom 11:36; Gal 1:5; Phil 4:20; Eph 3:20–21; 1 Tim 1:17; 6:16; 2 Tim 4:18). Jude 24–25, Rom 16:25–27, and 2 Peter 3:18 are the only extant examples of doxologies which close New Testament letters (yet see *1 Clem* 65.2; *Mart Pol.* 22.3; *Diogn.* 12.9). Nevertheless, Jude employs a traditional form, even if used in a nontraditional way.

In a recent study on the doxology to the Our Father, M. Black has revived an older form-critical study of biblical doxologies ("The Doxology to the *Pater Noster*," 327–32). On the basis of two different acclamations of God in 1 Chron 29:10–11, he concludes that there are two types of doxologies in biblical and related literature. First, he notes a hebraistic form, which typically begins with "Blessed . . ." (*eulogētos*); for example:

> Blessed art thou [*eulogētos*], O Lord God of Israel, Our Father, from everlasting to everlasting" [1 Chron 29:10 LXX].

A second type begins with "To you, O Lord, is greatness":

> To you, O Lord, is greatness, power, glory, victory and might [1 Chron 29:11 LXX].

The first form is found especially in the psalms and the worship of the temple, but also in New Testament documents such as Luke 1:68; 2 Cor 1:3; Eph 1:3; 1 Peter 1:3. The latter form occurs in Pss 28:1; 95:7; 103:31, as well as Gal 1:5; Rom 11:36; 16:27; Phil 4:20; Eph 3:21; 1 Peter 4:11; 2 Peter 3:18; Jude 25, and *Didache* and *1 Clement*.

According to other formal studies, doxologies typically contain four elements (Deichgräber, *Gotteshymnus*, 25–32):

(a) addressee, in dative case (*tōi, hōi, autōi, soi*)
(b) honor ascribed, either "glory" alone or in combination with synonyms
(c) duration of praise, usually "forever"
(d) "Amen," an invitation to hearers to affirm the praise

Although doxologies are generally composed of traditional elements, they are inevitably tailored to suit a particular circumstance. The following synopsis of four New Testament doxologies allows us to see the distinctiveness of Jude 24–25.

Rom 16:25–27	*Eph 3:20–21*	*Jude 24–25*	*2 Peter 3:18*
To him who is able to strengthen you . . . to the only wise God	To him . . . who is able to do . . . to him	To the One who can guard you . . . to the only God	To him
be glory	be glory	be glory, majesty, might, and authority	be the glory
forevermore	to all generations	before all ages, now and forever	both now and to the day of eternity
Amen	Amen	Amen	Amen

In Jude, God "is able to guard"; previously in the letter the wicked were "kept" by God in chains (v 6) and gloomy darkness is "kept" for wandering stars (v 13). Yet the saints are encouraged to "keep" themselves in God's favor (v 21). "Guarding" and "keeping," then, are characterisitic actions of God. In emphasizing the term "kept," Jude contrasts the constancy and faithfulness of the orthodox tradition with the wandering and faithlessness of his opponents. God guards what is pure and true, but "keeps" the wicked in judgment.

Jude honors God by acclaiming the Deity worthy of "glory, majesty, might, authority." This intensification of honor characterizes Jude's expansive style; it also represents his honoring of God in contrast to his perception of the scoffers' attempts to shame the Deity. He acclaims God's public reputation, "glory," which is challenged by those who disregard God's rule and judgment; they "murmur" (v 16) against God and go their own way. Jude attests God's "power," balancing his praise with their denial of God's judgment in the past and future. He confirms God's "authority," especially in light of the opponents' denial of Jesus' sovereign role, their flouting of authority, and their scoffing. Jude's honoring of God contrasts with his presentation of the opponents as "godless" (vv 4, 15, 18).

Jude praises God's honor as eternal both in the past and future. This accords with Jude's note that God is not shamed by the opponents, for "ages ago [they] were proscribed for judgment" (v 4), indicating God's honorable actions in the past. And they will suffer a future judgment (vv 9, 14–15), confirming God's honor in the age to come. God has vindicated his honor in the past, as the examples of biblical sinners who were judged indicate (vv 5–7, 11), which gives ground for a future divine vindication. Jude's sense of God's consistent past, present, and future power likewise replicates his sense of a tradition of morality and history which is ancient and still valid. It would appear, then, that Jude has adapted the traditional doxology to fit more specifically his situation.

God's Patronage and Honor

Jude regularly acclaims the benefactions of God and in so doing gives honor and praise to the divine Benefactor. As we have noted, he describes his addressees as "beloved" of God (v 1), that is, objects of divine favor. In the initial benediction in v 2, he prays for further benefaction on them, "mercy, peace, and love." He acknowledges God's "salvation" of them (v 3), which is in danger of being discredited and shamed by the opponents. The point is, patronage and benefaction must be publicly acknowledged or the patron is slighted and denied due recognition. The concluding doxology serves as a summary of benefaction by Jude's heavenly Patron. And by public praise of the Patron, Jude obligates him to continue acting graciously toward his clients. It belongs to this Patron to defend and protect this "chosen people," which will both benefit them and redound to the reputation of the Patron.

In his *Life*, Josephus tells a story of how those who give praise and honor thus share in that honor, a cultural phenomenon which has bearing on Jude's doxology. Josephus relates how a crowd of people "delighted in my honor [*timēs*] . . . my reputation [*doxan*] was a tribute to themselves" (*Vita* 273–74). As the honor of Jude's Patron is maintained, so Jude and his group are likewise honored. And their honoring of the Patron serves to maintain the divine benefaction, as God is the only one able to make them stand and be blameless so as to enjoy the fullness of heavenly blessings.

The various items in the doxology, quite traditional in themselves, should each be understood in terms of the cultural value of honor.

Glory (*doxa*) in the Greco-Roman world refers to opinion (see G. Kittel, "Doxa," *TDNT* 2.234–37); but if opinions about persons are to be known, they must be expressed publicly. Hence, *doxa* refers to the public reputation or fame of someone (Demosthenes, *Or.* 2.15; 3.24; Josephus, *Vita* 274). It indicates the worth of a person, his honor and standing. A person's glory may be replicated in his wealth and possessions (Gen 31:1; 45:13; Philo, *Op.* 79; *Leg. All.* 2.107) or in power and might (Pss 63:2; 96:7; Dan 2:37; 5:18). It may be manifested as brightness (Ezek 10:4; 43:2) or bold public appearance (Matt 6:29) or simply as "weight/heaviness" (*kabod*, Job 40:10).

But glory basically means the honorable reputation of a person, and so "glory and honor" appear as synonyms (Ps 8:5; Rom 2:7, 10; 1 Tim 1:17; Heb 2:7; 1 Peter 1:7; 2 Peter 1:17; Josephus, *Ant.* 2.268; 6.200; 11.217). And honor must be paid, publicly expressed and acclaimed, or it is not honor at all. Hence, mortals must declare God's good name (1 Chron 16:24) and give the Lord glory (Matt 9:8; 15:31; Luke 5:25–26; 7:16). This is most clearly expressed in the public acclamation of God in the psalms:

All thy works shall give thanks to thee, O Lord,
and all they saints shall bless thee!
They shall speak of the glory of thy kingdom
and tell of thy power,
to make known to the sons of men thy mighty deeds,
and the glorious splendor of thy kingdom [145:10–12].

Such glory is due the Lord (1 Chron 16:29; Ps 29:2) because of his benefaction. Thus "giving glory" occurs in conjunction with "praise" (Phil 1:11) or with "praise, blessing and thanksgiving" (1 Peter 1:7; Rev 4:9; 7:12). "Glory," then, is the inclusive term in doxologies which summarizes the good name, honor, and reputation of God.

Majesty (*megalōsynē*) is associated with monarchs, their thrones, and the public display of their wealth (Dan 5:18). "Throne of Majesty" serves as a substitute for the divine name (Heb 1:3; 8:1). Because it is the house of the Great King, the temple should have such greatness (1 Chron 22:5 LXX). Like "glory," "majesty" is the human response to divine benefaction (Tob 12:6). And like "glory," greatness is attached to one's name (Prov 18:10); it must be publicly acknowledged (Tob 13:3–4; Sir 39:15). Hence, ascribing "greatness" to God becomes part of the public honoring of the Deity (Deut 32:2; 1 Chron 29:11; Ps 145:3).

Might (*kratos*). In a warrior culture, honor is expressed by power, strength, and might; it is the ability to impose one's will and to defend one's house against challenge. In doxologies, God is the one who "is able" to act (*dynameōi*, Rom 16:25; Eph 3:20), who has power (*dynamis*) or strength (*ischus*); hence the psalms sing of God's "glory and power" (Pss 63:2; 96:7).

When "might" is honorably ascribed to God, it tends to appear in conjunction with other terms, especially the more explicit terms "honor" and "glory":

1 Tim 6:16	"honor and might [*kratos*]"
Rev 4:11	"glory, honor and power [*dynamin*]"
5:13	"blessing, honor, glory and might [*kratos*]"
19:1	"salvation, glory and power [*dynamin*]"
Mart. Pol. 20.1	"glory, honor, might [*kratos*] and majesty"

Authority (exousia) primarily rests in the most honorable persons on earth, namely, kings (2 Kg 20:13 LXX; 1 Esdr 4:28; Dan 7:27 LXX; Rev 17:12) or queens (Est 9:29), who enjoy power and sovereignty over all. Because of their high status and power, they have authority to make statutes and render judgments (Sir 45:17) and to impose taxes and collect tribute (1 Esdr 8:22; see W. Foerster, "Exousia," *TDNT* 2.562). This authority can be invested in royal officials or agents who in turn can command (Matt 8:9; Luke 4:36; 9:1), bind and loose (Mark 2:10; Luke 5:24), judge (John 5:27; Acts 9:14), and execute (John 19:10; Rev 6:8). The majordomo of the palace exercises great authority over the realm, as Joseph did in Egypt (see Tob 1:21). Rarely in the New Testament is "authority" ascribed to God. Moreover, except for 1 Esdr 4:40, it never occurs in a doxology (see Rom 13:1; John 17:2; Josephus *Ant.* 5.109), probably because it is simply assumed that the one God is sovereign over all. Yet God ascribes authority to others, either to the Son of Man (Dan 7:14) or to Jesus (Matt 7:29; Mark 1:27). "Authority" in Jude's doxology is a synonym for power and strength, which belong to the honorable person; for authority would be vain unless its claimant could back it up with power and strength (see Josephus, *Ant.* 14.302).

NOTES

STUMBLING

This term found only here in the New Testament reflects the commonplace of walking in the way either of righteousness or of wickedness. Some go astray from the right way (Jude 11, 18) and others stumble and fall along the way. Philo sums up the idea: "How difficult for runners after starting on the way of piety to finish the whole course without stumbling" (*Agr.* 177; see *Ep. Arist.* 187). The righteous, of course, walk according to wisdom (Prov 3:23; 4:12) or walk in the light (John 11:9–10) and do not stumble. Since standing and falling denote moral postures, an explicit note of divine judgment occurs in regard to "stumbling." Occasionally God is said to put a stumbling block before the wicked, i.e., a snare or trap (Isa 8:5; 1 Peter 2:8; Rom 11:9) or more simply the proud and mighty come to a bad end (Isa 28:7; Jer 50:32). But God is likewise acclaimed Israel's "keeper," who keeps their ways safe (Ps 121:3–8; 2 Thess 3:3) and guards them from the snares of enemies (Ps 141:9). Thus, when Jude acclaims God as able to keep the faithful from stumbling, he envisions God supporting the group in the way of righteousness. Hence, they will be "without blemish" (v 24). They will experience not God's trap or snare, but divine mercy (v 21); they will be objects of divine favor (*Sib. Or.* 3.289). Thus it is a great act of divine benefaction for God to support his clients and guard them from the shame of stumbling. In terms of body symbolism, an upright body, functioning as it should, denotes purity, whereas a prone body, which does not perform as it should, denotes pollution.

WITHOUT BLEMISH

Animal sacrifices offered to God must be "without blemish" (Exod 29:1; Lev 1:3; Num 6:14; Ezek 43:22). Jesus, who offered himself to God, is appropriately holy and blameless (Heb 9:14; 1 Peter 1:19). Because God is holy and blameless (2 Sam 22:31 LXX), all that comes before the Deity must likewise be totally pure and spotless, whether sacrifices or worshipers (Ps 15:2; Eph 1:4; Col 1:22) or priests (1 Macc 4:42). In the wisdom tradition this physical blamelessness becomes a moral quality of the righteous, who strive to be blameless (2 Sam 22:24 LXX/Ps 18:23) or to walk in God's ways blamelessly (2 Sam 22:33 LXX; Ezek 28:15; Prov 11:5, 20). Their heritage will endure (Ps 37:18; Rev 14:5). In the New Testament, the disciples of Jesus are described as blameless (Phil 2:15). Indeed, when the church is described as a virgin bride, she must be "without spot or wrinkle or any such thing . . . holy and without blemish" (Eph 5:27). The scenario envisioned is that of subjects brought before the throne of the great king, either in worship or to be judged there and admitted to the heavenly court. But in the presence of the sovereign, all must be in accord with the canons of that court, in this case, radical purity.

Blamelessness can be viewed profitably through the lens of cultural anthropology, namely, purity. Sacrificial animals without blemish are pure because they are whole and have all their members, thus fulfilling the definition of such an animal. Conversely, persons as well as animals with unwhole or defective bodies are unclean (see Lev 21:17–21); these may not come into the presence of

God. This is replicated in the social behavior of God's clients, who must be "holy as God is holy," that is, freed from all stain of sin. Only such perfect animals or persons may come into the presence of the perfect God. Thus "without blemish" is but one of the terms in the semantic word field of purity and pollution, as noted in the general introduction to this volume.

IN JOY

The cultural meaning of "joy" is much more than a private emotion of happiness. It is better understood as a public expression of honor in praise of the benefaction of a patron, such as when Jeremiah proclaims, "Sing aloud with gladness for Jacob, and raise shouts for the chief of the nations; proclaim, give praise" (Jer 31:7; see Isa 12:6; 61:10; Tob 13:13; Bar 4:37; 1 Peter 4:13; Rev 19:7). Since clients stand without confusion or fear in the presence of their patron, they too share in that honor, and so their rejoicing is their own public honor (Isa 60:5; 4 Ezra 7:98). If joy is related to public honor, its correlative is public shame, which is often expressed as "shame and confusion." Those who trust in God are not confounded or shamed (Pss 22:5; 69:6; Isa 45:17); in contrast, those upon whom divine judgment comes suffer shame and confusion (2 Kg 19:26; Ps 71:24; Isa 37:27; Jer 15:9; Ezek 36:32). In Jude this joy is the final honoring of God's clients with access to the divine presence; because they are judged blameless, they experience mercy, and so are greatly honored before their Sovereign and Patron.

ONLY GOD

The exclusivity of God is a traditional element in both Jewish and Christian confession of the Deity. The Hebrew Scriptures acclaim that God alone is the Deity who (a) spread out the heavens (2 Kg 19:15; Job 9:8; Neh 9:6; Isa 37:16; 44:24); (b) does wonders (Pss 72:18; 86:10); and (c) knows the secrets of the heart (1 Kg 8:39; 2 Chron 6:30; see G. Delling, "*Monos Theos*," *TLZ* 77 [1952]: 469–76). Christian usage is more simple in its confession of monotheism (Mark 12:32; John 5:44; 17:3; 1 Tim 1:17; 6:15–16). Jude's formula here confesses "the only savior God," acclaiming God as the unique benefactor. This note of benefaction too is a commonplace (see Philo, *Heres* 60; *Conf.* 93). In the letter's overall structure, the confession of the "only savior God" by the loyal disciples forms an inclusion with the "denial of the only master and lord" (v 4) by Jude's opponents.

BEFORE ALL AGES, NOW AND FOREVER

Typical doxologies acclaim God's glory endlessly into the future (*eis tous aiōnas*, Rom 11:36; Gal 1:5; Phil 4:20; 2 Tim 4:18). Yet this triple profession of glory in past, present, and future echoes Jewish theologoumena. For example, in Isa 48:12 God is both first and last, a remark which manifests God's absolute sovereignty (see Rev 21:6; Philo, *Plant.* 93; Josephus, *Ant.* 8.280). The targums to Exod 3:14 ("I am who I am") tend to elaborate the basic "I AM" as the figure who made the world and who will remake it at the end of time (see M. McNamara, *The New Testament and the Palestinian Targum to the Pentateuch* [AnBib 27. Rome: Biblical Institute Press, 1966] 97–112). For example, *Tg. Neof.* Exod 3:14 translated "I am has sent me to you" as "Who spoke and the world was from the beginning and shall say again to it Be! and it shall be." Similarly in Revelation, God is identified either as the Alpha and Omega (1:8) or as the figure who "is, was and is to come" (1:4, 8; see 4:8; 11:17). Thus Jude's remarks on God's eternity are typical Jewish attestations of the Deity's transcendence (see Pss 41:14; 106:48).

Yet they are also bound up with the honor of God. Not all kingdoms endure; monarchs on earth come and go (1 Kgs 2:15; 11:35; Dan 2:39–44; 4:31; 5:28; Isa 14:4–20). Their honor thus suffers limits, no matter what monuments they leave behind. Only God enjoys unlimited honor and knows no death or fading. Thus as part of giving God glory, the Deity's kingdom is acclaimed everlasting (Dan 4:3, 34; Ps 145:13) and God's name must be glorious forever (Ps 72:19).

BIBLIOGRAPHY

Black, Matthew, "The Doxology to the *Pater Noster* with a Note on Matthew 6:13b," A *Tribute to Geza Vermes* (Philip Davies and Richard White, eds.; Sheffield: JSOT Press, 1991), 327–38.

Deichgräber, Reinhard, *Gotteshymnus und Christushymnus in der frühen Christenheit* (Göttingen: Vandenhoeck & Ruprecht, 1967), 25–40, 97–102.

Elliott, J. K., "The Language and Style of the Concluding Doxology to the Epistle to the Romans," ZNW 72 (1981): 124–30.

Kamlah, E., *Traditionsgeschichtliche Untersuchungen zur Schlussdoxologie des Römerbriefes* (Unpublished dissertation: Tübingen, 1955), 66–87.

Neyrey, Jerome H., " 'Without Beginning of Days or End of Life' (Heb 7:3): Topos for a True Deity," *CBQ* 53 (1991): 441–46.

Jude: Bibliography

♦

Barnett, A. E., "The Epistle of Jude," *The Interpreter's Bible* (Nashville: Abingdon Press, 1957), 12.317–43.

Bauckham, Richard J., *Jude, 2 Peter* (Word Bible Commentary 50: Waco, TX: Word, Inc., 1983).

———, "James, 1 and 2 Peter, Jude," *It Is Written: Scripture Citing Scripture. Essays in Honour of Barnabas Lindars* (D. A. Carson and H. G. M. Williamson, eds; Cambridge: Cambridge University Press, 1988), 303–17.

———, "The Letter to Jude: An Account of Research," ANRW 2.25.5 (1988): 3791–827.

———, *Jude and the Relatives of Jesus in the Early Church* (Edinburgh: T. & T. Clark, 1991).

Bigg, Charles, A *Critical and Exegetical Commentary on the Epistles of St. Peter and St. Jude* (Edinburgh: T. & T. Clark, 1902).

Boobyer, G. H., "Jude," *Peake's Commentary on the Bible* (M. Black and H. H. Rowley, eds.; London: Thomas Nelson, 1962), 1041–42.

Busto, Saiz, J. R., "La cartas de Judas a la luz de algunos escritos judíos," *EstBib* 39 (1981): 83–105.

Cantinat, J. *Les Epîtres de Saint Jacques et de Saint Jude* (Paris: Gabalda, 1973).

Chaine, J., *Les Epîtres catholique: La seconde Epître de saint Pierre, les Epîtres de saint Jean, l'Epître de saint Jude* (EBib. 2d ed. Paris: Gabalda, 1939).

Charles, J. Daryl, " 'Those' and 'These': The Use of the Old Testament in the Epistle of Jude," *JSNT* 38 (1990): 109–24.

———, "Jude's Use of Pseudepigraphical Source-Material as Part of a Literary Strategy," *NTS* 37 (1991): 130–45.

———, "Literary Artifice in the Epistle of Jude," ZNW 82 (1991): 106–24.

Cranfield, C. E. W., *I & II Peter and Jude: Introduction and Commentary* (London: SCM Press, 1960).

Desjardins, M., "The Portrayal of the Dissidents in 2 Peter and Jude: Does It Tell Us More About the 'Godly' than the 'Ungodly'?" *JSNT* 30 (1987): 89–102.

Dunnett, W. M., "The Hermeneutics of Jude and 2 Peter: The Use of Ancient Jewish Traditions," *JETS* 31 (1988): 287–92.

Elliott, John H., *I–II Peter/Jude* (Augsburg Commentary on the New Testament. Minneapolis: Augsburg Publishing House, 1982), 161–85.

Eybers, I. H., "Aspects of the Background of the Letter of Jude," *Neot* 9 (1975): 113–23.

Fossum, Jarl, "Kyrios Jesus as the Angel of the Lord in Jude 5–7," *NTS* 33 (1987): 226–43.

Green, Michael, *The Second Epistle General of Peter and the General Epistle of Jude* (2d ed. Leicester: Inter-Varsity Press, 1987).

Gunther, J. J., "The Alexandrian Epistle of Jude," *NTS* 30 (1984): 549–62.

Hahn, F., "Randbemerkungen zum Judasbrief," *TZ* 37 (1981): 209–18.

Harm, H., "Logic Line in Jude: The Search of Syllogisms in a Hortatory Text," *OPTAT* 3.4 (1987): 147–72.

Hauck, F., *Die kathlischen Briefe* (NTD 10. 8th ed. Göttingen: Vandenhoeck and Ruprecht, 1957).

Heilgenthal, R., "Der Judasbrief: Aspekte der Forschung in den letzten Jahrzehnten," *TRu* 51 (1986): 117–29.

Hiebert, D. E., "Selected Studies from Jude. Part 1: An Exposition of Jude 3–4," *BSac* 142 (1985): 142–51.

———, "Selected Studies from Jude: Part 2: An Exposition of Jude 12–16," *BSac* 142 (1985): 238–49.

———, "Selected Studies from Jude: Part 2: An Exposition of Jude 17:23," *BSac* 142 (1985): 355–66.

James, M. R., "The Second Epistle General of Peter and the General Epistle of Jude (Cambridge: Cambridge University Press, 1912).

Joubert, S. J., "Language, Ideology and the Social Context of the Letter of Jude," *Neot* 24 (1990): 335–49.

Kelley, J. N. D., *The Epistles of Peter and of Jude* (London: Adam and Charles Black, 1969).

Klijn, A. F. J., "Jude 5–7," *The New Testament Age: Essays in Honor of Bo Reicke* (W. C. Weinrich, ed.; Macon, GA: Mercer University Press, 1984), 237–44.

Knopf, R., *Die Briefe Petri und Judä* (MeyerK 12. 7th ed. Göttingen: Vandenhoeck and Ruprecht, 1912).

Krodel, Gerhard, "The Letter of Jude," *Hebrews, James, 1 and 2 Peter, Jude, Revelation* (Philadelphia: Fortress Press, 1977).

Kubo, Sakae, "Jude 22–23: Two-division Form or Three?" *New Testament Text Criticism: Its Significance for Exegesis* (E. J. Epp and G. D. Fee, eds.; Oxford: Clarendon Press, 1981), 239–53.

Kugelman, Richard, *James and Jude* (New Testament Message 19. Wilmington, DE: Michael Glazier, 1980).

Kühl, Ernst, *Die Briefe Petri und Judae* (MeyerK 12. 6th ed. Göttingen: Vandenhoeck and Ruprecht, 1897).

Lawlor, G. L., *Translation and Exposition of the Epistle of Jude* (Nutley, NJ: Presbyterian and Reformed Publishing Co., 1976).

Leaney, A. R. C., *The Letters of Peter and Jude* (Cambridge: Cambridge University Press, 1967).

Magass, W., "Semiotik einer Ketzerpolemik am Beispeil von Judas 12f," *Linguistica Biblica* 19 (1972): 36–47.

Mayor, Joseph B., *The Epistles of St. Jude and the Second Epistle of St. Peter* (New York: Macmillan and Company, 1907).

Meier, John P., "The Brothers and Sisters of Jesus in Ecumenical Perspective," *CBQ* 54 (1992): 1–28.

Michl, J., *Die katholischen Briefe* (RNT 8. 2d ed. Regensburg: Frederich Pustet, 1968).

Moffatt, J., *The General Epistles: James, Peter and Judas* (MNTC. London: Hodder and Stoughton, 1928).

Oleson, J. P., "An Echo of Hesiod's *Theogony* vv. 190–2 in Jude 13," *NTS* (1979): 492–503.

Osborn, C. D., "The Christological Use of I Enoch i.9 in Jude 14–15," *NTS* 23 (1977): 334–41.

———, "The Text of Jude 5," *Bib* 62 (1981): 107–15.

———, "*I Enoch* 80:2–8 (67:5–7) and Jude 12–13," *CBQ* 47 (1985): 296–303.

Plummer, A., *The General Epistles of St. James and St. Jude* (London: Hodder and Stoughton, 1891).

Plumptre, E. H., *The General Epistles of St. Peter and St. Jude* (Cambridge: Cambridge University Press, 1926).

Reicke, R., *The Epistles of James, Peter and Jude* (AnB 37. Garden City, NY: Doubleday, 1964).

Ross, J. M., "Church Discipline in Jude 22–23," *ExpT* 100 (1989): 297–98.

Schelkle, K. H., *Die Petrusbriefe, der Judasbrief* (HTKNT 13/2. Freiburg: Herder, 1961).

Schlatter, A., *Die Briefe des Petrus, Judas, Jakobus, der Brief an die Hebräer* (Stuttgart: Calwer Verlag, 1964).

Schneider, J., *Die Briefe des Jakobus, Petrus, Judas und Johannes: Die katholischen Briefe* (NTD 10. 9th ed. Göttingen: Vandenhoeck and Ruprecht, 1961).

Schrage, W., *Die "katholischen" Briefe: Die Briefe des Jakobus, Petrus, Johannes, und Judas* (NTD 10. 11th ed. Göttingen: Vandenhoeck and Ruprecht, 1973).

Seethaler, P.-A., "Kleine Bemerkungen zum Judasbrief," *BZ* 31 (1987): 261–64.

Sellin, G., "Die Häretiker des Judasbriefes," ZNW 77 (1986): 206–25.

Senior, Donald, "The Letters of Jude and Second Peter," *BibT* 25 (1987): 209–14.

Sidebottom, E. M., *James, Jude and 2 Peter* (NCB. London: Thomas Nelson, 1967).

Soden, H. von, *Hebräerbrief, Briefe des Petrus, Jakobus, Judas* (HKNT 3/2. Freiburg: J. C. B. Mohr, 1899).

Spitta, F., *Der zweite Brief des Petrus und der Brief des Judas* (Halle: Verlag der Buchhandlung des Waisenhauses, 1885).

Staab, K., "Die griechischen Katenenkommentare zu den katholischen Briefen," *Bib* 5 (1924): 296–353.

Thekkekara, M., "Contend for the Faith: The Letter of Jude," *Biblebhashyam* 15 (1989): 182–98.

Wand, J. W. C., *The General Epistles of St. Peter and St. Jude* (London: Methuen, 1934).

Whallon, William, "Should We Keep, Omit or Alter the *hoi* in Jude 12?" *NTS* 34 (1988): 156–59.

Windisch, Hans *Die katholischen Briefe* (HNT 15. 3d ed. Tübingen: J. C. B. Mohr, 1951).

Wisse, Frederick, "The Epistle of Jude in the History of Heresiology," *Essays on the Nag Hammadi Texts in Honor of Alexander Boehlig* (Martin Krause, ed.; Leiden E. J. Brill, 1972), 133–43.

Wolthuis, T. R., "Jude and Jewish Traditions," *CTJ* 22 (1987): 21–41.

———, "Jude and Rhetoricism: A Dialogue on the Rhetorical Nature of the Epistle of Jude," *CTJ* 24 (1989): 126–34.

2 PETER
TRANSLATION AND OUTLINE

♦

I. Letter Opening: Address and Prayer (1:1–2)

1 1. Simeon Peter, servant and apostle of Jesus Christ, to those who
have received a faith as honorable as ours through the justice of
our God and Jesus Christ the Savior. 2. May favor and peace be
abundant in you by your acknowledgment of God and Jesus our
Lord.

II. Patron's Benefaction and Clients' Response (1:3–11)

1 3. As his divine power has bestowed on us everything for a life of
piety through the acknowledgment of the One who has called us
to his own glory and excellence, 4. in virtue of these, the
precious and greatest promises have been given us so that through
them you may become sharers of the divine nature and be freed
from the corruption in the world because of desire. 5. For this
reason be earnest to supplement your faith with excellence,
excellence with knowledge, 6. knowledge with self-control, self-
control with steadfastness, steadfastness with piety, 7. piety with
kinship affection, kinship affection with love. 8. For when you
possess these and increase in them, they will make you neither
useless nor fruitless for the acknowledgment of our Lord Jesus
Christ. 9. But whoever lacks them is blind, shortsighted and
forgets the purification of past sins. 10. All the more, brethren,
be zealous to make firm your call and election, for if you do this,
you will never stumble. 11. For in this way entry into the eternal
kingdom of our Lord and Savior Jesus Christ will be richly added
to you.

III. Occasion of the Letter: Peter's Farewell Address (1:12–15)

1 12. So then, I mean always to remind you about these things,
although you know them and are established in the truth present

to you. 13. I think it right, as long as I am in this tent, to keep
awakening you by reminders. 14. I know that the divesting of
my tent is near, as our Lord Jesus Christ has revealed to me.
15. I shall be zealous to enable you after my departure always to
remember these things.

IV. Reply to the First Slander: Prophecy of the Parousia Defended (1:16–18)

1 16. For we did not follow cleverly devised myths when we made
known to you the powerful coming of our Lord Jesus Christ, but
we were eyewitnesses of his majesty. 17. For he received from
God the Father honor and glory when the voice came to him
from the Majestic Glory: "This is my son, my beloved; on him
have I placed my favor." 18. And indeed we heard this voice
borne from heaven, when we were with him on the holy mountain.

V. Reply to the Second Slander: Prophecy and Interpretation Defended (1:19–21)

1 19. And we have a very certain prophetic word, to which you do
well to attend, as to a light shining in darkness until the day dawns
and the morning star rises in your hearts. 20. But first know that
no prophetic writing is a matter of personal interpretation;
21. because prophecy is not borne by the will of mortals, but
carried by the Holy Spirit, mortals spoke from God.

VI. The Third Slander: The Master Denied (2:1–3a)

2 1. But there appeared false prophets among the people, even as
among you there will be false teachers. They will introduce
ruinous doctrines, denying the Master who purchased them and
bringing upon themselves a rapid ruin. 2. And many will follow
their debauchery; because of them "the way of truth" will be
dishonored; 3a. and in their greed they will buy you with
specious arguments.

VII. Reply to the Third Slander: Divine Judgment Defended (2:3b–10a)

2 3b. Upon them judgment has not long been idle, nor does their
ruin sleep. 4. For if God did not spare the angels who sinned,
but handed them over, casting them into Tartarus in chains of
darkness to keep them for judgment, 5. and if God did not spare
the ancient world, but guarded Noah, herald of righteousness,
and seven others while bringing a deluge upon the world of the
impious, 6. and if God condemned and reduced to ashes the

cities of Sodom and Gomorrah, setting a warning for future
impious people, 7. but rescued the righteous Lot, worn down
by their lawless and licentious behavior. 8. (for day after day
that righteous man lived among them, in sight and sound tortured
in his just soul by their lawlessness), 9. then the Lord knows
how to rescue the godly from trial, but to keep the unrighteous
under punishment until the day of judgment, 10a. especially
those who follow the polluting desires of the flesh and who despise
authority.

VIII. Shame on the Opponents: Beasts, Lust, and Greed (2:10b–16)

2 10b. Audacious and arrogant, they are not afraid to insult the
glorious ones, 11. whereas the angels, greater in might and
power, do not bring an insulting judgment from the Lord against
them. 12. But these men, like beasts without reason, creatures
of instinct born for capture and destruction, insult what they do
not comprehend; in their destruction they too will be destroyed,
13. and will suffer wickedly the wages of their wickedness. They
reckon as pleasure daytime dissipation. Blots and blemishes, they
practice dissipation in their deceptions when they feast with you.
14. Their eyes are ceaselessly filled with adulteries and evils; they
entice the unstable; their own hearts are practiced in greed.
Accursed children! 15. Deceived themselves, they forsake the
straight way to follow the way of Balaam son of Bosor, who loved
the wages of wickedness. 16. He received rebuke for his lawlessness when his dumb donkey spoke in a human voice and hindered
the prophet's madness.

IX. More Shame on the Opponents: Hypocrisy and Harm (2:17–22)

2 17. These men are springs without water, mists driven by storms;
for them gloomy darkness is kept. 18. They mouth empty
boasts; they entice with debauchery and desires of the flesh those
who but recently fled from the company of those who live in
error. 19. They promise them freedom, but are themselves
slaves of destruction. For people are slaves to that which masters
them. 20. For if they, who fled the pollution of the world by
acknowledging our Lord and Savior Jesus Christ, again are entangled in evil company and are mastered by it, this last state is worse
than the first. 21. Far better for them that they should never
have acknowledged the way of righteousness, than acknowledging
it, to turn away from the holy rule given them. 22. For them
the proverb has proved true: "The dog returns to its vomit" and
"The pig, once washed, wallows in mud."

X. The Fourth Slander: God's Powerful Word Challenged (3:1–4)

3 1. Beloved, I am now writing you this second letter, in both of
which I arouse in your memory a correct understanding,
2. reminding you of the predictions by the holy prophets and the
command of the Lord and Savior through your apostles.
3. Know this first, that in the last days scoffers will come scoffing,
acting according to their peculiar passions, 4. and saying,
"Where is the promise of his coming? For, from the day the
fathers fell asleep, all has remained just as from the beginning of
creation."

XI. Reply to the Fourth Slander: Divine Word of Judgment Defended (3:5–7)

3 5. For in holding this, they forget that from of old by the word of
God the heavens were created and earth was put together out of
and through water. 6. Then by these the world was flooded with
water and destroyed. 7. By the same word the heavens and earth
are now stored up for fire, kept for the day of judgment and
destruction of the ungodly.

XII. The Fifth Slander and a Reply: Delay of Divine Judgment Defended (3:8–13)

3 8. Beloved, do not let this one fact escape your notice, that with
the Lord, one day is as a thousand years and a thousand years are
as one day. 9. The Lord does not delay about the promise, as
some reckon "delay," but is forbearing toward you. For he does
not wish any to be destroyed, but all to reach repentance.
10. For the day of the Lord will come like a thief. Then the
heavens will pass away with a roar; the elements will be burned up
and dissolved; and the earth and all its works will be found out.
11. Since all these will be dissolved in this way, what sort of
people ought you be, in holy and pious lives. 12. You await and
hasten the coming of the day of God, when the heavens will be
set on fire and dissolved and the elements burned and melted.
13. According to his promise, we await "new heavens and a new
earth," where righteousness will dwell.

XIII. Final Exhortation and Letter Closing: Stand Firm in the Tradition (3:14–18)

3 14. Therefore, beloved, as you look forward to this, strive to be
found by him spotless, unblemished, and at peace. 15. Reckon
the forbearance of the Lord as salvation, even as our beloved
brother Paul wrote to you according to the wisdom given him.

16. He speaks about these matters in all his letters, in which there
are things hard to interpret, and which the untutored and unstable
distort to their own ruin, as they do also with the other Scriptures.
17. But you, beloved, know this beforehand; guard lest you be led
astray by the deceit of the lawless and fall away from your proper
constancy. 18. Grow in the favor and knowledge of our Lord
and Savior Jesus Christ. To him be glory both now and on the day
of eternity.

2 Peter: Introduction

♦

1. Form and Literary Structure

2 Peter contains a number of literary forms (solemn decree—1:3–11; farewell address—1:12–15) but is cast in the form of a letter. Epistolographic conventions pertain basically to its introduction and conclusion. Like other NT letters, it begins with an introduction (1:1–11):

Opening (1:1–2)
Thanksgiving (1:3–4)
Exhortation (1:5–11)
—bad theology leads to bad ethics (1:5–7)
—two ways (1:8–11)

and ends with a conclusion (3:17–18):

Exhortation (3:17–18a)
Doxology (3:18b)

Even here there are significant variations in the conventions of letter writing found in other NT letters. This letter is not addressed to any specific individual or church, but generally "to those who have received a faith as honorable as ours" (1:1). Ordinarily NT letters contain a thanksgiving prayer, whether in Greek form (Pauline letters) or Jewish form (1 Peter 1:3–5). This document contains a list of divine benefactions for which the addressees ought to show honor (F. W. Danker, "2 Peter 1: A Solemn Decree," *CBQ* 40 [1978]: 64–82). In content this corresponds to literary thanksgivings, only here the explicit blessing or thanks is implied. Unusual is the immediate exhortation in 1:5–11. D. F. Watson argued that 1:3–15 be considered formally as a "miniature homily" (*Invention, Arrangement, and Style*, 96–101); but if Peder Borgen is correct in his assessment of the homily form (*Bread from Heaven* [NovTSup 10. Leiden: E. J. Brill, 1965], 28–58), then 1:3–15 lacks the introductory scripture text on which homilies are characteristically based. Moreover, Danker's argument that this is a "solemn decree" in which honor is owed to a benefactor seems more persuasive. In short, the letter form appears to be merely the literary fiction in which the author's remarks are cast.

The function of 2 Peter is primarily apology/polemic. In regard to letter type, the author suggests in 1:12–15 that it is the farewell address of the author to his addressees. This literary convention was well known to Greek as well as Jewish audiences. Letters of this formal type, however, are indeed rare (see 2 Tim 4:6–8). 2 Peter purports to be the final word of the author on matters which he considers vitally important. According to rhetorical argumentation, then, the situation appears urgent.

Ordinarily after the letter introduction we find the body of the letter. If the letter function is polemic and apology, then the treatment of five issues in the document can be said to comprise the body of this letter:

Reply to the first slander (1:16–18):
  Prophecy of the parousia defended
Reply to the second slander (1:19–21):
  Prophecy and interpretation defended
Reply to the third slander (2:1–3, 4–10a):
  Divine judgment defended
Reply to the fourth slander (3:1–3, 4–7):
  Divine word of judgment defended
Reply to the fifth slander (3:8–9, 10–13):
  Delay of divine judgment defended

In three of these the author casts the form of the polemic and apology in terms of a denial and then an affirmation: *not (ouk) . . . but (alla):*

1:16	*not* following cleverly devised myths	*but* we were eyewitnesses
1:21	*not* borne by the will of mortals	*but* carried by the Holy Spirit
3:9	the Lord does *not* delay as some reckon "delay"	*but* is forbearing

The author juxtaposes to the scoffing remarks of his opponents against prophecies of the parousia and divine judgment his affirmation of them. This rhetorical pattern, of course, is hardly unique to 2 Peter (see A. J. Malherbe, *Paul and the Thessalonians* [Philadelphia: Fortress, 1987], 3–4, 71), but seems to be a common mode of argumentation in antiquity. We have numerous examples of it in Philo's corpus, where he rejects polemical remarks about God and divine oracles and states his apologetic explanation clearly. For example,

This is *no* invention of mine	*but* a statement made by the most holy oracles [*Mut.* 152].

This is *not* a story invented by me	*but* an oracle inscribed upon the sacred tables [*Somn.* 1.172].

A variation of this rhetorical framing of polemic/apology is found in 2:3–9, where the author rejects the polemic that there is no divine judgment ("judgment is *not* idle, *nor* does ruin sleep," v 3) with his argument for divine judgment from biblical examples (vv 4–10a). A similar juxtaposition of denial and affirmation occurs in 3:4–7. The opponents deny divine action in the world to punish the wicked, casting their polemic in the form of a scoffing question, "Where is the promise of his coming?" This denial is bolstered by an argument beginning with "for": "For, from the day the fathers fell asleep, all has remained just as from the beginning of creation" (3:4). The author likewise begins his apologetic to this with the conjunction "for," arguing that they willfully forget the tradition which he then rehearses (3:5–7).

Thus, in following the argument of the author, we need to be aware of epistolographic conventions at the beginning and ending of the document, as well as conventions pertaining to a farewell address. But in terms of the document's thrust, it is a sustained defense of five basic items that have to do with God, in terms either of divine prophecies of the parousia or of divine judgment.

2. Rhetorical Structure

Formal epistolary conventions aside, we should also consider the rhetorical argument advanced in the document.

(a) Exordium. As we saw in the case of Jude, the document begins with an *exordium*. This initial part of an argument announces the hortatory intention of the speaker/writer, suggests the topics to be developed in the remainder of the writing, and requests a serious hearing. D. F. Watson (*Invention, Arrangement, and Style*, 87–101) argued that 2 Peter 1:3–15 be considered the *exordium* of the document. In this section the author indeed begins the exhortation to good theology and good morals which characterizes those disciples who are loyal to the tradition the author defends. Believing the promises and prophecies of God, they will imitate God's holiness and keep themselves in the way of virtue, which leads to entrance into God's kingdom. Furthermore, to gain the goodwill of the audience, he addresses them as clients of a great patron, who have been richly blessed with exceptional favors. God, the heavenly Patron, has not only granted them "all things" that pertain to life and godliness, but the greatest of divine gifts, a future share in the divine nature (1:3–4).

Moreover, the author mentions briefly a number of key topics and terms which will be developed in the course of the document.

1. Doctrine of God (1:3–4):
   2 Peter presents God as a generous benefactor, who has shown blessing in the past and who will bless those loyal to him by giving them a share in his kingdom (1:11) and divine nature (1:4). God's blessing is balanced by constant mention of divine judgment of the wicked (2:4–10, 16; 3:5–7, 9–13). Thus theodicy, divine justice, and judgment are presented as orthodox theology.
2. Human response: *piety* (*eusebeia*, 1:3, 6–7):
   God's benefaction entails divine rights and human duties. Indeed the pious are rescued by God (2:9); those who believe God's prophecies of judgment live worthy lives of holiness and piety (3:11). In contrast the scoffers, who deny God's just judgment, are presented as the "impious," upon whom divine judgment comes (2:5, 6; 3:7).
3. Acknowledgment of God (*epignōsis*, 1:3, 8):
   Those loyal to the tradition of God's just judgment indeed publicly acknowledge this and know it (3:18). In contrast, false teachers deny God's power and providence: they reject prophecies of the parousia (1:16); divine prophecies in general (1:19–21); divine judgment (2:3b; 3:9); and divine power over creation (3:4). Correct knowledge allows the loyal disciple to escape the world's corruption (2:20).
4. God's promises and prophecies (*epaggelmata*, 1:4):
   Loyal disciples honor God's prophecies of the parousia (1:16; 3:5–7, 9) as well as God's prophetic word (1:19–21; 2:4–9; 3:5–7). About these there can be no confusion, since all loyal followers—prophets of old, apostles, and even Paul (3:15–16)—agree. God's promises truly lead to life and so freedom from death and corruption, unlike the false promises of the opponents (2:19).
5. Freedom from corruption (*phthora*, 1:4):
   God is holy and incorrupt, and God's loyal disciples seek to live lives of incorruption (3:12–14) by walking in the way of virtue (1:5–7) and fleeing the way of vice (*apopheugein*, 1:4). Those who spurn God's prophecies of judgment are slaves of vice (2:20), mired in corruption and vice (2:22); many of their disciples had barely fled from a life of error (2:18, 20) before they became bound again to corruption. And so they are destined to destruction (2:1, 3; 3:7, 9) when the corrupt world will be destroyed (2:12, 19; 3:6, 12). Thus morally corrupt people are blots and blemishes (2:13) and so will be destroyed in the world's

corruption; but pious disciples are spotless (3:14) and are destined to share God's incorruption (1:4).

6. Desire (*epithymia*, 1:4):
The wicked are corrupted by the most seductive of the four cardinal vices, "desire"; they lead others into vice (2:18) and all such come to a just judgment (2:10). This "desire" is spoken of as passion and licentiousness (2:2, 7, 18); it results in stains, blemishes, and contagion (3:14).

7. Hastening on the way (*spoudē*, 1:5):
Those who acclaim God's just judgment hasten to live virtuously (1:5) and so hasten to confirm their call (1:10), to be found without blemish (3:14), and to bring the day of the Lord (3:12). The author himself hastens to leave a reminder of the true theology (1:15).

8. Two ways (1:5–10):
As the commentary will explain, the traditional doctrine of the two ways is announced here. The just walk in the way of virtue, which is also the "way of truth" (2:2, 15) and the "way of righteousness" (2:21); it is characterized by "self-control" (1:6). The wicked, however, walk in the way of vice (2:10–22), which is also called "the way of Balaam" (2:15). Their way is the vice of "desire" or sexual passion. Those who fear God walk in the way of virtue, but those who deny divine judgment walk in the way of vice.

9. Supplementing faith (*pistis*, 1:5):
This faith is correct theology, namely the true doctrine about God's prophecies and judgment. It is another way of "acknowledging" God (1:3, 8) and showing steadfastness in the truth (1:6).

10. Increasing (*plenazonta*, 1:8):
The upright increase in virtue as well as grow in grace and knowledge (3:18). The gain for the wicked is their greed (*pleonexia*, 2:3, 14).

11. Useless, fruitless (1:8):
Those who propose false theology are later called "waterless springs and mists" (2:17), who promise much and deliver little.

12. Blind, shortsighted, forgetful (*lēthēn*, 1:9):
Again the opponents who lack true theology and so true virtue are those who willfully forget the truth and distort it (3:5, 8). In contrast the author and the authentic disciples are those who remember correctly (1:12–13; 3:1).

13. A firm call (*bebaian*, 1:10):
Truth means standing firm and strong in the tradition (1:12; 3:17). Likewise, the prophetic word is made "most firm" (1:19) in virtue of

the testimony of the author. Indeed, the apology, with its rehearsal of eyewitness testimony and correct interpretation of prophecies and oracles, should make the tradition "firm."

14. Entering the eternal kingdom (1:11):
The great promises of God (1:3–4) are the advent of a new heaven and earth (3:13), which will be the home of the just. At the parousia of the Lord, the just will inherit the nature of God (1:4), which is incorruptibility and immortality. Hence, they hasten to do all that will insure their entrance into God's incorrupt and holy realm.

Thus the quasi-epistolary thanksgiving functions well as a typical *exordium* in which the topics and themes to be developed are put before the audience.

The rhetorical location of the prediction of death in 1:12–15 coheres with one of the functions of an *exordium*, namely, the ethos of the speaker and his request for a serious hearing. The author presents himself as a traditional elder of the group, who lives up to the duty of his role. He reaffirms the tradition in its fullness and leaves this letter as a permanent reminder of the truth. He does this in response to a revelation from the Lord Jesus Christ (1:14) that his life is coming to an end. Thus he presents himself as an honorable person who acts altruistically on behalf of the group. He is, moreover, one intimate with the Lord and familiar with special knowledge, as the revelation of his death indicates. Finally, the audience should heed this letter because it is his last word (1:14); as a dying patriarch, he reveals the future and leaves a legacy.

(b) Probatio. After the *exordium*, writers and speakers turn their attention to the proof of their case, the *probatio*. The task turns on persuading the audience of the legitimacy of the author's case (Watson, *Invention, Arrangement, and Style*, 101–35). In regard to 2 Peter, this will entail refutation of the opponents' arguments and assertions, as well as confirmation of the author's own position (see Cicero, *Inv. Rhet.* 1.24.34 and 1.42.78). The issue is *proof*, and what counts for proof or evidence in ancient rhetoric (see Quintilian, *Inst.* book 5).

As we noted above, the body of the letter contains five distinct arguments from the author. In the first proof (1:16–18), he refutes the opponents' slander about the prophecy of the parousia, confirming it by the proof of eyewitness testimony. In the second (1:19–21), he replies to the opponents' rationalizing of prophecy, defending the traditional position with an argument which Watson identifies as an enthymeme (*Invention, Arrangement, and Style*, 18, 105). The third proof (2:1–10b) contains a refutation of the opponents' denial of divine judgment through a series of examples confirming just what they deny.

The flow of proofs is interrupted by a *digressio* (2:10b–22), in which the author seeks to shame his opponents. This polemical material includes denunciations of them (2:10b–11), amplification of their ungodliness (2:12–14), examples of comparable sinners who were punished (2:15–16), more denunciations (2:17–18), and four maxims which put them in a bad light (2:19–22). In this *digressio*, the author seeks to portray a negative ethos for the false teachers troubling the church, even as he points to the seriousness of the situation by identifying such heinous malefactors.

In the fourth proof (3:4–7), the author refutes the scoffers' mocking of the prophecies of the end of the world by another enthymeme. This argument is based on examples of divine cosmological activity, such as were noted earlier in the proof section of 2:5–7. Finally, the opponents' denial of divine judgment is refuted and the author's tradition is confirmed (3:8–13); he appeals to traditions which the group presumably accepts and which are based on words of Jesus, the ancient prophets, and the gospel traditions from Jesus. Thus the author has left no slur or slander unexamined, and has labored to confirm his position with proofs drawn largely from the hallowed traditions held sacred by him and his audience. The effect of this *probatio* is to position himself as the honored elder who knows and defends the traditions of the group, while his opponents are cast negatively as scoffers at tradition.

(c) **Peroratio.** The document concludes with a *peroratio* (Watson, *Invention, Argument, and Style*, 135–41). It consists of two parts: (1) a recapitulation or *repetitio* (3:14–16) and (2) a final emotional appeal or *adfectus* (3:17–18). In the recapitulation, the author echoes both immediate materials and previous ones. Among the immediate repetitions we note:

- Awaiting (*prosdokōntes*): the addressees are urged to wait for the world's renewal (3:14), just as they waited for the day of God (3:12) and the new heavens and earth (3:13).
- Hastening (*spoudasate*): they hasten to be found pure (3:14), just as they hastened the coming of the day (3:12).
- Found (*eurethēnai*): they seek to be found pure (3:14), just as the earth and its deeds will be found at the day of judgment (3:10).
- Forbearance (*makrothymian*): they should reckon the Lord's delay of judgment as divine forbearance for salvation, just as the author interpreted delay of judgment in 3:9.

Besides these proximate repetitions, others can be observed which link the *peroratio* with both the *exordium* and the *probatio:*

- Hastening (*spoudasate*): the addressees hasten to be pure (3:14), even as they were exhorted to hasten to be virtuous (1:5) and to confirm their call (1:10).

- Without spot or blemish (*aspiloi, amōmētoi*): they should be pure, in contrast to the opponents who are denounced as "spots and blemishes" (2:13).
- Salvation (*sōtērian*): the forbearance of the Lord means salvation (3:15), even as the Lord has been repeatedly identified as their "Savior" (1:1, 11; 2:20; 3:2).
- Ignorant and unstable (*amatheis, astēriktoi*): the charge that some are ignorant (3:16) echoes the warning against being "blind and shortsighted" (1:9); the instability of the opponents (3:16) echoes the denunciation that they deceive other unstable folk (2:14) and contrasts with the exhortation to the faithful to stand firm (1:12).
- Destruction (*apōleian*): the opponents now court destruction (3:16) for their travesty of the tradition, just as the author declared that the end of their heterodoxy would be destruction (2:1, 3); destruction is the fate of the ungodly (3:7).

The repetitions of the *peroratio* capture many of the dualistic expressions which are integral to the two ways described by the author: those who know versus those who do not know; those who wait for the parousia versus those who deny it; those who keep pure versus those who are polluted; those who stand versus those who fall; those who come to salvation versus those who are destroyed.

The argument concludes with a direct, final appeal to the emotions of the addressees (*adfectus*), which can be framed both negatively and positively (Cicero, *Inv. Rhet.* 1.52.98, 100, 106). In 3:17 the negative appeal (*indignatio*) comes both in the repetition of the author's predictions of future heretics and especially in his warning (*phylassesthe*) that they not join the opponents and lose their standing with God. In the positive appeal (*conquestio*), they are exhorted to grow (*auxanete*) in correct knowledge and thus God's benefaction (3:18a). Thus the letter comes full circle, beginning with an appeal to loyalty to a benefactor (1:3–4) and ending with a similar appeal to grow in the benefaction of the heavenly Patron.

Thus by examining the rhetorical structure of 2 Peter we learn unmistakably that the document is a formal argument of praise and blame. Through rhetoric we gain greater clarity about just what is argued and how the argument is structured. And in the process we learn that the author was a rather skilled rhetorician, a person of formal education.

3. Vocabulary and Style

The most recent study of the vocabulary and style in 2 Peter was done by Bauckham (*Jude, 2 Peter*, 135–38). Of the vocabulary of this document, he notes the very high percentage of NT *hapax legomena* and gives a summary of his findings:

- Thirty-eight words occur but once or twice in the NT
- Fifty-seven words are not found in the NT
- Of these, thirty-two are not found in the LXX
- Half of the words found in the LXX are also found in Hellenistic Jewish writings of the period
- One third of the *hapax* occur also in the Apostolic Fathers

Unusual vocabulary, of course, may stem from the sources used. Although 2 Peter used Jude, which has a large number of rare words, of the thirty-eight words in 2 Peter which occur once or twice in the NT, only four are found in Jude (*asebein*, *empaiktēs*, *syneuōcheisthai*, and *hyperogkos*). Even assessing other possible sources, Bauckham concludes that the author himself possessed a very rich vocabulary, which indicates considerable formal education and a high degree of literacy.

Many words are repeated in 2 Peter, which has led some commentators to call the vocabulary "poor and inadequate." But in light of the two previous studies of the literary shape of the document and its formal rhetoric, repetition is often a function of literary technique such as catchwords and of rhetorical location in *exordium* or *peroratio* (see Bigg, *The Epistles of St. Peter and St. Jude*, 225–27). In an oral culture, it is expected that key terms in topic arguments are repeated and developed. Certain themes and the vocabulary in which they are expressed form the main topic which is both attacked and defended; it is expected that there be repetition of the vocabulary of this sort.

Many commentators at the turn of the last century negatively evaluated the style of this author, calling it "pompous" (Moulton, Howard, and Turner, *A Grammar of New Testament Greek*, 4.142) and "Baboo Greek" (E. A. Abbott, *Exp* 2/3 [1882]: 204–19). Other critics now tend to assess the style more historically as an example of the "Asiatic" style (Watson, *Invention, Arrangement, and Style*, 144–46). Hellenistic rhetoric distinguished "Attic" conciseness from "Asiatic" inflatedness:

> The distinction between the Attic and the Asiatic schools takes us back to antiquity. The former were regarded as concise and healthy, the latter as empty and inflated; the former were remarkable for the absence of all superfluity, while the latter were deficient in taste and restraint [Quintilian, *Inst.* 12.10.16; see Cicero, *Opt. Gen.* 3.8].

This overly negative view of Asiatic style is moderated in Cicero; while praising a certain Hortenius for his Asiatic style, he distinguished two types of Asiatic rhetoric:

> Of the Asiatic style there are two types, the one sententious and studied, less characterized by weight of thought than by the charm of balance and symmetry . . . The other type is not so notable for wealth of sententious phrase, as for swiftness and impetuosity—a general trait of Asia at the present time—combining with this rapid flow of speech a choice of words refined and ornate [*Brut.* 95.325].

This profile of ancient rhetoric helps us to identify the author of 2 Peter as a Greek writer of solid, but by no means aristocratic or Attic, eloquence. If, as Cicero remarks, the stereotype of this rhetoric truly belongs with Asian people, then the author is more easily located among the Hellenistic cities of Asia Minor.

It has been argued that there are some distinctive stylistic features of Christian literature, and our appreciation of 2 Peter is advanced by noting them. A. Wifstrand, ("Stylistic Problems in the Epistles of James and Peter," *ST* 1 [1948]: 171–80) identified four characteristic elements, which pertain as well to 2 Peter: (1) in-group vocabulary, (2) more intense and more intimate exhortation than typical diatribal style, (3) abundance of abstract substantive nouns, and (4) metaphoric language.

4. Literary Relationship to Jude

From the earliest times, the history of research on 2 Peter has been preoccupied both with its relationship to Jude and with the identification of its heretical opponents. According to early patristic evidence, 2 Peter was slow in becoming known and late in being accepted. There are no second-century commentaries on 2 Peter. Jude, however, was used by Clement of Alexandria, who argued against Carpocrates from Jude 8–17 (*Stromata* III.ii [GCS 15; Otto Stāhlin, ed.; Leipzig: J. C. Hinrichs, 1906], 197–200). Eusebius (*H.E.* 3.25.3) lists both 2 Peter and Jude with the "disputed books" (see Charles Bigg, *The Epistles of St. Peter and St. Jude,* 199–211).

As 2 Peter became known and accepted, it was assumed that Jude had in fact borrowed from him and that their opponents were the same. This judgment seems to have been influenced by the sense that the Apostle Peter would hardly have borrowed from a lesser figure, Jude, whereas the converse was quite plausible. Hence, for extrinsic reasons 2 Peter was thought to be prior to Jude and to be used by that author. Thus source-critical questions tended to be settled by appeal to prior judgments dealing with the honorable status of Peter and what was fitting for such a figure. This basic judgment prevailed until recent times when more critical investigations were made about the authorship of 2 Peter. With a decline in scholarly opinion about the authenticity of 2 Peter, the way was open to fresh investigation into its literary relationship to Jude. If 2 Peter was a pseudonymous writing, then the honor of "Peter" is not impugned if it can be shown that the author of 2 Peter borrowed from Jude.

It is to be expected that as scholarly questions about sources of biblical documents matured, the source-critical investigation of the relationship of Jude and 2 Peter would have its day. Bauckham (*Jude, 2 Peter,* 141) offers a convenient summary of the state of the question. The very close similarity between Jude and 2 Peter has led scholars to take one or another of the following four options. (1) Jude depends on 2 Peter, which position was found in the early church and was held by Luther and even modern scholars (e.g., Bigg, *The Epistles of St. Peter and St. Jude,* 216–23). (2) 2 Peter depends on Jude, which represents the viewpoint of most modern commentators (e.g., J. Chaine, *Les Epîtres catholiques* [Paris: Gabalda, 1939], 18–24; K. Schelkle, *Die Petrusbriefe, Der Judasbrief* [Freiburg: Herder, 1961], 138–39). (3) Both depend on a common source (e.g., B. Reicke, *The Epistles of James, Peter and Jude* [Garden City, NY: Doubleday, 1964], 189–90; C. Spicq, *Les Epîtres de Saint Pierre* [Paris: Gabalda, 1966], 197). (4) Both were written by the same author (e.g., J. A. T. Robinson, *Redating the New Testament* [London: SCM, 1976], 192–95).

The assertion of literary dependence has shifted from purely extrinsic arguments to judgments based on more complicated historical understandings of the two documents. Modern commentaries have traditionally contained discussions of the parallel passages in the two documents, which formed the bases for judgments about the priority of one document, usually that of Jude (e.g., J. B. Mayor, *The Epistle of Jude and the Second Epistle of St. Peter* [New York: Macmillan, 1907], i–xxv). With the maturation of redaction criticism, H. C. C. Cavallin called for a formal treatment of the relationship of the two documents from the perspective of redaction-critical methodology ("The False Teachers of 2 Pt," 263–64). Two recent studies of 2 Peter have offered just such a redactional comparison (Tord Fornberg, *An Early Church in a Pluralistic Society,* 33–59; and Jerome Neyrey, *The Form and Background of the Polemic in 2 Peter,* 119–67). And the recent commentary of R. Bauckham (*Jude, 2 Peter*) has offered still a third attempt at this.

It is relatively easy for a trained eye to discern both similarities and differences between Jude and 2 Peter, that is, the changes, omissions, and additions in the presumed derivative document. The difficulties for an accurate interpretation of the redaction lie in the historical and theological scenario which commentators imagine to be the background of each document. In short, redaction criticism itself operates in a context of presuppositions and hypotheses. In general, Fornberg, Neyrey, and Bauckman have worked from the hypothesis of the priority of Jude. And so all have argued concerning the use of and redaction of Jude by 2 Peter. These studies have all added weight to the hypothesis of Jude's priority by offering convincing interpretations of 2 Peter's use of Jude, but they have by no means proven it. This commentary operates on the current consensus that 2 Peter used Jude as a literary source and redacted that document in ways suitable to his historical situation. The redaction-critical comparisons in the commentary on 2 Peter will attempt to explain the scope and rationale of the changes made by 2 Peter in light of the historical and theological scenario which is explained in the next section of this introduction.

5. The Opponents of 2 Peter

Although letters were written in antiquity for a variety of reasons, 2 Peter states in 2:1 and 3:3–5 that he writes to refute false teachers and scoffers. Given the apologetic occasion for the document, we ask more specifically about the identity of his opponents. Who were they? What did they espouse? Why was that so dangerous as to warrant 2 Peter's response? It is the hypothesis of this commentary that the opponents were either Epicureans, who rejected traditional theodicy, or "scoffers" (*Apikoros*) who espoused a similar deviant theology.

(a) Epicurean Arguments Against Theodicy. It was characteristic of the ancient world to summarize knowledge in topoi, sententiae, or commonplaces, which extended even to thinkers such as Epicureans and Stoics (see J. H. Neyrey, "Acts 17, Epicureans and Theodicy," *Greeks, Romans, and Christians* [David Balch, ed.; Minneapolis: Fortress Press, 1990], 124–33). The ancient world knows Epicureans as those who deny the traditional doctrine of a provident Deity ("they pelt providence," Plutarch: *De Sera* 548C). Indeed, in literature ranging from Cicero's *Nat. Deor.*, Philo's *De Providentia*, and Seneca's *De Providentia* to Lactantius' *De Ira* and Origen's *Contra Celsum*, Epicureans were known in terms of their denial of divine judgment.

As we describe Epicurean theology, we should be aware of the point of view of the ancient records about it. Although their opponents called them "atheists" and reduced their doctrine about the Deity to a caricature of an immoral freethinker, Epicureans would give a more positive interpretation of their system. One of the central aims of Epicurus' system was "pleasure," which in context means "absence of trouble" or "freedom from pain and fear" (Diog. Laert. 10.128–32). Logically extending this system to the Deity, Epicurus argued that the Deity too should be free from trouble, that is, neither reacting in anger to punish the wicked nor blessing the good: "The blessed and eternal being has no trouble himself and brings no trouble upon any other being; hence he is exempt from movements of anger and kindness" (Diog. Laert. 10.139; see Cicero, *Nat. Deor.* 1.85; Lucretius, *R.N.* 1.44–49, 2.651; Plutarch, *Moralia* 1101B, 1102E, 1103D, 1125F).

In maintaining the transcendence of the Deity, Epicurus and his followers became the enemies of the prevailing doctrine of a provident Deity. Their opposition was based on four arguments: (1) cosmology: the world was made of chance occurrences of passing atoms, and not by a rational or divine power (Diog. Laert. 10.93–114); (2) freedom: traditional doctrine of providence destroys freedom and moral self-determination: "we would have no freedom whatsoever" (Cicero, *Fat.* 9.23; Diog. Laert. 10.133); (3) unfulfilled prophecy: since the cosmos comes about by chance, there can be no divination or foretelling (Plutarch, *Defectu* 434D; *Pythiae* 396E–F, 397C, 398B; *Non Posse* 1100D–E); and (4) injustice: justice is delayed; the just do not prosper, nor are the wicked punished: "this proscrastination and delay of the Deity . . . destroys belief in providence" (Plutarch *De Sera* 549B; 548C–D; Philo, *Prov* II.1; Lucian, *JConf.* 16; *JTr.* 46–49; Cicero, *Nat. Deor.* 3.79–85).

This doctrine about the Deity has ramifications in terms of human lives. According to Epicurus' Second Sovran Maxim: "Death is nothing to us; for the body, when it has been resolved into its elements, has no feeling; and that which has no feeling is nothing to us" (Diog. Laert. 10.139). This means that neither do the just and the wicked survive death nor are they rewarded or punished by the Deity in an afterlife. Indeed from reactions to Epicurean doctrines, more traditional thinkers articulated an intrinsic connection between their own espousal of a provident Deity and theodicy, i.e., the just judgment of the Deity after death. Thus Plutarch records this position:

> It is one and the same argument that establishes both the providence of God and the survival of the human soul, and it is impossible to upset the one contention and let the other stand . . . but if the soul survives, we must expect that its due in honour and in punishment is awarded after death rather than before [*De Sera* 560F].

Thus we can see the outlines both of a conventional attack on the providence of the Deity and of its defense. A topos emerged in antiquity which linked the providence of the Deity with afterlife and postmortem retribution. Epicureans were popularly known as those who rejected this doctrine and so as immoral people whose "theology" encouraged wickedness and vice. This popular caricature is noted by Lactantius:

> If any chieftain of pirates or leader of robbers were exhorting his men to acts of violence, what other language could he employ than to say the

> same things which Epicurus says: that the gods take no notice; that they are not affected with anger or kind feeling; that the punishment of a future state is not to be dreaded, because the souls die after death, and there is no future state of punishment at all [*Inst.* 3:17].

It is important to note that it is "one and the same argument" which establishes the Deity's providential action, the immortality of the soul, and postmortem retribution. The entire topos need not in every debate be stated in full; espousal of one part of it implies the whole argument. This may be important when examining the remarks of the opponents of 2 Peter, for the author may hear but one or two remarks and interpret them in terms of the topos on theodicy just described.

(b) Popular Polemics Against Theodicy. From both Jewish and Greek sources we learn that the argument of Epicurus and his followers became a popular doctrine. In its spread, it was no longer formally identified as "Epicurean" doctrine, but became a generalized popular statement of deviant theology. Sometimes a group such as the Sadducees was described to a Greco-Roman audience in terms that liken them to the Epicureans. Josephus' description of them as one of the four Jewish "philosophies" credits them with the same antitheodicy doctrine proposed by Epicurus and his followers:

> The Sadducees do away with Fate altogether, and remove God beyond, not merely the commission, but the very sight of evil . . . As for the persistence of the soul after death, penalties in the underworld and rewards, they will have none of them [*B.J.* 2.164–65; see *Ant.* 13.173; 18.16–17].

In other documents we read of the same polemic against theodicy, but without the Epicurean label. For example, in some of the targums to Gen 4:8, Cain propounds a theology which is formally identical with that of Epicurus (G. Vermes, "The Targumic Versions of Gen 4:3–16," *Post-Biblical Jewish Studies* [Leiden: Brill, 1975], 96–100):

> Cain answered and said to Abel:
> "I know that the world was not created by love,
> that it is not governed according to
>   the fruit of good deeds,
> and that there is favor in Judgement.
> Therefore your offering was accepted with delight,
> but my offering was not accepted from me with delight."

Cain answered and said to Abel:

"There is no Judgment,
there is no Judge,
there is no other world,
there is no gift of good reward for the just
and no punishment for the wicked."

First Cain denies that the Deity is provident, that is, that the Deity rewards and punishes; then he denies the three things that we have come to see form a commonplace: divine judgment, afterlife, and postmortem retribution.

Henry Fischel (*Rabbinic Literature and Greco-Roman Philosophy* [Leiden: E. J. Brill, 1973], 35–50) collected various forms of an "Epicurean Sententia on Providence and Divine Justice." In noting the variations of one sententia and its similarity to recognizable Epicurean remarks, Fischel is confident that the Jewish remark, "There will be no trial and there will be no [trial] judge," represents an Epicurean idea in Jewish language. Thus we learn of a commonplace on theodicy in the ancient world. Whether divine judgment is being denied or affirmed, a topos of three elements is commonly understood: divine judgment (providence), survival of death, and postmortem retribution.

Recognition of this material affords us with a well-known commonplace with which to compare both the polemical and apologetic remarks in 2 Peter. Since our author seems to quote his opponents explicitly in several places, we should give higher priority to those remarks than to mere allusions. Hence we note first of all the remark in 3:9 that "the Lord does not delay about the promise, as some reckon 'delay.'" The scoffing remark that the Lord is "slow" resembles the premier argument of the Epicureans in Plutarch's *De Sera Numinis Vindicta*, a formal debate over theodicy between Epicureans and other thinkers. The Epicurean in the debate "pelted providence" by calling attention to the delay of divine judgment. All the other speakers quickly affirm that "delay" of judgment constitutes the most telling argument against traditional theodicy: "The delay and procrastination of the Deity in punishing the wicked appears to me the most telling argument by far" (548C); "His slowness destroys belief in providence" (549B). In 2 Peter, the author reinterprets "delay" not as divine indolence, but as a gift of time for repentance: "but [the Lord] is forbearing toward you. For he does not wish any to be destroyed, but all to reach repentance." Thus he affirms in principle that God does act in justice, both to reward and to punish.

The author attributes a comparable deviant remark to his opponents in 2:1–3a. First he accuses them of introducing ruinous doctrines, "denying the Master who bought them" (v 1). As the commentary will explain, denying the Lord is not speculative atheism or mere change of formal allegiance, but a practical denial that this Lord exercises sovereignty and so does not reward or punish. As such, it resembles the denial of divine judgment we have noted in the topoi against traditional theodicy. Then the author affirms that God does in fact act in judgment. In response to their denial of judgment, he remarks: "Upon them judgment has not long been idle, nor does their ruin sleep" (v 3b). God is not slow to judge and to requite those who deny God's sovereignty.

In a second place, 2 Peter quotes his opponents. He records them scoffing at the predictions of a final coming and judgment: "Where is the promise of his coming? For, from the day the Fathers fell asleep, all has remained just as from the beginning of creation" (3:4). As the commentary will explain, such remarks both doubt and scoff at what they question; in this case, they call into question any divine action in the world, arguing from the sameness of experience that God does not intervene and so does not reward or punish. Our author responds by affirming what they deny, namely, that just as God once punished the wicked by water, so God will judge the wicked in the future with a fiery judgment (3:5–7).

This latter apology repeats the argument made in 2:4–9 that God acted in judgment both by water and fire according to ancient biblical traditions. Indeed, the author makes the formal point that these examples prove traditional notions of theodicy: "The Lord knows how to rescue the godly from trial, but to keep the unrighteous under punishment until the day of judgment" (2:9). Thus, the remarks in 2:4–9, which affirm God's actions to reward and punish, function as the warrant to the assertion that "judgment has not long been idle, nor does their ruin sleep" (2:3b). All of this serves as the author's response to the "denial of the Lord" by the false teachers in his church. Thus two positions are clearly delineated in 2 Peter: (a) opponents rejecting traditional notions of theodicy, namely, any divine action in the world, especially judgment, and (b) the author affirming traditional notions of theodicy, not only reward for the just, but especially judgment for the wicked.

Two other remarks in the document need to be examined in this attempt to describe the thought world of 2 Peter. And both reflect Epicurean notions about God. First, the author insists that his tradition about the coming of Jesus to judge is not a myth of cleverly concocted words: "For we did not follow cleverly devised myths when we made known to you the powerful coming of our Lord Jesus Christ" (1:16). Epicureans were notorious for their attack on myths of the underworld and its postmortem punishments (e.g., Lucretius, *R.N.* 3.978–1023; Lactantius, *Inst.* 7.13). Since for them death was the end of personal existence, there can be no afterlife and no retribution. Plutarch records some Epicureans scoffing and sneering at the doctrine of providence, "calling it nothing but a myth" (*Defectu* 420B); in another place he records Epicureans labeling the doctrine of providence, the all-seeing eye of God and justice, as a myth (*Adv. Colotem* 1124E–1125A).

We noted above that Epicurean cosmology precludes prophecy and oracles because it denies that a rational being providentially created the world and so can predict future events (Plutarch, *Defectu* 434D; *Pythiae* 414E; 418E; *Non Posse* 1100D–E; *Adv. Colotem* 1116E). Thus the attack on the prophecy of the parousia in 1:16 is both a rejection of theodicy and future judgment and also a denial of prophecy as such. Rejections of prophecy, of course, are explicit in the scoffing questions about "the promise of his coming" in 3:4–5. In contrast, 2 Peter constantly affirms the value of God's "promises" and the validity of the group's sacred prophecies and oracles.

Finally, the author asserts that his opponents "promise freedom" (2:19). From the Epicurean cosmological perspective, if the world were created and governed in an orderly fashion, there could be no human freedom but only Fate or determinism (Cicero, *Fat.* 9.23; Diog. Laert. 10.133; Lucian, *JConf.* 11, 12, 15; *JTr.* 25). Hence, one meaning of "freedom" would be free will and escape from the tyranny of Fate. Furthermore, from the Epicurean "pleasure" principle (*ataraxia*), freedom would be interpreted as "freedom" from fear as well as from punishment. The epitome of Epicurus' freedom from fear is found in his *tetrapharmakon*: "God is not to be feared. Death is not frightful. The good is easy to obtain. Evil is easy to tolerate" (F. Sbordone, *Philodemi Adversus Sophistas* [Naples: Loffredo, 1947], 87; Diog. Laert. 10.133). This meaning accords with the denial of divine judgment which we have seen above to describe the theology of the opponents. If God does not judge and there is no retribution, then mortals achieve "freedom." Even the author's reaction tends to confirm this Epicurean interpretation, for he ironically points out that while the opponents "promise freedom," they become "slaves of destruction." Instead of escape from judgment, they earn it by their false doctrine.

When the template of Epicurean doctrine about theodicy is placed over 2 Peter, we are able to discern the contours of the commonplace arguments, both denying the judgment of God and affirming it. But as we noted above, the same antitheodicy argument can be found in Jewish and Greek sources without the specific attribution to Epicurus. Hence it remains a probable argument that the opponents of 2 Peter voice a doctrine usually associated with "atheists" such as Epicureans. Moreover, it cannot be determined whether his opponents actually said all the things attributed to them or whether he perceived them in terms of this commonplace. But the materials discussed above clearly indicate that we look to popular skepticism about God's judgment as the background of the polemic in 2 Peter and not gnosticism or some other thought world.

(c) Greek Epicurean and Jewish Apikoros. There is a Jewish term for "scoffer," *Apikoros*, which appears to be related to the Greek word "Epicurean." Some scholars see the Jewish term as transliterating the Greek, and so meaning "Epicurean" (J. Geiger, "To the History of the Term *Apikoros*," *Tarbiz* 42 [1972–73]: 499–500; Samuel Krauss, *Griechische und lateinische Lehnwörter im Tal-*

mud, Midrasch und Targum [Hildesheim: Georg Olms, 1964], I. 207; II. 107). Others claim that *Apikoros* was "in no way associated with teachings supposed by the Jews to emanate from the philosopher Epicurus. To Jewish ears it conveys the sense of the root *pakar*, 'to be free from restraint,' and so licentious and sceptical" (H. Danby, *The Mishnah* [Oxford: Oxford University Press, 1933], 397).

In postbiblical Judaism, the term *Apikoros* is used of persons who hold opinions which indeed sound like variations of Epicurean themes. For example, an *Apikoros* is said to deny the resurrection (*m. Sanh.* 10.1; *t. Sanh.* 13.4–5; *b. Ros. Has* 17a) or to dispute over rewards and punishments (*m. Abot* 2.14). This *Apikoros* is charged with a polemic against Moses' lawmaking (*Sifre Deut* 12; *Sifre Num* 112 on Num 15:31) or with being an antinomian (*b. Ned.* 23a; *b. Sanh.* 99b). An *Apikoros* is generally considered a heretic (A. Marmorstein, "Les 'Epicuriens' dans la littérature talmudique," *REJ* 54 [1907]: 181).

The label *Apikoros* seems to presuppose some knowledge of Epicurean thought, even as brief as a doxographical summary, in regard to the specific positions associated with the Epicureans, namely, denial of resurrection and retribution. It functioned, moreover, as an indication that the position described was heretical or erroneous. While we cannot be certain that *Apikoros* derives directly from "Epicurean," the similarity of positions held by both indicates a rather widespread and so common antitheodicy stance in antiquity.

6. Social Location of the Author

As with the introduction to Jude, we ask a new and valuable question here from the sociology of knowledge and sociorhetorical criticism. Once more we adapt for 2 Peter the model developed by Vernon Robbins ("The Social Location of the Implied Author of Luke-Acts," *The Social World of Luke-Acts* [J. H. Neyrey, ed.; Peabody, MA: Hendrickson, 1991], 305–30). It is a commonplace of contemporary NT criticism that 2 Peter is pseudonymous (Meade, *Pseudonymity and Canon*, 179–80); hence we are concerned with the social location of the implied author. The model used here contains nine arenas of the possible social system in which 2 Peter is found; and our aim is to learn more about the precise social location of this author and the wider social context in which he worked.

(a) **Previous Events.** It is a commonplace that the past was considered normative for people in antiquity. They valued highly the *mos maiorum* or the traditions of the elders; they based their lives on sacred books which, because they contained the words of God, remain normative. Thus in the two basic institutions of antiquity, politics and kinship, what was said, done, or written in the past remained normative and influential on the present.

The author of 2 Peter begins with a celebration of the benefaction of the group's heavenly Patron (1:3–4). The solemn notation that everything needed for a life of piety has already been bestowed (v 3), including "precious promises" and a share in the divine nature (v 4), serves to remind the addressees of the persistent debt which they as clients owe their Patron. The past remains normative in the present, and so they owe acknowledgment of their Lord as well as to live a life worthy of their calling. It would be truly shameful to disregard the past benefactions and obligations owed to their Patron.

Past events play an important part of the argument of the document. First of all, the author makes constant appeal to past words as still normative in the present. Previous predictions of holy prophets and past commandments of the Lord and Savior need to be remembered (3:2). Although he does not quote any specific scriptural verse, the author employs past examples in his argument as having lasting value even in the present (i.e., *hypodeigma*, 2:6). God's past action in rescuing the godly and punishing the wicked (2:4–9) functions as warrant for God's current just judgment. Thus the author's riposte to present challenges to God's honor is based on past examples of divine behavior. Balaam (2:15–16) is likewise a past figure of wickedness whom God judged justly, and serves as another proof of past divine judgment.

The author's argument depends not only on past events as presently probative, but also on past personal experiences. In the debate over the prediction of "the coming of our Lord Jesus Christ" (1:16), the most formidable riposte the author can use is his appeal to being an "eyewitness" at that past event. What he saw and heard ground the truth and accuracy of the parousia prophecy, a past prediction which remains normative even in the present age of the persons of the document.

This appeal to past events, moreover, qualifies the author to speak normatively when he repeats past traditions. He states, moreover, that he has already written one letter to the addressees (3:1); and the current letter is mandated by another past event, a revelation from "our Lord Jesus Christ" of his own imminent death. The author's personal appeal to past events, then, serves a social function to give weight to his word and authority to his utterance.

In a document which argues about the future (i.e., the coming of the Lord, the fiery end of the world, the judgment of all, and the arrival of a new heaven and earth), the importance of the past remains cogent. Even the writings of a past figure like Paul (3:15–16) remain significant for the group, but only when they are properly interpreted according to the group's tradition. Hence, when the past actions of God, past prophetic words, and past traditions are mentioned, they are perceived as continuing in value and importance for the present. Thus, few past events are mentioned, and those that are all function in the argument of the document.

(b) Natural Environment. The author mentions no city or country; the only places about which he speaks belong to mythical or legendary realms. Certain places have a positive association for him: the "holy mountain" where Jesus was glorified (1:18), the kingdom of Jesus (1:11), and the new heavens and new earth (3:13). Other places carry a negative connotation: Sodom and Gomorrah (2:6–7) and the nether realm of gloom where the wicked are imprisoned (2:5). His opponents are censured because they are "placeless," like mists driven by a storm (2:17); by this he suggests that their mobility is deviant in his eyes. Although he mentions "ways" often, these are not the paved paths of the great Roman road network, but metaphorical ways of acting, either ways of righteousness (2:2, 15, 22) or ways of evil (2:15). Yet for other reasons, we would locate the author (a) in a city, not a village and (b) in Asia Minor, not Rome, Egypt, or Palestine.

(c) Population Structure. Various people in the document are addressed as "beloved" (*agapētos*). Jesus is "my son, my beloved" (1:17) and Paul is "beloved brother" (3:15); both of these are males. When the author collectively addresses the recipients of the letter as "beloved" or as "brethren," these terms would include women as well as men (1:10; 3:1, 8, 14). All of the other persons spoken of are clearly males.

The Lord Jesus is male by birth and by virtue of the gender-specific situations in which he is described. He is (a) the sovereign "Lord," whose state visit is predicted (1:16), (b) the beloved son, who is publicly honored by his Father (1:17), (c) the Master, who bought them from slavery (2:1), (d) the Lord, who commands (3:2), (e) the judge, who shows forbearance (3:9) or judgment, and (f) the thief prowling about at night (3:10).

Other figures of the group's present or past are likewise males. The author speaks simply about prophets (3:2) and apostles (1:16; 3:2), who appear to be the male figures noted in scripture and history. The examples he cites to prove God's power to judge are all males: Noah (2:5), Lot and the men of Sodom (2:6–7), and Balaam (2:15–16). Because of their mobility and their bold public speech, the opponents likewise appear to be males; they are accused of male vices, such as honor challenges, dissipation and carousing, boasting, and scoffing.

By presenting himself as "Simeon Peter, servant and apostle of Jesus Christ" (1:1), the author presents himself as a male. His behavior is likewise that of a typical male: challenge/riposte exchanges, public association with other males (1:16–18), paternal care of the group (3:1). He wishes to be honored as an elder, whose public word will carry authority. His literacy as well as scribal ability to write strong rhetoric would indicate that he is a male in a city, not a village.

(d) **Technology.** As noted earlier, this refers to knowledge for practical ends. Not surprisingly, all allusions to practical knowledge have to do with speech and writing. The physical letter presumably is made of papyrus. The author writes good Greek, in a mode which the ancients labeled "Asiatic style." His high degree of literacy means that he has been formally educated, presumably with access to a large body of scrolls such as the Hebrew scriptures. He has access to small documents such as Jude and certain Pauline letters. This suggests that he is located in a place where such documents were available and valued. As the commentary will note, the author does not claim to know the whole Pauline corpus that we now recognize; at best, it would seem that he knows Romans and 1 Thessalonians. Nevertheless, this suggests a certain scribal social location. His haggadic knowledge of Balaam indicates schooling in extrabiblical exegetical traditions, namely, access to both teachers and materials in which such traditions are written. We will have more to say about what the author knows; but in terms of writing technique, he appears to have been formally educated in Jewish and Christian traditions, with actual access to certain specific documents. His knowledge of the story of the Titans indicates familiarity with Greek materials, but nothing suggests that he has actual documents of Hellenistic literature.

(e) **Socialization and Personality.** The most distinctive thing about the author is his high degree of literacy. In a world in which perhaps 10 percent were literate, he demonstrates considerable reading and writing skills: (1) he displays a sophisticated vocabulary and writes in a recognizably elevated style; (2) he has notable rhetorical skills; (3) he knows a wide variety of lore and traditions, some of which are distinctive to Jews, others to Christians, and still more to Greeks; (4) he has access to a wide variety of Christian documents (i.e., letters of Jude, Paul, and Peter).

He presents himself as an eminent person easily recognized as enjoying special ascribed honor from the Lord Jesus: Simeon Peter, servant and apostle of Jesus Christ (1:1). He knows some of the Petrine traditions, especially the fact that Peter was the recipient of special revelations. He writes forcefully and with authority, presuming that his recognized status in the churches will prevail in the face of challenges to his authority.

Since slaves were occasionally quite literate, we cannot conclude to the social status of the implied author, whether a free person or a slave writing on behalf of a patron. Presumably he is a person of scribal training, but not an aristocrat; he lives in a city, not a village.

(f) **Culture.** This refers to the author's artistic, literary, historical, and aesthetic competencies. We noted above his high degree of literacy and rhetorical sophistication. He is clearly educated to express himself in a variety of literary forms: (1) a formal decree of honor (1:3–11); (2) letters; and (3) farewell address (1:12–15).

(1) *Multicultured Arguments*. Unlike Jude, the provenance of which document is distinctively Jewish, most of the material in 2 Peter would easily be recognized by educated Greek and Jew alike. There is a distinctively bicultural appeal made in the argument. The key to this lies in appreciating how the biblical story of the angels (2:4) is phrased to evoke in Greek ears echoes of the fall of the Titans who were cast into Tartarus (B. A. Pearson, "A Reminiscence of Classical Myth at II Peter 2.4," *GRBS* 10 [1969]: 71–80). Beginning with this we note other examples of materials which could be readily understood by Greek and Jew alike.

(a) *Opponents*. We noted above that the author perceives the heresy of his opponents according to a commonplace which rejects theodicy and providence. In Greek ears, this resembles the philosophy of Epicurus, who denied divine judgment, survival of death, and rewards and punishments in the underworld. Yet the same attack on theodicy is found in Jewish writings, and is ascribed to "scoffers" (*Apikoros*).

(b) *Examples*. The Jewish giants of Gen 6 are described to resemble the Titans of Greek lore, for they are "cast into Tartarus," not Gehenna. The Jewish Noah, who survived a flood which destroyed the world, has a counterpart, the Greek Deucalion. The fiery destruction of Sodom is paralleled in Greek lore by the demise of Phaeton. Jewish writings describe God's judgment both by water and by fire, which is known as well in Greek lore. The Jewish allusions to a new heaven and earth after the world's destruction resemble the Stoic "conflagration" and "regeneration" of the world.

Yet despite the bicultural character of this material in 2 Peter, we note that the author is truly steeped in Jewish biblical lore. Only three OT citations occur (2:22 = Prov 26:11; 3:8 = Ps 90:4; 3:13 = Isa 65:17); but commentators like Bauckham (*Jude, 2 Peter*, 138) note many allusions to biblical passages. The author indeed knows the Greek version of the Scriptures, and finds ready expression for his defense of theodicy and eschatological traditions in the very language in which these themes were expressed in the tradition of the group. As the commentary will show, he knows at least the Balaam story in its popular haggadic mode.

(2) *Traditions About Peter*. The author, moreover, has extensive knowledge of certain gospel traditions and especially those pertaining to Peter. This premier apostle was credited especially in Matthew's gospel with certain revelations from Jesus, a privilege on occasion shared with James and John but not with the remaining apostles. The following is a list of special revelations given Peter:

1:12–15	Peter's death revealed (John 21:18–19)
1:16–18	Transfiguration revelation (Matt 17:1–7)
1:20–21	Jesus' identity revealed (Matt 16:17)
2:1–3	Revelations about future false prophets (Matt 24:11, 24)
3:8	Revelation about unknowability of the time of the parousia (Matt 24:8, 36)
3:10–13	Revelations about the parousia (Matt 24:29–31)
3:10	Revelation about the thief in the night (Matt 24:43)
3:11–12	Revelation about cosmic regeneration (*paliggenesia*, Matt 19:28)

This plethora of revelations helps to define the author, not just as an elder who hands on old traditions, but as a prophet in his own right who has immediate revelations from the heavenly realm.

(3) *Knowledge of Paul.* The author claims to know several Pauline letters (3:15), and the following list indicates many of the identical terms shared between 2 Peter and certain letters.

Specific Terms from Paul's Letters

- acknowledgment (*epignōsis*, 1:2)—Rom 1:28
- faith, steadfastness, love (1:5–7)—1 Thess 1:3; 5:8
- kinship affection (*philadelphias*, 1:7)—Rom 12:10; 1 Thess 4:9
- entry into the kingdom (*eisodos*, 1:11)—although Paul speaks of an *eisodos* (1 Thess 1:9; 2:1), it is his own entry, not that of Christ; nevertheless, it is an unusual term
- the kingdom (*basileian*, 1:11) of the Lord—1 Cor 6:9
- fruitless (*akarpous*, 1:8)—1 Cor 14:14
- in this bodily tent (*skēnōmati*, 1:13, 14)—2 Cor 5:1–4
- the coming (*parousian*, 1:16) of the Lord Jesus—1 Thess 4:15
- the Master who bought them (*agorasanta*, 2:1)—1 Cor 6:20; 7:23
- stored up for fire (*tethēsaurismenoi*, 3:7)—Rom 2:5
- reckon "delay" as forbearance (*makrothymei*, 3:9)—Rom 2:4
- the day of the Lord will come like a thief (3:10)—1 Thess 5:2
- strive to be found by him (*heurethēnai*, 3:14)—1 Cor 4:2
- spotless and unblemished (*aspiloi kai amōmētoi*)—Phil 2:15
- fall away from your constancy (*stērigmou*, 3:17)—1 Thess 3:13
- according to the wisdom given him (3:16)—1 Cor 3:10; 15:10

There are, moreover, certain themes and topics shared by 2 Peter and certain Pauline letters. These are admittedly more subjective, but some attempt needs to be made to gain more precision about what letters 2 Peter might know.

Themes from Paul's Letters

- inheriting the divine nature (1:4)—Paul states in 1 Cor 15:50–56 that mortals must put on immortality, an equivalent expression
- sorites, chain of virtues (1:5–7)—Rom 5:1–5
- false prophets who deny judgment (2:3b)—in 1 Thess 5:3 Paul describes some people saying, "There is peace and security," even as judgment approaches
- freedom (2:19)—some in the Corinthian church understood their allegiance to Christ to mean freedom from law (1 Cor 6:12; 2 Cor 3:17) as well as freedom from judgment

To what letters of Paul might the author be referring? One must discount many of the parallels noted above as belonging to a shared tradition about the gospel; even Paul himself frequently depends on earlier traditions. Given the focus on the parousia and theodicy in 2 Peter, one would expect that the echoes of Paul be concentrated on these themes, which seems to be the case. 2 Peter 3:15 insists that the reinterpretation of the "delay" of judgment as a gift of forbearance is shared by Paul, which theme is found only in Rom 2:4–6. The reference to the "thief in the night" in 3:10 is found only in 1 Thess 5:4. Mention of "the wisdom given to him" (3:15) most closely resembles Paul's credentials as found in 1 Cor 3:10 and 15:10 (see also Rom 12:3 and 15:15). Thus we tentatively conclude that our author knows at least Romans and 1 Thessalonians, and possibly 1 Corinthians.

(4) *1 Peter and 2 Peter.* It is a commonplace that when the author states in 3:1–2 that he is now writing "this second letter," he alludes to 1 Peter. Commentators regularly list both similarities and dissimilarities between the two Petrine documents (e.g., Mayor, *The Epistles of Jude and Second Peter*, lxviii–cv); some argue for some literary dependency (G. H. Boobyer, "The Indebtedness of 2 Peter to 1 Peter," 36–50). The following list contains a number of the evident similarities between the two documents.

Some Shared Expressions in 1 and 2 Peter

- the epistolary greeting: 2 Peter 1:2 and 1 Peter 1:2
- prophetic inspiration confirmed: 2 Peter 1:16–21 and 1 Peter 1:10–12
- Noah and seven others saved: 2 Peter 2:5 and 1 Peter 3:20b

- mention of a previous Petrine document: 2 Peter 3:1
- forbearance and repentance: 2 Peter 3:9, 15 and 1 Peter 3:20a
- spotless and unblemished: 2 Peter 3:14 and 1 Peter 1:19
- affirmation of divine judgment: 2 Peter 2:4–9 and 1 Peter 1:17 and 4:5

It is not our intention to argue for common authorship of the two documents, but only to call attention to the fact that the author of 2 Peter claims to have written a previous letter. This presupposes that there is some basis for the pseudonymous attribution to "Peter." The allusions to revelations made to this Petrine figure argue strongly for this. More important, the author knows another Christian document, whether he penned it himself or merely alludes to it (see Bauckham, *Jude, 2 Peter*, 143–47).

(5) *Letter of Jude.* The author surely has a copy of Jude's letter before him, for he incorporates most of it into the middle of his own document. As the commentary will show, 2 Peter finds the materials about divine judgment in Jude congenial to his situation. Yet in discussing his use of Jude, we must attend to what appears to be the studied excision of esoteric materials from that document. 2 Peter seems purposefully to have omitted all references to *Enoch* and *T. Mos*. Given the criticism of his opponents against gospel and Pauline traditions about divine judgment, these two Jewish materials might have been considered to be too much like "cleverly devised myths" (1:16). Perhaps their omission from 2 Peter witnesses to a beginning sense of canon. We can only guess why they were omitted. In the case of Jude, then, we attend not only to what 2 Peter knew, but what he chose *not* to use.

In short, we should consider the author to be a collector of materials (Jude, Pauline letters, 1 Peter, gospel materials) and a preserver of common traditions. He is unusual among NT authors in that he expressly mentions other materials (yet see Luke 1:1–4). He makes no claim to be original, which would not be a particular virtue in a group-oriented culture; and he prides himself on being a trustworthy source and custodian of the treasured traditions of the group. He knows and guards the group's ideological patrimony. He probably should be thought of as a scribe in an urban environment situated where he would have ready access to diverse documents. He himself does not seem to have gathered them, but to have made extensive use of them.

(g) Foreign Affairs. We find no mention of the world of the Roman empire or the Jerusalem temple. In fact, the addressees are not named nor are they specifically located. From several elements in the document we conclude that the author writes in a city: (1) he has physical access to certain documents as well as knowledge of rhetoric and other school traditions, unlikely in a village of peasants; (2) he knows the importance of the patron-client relationship, casting God in the role of Benefactor-Patron; (3) he knows of the advent or parousia of dignitaries, more likely an urban than a rural phenomenon; (4) he appreciates investiture of "majesty . . . honor and glory" (1:16–17).

The world of 2 Peter appears to be exclusively the circle of disciples, whom he addresses. Even his opponents are known only in terms of their entrance into this group and their effect upon it (2:1–3; 3:3–4). The opponents presumably are of a social status comparable to the author. The world of the author enjoys a typical hierarchical arrangement. God, Benefactor and Patron, is honored above all; and Jesus Christ is acclaimed by status labels such as Lord, Savior, and Master. The author positions himself as an apostle and as "Peter," a figure with acknowledged authority in the group. He associates himself with other apostles and prophets. He links Paul to his cause, but considers himself superior to him by virtue of his "eyewitness" evidence of Jesus. The group addressed is correspondingly lower in status than the author. The author is at great pains to defend this precise arrangement of statuses and roles.

(h) Belief Systems and Ideology. Claiming as he does to represent the common and consistent traditions of the early disciples, the author's worldview and symbolic universe should sound similar to that of the evangelists, Paul and Peter. As with Jude, we have drawn upon anthropological categories suggested by Mary Douglas as lenses for viewing and organizing the various elements of the symbolic universe of 2 Peter.

(1) *Purity and Pollution.* The author perceives the cosmos to be an orderly place, where there is a proper place for everyone and everything. What is "in place" is pure and clean; what is "out of place" is polluted and unclean. We observe immediately that the author expresses great concern for the very categories of "pure" and "polluted." "Purity" is expressed in a variety of ways. Certain persons (3:2), places (1:18), and things (2:21; 3:11) are labeled "holy" (*hagios*) because they are associated with or authorized by God. True disciples will be "spotless, unblemished" (3:14), that is, living moral lives in accord with God's commands and in anticipation of God's just judgment. The "holy" disciples practice virtue (1:5–7), whereas the deviants "forget the 'purification' [*katharismou*] for sins" (1:9).

"Pollution" likewise finds expression in a variety of terms. Converts escaped the "defilement" (*miasma*, 2:20) of the world, and the author warns that those who continue to indulge in "defilement" will face God's judgment (2:10). Those who lapse from purity in Christ are likened to dogs returning to vomit and pigs to mire (2:22). Whereas true disciples flee "corruption" (*phthora*, 1:4), deviants in the group become "slaves of corruption" (2:19). They are both morally corrupted and will be physically corrupted (2:12). The opponents are labeled "spots and blemishes" (2:13), who pollute the holy gatherings of the saints. They are characterized as people of "passion" (*epithymia*, 2:18; 3:3), "debauchery" (*aselgeia*, 2:2, 18), and "adultery" (2:14). Thus the author classifies persons, places, times, and things as "pure" or "polluted."

The basis for his classification is the common tradition of God's own holiness as expressed especially in the ethical traditions of Judaism and early Christianity. This implies a shared sense of how the world should be ordered and how things should be labeled. We noted above the strong hierarchical arrangement of persons in the symbolic world of 2 Peter. This extends to places (holy mountains, holy meetings of the group), things, and times. But we note the powerful urge to label and classify, especially in terms of the native categories of "pure" and "polluted."

(2) *Characteristic Rituals*. Typical of NT writers, the author attends to the boundaries of the group. Operating from a very clear classification system, he distinguishes insiders from outsiders. Boundary making and maintenance thus seems to be the primary ritual here. It is expressed most clearly in the dualistic language pervading the document. Not only does it classify persons, places, things, and times, it indicates both who belongs and how they got there, as well as how others do not belong and how they will be removed. We attend here to the extensive and powerful dualistic language in the document, whereby the author distinguishes insiders and their characteristics and behavior from outsiders.

We noted above that the author distinguished and contrasted authentic members of the group from his opponents in terms of the labels (a) "pure" (*katharismos*, 1:9) and "polluted" (*miasma*, 2:20) and (b) spotless and unblemished (3:14) and spotted and blemished (2:13). The righteous acquire virtue (1:5–8), while the wicked practice vice (*epithymia*, 2:10, 18; 3:3; *aselgeia*, 2:2, 18). The true disciples are "full" and have everything needed (1:2, 3), whereas the opponents are empty, either "fruitless" trees (1:9) or waterless springs (2:17). Insiders are characterized as pious (*eusebeis*, *eusebeia*, 1:3, 6, 7; 3:11), but the outsiders as impious (*asebeis*, 2:5, 6; 3:7). The former walk in the straight way (2:15), the way of truth or righteousness (2:2, 21), the latter in the way of Balaam's greed (2:15). This means that the righteous flee the corruption of the world (2:20), while others return to their former corruption, as dogs to vomit and pigs to mire (2:22).

The author distinguished the two groups most clearly in terms of their knowledge and orthodoxy. Insiders respect authority, either God's or the teacher's, whereas outsiders defy authority (2:1, 10). The former have knowledge of God's promises and prophecies (1:5–6; 3:1–2), which are taught them by true prophets (1:16–21); they remember carefully the traditions (1:12–15; 3:1). The latter lack knowledge (2:12), reject prophecies (3:3–4), and act as false prophets

(2:1–3); they willfully forget the tradition (1:9; 3:5, 8). The true disciples acknowledge God's power to judge justly and to reward or punish (2:4–9), whereas the opponents deny all divine judgment (2:3b; 3:9). Hence, the insiders stand firm (*bebaios*, 1:10, 19) in the truth and enjoy stability (*stērigmos*, 3:17); their banner is truth (1:12; 2:2). The outsiders are unstable (*astēriktos*, 2:14; 3:16) and so fall (*ekpesēte*, 3:16); their hallmark is error (2:15, 17; 3:17).

All of this leads to contrasting postures toward the world. The holy ones flee from this world of corruption (2:20), which they expect to be destroyed in a fiery cataclysm (3:10). This world will be replaced by a pure world where righteousness dwells, a new heaven and a new earth (3:13). They await this and even hasten its coming (3:11). In contrast, the opponents are mired in corruption in a world which is corrupted by their presence and which will pass away (i.e., be corrupted). Yet they deny that this world will come to an end (3:3–4), for they proclaim "all has remained just as from the beginning." In short, they have no cosmological expectations. Different fates await these two groups. The insiders are promised a share in God's own immortality (1:4), which in another place is called "entrance into the eternal kingdom" (1:10). Fleeing corruption, they attain divine incorruptibility. The outsiders, however, face only destruction (*apōleia*, 2:1, 3; 3:7, 16).

The articulation of the letter's argument in such stark dualistic terms functions to draw boundaries. Boundaries were established earlier when disciples fled the company of those who live in error (2:18). At this time they received purification for their sins (1:9) and acknowledged Jesus both as Lord-Judge and as Savior (2:20). A clear boundary, then, separated insiders from their former associates, who are now outsiders. The letter is replete with spatial language denoting boundaries: one "flees from" a corrupt circle of friends or a corrupt world (*apopheugein*, 1:4; 2:18, 20) and "enters" (*eisodos*, 1:11) an eternal kingdom. Yet the boundary is not firm, for false teachers have entered the group and threaten to corrupt it by "introducing ruinous doctrines" (2:1–3). In this situation, the author sounds the alarm to warn of a life-threatening pollution in the group's midst. He identifies the hidden deceivers who are corrupting the group and thereby hopes to seal the breach in the boundary as well as to force the corrupting teachers to withdraw. And his primary strategy is to redraw the boundaries with sharp dualistic language which will appropriately classify every person, thing, and place as either pure or polluted.

(3) *Body*. The strong classification system (pure/polluted) and the intense concern to build and maintain boundaries indicate a strong sense of social control over the public assembly addressed by 2 Peter. This strong social control is replicated in the way the physical body is perceived, for it too is an object of vigorous control. The author exhorts the group in 1:6 to "self-control" (*egkrateia*), which in the commentary we will examine in terms of its centrality in

ancient moral exhortation. We focus here exclusively on the meaning of "self-control" as a code word for strong bodily control.

Philo offers a valuable illustration of "self-control" as the control or guarding of the bodily orifices, and therefore as evidence of popular appreciation of strong bodily control. He exhorts his audience to "bind up each of the [bodily] openings with adamantine chains of self-control [*egkrateias*]. For Moses says (Num 19.15) that 'every open vessel which hath no covering bound upon it is unclean' " (*Det.* 103). He then enumerates each bodily orifice and indicates what control is appropriate to it. Since this is an excellent example of this topic, we quote it at length:

> The *eye* is capable of seeing all colors and all forms, but let it see those that are meet for light and not for darkness . . . The *ear* is capable of apprehending all uttered words, but some let it refuse to hear, for countless things that are said are disgraceful . . . and because nature has given you *taste*, do not be like a cormorant and greedily devour all things . . . And because, with a view to the persistence of your race, you were endowed with *generative organs*, do not run after rapes and adulteries and other unhallowed forms of intercourse . . . and because a *tongue* and a *mouth* and *organs of speech* have been allotted to you, do not blurt out all things [*Det.* 101–2].

"Self-control," then, means strong bodily control, in particular, control of the orifices of the body.

This native understanding helps us appreciate the perception of the physical body in 2 Peter, for the author too believes that its orifices should likewise be subject to control. We compare and contrast how true disciples conduct their lives with how the opponents and those who follow their doctrine behave.

(1) *Eyes*: the author is an eyewitness (1:16) of holy visions. In contrast, he describes the eyes of his opponents as "ceaselessly filled with adulteries and evils" (2:14). If greed is an evil of the eye, they are uncontrolled here as well (2:3, 14). Those who do not see as the author sees are "blind and shortsighted" (1:9). Eyes, then, should see good things and see truly.

(2) *Mouth*: the mouth is for eating, and the opponents defile the group's meals with their "dissipation" and "deceptions" when they feast with the group (2:13). Those who follow their teachings are like dogs returning to their vomit (2:22). The mouth, moreover, is for speech, which too can be prescribed and proscribed. The author speaks inspired words prompted by God's spirit (1:20–21); he speaks in accord with the

words of prophets and apostles (3:1–2). His opponents, however, scoff at prophetic or traditional words (3:3–4). If the author's speech honors authority, his opponents defame it constantly (2:2, 10, 11, 12). They make empty boasts (2:18) and false promises (2:19). They teach false doctrines (2:1).

(3) *Genitals*: when disciples practice "self-control," they will be sexually moral (1:5), and the sexual organs will be strongly controlled. In contrast, the opponents are accused of totally unregulated intercourse: they are accused of adulteries (2:14), debauchery (2:2, 18), and "desire" (2:10, 18; 3:3).

Independently of the bodily orifices, the author contrasts bodily postures which are symbolic representatives of one's public confession. True disciples will "stand" at the coming of the Lord (1:12), for they are firm and stable in the truth. In contrast, the opponents are "unstable' (*astērikos*, 2:14; 3:16) and so will fall. The faithful will walk on the straight way (2:15), which is the way of truth (2:2) and righteousness (2:21), whereas the opponents walk in the way of Balaam (2:15). "Walking," of course, refers to a general pattern of behavior or actions controlled according to the group's customs and norms. Thus when 2 Peter urges "self-control" (1:6), he urges strong bodily control (of orifices as well as actions), which replicates his concern for strong social control of the group.

(4) *Sin*. All of the materials noted about pure/polluted and clean/unclean have a bearing on how the author understands sin. It is certainly the violation of laws and commandments accepted by the group, which brings God's just judgment (2:4–9). But since sin is also the destructive teaching of false teachers (2:1), the author understands it as well as a type of leaven or gangrene which is corrupting the pure church. A certain tolerance can be extended to rule-breakers, for God delays judgment to give time for repentance (3:9). But when sin is perceived as a form of corrupting pollution (2:18, 22), then intolerance is the appropriate social strategy. The issue is one of life and death, and haste and thoroughness are important. With such false doctrine there can be no tolerance or delay of judgment.

(5) *Suffering and Misfortune*. In some NT documents, authors perceive a cosmic war in progress, with the result that mortals are seen as the victims of attacks by Satan, demons, heavenly evil powers, and the like. Accusations of sorcery in the NT imply this, namely, that one is acting as an agent of Beelzebub (Mark 3:22–27) or Satan (John 13:2, 27). Paul was not speaking in metaphors when he spoke of "Death reigning" (Rom 5:14, 17) or "Sin reigning" (Rom 5:21), indicating that God's rule is challenged by the aggression of a rival or competitor. In this scenario suffering and misfortune are perceived either as

justly caused by God or unjustly inflicted by God's enemy. The wicked prosper because they are aided by their evil patron, Satan; but the just are unjustly attacked, shamed, harmed, and even killed (Matt 5:11–12; 23:34–37).

But in 2 Peter there is a clear and strong emphasis on the absolute sovereignty of God. Since the document is occasioned by scoffers denying the coming of Jesus and mocking the judgment of God, the author emphatically and repeatedly affirms the just judgment of God. God knows how to reward the just and requite the wicked (2:9), just as God always has in the past (2:4–8). The judgment of God is based on clear rules and norms which are known by all. The judgment of God is just, and so suffering and misfortune are depicted as the fitting retribution for shaming and disobeying God's just law. The strong focus on the issue of theodicy, the sovereignty of God to judge justly, admits no rival source of suffering or misfortune.

BIBLIOGRAPHY

Bauckham, Richard J., "The Delay of the Parousia." *TynB* 31 (1981): 3–36.

———, "2 Peter: A Supplementary Bibliography," *JETS* 25 (1982): 91–93.

———, "2 Peter: An Account of Research," *ANRW* 2.25.5 (1988): 3713–52.

———, "Pseudo-Apostolic Letters," *JBL* 107 (1988): 469–94.

Bigg, Charles, A *Critical and Exegetical Commentary on the Epistles of St. Peter and St. Jude* (Edinburgh: T. & T. Clark, 1901).

Boobyer, G. H., "The Indebtedness of 2 Peter to 1 Peter," in *New Testament Essays: Studies in Memory of T. W. Manson* (A. J. B. Higgins, ed.; Manchester, 1959), 34–53.

Cavallin, H. C. C. "The False Teachers of 2 Pt as Pseudo-prophets," *NovT* 21 (1979): 263–70.

Danker, F. W., "II Peter 3:10 and Psalm of Solomon 17:10," ZNW 53 (1962): 82–86.

Dunnett, W. M., "The Hermeneutics of Jude and 2 Peter: The Use of Ancient Jewish Traditions," *JETS* 31 (1988): 287–92.

Farkasfalvy, D., "The Ecclesial Setting of Pseudepigraphy in Second Peter and Its Role in the Formation of the Canon," *Second Century* 5 (1985): 3–29.

Fornberg, Tord, *An Early Church in a Pluralistic Society: A Study of 2 Peter* (ConBNT 9. Lund: C. W. K. Gleerup, 1977).

Käsemann, Ernst, "An Apologia for Primitive Christian Eschatology," in *Essays on New Testament Themes* (Philadelphia: Fortress Press, 1982), 169–95.

Meade, David G., *Pseudonymity and Canon* (Grand Rapids, MI: W. B. Eerdmans, 1986), 179–93.

Moulton, J. H., W. F. Howard, and Nigel Turner, A *Grammar of New Testament Greek* (Edinburgh: T. & T. Clark, 1907).

Neyrey, Jerome H., *The Form and Background of the Polemic in 2 Peter* (Unpublished dissertation, Yale University, 1977).

———, "The Form and Background of the Polemic in 2 Peter," *JBL* 99 (1980): 407–31.

Picirilli, Robert E., "Allusions to 2 Peter in the Apostolic Fathers," *JSNT* 33 (1988): 57–83.

Snyder, John, "A 2 Peter Bibliography," *JETS* 22 (1979): 265–67.

Soards, Marion L., "1 Peter, 2 Peter and Jude as Evidence for a Petrine School," *ANRW* II.25.5 (1988): 3828–49.

Talbert, C. H., "II Peter and the Delay of the Parousia," *VC* 20 (1966): 137–45.

Watson, Duane F., *Invention, Arrangement, and Style. Rhetorical Criticism of Jude and 2 Peter* (SBLDS 104. Atlanta: Scholars Press, 1988).

Wifstrand, A., "Stylistic Problems in the Epistles of James and Peter," *ST* 1 (1948): 170–82.

I.
Letter Opening: Address and Prayer (1:1–2)

◆

1 1. Simeon Peter, servant and apostle of Jesus Christ, to those who
have received a faith as honorable as ours through the justice of
our God and Jesus Christ the Savior. 2. May favor and peace be
abundant in you by your acknowledgment of God and Jesus our
Lord.

Epistolary Form

The document typically begins with a standard epistolary opening. The *sender* identifies himself by name ("Simeon Peter") and role and status ("servant and apostle of Jesus Christ"). The document is *addressed*, not to any specific church or person, but in general to all who share the same belief in the one true God and in Jesus. The typical *greeting* ("grace and peace") is conditioned by the recognition of and loyalty to the heavenly patrons, God and Jesus the Lord.

Letter openings, although highly conventional, often communicate important and specific clues about the particular occasion of the document. The sender identifies himself by a name which suggests a rich association in the past with the historical Jesus and a specific role and status among the followers of that Jesus. When the gospels first introduce the brother of Andrew, he is always "Simon Peter" (Matt 4:18; Mark 3:16; Luke 5:8; John 1:40), who is then recruited by Jesus and so takes the special name of "Peter." In various traditions he is called "fisher of men" (Mark 1:17; Luke 5:10), or "rock" (Matt 16:18), sobriquets which indicate his special role not just as a follower of Jesus, but as his agent/apostle. Links with Jesus become the source of his authority among the followers of Jesus, the church.

His role and status, however implicit in the name "Simeon Peter," are made explicit by the credentials claimed as "servant and apostle." Currently there is a trend to stress the serving role of leaders, and so "servant" might popularly be understood as it seems to be in Luke 22:26, "Let the greatest among you become as the youngest, and the leader as one who serves." But that obscures the tradition which labeled the special agents of God as "servants," be they kings, patriarchs, or prophets.

"Servants" of the Lord
Abraham, Isaac, and Jacob (Exod 32:13; Deut 9:27)
Jacob (Isa 44:1)
Moses (Deut 34:5; Josh 1:1–2; 1 Kgs 8:53, 56)
Samuel (1 Sam 3:9–10)
David (1 Sam 17:32; 2 Sam 3:18; 7:5, 8, 19–21, 25–29)
Ahijah (1 Kgs 15:29)

Likewise in Christian documents, the letter senders often identify themselves with this honorific label.

"Servants" of God
Paul (Rom 1:1; Gal 1:10; Phil 1:1; Titus 1:1)
James (1:1)
Jude (1)

All of these figures are "servants of God," trusted members of the circle that surrounds the sheik, pharaoh, the king, or God. As officials in the household of God they have an honorable and proper role and status in regard to other members of that household.

Modern readers tend to interpret "servant" and Christian leadership in terms of humble service, not hierarchy or power. But "servant" identifies special agents of God who were either kings, patriarchs, prophets, or kings: Moses, Samuel, David, and Ahijah. Courtiers at Saul's court call themselves "servants" (1 Sam 18:5, 30); King Ahaz addressed the king of Assyria as his "servant" (2 Kgs 16:7). Even Christian figures who are "servants of God" are trusted members of the circle that surrounds the group's sovereign. As officials in the household of God they have specific rights and duties (see J. N. Collins, *Diakonia. Reinterpreting the Ancient Sources* [Oxford: Oxford University Press, 1990], 92–95).

Simeon Peter is not only "servant" or majordomo over the household of the church, but "apostle." Over time, this label developed into a technical term for a formal agent, duly authorized by Christ. It is based on the commissioning by Jesus during his earthly career (Mark 3:14; Matt 16:18) and after his exaltation and enthronement (1 Cor 15:5; John 21:15–17; Luke 24:34, 36–50). To those familiar with Paul's letters, the two labels, "servant" and "apostle," would be easily recognized as claims to official church leadership roles and status (Rom 1:1; Titus 1:1).

The author, then, formally identifies himself as a person with an honorable status whose remarks should be taken seriously and whose role be duly acknowledged. Later in the document he will give a definitive interpretation of Jesus' word (1:15) and of Paul's letters (3:15–16). With his credentials clearly articulated, he can then proceed with the business of the communication.

The catholic addressees are given their due honor. The bond between Simeon Peter and them is a common faith in God and Jesus. This faith is described as *isotimē,* that is, precious or honorable. Moreover, Simeon Peter and his addressees share it equally in its fullness. He may have been an eyewitness of Jesus and also privileged to receive the revelation of the risen Lord, but he shares that faith with them, holding nothing back. They are further honored by Simeon Peter's acknowledgment that the churches are the beneficiaries of God's "justice."

In the notes we indicate that "justice," which is one of the four cardinal virtues, describes God's impartial and fair dealings with all peoples. In the same Greek literature that discusses this virtue, the authors there call attention to it in terms of benefaction and its place in patron-client relations. Part of "justice" is piety to the gods; and piety has to do with loving god and being loved by god (Menander Rhetor 361.22–363.3); being "beloved of god" means the grant of prosperity and protection, as well as being "honoured with the greatest or first or most numerous honours" (Menander Rhetor 362.4–7). Justice is likewise described as "mildness toward subjects, humanity toward petitioners, and accessibility" (Menander Rhetor 375.8–10). This is the language of benefaction by patrons to clients. In the letter opening God's justice-as-benefaction is stressed; for God granted "faith" and so membership in the covenant family (1:1), as well as numerous other blessings (1:3–4). Yet this premier aspect of God comprises just judgment as well, the reward of the righteous and the punishment of the wicked. This second sense of "justice" becomes the dominant issue which is debated in the letter. As we shall see, the sender mounts a formal defense of theodicy, God's impartial but strict judgment.

The greeting of "favor and peace" is regularly used in Christian letters, in all of the Pauline and Deutero-Pauline letters, as well as in 1 Pet 1:2; 2 John 3, and Rev 1:4. Simeon Peter has already noted that the addressees have been blessed with a precious faith, but now he continues his recognition of God's benefaction to them. He prays that God's favor and the fullness of blessings be theirs.

PATRON-CLIENT RELATIONSHIPS

The language is indeed formal, but quite appropriate when we consider the social relationships described here. God and Jesus are acclaimed as the heavenly patrons of the church. As generous patrons, they grant benefactions which honor and enrich their clients, the followers of Jesus. First and foremost among the benefactions is a precious faith, that is, recognition of them by God and gathering of them into God's covenant household. The initial benefaction will be augmented according to the prayer that "favor and fullness be multiplied" for these clients. The patrons, moreover, are identified simply but sufficiently as God and Jesus, who is both "savior" and "lord."

As with all patrons and clients, patronage implies a form of exchange or reciprocity. The church-as-client has been blessed "by the reliability" of God, and in return the client extends to the patron "acknowledgment" by way of confession, praise, and public acclamations of honor. Indeed, the relationship between the heavenly patrons and the church is an ongoing exchange. For according to the greeting, "favor and fullness" will indeed be multiplied "by the acknowledgment" of the group's heavenly patrons. Thus we see a symmetry in the way the faith was first given ("by the reliability of God") and the way that benefaction is maintained ("by the acknowledgment of God").

This exchange of a patron's favors and a client's honor of the patron may be illustrated by a passage from Josephus. He notes a public declaration of honor by the city of Athens for the Jewish king Hyrcanus. It proclaims that the city will "honor this man with a golden crown as a reward for merit . . . set up his statue in bronze in the precinct of the temple of Demos . . . announce the award of the crown in the theaters at the Dionysian festivals and at the Panathenaeum and Eleusinian festivals and at the gymnastic games." But the client city expects the patronage to be maintained, and so it publicly states that such honor will continue "so long as he continues to maintain good will toward us, everything we can devise shall be done to show honour and gratitude to this man" (*Ant.* 14.152). In terms of 2 Peter, the clients of the true God must honor God with public confession of his benefaction, and then the favor of the heavenly Patron will be multiplied in the clients.

NOTES

SIMEON/SIMON

The author reveals himself as "Simeon Peter." Simeon, the Greek transliteration of Simon, was an unusual form of the name in the first century. Simon Maccabeus, who was normally called Simon, was addressed as Simeon by his father (1 Macc 2:65); an ancestor of Jesus in Luke's genealogy is a certain Simeon (Luke 3:30); one of Jacob's sons was a Simeon, who left a testament (*T. Simeon*; A. E. Harvey, "The Testament of Simeon Peter," *A Tribute to Geza Vermes* [Sheffield: JSOT Press, 1990], 345–46). We know of a prophet Simeon in Jerusalem (Luke 2:25) and another prophet Simeon in Antioch (Acts 13:1).

Elsewhere in the New Testament Peter is always called Simon, except for Acts 15:14, where the more Semitic rendering is maintained. The use of the Hebrew form of the name is one more piece of evidence that the author was Jewish.

AS HONORABLE AS

The roots of this word are *iso* (equal) and *timē* (value, honor). It means "same kind" or "equal in value" according to parallel usages found in Strabo 15:3.20; Dio Chrys. 24(41) 2; Philo *Leg. All.* 2.18; *Sac.* 8; *Spec. Leg.* 1.181; Josephus, *Ant.* 12.119. Although some have claimed that it means that Peter's Jewish faith and their Gentile faith are on a par, that seems improbable in light of the absence of this idea in the rest of the letter; for the document really wants to affirm a common or catholic faith shared by all everywhere (Bauckham, *Jude, 2 Peter,* 176) and the generous benefaction bestowed impartially by God, the heavenly Patron. Philo occasionally uses *isotimos* to speak of the uniqueness of God: "no existing being is of equal honor to God" (*Conf.* 170; see *Sac.* 91; *Mut.* 57); in another place it connotes the highest rank or superlative quality of something (*Sac.* 131; *Sob.* 4). This uniqueness or superlative quality may also be intended as part of the *captatio benevolentiae* or the rhetorically crowd-pleasing technique of the writer: the addressees enjoy a unique and most valuable relationship with God.

JUSTICE

In popular Greek culture, *dikaiosynē* or "justice" is one of the four cardinal virtues, along with courage, wisdom, and temperance. Each of these virtues can be subdivided into its parts, on the order of genus and species; the parts then tell us the range of meaning of the primary virtue. In one place, the parts of justice are described as piety toward the gods, fair dealing toward men, and reverence toward the departed (Meander Rhetor 363.17–20). In another place, they consist of mildness toward subjects, humanity toward petitioners, and accessibility of justice (Menander Rhetor 375.8–10). In both places "justice" embraces benefaction, impartial treatment, just laws, and fairness to all. It is not accidental that God is first and foremost known in terms of "justice" in this letter, since the dominant issue throughout will be a defense of theodicy or God's just judgment. Yet God's judgment is both benevolent, as it is in the letter opening, and just, as it is defended in chapter 2.

OUR GOD AND [OUR] JESUS CHRIST THE SAVIOR

Many read this text as a reference to Jesus, God and Savior (Bauckham, *Jude, 2 Peter,* 168–69; Reumann, *Righteousness in the New Testament,* 171). The arguments supporting the confession here of Jesus as God are as follows: (1) Jesus is confessed in double terms elsewhere in the letter (1:11; 3:18); (2) the doxology to Jesus in 3:18 would seem to be an inclusio with 1:1, both attesting his exalted status; and (3) the phraseology here reflects Hellenistic usage (Fornberg, *An Early Church in a Pluralistic Society*, 142).

Yet there are arguments against this reading: (1) 1:2 distinguishes God and Jesus; and there appears to be an intended parallelism between 1:1 and 1:2:

en dikaiosynē tou theou hēmōn kai sōtēros Iēsou Christou (1:1)
en epignōsei tou theou kai Iēsou tou kyriou hēmōn (1:2).

(2) It is one thing to call Jesus "Lord," but a rare thing in the NT to call him "God" (John 1:1–3; 20:28). Admittedly in the late first and early second century he is increasingly acclaimed as divine with the title "God" (Ignatius *Eph.* 18:2; *Smyrn.* 1.1; see R. E. Brown, *Jesus God and Man* [Milwaukee, Bruce Publishing Co., 1967], 1–38). (3) With the possible exception of Phil 1:11, all references to *dikaiōsunē* in the New Testament refer to God's, not Christ's, righteousness. From the document itself, it would be unclear what is contextually meant by Jesus' "justice."

This document is concerned with God's justice, both as impartiality in benefaction (1:1) and as just judgment of saints and sinners. Granted that Jesus' parousia is the occasion for God's judgment, the letter defends God's justice (2:4, 9–10). When in 2:5, Noah is described as the "herald of justice," this surely refers to God's judgment, the rescue of the just and the punishment of the wicked. The focus of the rest of the document, then, is on God, and in particular on theodicy.

FAVOR (CHARIS)

Typically we read in the Old Testament that people regularly seek favor in the eyes of their lord, patriarch, king, or God (Gen 6:8; 32:5; 39:4; 47:25; Exod 33:13). Moreover, we are told that God's favor rested on certain people (Luke 2:40; Acts 4:33). In a world of limited goods which frequently depended on the benefaction of a patron, social standing and even survival depended on seeking and receiving such "favor." In secular Greek this term is generally used for a ruler's favors (H. Conzelmann, "Charis," *TDNT* 9.373–76). Here, although membership in the covenant community has already been granted by the heavenly Patron, favor and peace are further benefactions necessary to continued honorable living (see B. Malina, "Patron and Client," *Forum* 4.1 [1988]: 5–6).

In Jewish circles, the heavenly Patron, God, bestowed "grace/favor and truth," that is, a benefaction of kindness which is trustworthy (see John 1:14, 17). When the formula includes "peace," the concept is stretched to include *shalom*, or the fullness of blessings and prosperity. The combination of "grace and peace" is not exclusively Pauline (e.g., Z. *Bar.* 78:2), but belongs to the world of Semitic culture (Friedrich, "Lohmeyers These über das paulinische Briefpräskript," 346).

ACKNOWLEDGMENT

Recent discussion of this word indicates some distinction between *epignōsis* and *gnosis*. The former term suggests some particular point in regard to which knowledge is affirmed. In a recent study, Picirelli suggested a range of five meanings to it: (1) to know someone or something for who or what he or it really is; (2) to come to a realization or perception of something; (3) to learn or find out some fact; (4) realization or understanding that is already in existence; and (5) to give acknowledgment to someone or something ("The Meaning of 'Epignosis,' " 90).

In light of the contents of the letter and in view of the honor-shame dynamic of the letter opening, I favor the fifth meaning above, "acknowledgment of someone." "Favor and peace" will be increased in the clients of the heavenly Patron in relationship to their acknowledgment of the Patron's status and benefaction. In this regard, the meaning is similar to that found in Rom 1:28, where despite great benefaction, mortals "did not see fit to acknowledge God" (see Rom 1:20–21).

Yet what acknowledgment should be made? At this point in the letter the reader is not certain. Simeon Peter will shortly articulate clearly that the issue being contested and defended is the full honor of God as Sovereign, namely, God's power to judge and so to reward the good and punish the wicked.

BIBLIOGRAPHY

Brown, Raymond, et al., *Peter in the New Testament* (Minneapolis: Augsburg Publishing House/New York: Paulist Press, 1973), 154–56.

Doty, William, *Letters in Primitive Christianity* (Philadelphia: Fortress Press, 1973), 29–33.

Fitzmyer, Joseph, "The Name Simon," *Essays on the Semitic Background of the New Testament*. (SBLSBS 5. Missoula, MT: Scholars Press, 1974), 105–12.

Friedrich, Gerhard, "Lohmeyers These über das paulinische Briefpräskript kritisch beleuchtet," *TLZ* 81 (1956): 343–46.

Lohmeyer, Ernst, "Probleme paulinischer Theologie I. Briefliche Grussüberschriften," ZNW 26 (1927): 158–64.

Picirelli, Robert, "The Meaning of 'Epignosis,' " *EvQ* 47 (1975): 85–93.

Reumann, John, *Righteousness in the New Testament* (Philadelphia: Fortress Press, 1982), 170–77.

II.
Patron's Benefaction and Clients' Response (1:3–11)

♦

1 3. As his divine power has bestowed on us everything for a life of
piety through the acknowledgment of the One who has called us
to his own glory and excellence, 4. in virtue of these, the
precious and greatest promises have been given us so that through
them you may become sharers of the divine nature and be freed
from the corruption in the world because of desire. 5. For this
reason be earnest to supplement your faith with excellence,
excellence with knowledge, 6. knowledge with self-control, self-
control with steadfastness, steadfastness with piety, 7. piety with
kinship affection, kinship affection with love. 8. For when you
possess these and increase in them, they will make you neither
useless nor fruitless for the acknowledgment of our Lord Jesus
Christ. 9. But whoever lacks them is blind, shortsighted and
forgets the purification of past sins. 10. All the more, brethren,
be zealous to make firm your call and election, for if you do this,
you will never stumble. 11. For in this way entry into the eternal
kingdom of our Lord and Savior Jesus Christ will be richly added
to you.

Epistolary Form and Type of Letter

An epistolary "thanksgiving" prayer normally constitutes the typical opening convention of New Testament letters. It may begin with either a "thanksgiving" (*eucharistō:* Rom 1:8–15; 1 Cor 1:4–9; Phil 1:3–11; Col 1:3–8; 1 Thess 1:2–10) or with a more Semitic "blessing" (*eulogetos:* 2 Cor 1:3–7; Eph 1:3–10; 1 Peter 1:3–9). The thanksgiving prayer, moreover, frequently contains clues to the issues, tone, and key terms of the subsequent document. God's previous benefactions are praised in the expectation that the recipients will remain faithful to their heavenly patron.

Like Jude, this letter has no formal thanksgiving prayer. Yet 1:3–11 contains the same materials found in epistolary thanksgivings and functions in the same manner. It too acknowledges the benefaction of God (1:3–4) and exhorts God's clients to moral excellence as the proper way of honoring their patron by the exercise of recognized virtues (1:5–11). In this regard, it resembles the thanksgiving in 2 Tim 1:3–7, where the author describes the primary benefaction as "faith," a gift which he prays may be rekindled (1:6). If the gift is treasured, it will mean an exercise of "the spirit of power, love and self-control" (1:7).

While not a formal thanksgiving, 1:3–11 is cast in the language of a decree of honor to patrons and benefactors (Danker, "2 Peter 1: A Solemn Decree," 64–82). Cities frequently issued a decree which first acknowledged the gifts and virtues of a patron and then resolved on specific ways to recognize the patron. Danker noted twenty-seven specific phrases in 1:3–4 which correspond closely to the common language used in typical decrees of honor. (1) Such decrees begin with a phrase such as "Whereas . . ." to which "As . . ." (ōs) in 1:3 corresponds. (2) Similar to the acknowledgment of the patron's virtues and gifts in a decretal, our letter cites the benefaction of its heavenly patron: "His divine power has bestowed on us everything for a life of piety . . . precious and greatest promises given us . . . become sharers of the divine nature and be freed from the corruption of the world" (1:3–4). (3) By the recognition of specific benefactions the patron is acknowledged and so honored: ". . . . through the acknowledgment of the one who has called us" (1:3b). (4) Subsequently, as civic officials passed a resolution for specific recognition of the patron, 2 Peter exhorts the clients of God to honor their patron by living lives that will redound to God's praise and glory. Often people in the Bible are told "Be ye holy as God is holy" (1 Peter 1:17; see Lev 11:44–45) or "Live a life worthy of God who calls you into his own kingdom and glory" (1 Thess 2:12). Here the clients of God are exhorted to have excellence (*aretē*) in imitation of God's excellence (*aretē,* 1:3, 5). Moreover, they are to acquire other virtues, thus becoming holy and more honorable, which is a way of honoring their patron in return. And so the world will honor God by observing the honorable lives which flow from loyalty to such a patron (see 1 Cor 14:25; 1 Thess 4:12).

Danker's analysis undoubtedly proves that 1:3–11 is cast in the form of a decree of honor, a useful exegetical insight. Why begin this letter using such a form and language? As with epistolary thanksgivings, this passage introduces a reader to certain key terms and ideas which will become the issues argued and debated in the document. A full exposition of the summary character of 1:3–11 can be found in the *introduction*, but the following is offered as a convenient summary:

piety	3:11
promises	2:19; 3:4, 9, 13
corruption	2:12, 19, 3:10–12
lust	2:10, 18; 3:3
self-control	2:19 (false promise of "freedom")
purification	2:20–22; 3:14
forgetting	3:5, 8
entering the kingdom	3:13

To paraphrase 1:3–11 in terms of its relationship to the rest of the letter, Simeon Peter urges God's clients to acknowledge God's just judgment and the promise of it at the parousia of Jesus, a point denied by some in the group. Aware of this, the addressees will flee immorality, acknowledging that this world is corrupt and will be destroyed. Thus they will hold fast to God's cleansing of them from sin and strive to be blameless on the day of the Lord. In this they are contrasted with others who forget God's promises and their own baptism, and so come under God's just judgment. So they will await the Day of the Lord, when they will enter a new world in which God's judgment dwells.

Acknowledgment of God, which is the purpose of the decretal in 1:3–11, continues throughout the document. For the clients of God must acknowledge not just God's benefactions, but his full role and status as the world's Sovereign and Judge, a point which is apparently contested by those who deny this. And so the author's use of a decretal of honor and acknowledgment of the group's patron at the beginning of the document serves to establish a basic argument for the rest of the document, acknowledgment of the full role and status of the heavenly patron.

Socialization

The form in 1:3–11 is a secular decretal of honor; and much of the language sounds typically Hellenistic. Yet the scenario described here is Christian, and it functions to continue the socialization of new members into the symbolic world of those who acknowledge God and follow Jesus. First and foremost, the symbolic world is constituted by God and Jesus. God, the heavenly patron, has "bestowed on us everything for a life of piety . . . precious and greatest promises."

Hence, God is all sufficient for them; they need no other patrons, no other gods. They are Christians, moreover, who were cleansed of sin by baptism into Christ, who "acknowledge the Lord Jesus Christ" as Sovereign, and who strive for entrance into the eternal kingdom of this Christ. And so their past is rooted in God and Christ, as well as their future.

In terms of self-definition, they are different from the world. Theirs is a "call and election" that has set them apart. The world around them is described as corrupt in passion, yet they are cleansed of pollution and strive to remain blameless and spotless. This world is doomed to be destroyed along with sinners, but they are awaiting new heavens and a new earth where they will share in God's divine nature, immortality.

Finally, acknowledging their unique patron and distinguishing themselves from their neighbors, they are socialized to live a life worthy of their calling. As God has *aretê* (moral excellence), so must they. Yet their life is characterized by three particular virtues, distinctive to the followers of Jesus: "faith . . . steadfastness [hope] . . . love." They honor their holy God by their own holiness, which means flight from the cardinal vice of "desire" (*epithymia*) and practice of the great virtue of "self-control." Thus they are wholly pure, clean in heart and body and holy in action ("neither useless nor fruitless").

Purity, Classification, Separation, and Wholeness

As we learned in the general introduction, "purity" refers both to the general classification of all things in the world as well as to the specific cultural norms whereby some particular thing is labeled "holy" or "pure." In terms of general classification, 2 Peter perceives his world divided into two spheres, God and loyal disciples versus all others. He expresses his basic perception in dualistic language. First, he distinguishes the "holy" God from the "unholy" world. God's nature, as the notes below explain, is incorruptible and imperishable; loyal disciples are promised a share in it. The world on the other hand is "corrupt" because of vice; because corrupt, it will be destroyed. Second, people are classified in various ways: there are loyal disciples who remember all, in contrast to those others who forget (1:9); true disciples enjoy "everything" needed for a life of piety (1:3), in contrast to others who are "useless and fruitless" (1:8); some see, but others are blind; some are cleansed, others remain in sin (1:9).

Purity, moreover, is understood here in Jewish terms which indicate that what is "holy" is thereby separated from all that is evil or corrupt. Cleansed of sins, disciples continue to "escape" from this corrupt world (1:4) and seek "entry into the eternal kingdom" of heaven (1:11). Purity also has to do with wholeness and completeness. The author indicates that God supplies "everything" needed for piety, so that faithful clients may have "favor and peace" in abundance with them (1:2). The virtues described in the chain in 1:5–7 not only are holy actions, but the very chain indicates the fullness of holiness that they must strive for. Thus those who seek them will be completely holy. Their holiness, moreover, will mean body control (*egkrateia*), which means that all bodily members are "in place" and "separated" from uncleanness.

The author speaks of "purification of past sins" (1:9), which probably refers to a ritual such as baptism or some other *mikvoth* or washing rite. As he indicates how wrong it is to forget it, he suggests a continued concern to remember the past and principal act of becoming pure. Since it served as the past entrance ritual for becoming part of God's circle of clients, so remembrance of it will assist future entry into the eternal circle of the heavenly patrons.

CHAIN OF VIRTUES

New Testament documents frequently present the reader with lists of virtues and vices (Gal 5:19–23; Mark 7:21–22), a popular form of exhortation (O. J. F. Seitz, "Lists, Ethical," *IDB* 3:137–39; see Philo, *Sac.* 32). Each list is generally adapted in some way to the context in the document in which it is found, highlighting or responding to the specific situation of the group addressed. In general, we should formally classify the list of virtues in 1:5–8 as a typical list of virtues, with the added note that it is also cast in the rhetorical form of sorites or climax. Henry Fischel ("The Uses of Sorites," 119–51) gathered many examples of this in Hellenistic, Jewish, and Christian literature and classified them in terms of their content into six categories: (1) transmissional chains of authority, (2) catastrophic chains of disasters, (3) ethical and metaphysical chains of virtues, (4) circular chains, (5) defensive and commissioning chains, and (6) numerical chains of enumeration. He identified 1:5–7 not simply as a list of virtues, but a chain of them which progresses to a climax (from "faith" to "love"; see Wis 6:17–20; Seneca, *Ep.* 85:2; Cicero *Leg.* 1.7.22–23).

This chain, moreover, contains two different strands of virtues, some of which are specifically Christian (faith . . . hope . . . love) and some more properly Greco-Roman (self-control . . . piety . . . kinship affection). The triad of faith, hope, and love itself occurs frequently in Christian moral exhortations; the sequence may vary, with one or another in the last or climactic position:

faith, love, hope:	1 Thess 1:3; 5:8; 2 Thess 1:3–4; Rom 12:6–12; Eph 1:15–18; Col 1:4–5
faith, hope, love:	Rom 5:1–5; 1 Cor 13:6–7, 13
love, hope, faith:	Eph 4:2–5

Already in the Bible "love" and "faith" were linked in terms of *hesed* and *'emet*, that is, "steadfast kindness" in a covenant relationship (Gen 24:12; 2 Sam 2:5–6; Josh 2:12). The triad faith, hope, and love, even if not original to the followers of Jesus, quickly became characteristic of them and self-defining of their particular way of living. Evidently, we are reading "steadfastness" as "hope" (see 1 Thess 1:3; Titus 2:1).

The triad forms the determining framework within which other virtues are inserted, much the way it does in Rom 5:1–5.

Rom 5:1–5	2 Peter 1:5–7
faith	*faith*
peace	knowledge
	excellence
	self-control
hope	*steadfastness*
endurance	piety
character	kinship affection
love	*love*

Unlike Rom 5:1–5, however, group-specific virtues such as faith and love are supplemented by more popular ones. One might see this list looking in two directions, not unlike the Ten Commandments. First, certain virtues treat human relations with the divine: faithfulness to, knowledge of, and self-control in regard to the heavenly patron (i.e., *eusebia* or godliness); others deal with horizontal relationships among group members: piety (duty to ancestors and kin), kinship affection and love (i.e., *dikaiosynê* or righteousness).

The chain of virtues thus suggests a certain wholeness or completeness. Eight of them are listed, and the number eight was generally considered the complete number (see Philo, *Spec. Leg.* 2.212). All of the specifically Christian virtues are joined with more popular ones to suggest a completeness of moral response. The virtues look to honorable relations both with the heavenly patron and his earthly clients, thus embracing the whole world. Wholeness, moreover, is found in attention to virtues in regard to body (self-control) and spirit, as well as thought and action. In this wholeness, then, holiness is urged, a completeness of moral excellence to all.

NOTES

DIVINE POWER

All of the operations of God in the world were commonly grouped in terms of two powers in God: creative power (*dynamis poiētikē*) and executive power (*dynamis basilikē*). By God's creative power the world was made and kept in existence. By the divine executive power, God gave laws, ruled, and judged the world (see Philo, *Leg. All.* 2.68; *Cher.* 27–28; *Sac.* 59; *Plant.* 86–87; *Heres* 166; *Fuga* 95, 100; *Somn.* 1.159, 160–62; *Abr.* 124–25; *Mos.* 2.99; Rom 4:17). In time, God's executive power came to include eschatological events such as resurrection of the dead and final judgment. This document knows both powers of God: creative power is briefly alluded to in 3:4–5, whereas executive/eschatological power becomes the main topic of the document: 2:4–10; 3:6–7, 10–13. The divine power mentioned in 1:3 should be considered part of God's executive/eschatological power, for it refers not only to the "promises" of the parousia and final judgment, but especially to the sharing of the "divine nature" which God will grant to the just at the end of the world. This is the reward for holiness, the resurrection unto life. In virtue of this power the ultimate benefaction is bestowed on God's clients, a sharing in God's imperishability.

EXCELLENCE (ARETĒ)

The first occurrence of this term in 1:3 clearly belongs to the world of honor and shame. It can mean wealth, which an honorable person conspicuously displays, as well as achievements, for which he expects praise. It includes the meaning of virtue or excellence, the ground of praise. Or it can simply mean fame or reputation (Phil 4:8); frequently in Greek literature we find the combination *doxa kai aretē*, which is a sort of hendiadys meaning "famous valor" (Pausanius, *Arcad.* 52.6; Dionysus of Halicarnassus, *Ant. Rom.* 5.62.4; Diodorus of Sicily, 2.45.2; 3.70.5). Actions and excellence are not honorable in the ancient world until formally acknowledged as such. Hence, the honorable patron has displayed excellence by virtue of his benefactions and so rightly expects "acknowledgment" by "calling us to his own glory [for his] excellence" (Danker, *Benefactor*, 318). In this sense, "glory and praise" here resemble the conventional honoring of God in the Bible: "singing praise to God" (Pss 7:17; 9:2, 11; 30:12; 47:6–7; 75:9; etc.) and "declaring God's glory" (1 Chron 16:24–25; Pss 19:1; 22:2; 66:16; 73:28; 96:3; Isa 42:12; etc.).

Yet in 1:5 *aretē* takes on a slightly different meaning, for it means "virtue" here, rather than reputation for excellence. As the first thing to be added to "faith," it can probably be understood as a term inclusive of the four cardinal virtues recognized in popular philosophy (see Wis 8:7 and 4 Macc 1:18). Yet if the followers of Jesus pursue the moral perfection described in 1:5–7, they will begin to share God's excellence, as well as his "divine nature," and so be a credit to their God. Their *aretē* will redound to the *aretē* of God, that is, to God's praise and glory. Thus, the two meanings complement each other when seen as expressions of honor in that world.

DESIRE (EPITHYMIA)

In regard to 1:1, we noted that people acknowledged four cardinal virtues, one of which is "justice." Correspondingly, there were four cardinal vices, desire, pleasure, fear, and grief (Diog. Laert. 7.110; Plato, *Phaedo* 83b). Given the reference in 1:5 to *aretē*, Greek readers would recognize the term "desire" (*epithymia*) as one of the four vices. The hearers of this letter are urged to develop the virtue of "self-control" (1:6), which offsets the vice of "desire": "To self-control [*egkrateias*] belongs the ability to restrain desire [*epithymian*] by reason" (Aristotle, *Virtues and Vices* 5.1 1250b 12–16). Later in the letter, Simeon Peter will condemn a second of these cardinal vices, "pleasure," (*hēdonē*; see 2:13). See note on "self-control" below.

CORRUPTION (PHTHORA)

A full understanding of this term requires that we understand it as an expression both of the strong purity concerns of the author and of his cosmology. Since in the context the addressees are urged to flee from "corruption" to participate in the divine nature, it must refer to destruction as opposed to imperishability. This is borne out by its use in 2:12 and comparable descriptions of this world which is doomed to destruction (2:5–6; 3:4–7, 10–12). Yet this cosmology of a doomed world is replicated in the description of it as a place of corruption (2:19), which is enslaved to vices such as "desire" (1:4) and "pleasure" (2:13). In this world are found defiling passion (2:10) and defilement (2:20). This double meaning of *phthora* corresponds to typical New Testament usage: (1) destruction and perishability (Rom 8:21; 1 Cor 15:42, 50; Col 2:22) and (2) moral corruption (Gal 6:7).

In proportion as disciples of Jesus "flee" from this corrupt world which is doomed to destruction, they will become spotless and so be full of virtue (1:8). Thus they will be able to enter another world, "the eternal kingdom of our Lord" (1:11; see 3:13). In the next note, we will indicate that the "divine nature" to which God invites his clients is characterized as "incorruptibility" (*aphtharsia*), just as God is "incorruptible" (*aphthartos*). Hence, corruption serves to contrast God and God's world with the world of mortals. Yet God's world is accessible to mortals by benefaction from the divine patron.

DIVINE NATURE

It is not unusual in Hellenistic literature to find mention of mortals sharing in the divine nature, either in God's prophetic powers (Josephus, *Ag. Ap.* 1.232) or blessedness (Philo, *Decal.* 104; see Plutarch, *Defect.* 415C; Josephus, *Ant.* 8.107; Philo, *Abr.* 144). Yet it was axiomatic to describe the nature of a true god as "eternal and imperishable": "With regard to the gods . . . some of them have a nature which is eternal and imperishable" (Diodorus of Sicily 3.9.1; see J. H. Neyrey, "'Without Beginning of Days or End of Life' [Hebrews 7:3]: Topos for a True Deity," *CBQ* 53 [1991]: 441–45). When discussing how mortals necessarily understand the divine, Plutarch remarks that the nature of the Deity is to be blessed and imperishable (*De Iside* 358E). And the Christian apologist Aristides compares and contrasts mortals with the Deity in terms of divine imperishability:

> Man is constituted of the four elements and of a soul and a spirit and without any one of these parts he could not consist . . . But God has none of these things in his nature, but is uncreated and imperishable. And hence it is not possible that we set up man to be of the nature of God [*Apol.* 7:1–2].

The sharing in 1:4 pertains to God's imperishability (see "sharers in that which is incorruptible," *Barn.* 19.8). As the readers are urged to flee from a corrupt world doomed to destruction, they will correspondingly "enter the eternal kingdom" (1:11), which is imperishable and eternal.

According to Gen 1:26, God created humankind in the divine image, which was popularly understood as sharing in God's imperishability (J. Jervell, *Imago Dei* [Göttingen: Vandenhoeck and Ruprecht, 1960], 113–19). Wis 2:23 expresses this clearly: "God created man for incorruption [*ep' aphtharsiai*], and made him in the image of his own eternity" (see 4 Macc 18:3). Paul argues that mortals of flesh and blood may not come into the presence of the holy God, who is imperishable and immortal; hence "the dead will be raised imperishable . . . this perishable nature must put on imperishability, and this mortal nature must put on immortality" (1 Cor 15:52–53; see Joachim Jeremias, "Flesh and Blood Cannot Inherit the Kingdom of God (1 Cor XV.50)," *NTS* 2 [1955]: 151–59). Even here, this is considered a benefaction of God.

Some Greek heroes received immortal honors because of their benefactions to humankind (Diodorus of Sicily 1.12.10–13.1; 3.9.1; 6.1.2; Plutarch, *Pelop.* 16; *Malice of Herodotus* 857D). However, in the perspective of 2 Peter and other Jewish and Christian writings, imperishability is related to sinlessness; for death and corruption entered the world through sin (Gen 2:17). Hence, in the new creation, God's clients are being cleansed of their sins (1:9); remaining spotless, they will be restored to the benefaction given the first Adam. Thus, they become deathless because sinless. This understanding precludes any sense of pantheism. And so the Hellenistic phrase "divine nature" contains concepts which are thoroughly biblical, although quite compatible with popular theology (J. H. Neyrey, "'I SAID: YOU ARE GODS': Psalm 82:6 and John 10," *JBL* 108 [1989]: 655–59). The scenario whereby mortals share God's imperishability is cast in Christian terms, namely, the end of the world, when sinlessness is rewarded by entrance into the eternal kingdom and participation in divine imperishability.

FAITH

As Danker has shown, "faith" (*pistis*) belongs to the chancery language of benefaction and should be translated as "faithfulness" or "fidelity." When a worthy patron has acted as benefactor, some appropriate response is expected, which is generally some form of public honor as well as loyalty or commitment (*Benefactor,* 460). According to Josephus the jailor of the patriarch Joseph praised him for showing "fidelity [*pistin*] to the tasks committed to him" (*Ant.* 2.61). More to the point, Xenophon remarked that a certain letter "contained reminders of former friendship and fidelity" (*pisteōs; An.* 1.6.3). "Friendship" is the code word here for a patron-client relationship, whose hallmark is "fidelity." Concerning the importance of "faithfulness" in patron-client relations, Aristotle remarked: "There is no stable friendship without fidelity [*aneu pisteōs*], and fidelity [*pistis*] comes with time" (*Eud. Eth.* 7.2.39 1237b 12–13). In the NT, God's faithfulness is often praised in contexts where divine benefaction is noted (1 Cor 1:9; 1 Thess 5:24). And this divine faithfulness or loyalty must, of course, be balanced with a corresponding faithfulness and loyalty on the part of God's clients (see Prov 12:22 LXX).

SELF-CONTROL (EGKRATEIA)

Some ancient authors considered "self-control" as "the foundation of all virtue" (Xenophon, *Mem.* 1.5.4), although it was generally ranked after the four cardinal virtues (Diog. Laert. 7.92). It was popularly defined as "a disposition never overcome in that which concerns right reason or a habit which no pleasure can get the better of" (Diog. Laert. 7.93). In practice "self-control" expresses the strong bodily control that the ancients valued (see introduction to 2 Peter 6 [h] [3]. Philo was typical in describing it as the antithesis to "desire" (*epithymia*) and "pleasure" (*hēdonē; Sp. Leg.* 1.149; see Sir 18:30) as well as to "money" (Xenophon, *Mem.* 1.5.6; Philo, *Sp. Leg.* 1.150). It is frequently linked with "endurance" as it is in 2 Peter 1:6 (Aristotle, *N.E.* 7.1.6; Plutarch, *Virt. Mor.* 449C) or "faithfulness" (*pistis,* Josephus, *Ant.* 16.246). Specifically it was understood to be the guardian of the bodily orifices (Philo, *Det.* 101–3; *Sp. Leg.* 2.195). Although commonly discussed in Greek authors (Aristotle, *N.E.* 7.1–14 1145a–1145b; Stobaeus, *Ecl.* 2.60.9; Sextus Empiricus, *Adv. Math.* 8.153; see W. Grundmann, "Egkrateia," *TDNT* 2.339–42), "self-control" occurs in Jewish writings, especially those of Hellenistic Judaism (*Ep. Aris.* 278; Josephus, *B.J.* 2.120; 4.373). Luke says that it constitutes a key element in Paul's preaching (Acts 24:25; see 1 Cor 9:25 and Titus 1:8).

Philo described "self-control" as the virtue into which converts who experience repentance (*metanoia*) transferred as they left a life of vice (*Abr.* 24; *Virt.* 180; *Praem.* 116). And since it functions as the key antidote to "pleasure" and "desire," we should notice how it functions in 2 Peter as the antithesis to all that the author's opponents do and stand for. Converts to the holy God have fled a world corrupted by "desire" (*epithymia,* 1:4); and God judges those who "follow polluting desires of the flesh" (2:10). But it is the opponents who entice people back to that life of "debauchery and desires of the flesh" (2:18); they scoff at the truth because of their "desires" (3:3). Moreover, they pursue "pleasure" (*hēdonē*, 2:13). Holy disciples will guard their bodily orifices by practicing "self-control," and so distinguish themselves from the opponents, who are notorious for their lack of control in all the windows of the soul:

(1) *eyes:* "their eyes are . . . filled with adulteries and evils" (2:13);
(2) *mouth for speech:* "insult [*blasphēmountes*] what they do not comprehend" (2:12; see 2:2, 10); *mouth for eating:* dissipation at common feasts (2:13); return to vomit (2:22);
(3) *genitals:* debauchery (2:2, 18) and adultery (2:14).

They are also accused of greed (*pleonexia*, 2:3, 14), for which "self-control" is considered the appropriate prophylactic (Philo, *Sp. Leg.* 1.163; Xenophon, *Mem.* 1.5.6).

The importance of "self-control," then, lies in recognition of it as a premier virtue for Jews as well as Greeks. Considered as "pure and stainless," it serves as the antidote for "desire" and "pleasure," which are "profane, impure and unholy" (Philo, *Sp. Leg.* 1.150). In this document it summarizes the strong bodily control which makes disciples able to stand at God's judgment and enter the kingdom of Jesus. Alternately, it contrasts the true disciple with the opponents who are credited with living a life of "freedom," presumably from law and rule as well as freedom from judgment.

PIETY (EUSEBEIA)

The virtue of "piety," which is a division of "justice," contains three parts: duty to the gods, to one's dead ancestors, and to family/parents (see Aristotle, *Virtues and Vices* 5.2 1250b 23–25; W. Foerster, "Eusebeia," *TDNT* 7.176–78). Danker (*Benefactor*, 343–45) indicates that it refers to the attitude or performance relative to "gods, heads of state, civic entities or other authority figures." It tends to describe the vertical dimension of human relations, whereas terms like *dikaiosynē* or *philadelphia* (2 Peter 1:7) cover horizontal relationships. Philo makes this distinction clear: "Among the vast number of particular truths and principles, there stand out high above the others two main heads: one of duty to God as shown by piety [*eusebeias*] and holiness [*hosiotētos*], one of duty to men as shown by humanity [*philanthrōpias*] and justice [*dikaiosynē*]" (*Spec. Leg.* 2.63). Several meanings of piety are operative in 1:3–11. Since God grants "all needed for life and piety," clients should first and foremost honor their heavenly patron and pay their dues to God. But in 1:7, piety is linked with "kinship affection" (*philanthropia*) and "love" (*agapē*), which suggest horizontal duties to fictive kin in the Christian covenant family. In the sense of rights and duties, clients should honor their patron and praise his benefaction, as well as give him his full due, even acknowledgment of his power as just judge. Thus true disciples will loyally acclaim God, while false disciples despise authority (2:10). It should be noted that just as the ancients listed four cardinal vices, they knew of four cardinal virtues. At one point in the tradition "piety" (*eusebeia*) was considered one of the four virtues (S. C. Mott, "Greek Ethics and Christian Conversion: The Philonic Background of Titus II.10–14 and III.3–7," *NovT* 20 [1978]: 23–30).

KINSHIP AFFECTION (PHILADELPHIA)

In the NT disciples are called "brothers and sisters," a remark which encourages them to think of one another as kin, with all the rights and duties of kin (K. H. Shelkle, "Bruder," *RAC* 2 [1954]: 632–39). In secular Greek and the LXX this term is typically used of examples of noteworthy generosity between actual brothers (4 Macc 13:23, 26; 14:1; Philo, *Jos.* 218; Josephus, *B.J.* 1.275, 485; *Ant.* 2.161; Lucian, *Dial. Deo.* 286), but it can be extended to "kinship" based either on ethnic affinity (2 Macc 15:14) or on treaties of friendship between rulers (1 Macc 12:10, 17). In contrast, Christians were regularly exhorted to treat each other as kin (Rom 12:10; 1 Thess 4:9; Heb 13:1; 1 Peter 1.22; 3:8). This generous way of dealing with each other was frequently commented on by outsiders, usually in a pejorative way (Lucian, *Peregrinus* 13; Minucius Felix, *Octavius* 31.8; Tertullian, *Apology* 39). Thus "kinship affection" in the NT is in the process of becoming a distinguishing trait of disciples. In general this term is found primarily at Greek sources (Xenophon, *Mem.* 2.3.17; Plutarch, *Frat. Amor.* 478B–492D; *Solon* 27.5; *Lucullus* 43.3) and in Hellenistic Jewish writings.

FRUITLESS (AKARPOS)

Barren women and parched fields were called "fruitless," as well as wasted effort (4 Macc 16:7). The metaphorical usage here characterizes typical NT exhortation. Correct knowledge of God (i.e., loyalty to God's authority) leads to honorable behavior, which is called "bearing fruit" (Matt. 21:43; Mark 4:20; Gal 5:22; James 3:17–18). In one classic place, disciples are exhorted "to lead a life worthy of the Lord, fully pleasing to him, bearing fruit in every good work" (Col 1:11). This illustrates how honorable actions honor the patron. Here "fruitlessness" is linked with failing to "acknowledge the Lord Jesus Christ," that is, disloyalty to his authority and his role as judge. "Fruitlessness" also describes bad deeds (Eph 5:11); failure to "bring forth fruit" leads to judgment (Matt 3:8, 10). Fruitlessness, then, dishonors the patron and leads to vindication of honor by him in a requiting judgment, when the ax will be laid to the roots.

FORGETS (LĒTHĒN LABŌN)

In the dialectic of the exhortation, the author presents himself as the "reminder" of the proper attitude toward God and the content of the tradition

(1:13; 3:1–2). He thus positions himself as the opposite of his opponents who willfully "forget" God and the traditions of correct thinking about God. Here "forgetting" is linked with forgiveness of sins, and takes on the quality of dishonoring God. Danker (*Benefactor* 463) indicates how important in patron-client relationships was "remembrance" of benefaction, either tax relief, cancellation of debts, or forgiveness of crimes. Honorable clients remember and thus manifest piety (*eusebeia*), whereas dishonorable clients forget and shame their patron.

STUMBLE (PTAISĒTE)

This is no mere "suffering reversal of fortune" (Philo, *Jos.* 144), but sinning (Sir 37:12; Rom 11:11). Philo describes a bad judge "stumbling like a blind man, proceeding without staff or others to guide his feet" (*Spec. Leg.* 4.70), a meaning that fits with 2 Peter's earlier remark about the blindness and shortsightedness of those who do not follow the tradition. In another place Philo describes a certain kind of stumbling because of deception (*Leg. All.* 3.66). True disciples have guides to instruct them on the correct way, whereas the disciples of the opponents lack sight, suffer deception, and deviate from the way of truth.

BIBLIOGRAPHY

Chadwick, Henry, "Enkrateia," *RAC* 5 (1962): 343–65.

Danker, F. W., "2 Peter 1: A Solemn Decree" *CBQ* 40 (1978): 64–82. Reprinted in his *Benefactor* (St. Louis: Clayton Publishing House, 1982), 453–67.

Easton, B. S., "New Testament Ethical Lists," *JBL* 51 (1932): 1–12.

Fischel, H. A., "The Uses of Sorites (*Climax*, *Gradatio*) in the Tannaitic Period," *HUCA* 44 (1973): 119–51.

Hiebert, D. E., "Selected Studies from 2 Peter. Part 1: The Necessary Growth in the Christian Life: An Exposition of 2 Peter 1:5–11," *BSac* (1984): 43–54.

O'Brien, P. T., *Introductory Thanksgivings in the Letters of Paul* (NovTSup 49. Leiden: E. J. Brill 1977).

Schubert, Paul, *Form and Function of the Pauline Thanksgivings*. BZNW 20. Berlin: Alfred Töpelmann, 1939.

Wolters, A., "'Partners of the Deity': A Covenantal Reading of 2 Peter 1:4," *CTJ* 25 (1990): 28–44.

III.
Occasion of the Letter: Peter's Farewell Address (1:12–15)

♦

1 12. So then, I mean always to remind you about these things,
although you know them and are established in the truth present
to you. 13. I think it right, as long as I am in this tent, to keep
awakening you by reminders. 14. I know that the divesting of
my tent is near, as our Lord Jesus Christ has revealed to me.
15. I shall be zealous to enable you after my departure always to
remember these things.

Farewell Address/Testament

When the author states that Jesus revealed to him his imminent death, we are prompted to read 1:12–15 in light of the genre of farewell addresses and testaments. Jewish and Christian literature frequently records how on the departure or death of a leader, he speaks to his children or followers and leaves them his final words or testament. Jacob gives a final address to his twelve sons (Gen 49), Moses to Israel (Deut 33:1–29; Josephus, *Ant.* 4.177–93), Joshua to his followers (Josh 24). Each of Jacob's twelve sons leaves a testament (Testament of the XII Patriarchs; see A. E. Harvey, "The Testament of Simeon Peter," 343–49). In the NT Jesus is reported to have given a farewell address in Luke 22:14–36 and John 13–17, as well as Paul to the elders at Miletus (Acts 20:17–35). This letter purports to be Peter's farewell address.

Formal analysis of the regular elements of a testament or farewell address has proved difficult to establish because of the variety of examples available to us.

But certain common features can be identified, which aid in the interpretation of 2 Peter.

Formal Elements of Farewell Addresses/Testaments

1. Prediction of death or departure
2. Predictions of future crises for followers
3. Virtues urged; ideal behavior prescribed
4. Commission
5. Legacy

The author indicates his imminent death in 1:14, which is the occasion for writing this document. In the letter, he predicts future attacks on the group by false teachers and false prophets (2:1–3; 3:1–7). Given the nature of the attacks, he urges the virtue of faithfulness to the true tradition (1:4, 16–18; 3:1–2) and he encourages a moral uprightness which flows from living according to the truth (1:5–11; 3:11–13). A commission is implied in that someone will read this document to the church and remind its members of it constantly; this person can only be an official who can speak in Peter's name and in support of the tradition it embodied. Finally, he leaves a legacy, in this case, the truth about God's just judgment (2:4–10; 3:8–10) and the correct reading of Paul's letters (3:15–16). This letter, then may profitably be interpreted in formal terms as a farewell address or testament.

Honor and Shame

In delivering a testamentary farewell address, the author claims a particular honorable role and status. According to literary parallels, testaments were delivered by patriarchs and leaders (Jacob, Moses, Joshua, and Jesus). The delivery of their testaments is likewise a ritualized ceremony, whereby their particular role and status is confirmed in the kinship group of family members or disciples. Thus Peter's honor as a chief apostle and patriarch among the churches is both claimed and acknowledged by his testament.

Patron, Mediator, and Client Relationships

"Peter" is himself the recipient of the benefactions of Christ, in this case, a revelation of his imminent death (1:14). And so he acts as client to his patron, "our Lord Jesus Christ." Yet in turn he acts as benefactor and patron to the churches, for he passes on to them a permanent and clear legacy of "the truth present to them" (1:12). Technically, he functions as a mediator in patron-client relationships depicted here; as recipient himself of eyewitness experiences (1:16–17), he passes on these to the true clients of Christ, the churches.

According to ancient literature on patron-client relationships, some reciprocity is always due when a benefaction is bestowed. When cities inscribe notice of benefaction, their public "remembering" is formally understood as the appropriate and expected response of honorable clients (F. W. Danker, *Benefactor* [St. Louis: Clayton Publishing House, 1982], 436). Recipients of benefaction should never forget their patrons (Seneca, *Ben.* 7.22.1; 2.10.4). Indeed, failure to remember is tantamount to lack of loyalty (*fides* or *pistis*; Seneca, *Ep.* 81.12). Thus when the author states that he will leave a reminder of certain things, he acts as God's broker to leave a public testimony to the benefaction of the divine Patron. His document will function as testimony to the Patron's benefaction comparable to public inscriptions of civic benefaction. Recipients, moreover, are thus solemnly obligated to "remember" this benefaction.

Tents and Ritual Language

When the author speaks of being in a "tent" and "divesting myself of this tent" he speaks metaphorically of life and death respectively. In the NT we occasionally hear of the body described as a dwelling place, often a temple (John 2:21). In a peasant world, one would not be surprised at reference to tents as places of residence (see Isa 38:12). The remarks in 1:13–14 resemble Paul's comments in 2 Cor 5:1–4, where he speaks of his death as the leaving of a tent dwelling. The living body is described as a tent (*Para. Jer.* 6:6–7), as is the dead body (Sentences of Sextus 320; Eusebius, *H.E.* 3.31). Whence this type of understanding? Does it imply a form of body/soul dualism? Most of the evidence which speaks of the body as a tent comes from the Hellenistic world, traditions which have also influenced Jewish thought (see Wis 9:15). Diognetus speaks of "the immortal soul dwelling in a mortal tent" (6.8). Since this metaphor is found in both Hellenistic and Jewish materials, it may be one more example of the author's strategy to talk of the Christian gospel in multicultural terms.

The metaphor of putting off of this earthly tent may fruitfully be examined in the light of ritual process. Greek mysteries as well as Christian baptismal practices spoke of the initiation of the neophyte as "putting off of the body of flesh" and "putting on a new nature" (Col 2:11; 3:10; see Philo, *Leg. All.* 2.55). Former role and status, symbolized by the old garment of the old dwelling place, are abandoned. And in terms of the language world of 2 Peter, the earthly body belongs to corruption, something all followers of Jesus flee and seek to escape.

Yet nudity is not a normal state for those who dwell in ancient villages and cities. Thus, the person who ritually assumes a new role or status puts on garments symbolic of this or takes up residence in a dwelling signifying this new status. When Paul speaks of putting off the earthly tent, he is ashamed "to be found naked," and so "longs to put on our heavenly dwelling" (2 Cor 5:2–3). Paul stated that flesh and blood cannot inherit the kingdom of God; but through a change, "this perishable nature must put on imperishability and this mortal nature must put on immortality" (1 Cor 15:53–54). Although the author here describes his death as the putting off of the bodily tent, he does not explicitly describe the completion of the ritual process whereby he would put on a new garment or take up residence in a new tent. At least he does not say this in so many words. But he has indicated that God allows participation in the divine nature which is incorruptible. One might expect some reference to putting on the garments of glory or taking up residence in the heavenly tent (see Luke 16:9). Perhaps his anticipation of "new heavens and a new earth" (3:13) implies his expectation of putting on a new garment or dwelling in a new, glorious tent. Yet the language reflects ritual process and its metaphors of divesting and investing, which are equally applicable to the status transformation rituals of baptism/initiation or death (W. A. Meeks, *First Urban Christians* [New Haven, CT: Yale University Press, 1983], 155, 157).

NOTES

REMEMBERING/REMINDING AND THE IMPORTANCE OF THE PAST

Three times the author identifies his task as assisting the churches to remember (1:12, 13) and as reminding them (1:15) of the tradition. This task offsets the willful forgetting of the tradition by the false teachers (3:5, 8). He reminds them of "the truth" of their faith in God, which is the Christian doctrine of theodicy or God's just judgment. He reminds them also of the "promises" of God, which have to do with God's prediction of the world's end and the redemption of the faithful to share eternal life with God.

Implicit in the author's remarks is a profound valuing of the past, which is a typical feature of the culture of the ancient world. Unlike our more evolutionary model of time, in which we see progress and development which point to the future as the golden age, the ancients evaluated history in terms of a gradual degeneration model (A. Y. Collins, "Numerical Symbolism in Jewish and Early Christian Apocalyptic Literature," *ANRW* 2.21.2 [1984], 1239–41). First came the golden, then the silver and bronze, ages. In a culture which valued authority, what was older was valued over what was new; the past was more important than the present. Hence, when the author speaks of reminding and giving remembrance of things past, this makes cultural sense, for it points to the golden age when Jesus was manifested in glory before the people (1:16–17) and when the promises of God were delivered. The past, moreover, serves as the norm for the present and the future, as we shall see in the rehearsing of biblical examples in 2:4–10 and 3:4–7.

REVELATION

The author claims that Jesus revealed to him his imminent death (1:14). Predictions of the future sufferings and deaths of NT figures are not uncommon (John 13:36; 21:19; Acts 9:16; 21:11). But the author's remarks take on special significance in this document for Peter is portrayed here, as he is in the tradition, as the recipient of heavenly revelation (see 1:16–17). Yet this particular revelation of Peter's death functions uniquely here as the trigger for the patriarch's farewell address. Hence, even the authority of Jesus is borrowed in support of the present reminding of the traditional faith. The author speaks to confirm the truth because it was revealed by his heavenly Lord.

Scholars have exercised themselves over what biblical text might be alluded to in 1:14. John 21:19 remains the popular favorite, for there Jesus predicts Peter's following Jesus even in his death, a prediction which offsets Peter's earlier denial of the Lord (see John 13:36–38). Later legends about Peter tend to contain just such a prediction by Jesus, although they may depend on the notice in 2 Peter 1:14, rather than on an independent tradition (Bauckham, *Jude, 2 Peter,* 200–10).

DEPARTURE (EXODUS)/DEATH

Just as Moses in his farewell address spoke of his death as his exodus from life (Josephus, *Ant.* 4.189), so the author speaks of his departure from this life as an exodus. This is a common metaphor for death in Jewish writings (Wis 3:2; 7:6; *T. Naph.* 1:1), in some way derivative from the historical "exodus" from slavery in Egypt. Independently of this document Irenaeus spoke of the deaths of Peter and Paul as an exodus (*Adv. Haer.* 3.3.1; cited by Eusebius, *H.E.* 5.8.2). Yet the term occasionally means simply "departure" (Philo, *Mos.* 1.268; *Virt.* 76–77) or "escape." Here it should be seen in combination with the term of entrance (*eisodos*) used in 1:11. Just as there is an *exodos* from this perishable, temporary world, so there is a corresponding *eisodos* into the imperishable, eternal world (see Wis 7:6). Just as one "puts off" the tent of flesh (1:13–14) and "puts on" immortality, so one experiences an *exodos* from this dwelling and an *eisodos* into a new kingdom. The heightened language used to describe death as a passage or transition serves to give greater value to the richness of the promises of God for a future life which will come with the parousia of Christ. In 1:4 the author called these promises "precious and greatest," an evaluation which is continued with remarks about an *exodos* from this world and an *eisodos* into a superior world.

BIBLIOGRAPHY

Bauckham, Richard, "Pseudo-Apostolic Letters," *JBL* 107 (1988): 469–94.

Boobyer, G. H., "The Indebtedness of 2 Peter to 1 Peter," *New Testament Essays, Studies in Memory of Thomas Walter Manson* (A. J. B. Higgins, ed.; Manchester: Manchester University Press, 1959), 44–51.

Collins, John J., "The Testamentary Literature in Recent Scholarship," *Early Judaism and Its Modern Interpreters* (Robert A. Kraft and George W. E. Nickelsburg, eds.; Philadelphia: Fortress Press/Atlanta: Scholars Press, 1986), 268–85.

Harvey, A. E., "The Testament of Simeon Peter," *A Tribute to Geza Vermes, Essays on Jewish and Christian Literature and History* (P. R. Davies and R. T. White, eds.; Scheffield: JSOT Press, 1990), 339–54.

Knoch, O., "Das Vermächtnis des Petrus: Der 2. Petrusbrief," *Wort Gottes in der Zeit, Festschrift für K. H. Schelkle* (H. Feld and J. Nolte, eds.; Düsseldorf: Patmos-Verlag, 1973), 149–65.

Kolenkow, Anitra B., "The Literary Genre 'Testament,' " *Early Judaism and Its Modern Interpreters* (Robert A. Kraft and George W. E. Nickelsburg, eds.; Philadelphia: Fortress Press/Atlanta: Scholars Press, 1986), 259–67.

Vögtle, A., "Die Schriftwerdung der apostolischen Paradosis nach 2. Petr 1, 12–15," *Neues Testament und Geschichte: Historisches Geschehen und Deutung im Neuen Testament* (H. Baltensweiler and B. Riecke, eds.; Zürich: Theologischer Verlag, 1972), 297–305.

Zmijewski, J., "Apostolische Paradosis und Pseudepigraphie im Neuen Testament: 'Durch Erinnerung wachhalten' (2 Petr 1, 13; 3, 1)," *BZ* 23 (1979): 161–71.

IV.
Reply to the First Slander: Prophecy of the Parousia Defended (1:16–18)

♦

1 16. For we did not follow cleverly devised myths when we made
known to you the powerful coming of our Lord Jesus Christ, but
we were eyewitnesses of his majesty. 17. For he received from
God the Father honor and glory when the voice came to him
from the Majestic Glory: "This is my son, my beloved; on him
have I placed my favor." 18. And indeed we heard this voice
borne from heaven, when we were with him on the holy mountain.

Context of the Argument

The author praised God's benefaction of "the precious and greatest promises" (1:4); he himself promised to give the addressees the legacy of a clear reminder of the truth (1:12–15). Now in 1:16–18 he begins to specify just what those promises are and of what he reminds them. He focuses on "the powerful coming of our Lord Jesus Christ," the event we call the parousia, when Jesus will judge the living and the dead. Yet the author describes a scene we have come to call the transfiguration (1:17–18). And he prefaces his description with a denial that the parousia of Jesus is a mere human invention (v 16). The key to 1:16–18, then, lies in appreciating the prophetic character of the transfiguration, how the author interprets it as a commissioning of Jesus as Lord and as a bestowal of a new role and status (power and glory) on Jesus. Of this event and its prophetic character, the author is an eyewitness. Yet his proclamation of the prophecy of

Christ's return is mocked by some in the group who scoff at "the promise of his coming" (3:4). Hence, the author takes a defensive tone in regard to this permanent reminder of the tradition he promised in 1:12–15 to leave the churches.

FORENSIC RHETORIC

Much of what follows depends on a reader's appreciation of the apologetic nature of this document. Clearly in 2:1–19; 3:3–7, 8–10, 15–16 the author both refutes false teachers who are subverting the truth and defends the tradition for which he is an authorized witness. In this we should not find it surprising that aspects of forensic rhetoric are employed in the discourse, for most literate persons were taught basic principles of rhetoric as part of their education in writing and speaking (Neyrey, "Forensic Defense Speech," 213–18).

The author responds as one charged with deceit, namely, that his remarks on Christ's coming and God's judgment are "cleverly devised myths." Testifying on his own behalf, he denies that his proclamation was concocted for purposes of deceit. To the point, he claims to be an eyewitness (*epoptai*) at the giving of the prophecy. The third structural part of the forensic defense speech contains the proof (*probatio/pistis*), in which witnesses, arguments, and evidence are brought forth (Cicero, *Inv. Rhet.* 1.24.34; Quintilian, *Inst.* 5.3.1–5.28). Rhetorical handbooks instruct orators to organize their proofs in accord with forensic procedure. "First among the proofs must be placed the evidence of witnesses and confessions that are obtained by torture" (*Rh. Al.* 36 1442b37). The author claims to have seen and heard the events on the holy mountain; he was not alone, and so his testimony is confirmed by the weight of other witnesses. His remarks on Christ's coming and God's judgment, then, are eyewitness testimony, not rumor or secondhand reports (see Demosthenes, "Against Eubulides," 4; Philo, *Spec. Leg.* 4.59; *Conf.* 141; *t. Sanh.* 8.3).

The rhetorical handbooks indicate that such formal testimony can be confirmed by "probability, examples, tokens, signs and maxims" (*Rh. Al.* 36 1442b39–1443a6). The best proofs are tokens (*tekmēria*) and signs (*sēmeia*), that is, irrefutable proof from which cogent syllogisms are made (*tekmēria*) or probable proof which allows valid inference (*sēmeia*) (Quintilian, *Inst.* 5.9.3–9; see Aristotle, *Rh.* 1.2.16–17 1357b1–10). The vision of Christ's glory and the hearing of God's word should be interpreted as forensic proof, as tokens and signs of Christ's status and role in God's plan of judgment. These tokens and signs were seen and heard by many witnesses; their probative force is indisputable.

Forensic speeches all contain a part which is called *narratio*, where the nature of the case is stated (Cicero, *Her.* 1.3.4; Quintilian, *Inst.* 3.9.1, 4.2.31). Chief among the points made here is the focus on what must be judged (*iudicatio/krinomenon*), that is, affirmed or denied (Cicero, *Inv. Rhet.* 1.13.18; Quintilian, *Inst.* 3.11.5–6). In this document the author asserts that the issue to be judged is the veracity of the prophecies of God's day of judgment and Christ's parousia, that is, the issue of theodicy.

An eyewitness, then, testifies to the truth. He defines the issue to be judged: God's appointment of Jesus as the Lord who would come on the day of judgment and assist God in rewarding and punishing. This testimony is supported by tokens and signs seen and heard on the holy mountain. The author, then, begins the defense of the tradition in terms of accepted forensic procedure.

The Honor of Peter

The author responds in 1:16–18 to attacks on his authority, either real or perceived. He is accused of fabricating myths about the future. In the cultural world of the New Testament his claim to be Christ's spokesman is challenged and his honor is threatened as his role and status are called into question. Like Jesus in the gospel stories, he delivers a riposte to this challenge, thus defending his honor and that of the one who sent him (see Matt 10:40–41; John 5:23; 8:49–50). To fail to do so would be shameful.

In what does the author's honor consist? Evidently he presents himself as an intimate associate of "our Lord Jesus Christ." Tradition tells us that he was one of the three people favored to be with Jesus at the theophany we label the transfiguration (Mark 9:2; Matt 17:1; Luke 9:28). But his honor further rests on the portrayal of him as a frequent recipient of revelations and as an eyewitness to special events in the life of Jesus. For example, Peter, along with James and John, are special eyewitnesses not only of the transfiguration, but the raising of Jairus' daughter (Mark 5:37) and the revelation about the final times (Mark 13:3). Jesus declares Peter blessed because "flesh and blood did not reveal it to you, but my Father in heaven" (Matt 16:17). Later Jesus gives Peter special instructions about paying the temple tax (Matt 17:24–27). Along with the revelation of the Risen Lord to the elite circle of the apostles (Matt 28:16–20), tradition records a special Easter revelation to Peter (Luke 24:34; 1 Cor 15:5). Peter, then, is cast in his traditional role as the honored recipient of heavenly revelations. His response in 1:16 that his report of the parousia material is not a cleverly devised myth constitutes a fitting defense of this traditional ascription of honor. To fail to respond here could bring shame upon him and discredit his basic role and status in the transmission of these traditions.

Yet it should be remembered that in the synoptic accounts of Jesus' transfiguration, Peter is portrayed in a less than admirable light. The evangelists comment that when Peter offered to make three booths, "he did not know what he said" (Luke 9:34; see Mark 9:6). And descending from the mountain, Peter and the others did not understand the words of Jesus (Mark 9:10). The present version of those events presents Peter in a more favorable light: he claims to have seen and heard clearly, and he claims to know how to understand the prophetic import of the event (1:20–21).

The Honor of God and Christ

The description of the theophany on the holy mountain contains numerous instances of the language of honor. God is depicted as "the Majestic Glory," a circumlocution for God which emphasizes the divine transcendence and honor; it is not uncommon in biblical literature to refer to God as "Majesty" (Heb 1:3; 8:1) or "Glory" (*1 Enoch* 14:20; 102:3; *T. Levi.* 3:4). We read of "the glory of his voice" (Sir 17:13); the voice of God is powerful, and so it is "full of majesty" (Ps 29:4). God's "majesty" is equated with power (Pss 68:34; 96:6; 111:3; see F. W. Danker, *Benefactor* [St. Louis: Clayton Publishing House, 1982], 466).

God, of course, ascribes honor to Jesus. He bestows on him "honor and glory" and publicly proclaims that "on him I have put my favor." Jesus' honor is made clearer in the actual pronouncement where God articulates Jesus' role and status: "My son, my beloved." The voice from heaven echoes Ps 2:7 and Isa 42:1, texts which have to do with divine commissionings. And indeed, most theophanies in the Scriptures function as commissioning (see R. H. Fuller, *The Formation of the Resurrection Narratives* [New York: Macmillan Co., 1971], 35, 83–84, 140), hence as the ascription of honorable role and status. This theophany, although honoring Jesus in the past, is the basis for his future honor, when he will come "in power" as "the Lord Jesus Christ." At stake, then, is God's honor in designating Jesus as Lord and Jesus' honor in the role and status of the one who will come in power. Thus God's honor is challenged if the honor of his agent is rejected (P. Borgen, "Agency in the Fourth Gospel," *Religions in Antiquity* [J. Neusner, ed.; Leiden: E. J. Brill, 1968], 137–48). As Jesus' agent, Peter is honor bound to defend his patron, which is what he does with vigor.

Theophany to Jesus/ the Transfiguration

The event described in 1:17–18 should be formally identified as a theophany. Like other biblical theophanies it occurs on a mountain (Sinai, Exod 19–20; 34;

Horeb, 1 Kgs 19:8–18); and like them, it functions as a commissioning by God of the person who receives the theophany. The tableau here resembles the narrative in the synoptic gospels which we label the "transfiguration," which is also a theophany of God to Jesus. Like the gospel account of the transfiguration, it includes: (1) a mountain setting (Mark 9:2); (2) Peter and other "eyewitnesses" (Mark 9:2b). (3) Whereas our author speaks of Jesus' "honor and glory," the gospel events speak of his "transfiguration" (Mark 9:2c), his "facing shining like the sun" (Matt 17:2), "his garments glistening, intensely white" (Mark 9:3). Luke 9:32, however, states that they saw his "glory." (4) God appears and his voice proclaims, "This is my beloved son, on him have I placed my favor" (Matt 17:5). 2 Peter does not seem to follow any particular synoptic version, but contains elements found uniquely in each of them.

Yet this version is in many ways different from that found in the synoptic gospels. For example: (1) Peter is presented here alert, not fearful, and understanding of the event, unlike his reaction in Mark 9:6 and 9–10. (2) In addition to the divine word, "This is my son," we find echoes of the baptismal theophany where God commissioned Jesus as "My beloved." (3) God, although never described in the synoptic accounts, is described here as "the Majestic Glory," highlighting the divine honor and transcendence. (4) The meaning and function of the theophany in 1:17–18 appear to be different from that of the synoptic event.

How was the transfiguration understood in the synoptic gospels? What was its function in the narrative? Structurally, it balances the theophany-commissioning at Jesus' baptism; God's appearance at Jesus' baptism authorized his preaching and acts of power (Mark 1:15–8:30), whereas God's theophany at the transfiguration authorizes his way to Jerusalem, his cross and vindication (Mark 8:31–16:8). Yet this version of that event is understood as related to "the powerful coming of our Lord Jesus Christ" (1:16), and so is perceived as a prophecy of his parousia. Yet even here as in the synoptics, God officially commissions Jesus by way of a theophany.

Commentators on the synoptic version of the transfiguration have argued for a link between it and Jesus' future coming in glory to judge. In the early church there was a widespread interpretation of the transfiguration as the fulfillment of a prophecy made by Jesus that "those standing here would not taste death until they saw the kingdom of God come in power" (Mark 9:1). Clement of Alexandria pointed out that Jesus was proclaimed as "the Power" at the transfiguration because it was necessary that the Lord's word be fulfilled which said: " 'There are some of those standing here who will not taste death until they see the Son of Man in glory.' Therefore Peter and James and John saw and fell asleep" (*Excerpta ex Theodoto* 4.2–3; Origen, *Comm. in Matt.* 12.31 [P.G. 13.1052–54]). In recent times, the transfiguration was viewed as a prophecy of the parousia, "a miniature picture of the whole second advent scene" (Boobyer, *St.*

Mark and the Transfiguration Story, 87), a prelude to it (J. Höller, *Die Verklärung Jesu* [Freiburg: Herder, 1937], 172), a foreshadowing of it (J. Moffatt, *The General Epistles* [Garden City, N.Y.: Doubleday, 1928], 187).

We are accustomed to understanding the transfiguration as occurring in the middle of Jesus' ministry. Some commentators argued that it is a misplaced resurrection appearance of Jesus, which occurred at a different time in his career (W. Schmithals, "Der Markusschluss, die Verklärungsgeschichte und die Aussendung der Zwölf," *ZTK* 69 [1972]: 395–97), but this has met with telling criticism (R. H. Stein, "Is the Transfiguration [Mark 9:2–8] a Misplaced Resurrection Account?" 88–89). Yet an ancient document, the *Apocalypse of Peter*, which developed out of a Petrine tradition, described the transfiguration as occurring on the Mount of Olives when the disciples ask Jesus, "What are the signs of thy parousia and of the end of the world?" (v 1). Jesus answers with a pastiche of gospel descriptions of the parousia and the return of the Son of Man (vv 1, 6); his discourse describes the punishment of the wicked (vv 2–14) and the glories of those saved (vv 15–16). Jesus then takes them up a "holy mountain," which is seemingly different from the Mount of Olives where they were standing. Two glorious men, presumably Moses and Elijah, appear and Jesus is himself apparently transfigured. When Peter asks about the "other righteous fathers," Jesus shows him paradise and explains that "honor and glory" await all who will be persecuted for Jesus' sake (v 16). After this vision of the future, God's voice is heard saying, "This is my Son, my beloved, on him have I placed my favor"; after this, God bore away the Lord into heaven" (v 17).

The *Apocalypse of Peter* witnesses to a tradition which located the transfiguration at a different time in Jesus' career and interpreted it as a prediction of his parousia (see A. E. Simms, "Second Peter and the Apocalypse of Peter," *Expositor* 8 [1898]: 460–71; F. Spitta, "Die Petrusapokalypse und der zweite Petrusbrief," *ZNW* 12 [1911]: 237–42; M. R. James, "A New Text of the Apocalypse of Peter," *JTS* 12 [1910–11]: 36–54, 363–83, 573–83). It helps modern readers imagine a scenario similar to that in 1:17–18 for the following reasons: (1) The "transfiguration" in the *Apocalypse of Peter* is Jesus' formal occasion to discourse on theodicy, the reward of the just and the punishment of the wicked. (2) It is the occasion when Jesus prophesies his parousia: "I will come in my glory, shining seven times as bright as the sun will I come in my glory, with all my saints, my angels, when my Father will place a crown on my head, that I may judge the living and the dead and recompense every man according to his works" (v 1). (3) As a theophany it functions as God's ascription to Jesus of a new role and status. This is just the understanding of the transfiguration which satisfies the details of the argument in 1:16–18.

NOTES

CLEVERLY DEVISED MYTHS

"Myth," while it can mean "story" as distinguished from *logos* or argument, often has the polemical connotation of something untrue or unseemly (C. K. Barrett, "Myth and the New Testament. The Greek Word *mythos*," *ExpT* 68 [1957]: 345–48). Rationalist thinkers in the ancient world commonly criticized the stories of fantastic postmortem punishments in the underworld as myths fabricated for moral and social control of naive people (see Epictetus, "Against Epicureans and Academics," 2.20.23; Sextus Empiricus, *Adv. Phy.* 1.53–54; Oenomaeus of Gadara in Eusebius, *Prep. Evan.* 5.21; Lucretius *R.N.* 3.978–1023; Philo, *Det.* 72–73). Diodorus of Sicily sums it up well: "For it is true that the myths (*mythologia*) which are related about Hades, in spite of the fact that their subject-matter is fictitious (*peplasmenēn hypothesin*), contribute greatly to fostering piety (*eusebeian*) and justice (*dikaiosynēn*) among men" (1.2.2).

The negative connotation of myth here is accentuated by its description as something "cleverly concocted" (G. Stählin, "Mythos," *TDNT* 4.789–90). *Sophizō* conveys the sense of deception (*Barn.* 9:4; Josephus, *B.J.* 4.103; 5.452) or lying (Philo, *Mut.* 240), and so indicates that the myths or stories are of human origin for purposes of deception (Plutarch, *Defect.* 431A). It was a typical slander to label stories, both Greek and Jewish, as humanly concocted or fabricated (*plasteō, plastos*):

(1) to invent fables (*mythoplasteō*):
Philo, *Post.* 52; *Gig.* 58; *Fuga* 121

(2) an inventor of fables (*mythoplastēs*):
Philo, *Conf.* 6; *Aet.* 56, 68; Plutarch, *Pyth.* 395C

(3) making of fables (*mythou plasma*):
Philo, *Op.* 1, 2, 157; *Det.* 125; *Cong.* 61; *Abr.* 243; *Mos.* 2.271; *Dec.* 156; *Praem.* 8, 162; *Vit. Cont.* 63

(4) to invent/relate fables (*mythopoiia*):
Philo, *Sac.* 13, 76; *Mut.* 59

The author rejects the real or imagined slander against the prophecy of Jesus' parousia in a form also used by Philo to affirm the truth of Scripture against comparable slanders: not human inventions, but divine oracles:

This is *no* invention of mine [*mythos*]
but a statement made by the most holy oracles [*chrēsmōn*] [*Fuga* 152].
This is *not* a story invented by me [*mythos*],
but an oracle [*chrēmos*] inscribed on the sacred tables
[*Somn.* 1.172; see *Fuga* 121; *Abr.* 243].

Speaking of the Delphi oracles, Plutarch remarked in defense that even if "these matters appear to be myths," there are witnesses to them in events of history (*Pyth.* 398D).

THE POWERFUL COMING

Parousia is the common term in the Hellenistic world which describes the visit of a ruler or the presence of the gods or rulers or prominent persons (1 Cor 16:17; see A. Oepke, "Parousia," *TDNT* 5.859–61). It gradually became the technical term used by Christians for the return of Jesus in glory to judge the living and the dead (Matt 24:3, 27; 1 Thess 2:19) or to raise the dead (1 Thess 4:15; 1 Cor 15:23), a time when rewards and punishments would be meted out (1 John 2:28). Jesus, then, is described as a royal person coming in state (i.e., "power" and "glory"). The affirmation of this in 1:16 is balanced by its questioning by scoffers in 3:4, who mock the "promise of the parousia" because of its delay. The honor of Jesus, then, is at stake, his role as ruler and judge.

EYEWITNESSES

The term *epoptēs* occasionally describes God's all-seeing knowledge of human affairs (2 Macc 3:39; 7:35; 3 Macc 2:21; *1 Clem* 59:3); some inscriptions apply it to rulers such as Pompey and Augustus (M-M, 251). It is also the term for someone initiated into the mysteries, who sees the highest of revelations (Plato, *Phaed.* 250C; Plutarch, *Demet.* 26.1–2). Along with *autoptos*, it can mean not just a spectator (Aeschylus, *Prom.* 298–99), but a supervisor (Josephus, *Ap.* 2.187). The note of authority seems important here, just as it is for composers of history who write of what they have firsthand experience (Polybius 3.4.13, 12.25g.3; see H. J. Cadbury, *Beginnings of Christianity* [Grand Rapids, MI: Baker Book House, 1979], 2.498–500). The author claims authority to speak precisely because of his firsthand knowledge, just as other New Testament writers testify of their records (John 19:35; 21:24; 1 John 1:1–3; see D. E. Nineham, "Eyewitness Testimony and the Gospel Tradition III," 254–64). In fact, Peter defends his remarks with the claim to be an eyewitness, just as Josephus did in regard to his history (*Ap.* 1.53–56). The term, then, resonates in Jewish and Greek ears; it suggests authoritative knowledge of mysteries revealed; it is used here in defense of the author's experience (versus secondhand reporting). It is best interpreted as part of the forensic defense mounted on behalf of the parousia prophecy, as indicated in the exposition above.

VOICE OF GOD

After the destruction of the temple, Jewish traditions tell how God caused a "voice from heaven" (*Bat Kol*) to come forth, a voice which did not add anything to God's revelation so much as to render judgments on specific issues or to indicate a specific role for community members (*J.E.* 2.588–92; Otto Betz,

"Phōnē," *TDNT* 9.288–90). New Testament documents tell of a heavenly voice which ascribes honor and status to Jesus both at his baptism (Mark 1:11) and at the transfiguration (Mark 9:7). John's gospel relates how a voice from heaven proclaimed "glory" as Jesus accepts God's commissioning to the cross (12:28; see *Mart. Poly.* 9.1). While some Jewish traditions indicate that the voice of God was visible (Exod 20:18; Philo, *Migr.* 47), our author clearly indicates that he heard the voice from the Majestic Glory, but does not claim to have seen it or God; on the contrary, he saw the "honor and glory" given Christ.

THE HOLY MOUNTAIN

The gospels report that Jesus frequently went up mountains to reveal his teaching to his disciples: (1) the mount from which he delivered the Great Sermon (Matt 5:1), (2) the Mount of Olives, from which he gave an eschatological discourse (Matt 24:3), and (3) a high mountain in Galilee where he commissioned the disciples (Matt 28:16). Mountains, as we noted above, are the traditional sites of theophanies: Sinai, Horeb, and the mount of the transfiguration (Mark 9:2). The author is surely drawing on the biblical tradition which associates mountains as the typical site of theophanies and revelations, although by identifying this site as "the holy mountain," a specific locus is implied.

BIBLIOGRAPHY

Boobyer, G. H., *St. Mark and the Transfiguration Story* (Edinburgh: T. & T. Clark, 1942).

Hennecke, Edgar, and Schneemelcher, Wilhelm (eds.), "The Apocalypse of Peter," *NT Apoc.* 2.663–83.

Kee, Howard C., "The Transfiguration in Mark: Epiphany or Apocalyptic Vision?" *Understanding the Sacred Text* (John Reumann, ed.; Valley Forge, PA: Judson Press, 1972), 137–52.

Neyrey, Jerome H., "The Apologetic Use of the Transfiguration in 2 Peter 1:16–21," *CBQ* 42 (1980): 504–19.

———, "The Forensic Defense Speech and Paul's Trial Speeches in Acts 22–26: Form and Function," *Luke-Acts: New Perspectives from the Society of Biblical Literature Seminar* (C. H. Talbert, ed.; New York: Crossroad, 1984), 210–24.

Nineham, D. E., "Eyewitness Testimony and the Gospel Tradition III," *JTS* 11 (1960): 254–64.

Stein, R. H., "Is the Transfiguration (Mark 9:2–8) a Misplaced Resurrection Account?" *JBL* 95 (1976): 79–95.

V. Reply to the Second Slander: Prophecy and Interpretation Defended (1:19–21)

♦

1 19. And we have a very certain prophetic word, to which you do
well to attend, as to a light shining in darkness until the day dawns
and the morning star rises in your hearts. 20. But first know that
no prophetic writing is a matter of personal interpretation,
21. because prophecy is not borne by the will of mortals; but
carried by the Holy Spirit, mortals spoke from God.

The Prophetic Word

This verse has long been a *crux interpretum* for commentators on 2 Peter. Some have argued that it refers to OT prophecies (C. Bigg, A *Critical and Exegetical Commentary on the Epistles of St. Peter and St. Jude* [Edinburgh: T. & T. Clark, 1902], 267; Joseph B. Mayor, *The Epistles of St. Jude and the Second Epistle of St. Peter* [New York: Macmillan and Company, 1907], 108; R. Knopf, *Die Briefe Petri und Judä* [MeyerK 12. 7th ed.: Göttingen: Vandenhoeck and Ruprecht, 1912], 218–82) or to NT prophecies of the parousia, such as Mark 13:26 and 1 Thess 5:2 (E. H. Plumptre, *The General Epistles of St. Peter and St. Jude* [Cambridge: Cambridge University Press, 1926], 174; Curran, "The Teaching of 2 Peter i:20," 349). Equally debated is the meaning of *bebaioteron;* for some it means that the parousia prophecy is a *surer* prophecy *than* the transfiguration (Bigg, 268) or that the OT prophecies are now *surer* after the transfiguration, either because we comprehend now what was meant by the predicted glory of Jesus (J. Chaine, *Les Epîtres catholique: La seconde Epître de saint Pierre, les Epîtres de saint Jean, l'Epître de saint Jude* [EBib. 2d ed. Paris: Gabalda, 1939], 54) or because we have some surety of its fulfillment (K. H. Schelkle, *Die Petrusbriefe, der Judasbrief* [HTKNT 13/2: Freiburg: Herder, 1961], 200).

If 1:19 refers to OT prophecies, is the reference vague and generic, or does the letter indicate what those prophecies are? The author cites examples of God's judgment in 2:4–8 and concludes to the principle that God rewards the just and punishes the wicked (2:9–10). Yet the biblical examples of theodicy there do not seem to be prophecies of the parousia. God's word, by which the world was created from water, is likewise the word whereby the world will be judged by fire (3:7). This functions as a generic statement of "word" and theodicy, and it could account for the content of the "prophetic word" in 1:19. The remarks about the thief in the night and the dissolving of the world in fire (3:10–11) are prophetic of God's day of judgment, although they are not strictly labeled as prophecies there. Paul's letters, which the scoffers misconstrue, tell the truth about Jesus' parousia and God's judgment (3:15–16). All of these statements in one way or another function as the contents of the generic prophecy of the parousia of Jesus and the day of God's judgment.

But what is meant in 1:19 by the "prophetic word" and how is it "very certain"? Peter began to fulfill his stated aim to leave a clear reminder by claiming to have firsthand experience of the prophecy of "the powerful coming of Jesus" (1:16). This experience rests on being an eyewitness to the transfiguration event, which he understands as a prophecy of Christ's return in glory and power to judge the living and the dead (1:17–18). This, at least, is an unmistakable prophecy, one which is found in the gospel traditions about Jesus, and so can be considered "a writing," or Scripture. And it is located here in the argument; it is not a hypothetical prophecy.

A Confirmed Prophetic Word (bebaioteron)

What confirms a prophecy? What is the force of *bebaios?* In regard to legal matters, *bebaios* may refer to matters with guaranteed security (M-M, 107–8). In philosophy, an argument (*logos*) might be "firm, sure, well-grounded" (H. Schlier, "Bebaios," *TDNT* 1.601); it is the task of philosophy to establish principles (Epictetus 2.11.24). In Philo's epistemological scheme we find extensive use of *a-bebaios* in contexts which shed light on our inquiry. Sense knowledge is *unstable* (*abebaios*; *Op*. 156; *Abr*. 84, 269; *Jos*. 130, 142). Philo considers myths as *baseless* guesswork (*Sac*. 13); certain hopes are *ungrounded* (*Gig*. 39; *Flac*. 109), as are certain *unfounded* conjectures (*Conf*. 140, 159); mere human judgments are *unstable* (*Virt*. 56). What is only heard is *abebaios*, but what is seen is *bebaios* (*Post*. 13); hearsay gives no sure ground for belief (*Ebr*. 188). For the certitude of sight must be held better than the deceitfulness of hearing (*Conf*. 140; *Abr*. 60; see also Herodotus 1.8 and Polybius 12.27.1).

But what specifically confirms a prophecy? Philo indicates that prophecies are confirmed in two ways. As noted above, prophecies have eyewitnesses to them which prove them to be authentic (*Det*. 124; *Migr*. 139; *Heres* 4; *Sp. Leg*. 1.273, 341; 4.32). No testimony is so certain as personal experience (*Ebr*. 97–98; *Cong*. 73; *Mos*. 2.280). Prophecies which have God as witness are the most confirmed of all (*Migr*. 115; *Somn*. 2.22).

In comparison with Philo's use of *bebaios*, we suggest that Peter evaluates "the prophetic word" as "very confirmed" because: (1) God, who is infallible, is the author of the prophecy (vv 17–18), and (2) the prophecy enjoys eyewitnesses who have visual experience of it (v 16). It is, then, well grounded; it certainly is not conjecture or myth.

Structure of Hellenistic Prophecy

D. E. Aune (*Prophecy in Early Christianity*, 23–48) provides an important framework for understanding the structure of popular prophecy. Ordinarily oracles were delivered at a sacred shrine by a person recognized as a *mantis*. While the oracle on occasion was delivered directly to those petitioning it, customarily intermediaries were used, whose title was "prophet" (*prophētēs* or *theopropos*). This intermediary might interpret in some way the vague utterance of the *mantis*, put it into poetry, or simply record it. It was assumed and never questioned that the *mantis* was "possessed" by the revealing Deity (W. D. Smith, "So-called Possession in Pre-Christian Greece," *TAPA* 96 [1965]: 403–36), so that all utterances were authentic words from the Deity (Dio Chrysostom, *Disc*. 1.57). Yet there is a body of evidence that the *mantis* did not always speak clearly; Plutarch remarks that the *mantis* at Delphi "obstructed the understanding of these [oracles] in their true meaning and combined vagueness and obscurity with the communication" (*Pyth*. 407A). In one of Lucian's satires, a character criticizes Apollo, "In your oracles you are ambiguous and riddling and you unconcernedly toss most of them into the debatable ground so that your hearers need another Apollo to interpret them" (*Jup. Trag*. 28). The *mantis*, moreover, was often said to "understand nothing" when possessed (Philo, *Mos*. 1.283). Therefore, the source may be the Deity, and thus true, but the *mantis* may not be the best of channels (Plutarch, *Pyth.* 397A). Hence, the *prophētēs* or intermediary or interpreter was often a necessary figure (Plato, *Tim.* 71E–72B). Thus two figures regularly occur in the transmission of oracles: a source (*mantis*) and an interpreter (*prophētēs*). The author of 2 Peter has already positioned himself as the source or *mantis* when he claimed to be an eyewitness to the oracle about Jesus' parousia (1:16–18). Now he claims to function as well as a valid intermediary and interpreter of that oracle.

In his typology of oracular persons, Aune distinguishes oracular figures attached to fixed civic or national shrines from "free" prophets (*Prophecy in Early Christianity*, 35–46). 2 Peter is clearly not an attached prophet, but a "free" one. Aune further distinguishes the latter into four categories: (a) technical diviner, (b) inspired diviner, (c) collector and interpreter of oracles, and (d) magical diviner. The technical diviner was a religious adept who professed the ability to deal with the ambiguity of oracular signs and symbols such as dreams; such a person was steeped in the lore of divination. The inspired diviner was the ecstatic and spontaneous vehicle of divine utterances. The collector and interpreter of oracles (*chrēsmologos*) offered appropriate oracles from his collection (Herodotus 7.6). This controversial figure was often berated for pronouncing oracles without specification about time of fulfillment. The last type dealt with revelatory magic. "Peter" in the New Testament is the frequent recipient of revelations from Jesus; in 1:16–18 he is best understood as an "inspired diviner." Yet in 1:20–21, appeal is made to "prophetic *writing*" (*graphēs*); and according to 3:1–2 and 15–16 other prophetic writings are cited. Hence, the author might well be understood as a "collector and interpreter of oracles," a *chrēsmologos*. This comparison with common Hellenistic understandings of oracles and prophets indicates one more instance of the author's attempt to express himself in multicultural terms.

INDIVIDUALISM AND PERSONAL INTERPRETATION

Implied in the argument in 1:19–21 is the value put in the ancient Mediterranean culture on being a group-oriented person rather than an individualist. This general social science scenario necessary for interpreting the cultural world of the NT was sketched in the general introduction. Here we can see its importance. Among others, Plutarch comments on the phenomenon of "tribes of wandering soothsayers and rogues" who made up oracles and pandered to the crowds (*Pyth.* 407C). Such unattached people acted independently of any shrine or fixed tradition; they acted on their own and for their own benefit. Paul, on the other hand, commends prophecy because it serves the group and builds it up (1 Cor 14:3, 5, 12, 26). Speakers in tongues are idiosyncratic, building up only themselves (14:4), and thus not fitting into the ideal of a group-oriented person. Thus one cultural factor in the giving and understanding of prophecy was the way in which it functioned in the building up of the life of the group. Prophecies about the parousia and God's judgment lead to holiness, and so benefit the group. Not so "promises of freedom" (2:19).

But more is implied here that concerns a group-oriented person. The *mantis* and the interpreter both act as clients of the revealing Deity. They do not act on their own, but as agents of the revealer. Philo makes this quite clear: "For no pronouncement of a prophet is ever his own; he is an interpreter prompted by another in all his utterances, when knowing not what he does he is filled with inspiration, as the reason withdraws and surrenders the citadel of the soul to a new visitor and tenant, the Divine Spirit which plays upon the vocal organism and dictates words which clearly express its prophetic message" (*Sp. Leg.* 4.49). He contrasts this with the self-generated and self-serving prophet. Philo's treatment of Balaam illustrates this principle. That prophet was hired by Balak to act for the king's private purposes in cursing Israel; but Balaam "said nothing which was his own, but the divinely inspired version of the prompting of another" (*Mos.* 1.286). Explaining his failure to act idiosyncratically, Balaam told the king: "I say nothing that is my own, but only what is prompted by God" (*Mos.* 1.281).

The issue in 1:20–21, however, is not the source of prophecy but its interpretation. The claim is made that the author's interpretation is correct (i.e., "inspired"), but no rationale is given. Yet the understanding of tradition for a group-oriented culture can illuminate how a correct interpretation can be known. The author appeals to traditions about both God's judgment and Jesus' parousia. He appeals to this tradition in regard to the prophecies being disputed when he "reminds you of the predictions by the holy prophets and the command of the Lord through your apostles" (3:2). Even Paul supports these (3:15–16). Thus his interpretation of the prophecies can be measured according to group norms; his version is truly in accord with what has been proclaimed *semper, ab omnibus, ubique,* always, by all, and everywhere. It accords, moreover, with Scripture as alluded to in 2:4–9 and 3:5–7 and with dominical traditions (3:10–12). Although some oracle-mongers tailored their materials to leave out threatening prophecies (Thucydides 2.8.2; 2.21.3; 8.1.1), Paul criticizes those who say "Peace and security" (1 Thess 5:2). Hence, if distortion took place in the selection and presentation of oracles, it tended to be in the omission of disturbing material, which is not the case with 2 Peter. Thus the claim is made to know the collective wisdom of the group and to adhere to it. The author's interpretation is *not* self-serving or idiosyncratic.

NOTES

VERY CERTAIN

The grammatical form *bebaioteros* is the comparative degree of the adjective, but it is not uncommon for such comparatives to be read as superlatives. Hence, it is translated here as "very certain" (BDF # 60, 16; see 1 Cor 13:13 and Matt 8:12; E. Goetchius, *The Language of the New Testament* [New York: Scribner's, 1965], 212–13). Scoffers dismiss the "promise of his coming" (3:4), judging it an unconfirmed or groundless prophecy. In defense, the author acclaims it "very certain."

THE DAY

Because this document defends the day of God's judgment, the reference to "day dawning" in 1:19 probably should be linked with "day of judgment" (2:9; 3:7), "day of the Lord" (3:10), and "day of God" (3:12). But the usage here is basically metaphorical: disciples guide themselves by a lesser light (a lamp) at night, until the full light of day (the sun) arises. The lamp is the prophecy of the Lord's parousia and God's day of judgment, which guides us during a time of darkness (see Matt 25:1–13). But we wait for its fulfillment, when a lamp will no longer be needed, for we will see clearly then. This also implies that true believers are people of the light, people of the day (1 Thess 5:5, 8).

MORNING STAR (PHŌSPHOROS)

The word for the morning star is the Greek term *Phōsphoros* or "Light-Bringer" (Aristophanes, *Ra.* 342; Plutarch, *Defectu.* 430A; *Exilio* 601A). Astrology was an extremely important part of the lives of most people in antiquity. The movement of the heavens told time for them: when day began or ended, when to plant or harvest, etc. And the stars were identified with heavenly persons who exercised influence on the earth, either for good (Rev 1:20) or evil (see "moonstruck" in Matt 4:24; 17:15 and "Wormwood" in Rev 8:11). Thus a certain star might exercise power over mortals on earth, as is the case of Jesus *Phōsphoros* in Rev 22:16. Yet this star serves another function, one which is fully in keeping with its name as "Light-Bringer." Cicero's remarks are useful here: "Lowest of the five planets and nearest to the earth is the star of Venus, called in Greek *Phōsphoros* and in Latin Lucifer when it precedes the sun" (*Nat. Deor.* 2.20.53). The context of its mention in 1:19 has to do with our looking to prophecies about the arrival of Jesus, the Morning Star, as one uses a lamp for illumination in darkness. Thus Jesus is truly Lucifer and *Phōsphoros*, i.e., "Light-Bringer." This thoroughly Greek casting of the image makes less likely an allusion to the star of Jacob in Num 24:17; this popular star was interpreted as heralding an anointed king (*T. Levi* 18:3; *T. Judah* 24:1; CD 7:18–20). The "Day Star" in Isa 14:12 is the king of Babylon whose destruction the prophet heralds; although this is a Semitic instance of "Light-Bringer," it hardly influences the positive presentation of Jesus as the authentic Light-Bringer. In Rev 22:16 the arriving Lord Jesus is called *Phōsphoros* and is connected with David, so both meanings can be linked. However, the usage here is decidedly Greek and capitalizes on the image of "Light-Bringer," not Jewish messianic ruler. The use here is surely metaphorical. Until the true light ("day" and "morning star") come to fulfill the prophecy of the parousia, believers must cling to the prophecy itself as a lamp shining in the dark night of waiting in faith (see Mayor, 109–11). The fulfillment of God's prophecy of salvation is compared to "day dawning from on high" (Luke 1:78–79; see Eph 5:14).

INTERPRETATION

The Greek term *epilysis* derives from the verb *epilyō*, which suggests that riddles are solved (Josephus, *Ant.* 8.167) or ambiguities resolved (Philo, *Agr.* 16) or sophistries exposed (Sextus, *Adv. Pyrrh.* 2.246) or hidden meanings revealed (Mark 4:34). *Epilysis* basically means explanation or interpretation (Vettius Valens 221.9; 330.10; Gen 40:8 Aquila; Clement, *Paed.* 2.1.14). Later the author admits that Paul's writings are "hard to understand" (3:16) and require careful interpretation. And in both of his letters, he himself is giving them a "correct understanding" of the words of the prophets (3:1). Hence, in 1:20 he indicates the need for correct or traditional interpretation of obscure prophetic materials, claiming that capability while denying it to his adversaries.

BIBLIOGRAPHY

Aune, David E., *Prophecy in Early Christianity and the Ancient Mediterranean World* (Grand Rapids, MI: W. B. Eerdmans, 1983).

Baasland, E., "2 Peters brev og urkristelig profeti. Eksegese av 2, Pet. 1,12–21," *Tidsskrift for Teologi og Kirke* 53 (1982): 19–35.

Böhmer, J., "Tag und Morgenstern? Zu II Petr i 19," *ZNW* 22 (1923): 228–33.

Cox, S., "From Starlight to Sunlight: 2 Peter i. 16–20," *The Expositor* 1/1 (1875): 169–85.

Curran, J. T., "The Teaching of 2 Peter i.20," *TS* 4 (1943): 347–68.

Dautzenberg, Gerhard, *Urchristliche Prophetie: Ihre Erforschung, ihre Voraussetzung im Judentum and ihre Struktur im ersten Korintherbrief* (Stuttgart: Kohlhammer, 1975), 118–21, 290–91.

Durand, A., "Le Sens de IIa Petri, I.20," *RSR* 2 (1911): 187–89.

Hiebert, D. E., "Selected Studies from 2 Peter. Part 2: The Prophetic Foundation for the Christian Life: An Exposition of 2 Peter 1:19–21," *BSac* 141 (1984): 158–68.

Lonning, I., "Tradisjon og skrift. Eksegese av 2 Petr 1,19–21," *NorTT* 72 (1971): 129–54.

Louw, J., "Wat Wordt in II Petrus 1:20 Gesteldt?" *NedTTs* 19 (1965): 202–12.

Molland, E., "La thèse 'La prophétie n'est jamais venue de la volonté de l'homme' (2 Pierre I,21) et les Pseudo-Clémentines," *Opuscula Patristica* (Oslo: Universitetsforlaget, 1970 = *ST* 9 [1955]): 67–85.

Neyrey, J. H., "The Apologetic Use of the Transfiguration in 2 Peter 1:16–21," *CBQ* 42 (1980): 504–19.

Sibinga, J. Smit, "Une citation du Cantique dans la Secunda Petri," *RB* 73 (1966): 107–18.

VI.
The Third Slander: The Master Denied (2:1–3a)

♦

2 1. But there appeared false prophets among the people, even as among you there will be false teachers. They will introduce ruinous doctrines, denying the Master who purchased them and bringing upon themselves a rapid ruin. 2. And many will follow their debauchery; because of them "the way of truth" will be dishonored; 3a. and in their greed they will buy you with specious arguments.

Form Criticism

We recall from 1:12–15 that the author of this document formally presents himself as writing a testament or farewell address. Typically the dying patriarch predicts future hard times for his descendants, often their lapse from the clan's religious traditions. Here Peter predicts deviant teachers leading the faithful astray, a prediction proved true in 3:3–4. In terms of literary criticism, 2:1–3a serves as the topic sentence for the subsequent polemic against the author's opponents; it presents and rebuts basic elements of their doctrine while reaffirming the tradition of God's just judgment, which they denied.

As a topic statement, 2:1–3a contains most of the important elements which will subsequently be treated in the remainder of the document. It contains references to:

(1) false teachers (see 2:15, 19; 3:3–4, 15–17)

(2) denial of authority and judgment (see 2:10–11, 20; 3:4, 9)

(3) polemical accusation that bad theology leads to bad morals (see 2:13–14, 18, 20–22)

(4) immediate judgment affirmed (see 2:4–10, 12, 16, 17; 3:5–7, 8, 10)

(5) ruin affirmed (see 3:7, 16)

The author previously affirmed "promises" of God's rewards and confirmed predictions of the parousia with its just judgment (1:16–17). That affirmation and its restatement in 3:1–13 are the formal response to the challenge of the false teachers who deny the parousia and divine retribution. The opponents in 3:4 explicitly deny the ruin and destruction of the world in the scenario of God's judgment. In response the author articulates the traditional doctrine of theodicy, a quid-pro-quo judgment against them: for introducing *ruinous* doctrines, they bring *ruin* upon themselves, a *ruin* which does not sleep.

Moreover, just as his opponents accused Peter of fabricating doctrines of judgment for control of the church (1:16), he returns the compliment by labeling their teaching a fabrication (*plastois logois*, 2:3). His teaching is a benefaction which benefits the church, whereas theirs is done out of greed. His leads to purity and godliness, theirs to debauchery. A certain dualistic perception serves to distinguish the rival teachers, creating a world of truth and goodness which contrasts with one of deceit and debauchery.

Redaction: Relationship to Jude

Redaction-critical comparison of 2 Peter and Jude indicates a close relationship between 2 Pet 2:1–3a and Jude 4:

2 Peter 2:1–3a	*Jude 4*
1. But there appeared false prophets among the people, even as among you there will be false teachers. They will introduce ruinous doctrines, *denying the Master* who purchased them and bringing upon themselves a rapid ruin.	For certain men have crept in, who ages ago were proscribed for judgment. Godless men, they turn away from God's favor to debauchery and *deny* our only *Master* and Lord Jesus Christ.
2. And many will follow their debauchery; because of them "the way of truth" will be dishonored . . .	

The author directly borrows the phrase "they . . . deny our only Master" from Jude, but uses it differently. For him it summarizes their denial of theodicy and rejection of divine judgment. Whereas Jude spoke about these men as "ages ago . . . proscribed for judgment," 2 Peter changes that to emphasize their imminent ruin, a proof of divine judgment. This seems to be his riposte to their scoffing at the "delay" of judgment (3:9) and their proclamation of freedom from judgment (2:3, 19). Both Jude and Peter accuse them of "debauchery," but in different senses. Jude notes the ingratitude of God's clients who swap holy favor (*charita*) for unclean vice, whereas 2 Peter indicates how the false doctrine of his opponents becomes a moral poison to some and leads to their shaming of their heavenly Patron. 2 Peter, who seems to have specific opponents in view, is decidedly more precise about describing them as "false teachers" and associating them with "false prophets" who proclaimed "peace and security" rather than God's imminent judgment. Thus the redactional changes serve the author's riposte to his opponents by making quite specific their ideological error and its deleterious effect on church members.

Deny the Master

This is probably not a total denial of allegiance to Christ so much as a rejection of certain aspects of that relationship. In the Bible we read of many practical, not theoretical, denials of God. In the psalms, denials of God are linked with rejection of divine retribution and punishment. The problem in Ps 9 LXX lies in the embarrassing absence of divine judgment on sinners; the psalmist records the wicked saying:

ouk ekzētēsei
ouk estin ho theos enōpion autou [9:25 LXX].
He [God] will not require.
There is no God before him.

The Vulgate captured the psalm perfectly by translating it:

Ait impius in superbia mentis:
"Non vindicabit! Non est Deus"
The wicked says in his proud heart:
"[God] will not requite! There is no God!"

That is, the wicked man denies that God requites or judges, and so when he claims "There is no God," he speaks as a practical atheist who basically denies

God's providence or judgment. The Jewish midrash on this psalm likewise interprets these verses as a denial of divine judgment: "There is no judgment and there is no Judge. The Only One, blessed be He, has gone away and sits in heaven" (*Midr. Psalms* 10.6). Thus a certain stream of atheism is tied to denial of divine judgment.

Ps 9 LXX records numerous denials of divine judgment by the foolish sinner: "He will not require" (9:25); "I shall not be moved" (v 27); "God has forgotten" (v 32); "He has turned away his face so as never to look" (v 32); "He will not require it" (v 34). Similarly Ps 13:1 LXX begins with a denial of God, which is followed by a list of corrupt deeds for which the sinner does not expect recompense. Twice the psalmist accuses the sinner of "not fearing God": "There is no fear of God before their eyes" (10:3 LXX) . . . "there is no fear" (10:5). Denial of God, then, means rejection of divine judgment and pursuit of wickedness without fear.

The reader is reminded of the argument in the introduction to 2 Peter, where Epicurean denials of divine judgment were described. It was also noted there that such denials were common among Greeks and Jews, as the materials from the psalms just described testify. Although in that introduction it was stated that denial of divine judgment was a common argument which contained three related elements (no judge, no afterlife, no postmortem retribution), only one of those elements is found in 2:1–3a, the denial of a judge. But as Pss 9, 10, and 13 LXX indicate, when people "denied God," they also denied God's future judgment. Thus "denial of the Lord" may be understood as a cryptic remark which implies a fuller denial of theodicy.

HONOR AND SHAME

How honorable are the author's God and his Lord Jesus Christ. While the author acknowledges this honor, he bristles because others do not give God and Christ their due respect. They shame Christ by denying him judgmental authority, as traditionally predicted in prophecies of the parousia. They shame him in particular because such honor and respect are his right, especially since he has acted as benefactor to them by "purchasing them" from sin and slavery. They shame him, moreover, because their teaching brings "the way of truth," that is, the "way of Jesus," into disrepute for immorality. The Greek word *blasthēmēthēsetai* is best understood here in terms of dishonor and loss of reputation (see Isa 52:5). Indeed, Paul and later authors are greatly concerned with the reputation of the community, and so urge conformity to accepted moral behavior, lest church members dishonor the gospel and its Lord (1 Cor 14:23; 1 Tim 6:1; Titus 2:5; 1 Clem 47:7).

The denial of the Master who purchased them constitutes a serious honor challenge to which the author, because he is the Lord's deputized agent, must respond. Failure to answer the challenge would likewise mean dishonor. The full response to this dishonor follows in 2:4–10 and elsewhere, but here it is sufficient for the author to affirm what the challengers deny. Their denial of the Lord's just judgment is affirmed by him; their comeuppance is assuredly near. Honor denied is thus defended.

NOTES

FALSE PROPHETS/FALSE TEACHERS

By paralleling contemporary false teachers with the false prophets of old, the author evokes the biblical tradition about them. Jeremiah's description of false prophets contained three elements: (1) their message was contrary to his own; they cried "Peace, peace!" and "No evil shall come upon you" (Jer 4:10; 6:14; 14:13; 23:17; 27:9, 16ff.; see 1 Thess 5:3); (2) only true prophets were authorized by God; false prophets have no such ascribed authority; (3) when false prophets are accused, Jeremiah often conducts a lawsuit against them (*rib*), charging them with evil and decreeing their punishment. False prophets, then, speak on their own authority, preach freedom from fear and judgment, but are condemned by God. Peter accuses the false teachers of his group with fabricating false doctrine on their own; one of their themes was the "denial of the Master," namely, his judgment. And he prosecutes them and proclaims their punishment.

INTRODUCE (PAREISAXOUSIN)

The term can be used neutrally, as in the case of "suggesting" a successor (Plutarch, *Galba* 21.1) or "representing" someone (Philo, *Sac.* 94) or "proposing" a doctrine (Polybius 6.56.12). But it often conveys the sense of something done secretly and maliciously. Socrates, for example, was tried "for introducing foreign deities" (Plutarch, *Alex. Magn. Fort.* 328D); Polybius uses it to describe supplies secretly slipped into a city (1.18.3) or betrayal (2.7.8); Orpheus was said to introduce fantastic ideas (Diodorus of Sicily 1.96.5). In later Christian writings, it describes heresy being spread (Eusebius, *H.E.* 4.22.5). The usage in 2 Peter is comparable to the labeling of deviant doctrines elsewhere in the New Testament, i.e., the "leaven" of the Pharisees (Matt 16:6, 12) or the "gangrenous" bad talk of some (2 Tim 2:17). Hence, the new doctrine of these false teachers is a "pollution." By labeling it as such, the author can evoke an attitude of intolerance toward his opponents. For the classification of deviant doctrine as a pollution ensures its negative reception as well as a hostile reaction toward its proponents.

RUINOUS DOCTRINES

Literally the author accuses his opponents of a "doctrine of destruction." They are *not* proclaiming either the destruction of the world (see 3:4) or God's judgment (see 3:9); in fact, they promise freedom from all such (2:19). Rather, this reflects the author's ironic verdict on their teaching: it leads to destruction, even as it leads to corruption. Although the term "doctrine" (*heiresis*) comes to mean "heresy," the Greek word refers to a school of thought or party allegiance for Jews and Greeks alike (see Josephus, *B.J.* 2.118; *Ant.* 13.171; *Life* 12; Acts 5:17; 15:5; 26:5).

MASTER

"Master" (*despotēs*) typically refers either to the head of the household, who has absolute rights over his family and slaves (2 Tim 2:21; Titus 2:9; 1 Peter 2:18) or to a ruler with sovereign power, such as the Roman emperors. It was used of Greek deities and the Hebrew God, especially in terms of God's absolute sovereignty and omnipotence (Josh 5:14; Wis 6:7; Job 5:8). Both the Greek Xenophon and the Jew Josephus remark on the reservation of the term "master" for the Deity: "To no human creature do you pay homage as master [*despotēn*], but to the gods alone" (*An.* 3.2.13; see Josephus, *B.J.* 7.418–19). Occasionally in the LXX God is called "Master" (*despotēs;* Gen 15:2; Isa 1:24; Jer 4:10), which usage can be found in Luke 2:29; Acts 4:24, and Rev 6:10.

Inasmuch as Jesus is said to be the "Master who purchased them," the image here is of a head of the household and his slaves. Slaves, whether under the authority of their masters or manumitted by them, nevertheless owe them honor: "Let all who are under the yoke of slavery regard their masters as worthy of all honor" (1 Tim 6:1). Thus Jesus will be shamed if the slaves of his household do not honor and obey him. This reference to Jesus' buying them is the only mention of his saving death in the document, but it echoes a traditional formula (see 1 Cor 6:20; 7:23; Rev 5:9; 14:3–4). The remark here is striking in that Jesus is beginning to be acclaimed by a term reserved for the most powerful earthly and heavenly rulers (K. Rengstorf, "Despotēs," *TDNT* 2.44–47). A fuller exposition of the Hellenistic and Jewish background of the term "master" can be found in the notes to Jude 4, where a similar phrase is recorded.

PURCHASED THEM (AGORASANTA)

New Testament writers, especially Paul, speak of Christ purchasing the freedom of his disciples, often at the price of his blood (1 Cor 6:20; 7:23; 1 Peter 1:18–19; Rev 5:9; 14:3–4; see I. H. Marshall, "The Development of the Concept of Redemption in the New Testament," *Reconciliation and Hope* [R. Banks, ed.; Grand Rapids, MI: W. B. Eerdmans, 1974], 154–60). This reflects a distinctively Hellenistic practice of sacral manumission of slaves; A. Deissman (*Light from the Ancient East* [Grand Rapids, MI: Baker Book House, 1965], 322) cites a typical formula for this: "N.N. sold to the Pythian Apollo a male slave named X.Y. at a price ___ minae, for freedom." By purchasing their freedom, Jesus assumed the role of Patron, to whom his clients owed an eternal indebtedness, so that failure to remember this and repay loyalty and honor to the Patron would mean shameful behavior on the part of the clients. Disciples were purchased from slavery to an evil taskmaster (Sin or Death), so as to become the slaves of Jesus (Rom 6:17–18; see Dale Martin, *Slavery as Salvation* [New Haven: Yale University Press, 1990], 62–63, and *Sif. Num.* 115). "Denying" the Lord who "purchased" them, then, betokens shameful behavior.

DEBAUCHERY, GREED

Polemics in the ancient world, like most other forms of speech, were quite stereotypical. Hence, accusations of the sort made in 2:1–3a need to be seen less as actual statements of what the author's opponents did or said than as projections of what their errors lead to. Given the strong purity concerns of ancient Jews and Christians, one of the worst polemical charges made was the accusation that bad theology leads to bad morals, in particular sexual immorality. Illustrative is Paul's triple charge that sinners invariably lapsed into sexual uncleanness (Rom 1:25, 26–27, 28). Debauchery remained one of the capital sins (see Mark 7:22; Rom 13:13; Gal 5:19; Eph 4:19; 1 Peter 4:3), certainly a favorite accusation with which Peter chastens his opponents (see 2:7, 10, 13, 18). Similarly, since love of money was the root of all evil (1 Tim 6:10), opponents could be pilloried by accusing them of acting out of greed. The commonplace description of an unconverted pagan in Eph 4:19 links greed with licentiousness: "they have given themselves up to licentiousness, greedy to practice every find of uncleanness."

WAY OF TRUTH

The disciples of Jesus not only followed his way, the way of the Cross, but came to be known as "the Way" (Acts 9:2; 19:19, 23; 22:4; 24:14, 24). This builds on the Jewish tradition of walking in the way of the Lord, that is, following the halakah of the tradition (*hlk* = to walk; see W. Michaelis, "Hodos," *TDNT* 5.50–64). Paul describes discipleship as "walking" (Gal 5:16; Rom 6:4; 13:13; 14:15; Phil 3:17; 1 Thess 2:12), and thus implies that disciples walk in a certain way. Accordingly, two ways were often contrasted, the way of truth and the way of falsehood (*Barn.* 18–20; *Did.* 1–5; *1 Clem* 35:5; 1QS 3:13–4:26). Peter is particularly fond of this term, for he regularly speaks of the authentic tradition as "the straight way" (2:15) or "the way of righteousness" (2:21), in contrast to "the way of Balaam," which is greed (2:15) or the "way of the false teachers," which leads to debauchery (2:2). Here the authentic way of Jesus could not mean denial of the Master's law and his just judgment; for the way of truth means a pure moral life filled with all virtue (see 1:4–7).

DISHONORED (BLASPHĒMĒTHĒSETAI)

The term *blasphēmein* is best understood here in terms of shame or dishonor. Paul remarks that sinners "dishonor [*atimazeis*] God by breaking the law" (Rom 2:23). He then cites Isa 52:5 apropos of this: "For as it is written, 'The name of God is blasphemed [*blasphēmeitai*] among the Gentiles because of you' " (Rom 2:24; Hermas, *Sim*. 6.2.3). Thus "blaspheme" is linked with "dishonor." 2 Peter expresses the same sense of dishonor in two ways. First the heavenly Patron is dishonored by denial of his authority, but he is also dishonored by the shameful actions of his clients in the church. The author reflects a very common concern among the early churches for their honor or good name (1 Thess 4:12; 1 Cor 14:23) and their fear that it will be dishonored (1 Tim 6:1; Titus 2:5; Ignatius, *Trall*. 8:2; *1 Clem* 47:7; Polycarp, *Phil*. 10:2–3).

SPECIOUS ARGUMENTS (PLASTOIS LOGOIS)

Although the term *plastos* can mean something molded, like a statue (Philo, *Leg. All*. 2.54–55), it connotes the sense of something fictitious and deceitful. Either as "feigning" something (Euripides, *Bacch*. 218), or "appearing" to be someone (Sophocles, *Oed. Tyr*. 780) or "making pretense" of something (Herodotus 1.68), this term can be used to describe forgeries (Josephus, *Vita* 177, 337) and deception (Philo, *Somn*. 2.140). In this context it contains a note of shame, for it functions as the riposte to the challenge of the opponents in 1:16. They challenged the author with concocting the story of Jesus' parousia (*sesophismenois mythois*), thus attempting to shame him; but in his response, he accuses them of the same thing (*plastois logois*) and thus defends his honor while shaming them. There is also a note of "uncleanness" here, for their doctrines are perceived as a pollution by the author, yet the evil is disguised as good. They "promise freedom" (2:19), which appears to be a good thing, but in truth they are "slaves of corruption." And those seduced by their polluting doctrine become entangled again in the defilements of the world (2:20). Thus he unmasks hidden corruption, even as he defends his honor.

BIBLIOGRAPHY

Barrett, C. K., "*Pseudapostoloi* (2 Cor 11,13)," *Mélanges Bibliques en hommage au R. P. Béda Rigaux* (A.-L. Descamps and A. de Halleux, eds.; Gembloux: J. Duculot, 1970), 377–96.

Cavallin, H. C. C., "The False Teachers of 2 Peter as Pseudo-Prophets," *NovT* 21 (1979): 263–70.

Chang, A. D., "Second Peter 2:1 and the Extent of the Atonement," *BSac* 142 (1985): 52–63.

Hiebert, D. E., "Selected Studies from 2 Peter. Part 3: A Portrayal of False Teachers: An Exposition of 2 Peter 2:1–3," *BSac* 141 (1984): 255–65.
Karris, R. J., "The Background and Significance of the Polemic of the Pastoral Epistles," *JBL* 92 (1973): 549–64.
Neyrey, J. H., *The Form and Background of the Polemic in 2 Peter* (Unpublished dissertation: Yale University, 1977), 27–30, 33–42.

VII.
Reply to the Third Slander: Divine Judgment Defended (2:3b–10a)

♦

2 3b. Upon them judgment has not long been idle, nor does their
ruin sleep. 4. For if God did not spare the angels who sinned,
but handed them over, casting them into Tartarus in chains of
darkness to keep them for judgment, 5. and if God did not spare
the ancient world, but guarded Noah, herald of righteousness,
and seven others while bringing a deluge upon the world of the
impious, 6. and if God condemned and reduced to ashes the
cities of Sodom and Gomorrah, setting a warning for future
impious people, 7. but rescued the righteous Lot, worn down
by their lawless and licentious behavior 8. (for day after day that
righteous man lived among them, in sight and sound tortured in
his just soul by their lawlessness), 9. then the Lord knows how
to rescue the godly from trial, but to keep the unrighteous under
punishment until the day of judgment, 10a. especially those
who follow the polluting desires of the flesh and who despise
authority.

Rhetorical Power and Basic Argument

The Greek text of 2:3b–10 contains a single sentence of several balanced and repetitious clauses. It constitutes the author's riposte to the opponents' challenge that God does not judge wickedness. The opening verse contains the topic and argument of the sentence: judgment is not idle, nor does ruin sleep. As proof, the author cites three examples from the Bible which testify to God's just judgment. Goes does not spare the wicked (e.g., the angels, Noah's generation, Sodom and Gomorrah), but rescues the just (Noah and Lot). A summary conclusion in vv 9–10 balances the topic statement. Given these three examples, it is evident that God judges justly, both by rescuing the good and punishing the wicked.

In addition to a topic and concluding statement, this elegant sentence presents its proof through the steady repetition of three conditional sentences ("if . . . if . . . if . . .). These proofs are themselves composed of balanced statements which affirm both the judgment of the wicked ("did not spare . . . did not spare . . . condemned") and the reward of the righteous ("guarded . . . rescued"). The argument builds from a simple statement about God's judgment of the angels, to a longer statement about Noah and his world, to the lengthy presentation of Lot and the sinful cities.

Much of the power and clarity of the rhetoric derives from the repetition of key dualistic terms in the sentence. Condemnation contrasts with reward, the righteous with the lawless, the godly with the ungodly; destruction by fire balances that by water. The cadence builds with the repetition of phrases such as "did not spare . . . did not spare"; God "guarded . . . rescued . . . rescue" and "keep . . . keep." Divine judgment is ever in focus: God keeps the wicked "for judgment . . . condemned . . . to keep . . . until the day of judgment."

Yet for all of his eloquence, the author taps into a tradition which appears to be a commonplace in antiquity. There are similarities between 2:4–9 and Sirach 16:6–23 that are worth noting. Like 2 Peter, the formal setting of the passage in Sirach is a debate over whether God judges and requites. In the polemical part (16:17–23), a sinner boasts that he is hidden from God and so his wickedness goes undetected and unpunished:

> I shall be hidden from the Lord and who from on high will remember me? Among so many people I shall not be known [16:17].

By way of refutation (16:6–16), the author defends the common tradition by presenting a list of biblical figures who did *not* escape divine judgment. This list argues for the future fate of the wicked on the basis of past examples. An analogy is established in 16:6 at the head of the list, which asserts that the past action of God is prophetic of the future. The list of those punished contains the examples of the giants of Gen 6:3 and Sodom. The vocabulary there likewise employs the same verbs and the same grammatical structure found in 2 Peter 2:4–5.

2 Peter 2:4–5	*Sirach 16:7–9*
v 4 God did not spare the angels who sinned v 5 God did not spare the ancient world	v 7 God was not propitiated for the ancient giants v 8 He did not spare the neighbors of Lot v 9 He showed no pity for a nation devoted to destruction

Finally, Sirach contains a general affirmation of the traditional theodicy doctrine; after the list of people "not spared" by God, we read:

> For mercy and wrath are with the Lord,
> He is mighty to forgive, and he pours out wrath.
> As great as his mercy, so great also is his reproof.
> He judges a man according to his deeds [16:11–12].

2 Peter is not quoting Sirach, but rather both of them articulate a defense of traditional theodicy, drawing upon common examples and reflecting a common understanding of God.

Redaction: Relationship to Jude

Although 2 Peter borrows heavily from Jude 5–8, he redacts his source to fit his argument and context.

2 Peter 2:3b–10a	*Jude 5–8*
3. Upon them judgment has not long been idle, nor does their ruin sleep.	5. . . . although Jesus saved a people from the land of Egypt, he afterward destroyed those who were unfaithful.
4. For if God did not spare the *angels* who sinned, but handed them over, casting them into Tartarus *in chains* of *darkness* to keep them *for judgment*, 5. and if God did not spare the ancient world, but guarded Noah,	6. And *angels*, who did not keep to their own position but left their proper abode, he is keeping with everlasting *chains* in *darkness for the judgment* of the great day.

2 Peter 2:3b–10a	*Jude 5–8*
herald of righteousness, and seven others while bringing a deluge upon the world of the impious,	
6. and if God condemned and reduced to ashes the cities of *Sodom and Gomorrah*, setting a *warning* for future impious people,	7. Similarly, *Sodom and Gomorrah* and the villages around them likewise committed fornication and went after other flesh; they are set as *examples*, suffering a punishment of eternal fire.
7. but rescued the righteous Lot, worn down by their lawless and licentious behavior	
8. (for day after day that righteous man lived among them, in sight and sound tortured in his just soul by their lawlessness),	
9. then the Lord knows how to rescue the godly from trial, but to keep the unrighteous under punishment until the day of judgment,	
10. especially those who follow the *polluting* desires of the *flesh* and who *despise authority*.	8. Nevertheless, these dreamers *defile the flesh* and *flout authority*.

Although both authors turn to biblical examples of God's judgment, Jude's first and best example indicates his concern with the subsequent judgment visited on those who fell from grace, namely, the Exodus generation. 2 Peter argues more generally for the principle of God's just judgment against those who formally deny it. Jude's list (Exodus generation, angels, Sodom) is unconcerned with historical sequence and focuses only on judgment of the wicked. 2 Peter purposely follows the sequence of events in the early part of Genesis; he stresses God's just judgment, which both rescues the righteous and requites the wicked. 2 Peter follows Jude's account of the punishment of the "angels," repeating how God "keeps" them "in chains" and "darkness" for "judgment." 2 Peter, however, puts them in Tartarus, the Greek name for the underworld, signaling his attempt to address a multicultured audience, which does not seem to be Jude's interest. 2 Peter substitutes the story of Noah for Jude's mention of the Exodus generation. Since his interest goes beyond Jude's illustration that those who are called can subsequently be rejected, he chooses an example which tells specifically of the rescue and reward of the just (Noah) and the punishment of the wicked (the ancient world). In content, this resembles the way he also casts the stories of Lot and Sodom and Gomorrah.

Whereas Jude spoke of Sodom, Gomorrah, and the "cities" around them, 2 Peter simplifies this to "the cities of Sodom and Gomorrah." Whereas Jude highlighted them as "examples" of "punishment by fire," 2 Peter begins by noting that God "reduced them to ashes" as an "example." Jude's note that they practiced "fornication and went after other flesh" is reduced in 2 Peter to "debauchery," a regular charge made against his own opponents (2:2, 18). Jude says nothing about Lot, for his interest is only in examples of punishment. But since 2 Peter also defends God's just judgment, which includes rewards to the righteous, he contrasts Lot with Sodom and Gomorrah, just as he juxtaposed Noah with his world. Both authors label their materials "examples," but they prove different things. Jude's samples (*deigma*) are general warnings against backsliding, whereas 2 Peter's examples (*hypodeigma*) serve as the formal riposte to explicit challenges to God's day of judgment.

Whereas Jude's examples function as general warnings about backsliding, those in 2 Peter are explicitly said to prove what is being theoretically contested, namely, theodicy or God's just judgment. What was challenged (2:3b) is refuted by these three examples of judgment ("God did not spare . . ."); and the argument concludes with a formal summary statement that God knows how to rescue the godly and to punish the unrighteous (v 9). Hence, the material in 2 Peter serves as a formal riposte to the challenge to God's honor, which was not the case in Jude.

Jude moved from his examples to the situation of his opponents in v 8, likening their flouting of authority to the arrogance of the angels and their defilement of the flesh to Sodom's going after other flesh. 2 Peter attaches this material to his summary about God's punishment of the wicked, but indicates that God especially requites sinners who pollute the flesh and flout authority. Thus he advances his polemic by singling out what he considers the two major evils of his opponents. Both authors speak of "pollution" (*miasmou, miainousin*) of the "flesh" (*sarx*). 2 Peter, when noting this pollution of the flesh, seems to be picking up Jude's earlier remark about Sodom's going after other flesh. Both declaim the rejection of "authority" (*kyriotēs*).

God's Honor Defended: Riposte to Opponents' Challenge

As we noted in regard to 2:1–3, the opponents effectively reject God's judgment by "denying the Lord." The author perceives this denial as a challenge to God's honor, which he in turn is honor bound to defend as God's agent. How is honor related to judgment? In one of his summaries, Aulus Gellius lists three reasons for punishment: (1) correction and reformation of the wicked (*kolasis*), (2) defense of the honor of the lawgiver (*timōria*), and (3) exemplary warning to others (*paradeigma*). A similar topos is found in Clement, *Strom.* 4.24. 2 Peter uses two of these technical terms in his argument: God punishes the wicked (*kolazomenous*, v 9) and makes an example of Sodom (*hypodeigma*, v 6). But the argument here focuses on the defense of the honor of the lawgiver, although the term *timōria* does not appear. Aulus Gellius states: "That reason for punishment exists when the dignity and prestige of the one who is sinned against must be maintained, lest the omission of punishment bring him into contempt and diminish the esteem in which he is held; and therefore they think that it was given a name derived from the preservation of honour" (*Attic Nights* 7.3).

How is God's honor challenged? Basically God is the orderer of the cosmos, its lawgiver whose laws proscribe sin and evil. Just as God is a generous benefactor (1:3–4), so too God is a just lawmaker. Yet the author perceives his opponents despising God's benefactions, especially the promises and laws that lead to sharing the divine nature. Moreover, he understands their "denial of the Master" and their dishonoring of authority (2:10a) as a rejection of God's role as lawgiver and just judge. Twice in 2:3b–10a he calls attention to "lawlessness" (*athesmōn*, v 7; *anomois*, v 8). Shortly he will ridicule the promise of freedom they make (2:19), which we interpret as freedom from God's laws and from divine judgment. Thus God's honor, respect, and power are challenged; divine authority is despised; God is being mocked.

The challenge must be answered. What is denied must be affirmed (v 3a). God's active power must be demonstrated by three indisputable examples from the group's sacred traditions. The author not only argues for the fact of divine punishment of the wicked, but honors God by insisting on the justness of that judgment. God rewards those who honor him by walking in his ways, but requites those who walk in ways that dishonor God. In conclusion, God defends his honor by public disgrace of those who "despise authority" (2:10). The three examples of God's just judgment not only defend the honorable principle of God's sovereignty, but explicitly support the group's tradition of divine judgment on a future day of recompense, the parousia. Hence, the reference in v 9 to "the day of judgment" focuses the riposte to the attacks on God's honor. God's judgment will be emphatically challenged and defended once more in 3:3–9.

Pollution

When the author states that God punishes especially those who "follow the polluting desires of the flesh" (2:10), the term *miasmos* evokes a cultural scenario familiar to Jew and Greek in antiquity. Philo's writings offer a convenient sense of the cultural world suggested by this term. "Pollution" is perceived in contrast to purity or cleanness (Philo, *Cher.* 16; *Mos.* 2.231); the ideal in the New Testament is to be "free from pollution" (*amiantos*: James 1:27; 1 Peter 1:4; *T. Benj.* 8:1–3), which is the equivalent of "spotless and blameless" (see 2 Peter 3:14). A variety of things could cause pollution: sacrifice of children (*Abr.* 181), fratricide or any spilling of blood (*Jos.* 13; *Praem.* 68; Josephus, *B.J.* 4.201, 215; *Ant.* 2.33), adultery and sexual immorality (*Jos.* 45; *Spec. Leg.* 3.49; Jer 3:1, 2, 9). Pollution is never merely personal, but contaminates the group or the nation (*Mos.* 1.303, 304; *Spec. Leg.* 3.42; Josephus, *B.J.* 2.455; see F. Hauck, "Miainō," *TDNT* 4.645). Because it is thought to contaminate the people or the land, it is a life-and-death moral issue, which evokes intolerance, and so it must always be purged. Cleansing or purging means removing the cause of pollution, either by separating from it (Ezra 6:21), removing it from one's midst (Josephus, *Ant.* 9.262, 263, 273; 1 Macc 4:43; 13:50), casting it out (Josephus, *Ant.* 12.286), purging it (Josephus, *B.J.* 6.110), or killing it (Philo, *Spec. Leg.* 3.51). In some places purity and pollution are linked with honor and shame. Philo stated that what is pure and undefiled deserves honor, whereas what is polluted should be punished, i.e., shamed (*Det.* 131). Indeed he considers punishment an appropriate way of dealing with pollution (*Mos.* 1.303). In reverse, Josephus spoke once of "polluting God's providence" (*Ant.* 2.24), that is, shaming God.

In regard to 2 Peter 2:10a, when the term *miasmos* occurs, it too participates in the larger cultural understanding of "pollution." Here the source of pollution is sexual immorality (following "the polluting desires of the flesh"). The pollution of the opponents is not theirs alone, but corrupts others (2:13–14, 18–19), causing them to lose their holiness (2:20). Thus God is shamed by this loss of loyal followers and so God appropriately acts to shame the polluters. This God does according to 2:10 by punishing the wicked, thus purging the group and the world. By labeling certain behavior as "pollution," the author encourages a certain intolerance toward the source of pollution. Even if he cannot ensure its expulsion, God knows how to accomplish it.

NOTES

JUDGMENT NOT IDLE, RUIN NOT SLEEPING

Occasionally scoffers claim that "God slumbers." Elijah mocked the god Baal with a taunt that the rival Deity "is asleep and must be wakened" (1 Kgs 18:27). Such remarks about the Deity's sleep serve to deny either the Deity's existence or sovereignty (see Origen, *Celsum* 4.72). Accordingly Israel prays that "God awake" from sleep (Ps 44:23) to execute judgment for the poor (Pss 3:7;

12:5; 4:23–26; 82:8) and to smite the wicked (Pss 9:19; 17:3; 68:1; 74:22). There is a strong denial that God does *not* sleep (Ps 121:4), nor do his agents of judgment (Isa 5:27). As noted in the introduction to 2 Peter (4.a), Epicureans typically denied that the Deity either rewarded or punished, thus acclaiming the inactivity of God (Cicero, *Nat. Deor.* 1.9.51; Oenomaus of Gadara, cited in Eusebius, *Praep. Evan.* 5.19; see Origen, *Celsum* 6.78). The affirmation of imminent judgment in 2:3b should be seen in tandem with the assertion that there is no "delay" in divine judgment in 3:9. In terms of honor, the opponents are perceived as challenging the honor of God (denial of God's judgment); and the author delivers the obligatory riposte (denial of their denial).

TARTARUS

Instead of the Jewish word for hell (Gehenna), the author uses the Greek term, Tartarus. The verbal form used is "cast into Tartarus" (see Sextus Empiricus, *Pyrrh.* 3.210). He alludes here to the story of the Giants in Genesis 6, which forms a unity with other examples from Genesis, Noah, and Lot. With the hellenization even of Israel, "Tartarus" entered Jewish culture and literature, finding its way into the LXX Job 40:20; 41:24; Prov 30:16, as well as *Sib. Orac.* 2.302; 4:186; *1 Enoch* 20:2, and Philo, *Leg.* 103; *Praem.* 152.

The remarks about the biblical angels seem tailored here to evoke a reminiscence of the Greek story of punishment of the Titans in Tartarus. In Hesiod's version, the Titans are defeated in war and hurled under the earth in chains into gloomy Tartarus, details identical with the author's version in 2:4 (Hesiod, *Theog.* 617–735). Josephus recognized the similarities between the angels of Genesis 6 and the Greek giants: "The deeds that tradition ascribes to them resemble the audacious exploits told by the Greeks of the giants" (*Ant.* 1.73). The use of an example readily recognized by Greek and Jewish hearers seems calculated to appeal to common knowledge about divine punishment of the wicked. This suggests a pluralistic audience of Jew and Gentile, as well as an author familiar with and eager to employ pagan stories which reinforce the Bible.

NOAH

Although Genesis is silent on Noah's preaching, a common midrashic tradition developed around this point. Aware of God's coming judgment, Noah calls on his world to repent and so escape judgment: "Noah, indignant at their conduct and viewing their counsels with displeasure, urged them to come to a better frame of mind and amend their ways" (Josephus, *Ant.* 1.74); this tradition of Noah as a preacher of repentance was a commonplace in Jewish writings (see *Sib. Orac.* 1.128–29; *b. Sanh.* 108a–b; *1 Clem* 7:6 (see Bauckham, *Jude, 2 Peter*, 250–51; Lewis, *A Study of Noah and the Flood*, 102–4). Several points need to be made; the watery flood in Noah's time is balanced with the fiery ruin in Lot's. Greek myths likewise know of both a watery destruction when Deucalion and Pyrrha alone survived the judgment of God and a fiery punishment of Phaethon. Again, the proofs of divine judgment are found in traditions common to Jewish and Greek members of the church. Noah exemplifies for 2 Peter the ideal response to God's predictions of ruin and judgment: speedy preparations to escape disaster. Hence, the suggestion that Noah's preaching depends upon or interprets the preaching of Jesus to the spirits in prison (1 Peter 3:19) seems improbable (see Dalton, "The Interpretation of 1 Peter 3, 19 and 46," 550). And so Noah serves as a model to the church of the author to heed the prophecies of the parousia by lives as spotless as Noah's, who is "perfect" and "righteous" (Gen 6:9; *Jub* 5:19; Sir 44:17). Moreover, Noah illustrates the principle that "many are called and few are chosen"; only Noah and seven others were spared.

SETTING A WARNING (HYPODEIGMA)

Although this term can mean the pattern after which something is built (Ezek 42:15; 1 Chron 28:11; Heb 8:5; 9:23), the sense here is that of an example or even proof (E. K. Lee, "Words Denoting 'Pattern' in the New Testament," *NTS* 8 [1961]: 167–69). Just as the author offered his eyewitness testimony (1:16) as proof of the parousia prophecy, now he offers proof from a historical example (Polybius 3.54.6; for the use of "example" in rhetoric, see S. K. Stowers, *The Diatribe and Paul's Letter to the Romans* [SBLDS 57. Chico, CA: Scholars Press, 1981], 168–74). Josephus indicates how Rome will "make an example" of rebellious Jews by crushing their revolt (*B.J.* 2.397), the same meaning found here as in Heb 4:11. Sodom and Gomorrah, of course, were frequently cited as examples of wickedness punished by God (Deut 29:22–28; Wis 10:6–8; 3 Macc 2:5; Matt 10:15; 11:23–24). Thus God's action is proof that God indeed judges as well as an example or pattern of the judgment by fire which is in store for the world (3:10–12). The use of such common examples is one more element in the socialization of the group, namely, the appeal to traditional examples for governing group behavior.

WATER AND FIRE

Divine judgment by water and fire was a commonplace among Greeks as well as Jews. The two are joined together in tradition and appear together as one example or proof: (a) Jewish tradition (Luke 17:26–30; *T. Naph.* 3:4–5; Josephus, *B.J.* 5.566; Philo, *Mos.* 2.53–65) and (b) Hellenistic tradition (Plato, *Tim.* 22B–C; Lucretius, *R.N.* 5.341–44, 383–415; 6.660–737; Seneca, *Nat. Ou.* 3.27–30; Origen, *Celsum* 1.19–20). The choice of examples that resonate in both Jewish and Greek ears seems intentional and is another example of the multicultural casting of the Christian message by the author.

BIBLIOGRAPHY

Alexander, T. D., "Lot's Hospitality: A Clue to His Righteousness," *JBL* 104 (1985): 289–91.

Bauckham, Richard, *Jude, 2 Peter* (Waco, TX: Word Books, 1983).

Cox, S., "Lot. 2 Peter II. 7,8," *The Expositor* 2/8 (1884): 270–80.

Dalton, W. J., "The Interpretation of 1 Peter 3,19 and 4,6: Light from 2 Peter," *Bib* 60 (1979): 547–55.

Lewis, Jack P., A *Study of the Interpretation of Noah and the Flood in Jewish Literature* (Leiden: E. J. Brill, 1968), 101–20.

Lührmann, D., "Noah und Lot (Lk 17:26–29)—ein Nachtrag," ZNW 63 (1972): 130–32.

Pearson, B. A., "A Reminiscence of Classical Myth at *II Peter* 2.4," *GRBS* 10 (1960): 71–80.

Rappaport, S., "Der gerechte Lot," *ZNW* 29 (1930): 299–304.

Schlosser, J., "Les jours de Noé et de Lot: A propos de *Luc*, xvii,26–30," *RB* 80 (1973): 13–36.

VIII.
Shame on the Opponents: Beasts, Lust, and Greed (2:10b–16)

♦

2 10b. Audacious and arrogant, they are not afraid to insult the
glorious ones, 11. whereas the angels, greater in might and
power, do not bring an insulting judgment from the Lord against
them. 12. But these men, like beasts without reason, creatures
of instinct born for capture and destruction, insult what they do
not comprehend; in their destruction they too will be destroyed,
13. and will suffer wickedly the wages of their wickedness. They
reckon as pleasure daytime dissipation. Blots and blemishes, they
practice dissipation in their deceptions when they feast with you.
14. Their eyes are ceaselessly filled with adulteries and evils; they
entice the unstable; their own hearts are practiced in greed.
Accursed children! 15. Deceived themselves, they forsake the
straight way to follow the way of Balaam son of Bosor, who loved
the wages of wickedness. 16. He received rebuke for his lawlessness when his dumb donkey spoke in a human voice and hindered
the prophet's madness.

Rhetoric and Basic Argument

Polemical challenges to the orthodox tradition cited in 2:1–3a are emphatically answered first in 2:3b–10a and again in 10b–16. Denial of the Master (2:1) and despising of authority (2:10a) are linked with the dishonoring of the majestic angels (2:10b). Just as the author cataloged examples of divine judgments in vv

4–9, so he predicts here their destruction like dumb beasts and compares their fate to that of Balaam, who was rebuked by his donkey. The judgment which the opponents deny the author affirms.

The repetition of three phrases at the beginning and end of this section embodies the author's polemical argument. The opponents are likened to dumb beasts (*aloga zōia*, v 12); Balaam is rebuked by a dumb donkey (*aphōnon*, v 16). The "wages of their wickedness" (*misthon adikias*) will be repaid to the scoffers (v 13); Balaam, who was rebuked, loved just such wages (v 15). The opponents who insult the majestic beings and despise dominion will be destroyed for what they despise (v 10), just as Balaam was rebuked when he sought to pervert his prophetic powers (v 16). Twice we are told that arrogant speech, done for love of money, is requited. The author, then, introduces and concludes the passage with remarks about arrogant speech which is requited, thus reinforcing the catalog of examples of divine justice in 2:4–9.

As the audience hears the passage, they are aided in holding its complex sentences together by the repetition of words and patterns of assonance. The initial remarks are linked by the catchword "insult" (*blasphēmountes*, v 10b . . . *blasphemon*, v 11 . . . *blasphēmountes*, v 12). This evil leads to "destruction" (*phthoran* . . . *en phthorai* . . . *phtharēsontai*, v 12). The *lex talionis* continues this: "they will suffer wickedly the wages of their wickedness" (*adikoumenoi* . . . *adikias*, v 13). The impurity of the opponents is stressed through repeated synonyms ("blots, blemishes") and by repetition of the charge of "dissipation" (*tryphēn* . . . *entryphōntes*, v 13). Truth and falsehood are contrasted in the juxtaposition of the "straight way" and the "way of Balaam" (v 15). Moreover, internal assonance likewise binds phrases together and aids in their comprehension and retention. For example:

*hē*donen *hē*goumenoi en *hē*merai (v 13)
*m*estous *m*oichalidos (v 14)
*a*katapaustous . . . *ha*martias *a*stērikous (v 14)
a*ph*ōnon *ph*ōnēi *ph*thegxamenon (v 16)

HONOR AND SHAME/ CHALLENGE AND RIPOSTE

The author has already exposed the opponents' challenge to God, namely, their "denial" of divine sovereignty and their despising of authority, both that of God and of his agents. The honor of God is challenged, and the author understands his role as the deliverer of an appropriate riposte. He begins by labeling the challengers as seekers of honor, that is, "audacious" and "arrogant." *Tolmaō* denotes presumption of status and power (Rom 15:18; 2 Cor 10:12; Jude 9; Philo, *Somn.* 1.54); *authadēs* means arrogance (Titus 1:7; Prov 21:24; Josephus, *Ant.* 1.189). By labeling the opponents in this way, the author portrays them as claiming honor which is not theirs. They extend themselves beyond what God assigned, thus infringing on God's honor and that of his agents. Their arrogance takes the form of "not fearing," that is, not respecting the role and status of their betters, namely, "the majestic beings" who are superior to them in the honorable qualities of might and power. Typical of that culture, the opponents express their honor challenge verbally by "insulting" others. The root meaning of *blasphēmein* has to do with injuring the reputation of another by speech (Titus 3:2; Josephus, *Vita* 232; Philo, *Spec. Leg.* 4.197; Isocrates 10.45). As we have seen, part of the dishonor lies in their rejection of God's laws and his future judgment. The opponents, then, dishonor the most honorable people in the cosmos, God, the majestic angels, and deputized leaders in the group. Their dishonor of God is also reflected in the harm they do to God's family (deceive, pollute, lead astray). It belongs to the head or leader to defend the honor and well-being of the group; God's covenant family is being harmed, which is insulting as well to the one charged with guarding it. This challenge cannot be ignored.

An appropriate riposte follows. Despite the opponents' claims to wisdom and insight, the author compares them with dumb beasts. Despite their claim of freedom from judgment, he declares them born for capture and destruction. They will most surely experience God's justice according to a *lex talionis:* for the harm they caused, they will receive a reward of harm. The example of Balaam functions as part of the riposte; for like the opponents, Balaam left the straight way of truth and greedily accepted money to harm others, thus shaming God's prophetic spirit by attempting to harm God's people. His riposte came from a dumb donkey, making his disgrace that much more shameful. Recall that the author earlier claimed that the disciples of Jesus are destined to share the divine nature (1:4); but by being called dumb beasts destined for destruction, these people forfeit the honor of immortality. They are now branded as "accursed."

The riposte contains many traditional polemical slanders, especially accusations of greed and immorality. The opponents are motivated by love of money, the root of all evil; their self-proclaimed wisdom is false theology which leads to pollution and debauchery. Thus their challenge to God's honor begins and ends in evil. To a community called to be "holy as God is holy," accusations of dissipation, pollution, and adultery function to discredit claims to freedom and enlightenment.

Redaction: Relationship to Jude

Some borrowing and dependency are evident here. Jude 8–12 is reproduced in 2 Peter 2:10b–16 in virtually the same order, although Jude 11 and 12 are transposed in 2 Peter. As we noted in "Rhetoric and Basic Argument" above, 2 Peter seems to begin and end this part of his polemic with certain phrases and remarks, which account for the slightly different order of the material in Jude.

2 Peter 2:10b–11	*Jude 8–9*
10b. *Audacious* and arrogant, they are not afraid to *insult the glorious ones*,	8. . . . these dreamers defile the flesh, flout authority, and *insult the glorious ones*.
11. whereas the *angels*, greater in might and power, *do not bring* an *insulting judgment* from the Lord against them.	9. But Michael the arch*angel*, when he argued with the devil and disputed over the body of Moses, *did not* himself *dare bring* a *judgment* against *insult*, but he said: "The Lord will rebuke you."

2 Peter borrows heavily from Jude at this point, although he redacts the material cleverly to fit his particular situation. Whereas in Jude, Michael did not dare (*etolmēsen*), 2 Peter's opponents are quite daring (*tolmētai*). In both documents, evil people "insult the glorious ones," namely, the angels. In Jude, the archangel Michael does not himself "bring a judgment" (*epenegken krisin*) for the insult, whereas in 2 Peter the angels in general do not bring a judgment (*pherousin krisin*) in riposte for their insult. In Jude, the riposte will be given by the Lord; Michael quotes Enoch to the effect that "the Lord will rebuke you." 2 Peter merely remarks that the angels do not bring a judgment "from the Lord." In general, 2 Peter repeats the insults against God's angels, because he perceives this as part of the opponents' scoffing at any notion of divine judgment; but he omits the contest between Michael and Satan as well as the citation of *1 Enoch*. We can only guess that in his situation, although many documents and sources are indicated in the letter, mention of *1 Enoch* was in some way unsuitable. His use of Jude, then, focuses on "insult" against authority figures, in particular ones who are said to play a role in the heavenly judgment of the wicked.

2 Peter 2:12–13	Jude 10
12. *But these men, like beasts without reason*, creatures of instinct born for capture and destruction, *insult what they do not comprehend;* in their destruction they too will be *destroyed.* 13. and will suffer wickedly the wages of their wickedness.	10. *But these men insult whatever they do not know;* by nature they understand *like animals without reason*, and are *destroyed* in this.

2 Peter follows Jude quite closely here. Both begin with the pejorative description of their opponents as "these men" (*houtoi de*) and both note that their opponents "insult" what "they do not know." The two authors label their opponents "beasts without reason" (*aloga zōia*), who are only acting according to their bestial nature (*physika*, 2:12; *physikōs*, v 10). Their fate is similar, "destruction" (*phtharēsontai*, 2:12; *phtheirontai*, v 10).

Thus, both authors deliver a strong polemic against the opponents, who present themselves as enlightened and who command attention for their arguments. The authors liken them to reasonless beasts. Hence, their "insults" are bestial actions, not to be taken seriously; they cannot by nature know anything. 2 Peter's redaction thrice mentions destruction: the beasts are born for destruction (*eis phthoran*); in their destruction (*en phthorai*) they will be destroyed (*phtharēsontai*). It is possible to read the last phrase as a type of *lex talionis* pronounced against them: "in their destruction [of others] they will be destroyed." Then it would directly parallel the next phrase in the document, which is itself another *lex talionis* judgment: they "will suffer wickedly [*adikoumenoi*] the wages of wickedness [*adikias*]." 2 Peter, then, redacts Jude to emphasize the imminent retribution which awaits those who deny it.

2 Peter 2:13–14	Jude 12
13. They reckon as pleasure daytime dissipation. *Blots* and blemishes, they practice dissipation in their deceptions when they *feast with you.* 14. Their eyes are ceaselessly filled with adulteries and evils; they entice the unstable; their own hearts are practiced in greed. Accursed children!	12. These men are *stains* on your fellowship meals; they *feast* fearlessly *with you* and pasture only themselves.

Both authors indicate that their opponents are inside the group, for they both "feast with you" (*syneuōchoumenoi*). Both label their opponents as a pollution threatening the holy group: Jude = "stains" (*spilades*), 2 Peter = "blots and blemishes" (*spiloi kai mōmoi*). 2 Peter elaborates on the impurity of his opponents, stressing their dissipation (v 13), adultery (v 14), and greed (v 14). He says that they are "trained" in wickedness (*gegymnasmenēn*). Indeed, their wickedness is complete: they "ceaselessly" do evil and their eyes are "filled" with adulteries. Thus while both authors alert their audiences to a pollution in their midst, 2 Peter uses the occasion to stress just how polluted his opponents are and what a corrupting effect they have on others by "enticing the unstable."

2 Peter 2:15–16	*Jude 11*
15. *Deceived* themselves, they forsake the straight way to follow *the way of Balaam* son of Bosor, who loved the *wages* of wickedness.	11. Woe to these who have gone *the way of* Cain, and abandoned themselves for *gain* to the *deceit* of *Balaam*, and are destroyed in the rebellion of Korah.
16. He received rebuke for his lawlessness when his dumb donkey spoke in a human voice and hindered the prophet's madness.	

2 Peter reduces Jude's triad of Cain, Balaam, and Korah to the single example of Balaam. Both authors agree that a deviant "way" (*hodos*) is followed by the opponents, either the way of Cain (Jude) or of Balaam (2 Peter). 2 Peter contrasts the wrong way with "the straight way" of orthodox tradition. Both see "deception" (*planaō*) practiced: in Jude, Balaam deceives others, whereas in 2 Peter the opponents are themselves deceived, presumably by the Evil One. "Wages" (*misthoi*) figure in both descriptions of Balaam; in Jude, the opponents abandon themselves to Balaam's way for gain or greed, whereas in 2 Peter Balaam himself loved gain, or the wages of his wickedness. 2 Peter both expands the caricature of Balaam ("way of Balaam . . . wages of wickedness . . . lawlessness") and adds mention of the rebuke he suffered. Indeed, it is the rebuke which figures prominently in the controversy over judgment and retribution. Heavenly rebuke does come, either directly from God (2:4–9) or from creatures used by God, despite what the opponents deny.

Balaam Rebuked

The author, while borrowing the example of Balaam from Jude 11, highlights only a part of the story of that prophet. For purposes of analysis we identify five elements in the account of Balaam in 2 Peter 2:15–16.

(a) **Follow the way of Balaam:** in legend, he was known for *lying* (the targums to Num 22:30 claim that Balaam denied that the ass who rebuked him was his) and *flattery* (*Deut. R.* I.2), and *sexual immorality* (in Philo's *Mos.* 1.293–99 Balaam advises Balak to seduce the Israelites).

(b) **Loved the wages of wickedness:** passing mention is made in Num 22:16–9 of Balak's gold and silver offered to Balaam; but in legend he is known for his avarice and greed (Philo, *Mos.* 1.267–68; *Cher.* 33–34; see *Num. R.* XX.7, 10). Ironically, although Balak refused to reward him when he blessed Israel, nevertheless he received a recompense for his seduction of Israel when he was slain with the sword (Num 31:8); the legends see this as a fitting "reward" for his harm: "They also killed Balaam son of Beor with the sword. The Israelites paid him his full salary, and did not deprive him because he had come to give them [the Moabites] counsel" (*Sifre Num.* 157; see *Num. R.* XXII.9). In fact, some legends see Balaam illustrating the proverb "as you sow, so you reap": "What was Balaam doing there? He came to take his reward for the slaughter of the 24,000 (Num 25:9). Of him it says 'Whoso diggeth a pit shall fall therein; and he that rolleth a stone, it shall return upon him' (Prov 26:27)" (*Num. R.* XXII.4).

(c) **Rebuke for his lawlessness:** in Num 22:28 and 30, Balaam's donkey rebuked him for striking her; but in haggadic legends that rebuke was inflated to include a note of divine judement: "Woe to us for the day of judgment, woe to us for the day of rebuke! Balaam was the wisest of the heathens, yet he could not withstand his ass' rebuke: 'Was I ever wont to do so to thee? and he said: Nay' (Num 22:30) . . . How much more when the Holy One, blessed be He, comes and rebukes each man according to his deserts, as it says 'But I will reprove thee, and set the cause before thine eyes' (Ps 50:12)" (*Gen. R.* XCIII.10).

(d) **His dumb donkey spoke in a human voice:** although Num 22:28 records Balaam's donkey reproaching him for beating her, *Tgs. Ps.-J.* and *Yer. I* record a full censure by the donkey of Balaam's deception of the people and his misuse of his prophetic powers.

(e) **Hindered the prophet's madness:** in the targums to Num 22:30, the ass argued about the vanity of Balaam's power to curse. She ultimately did not prevent his pursuing his wickedness, but berated him for having no understanding and no wisdom. Her function seemed mainly to shame him.

The author is not merely repeating midrashic legends, but selecting and editing them so that Balaam functions polemically against the author's own opponents in his letter. The *rebuke* of this sinner recalls the divine judgment of the wicked in 2:4–9; despite their denial of judgment, Balaam's ass is one more proof of accountability for one's actions and for divine judgment. The rebuke was administered by a "dumb donkey," which takes the reader back to the reference to "speechless beasts" (2:12) who are destined for destruction. The "way of Balaam" is contrasted with the "straight way" (2:15), thus the traditional doctrine of the "two ways" contrasts the way of greed and debauchery with the way of self-control and purity. Although Balaam acted alone, here he is said to deceive others and lead "followers" astray, which reminds us of disciples "following their debauchery" (2:2). Balaam's "lawlessness" (*paranomia*) parallels the "lawless" behavior (*athesmōn*) of the Sodomites who were punished (2:7–8); true disciples are warned of "lawlessness" (*athesmōn*) in the letter's ending (3:17). Balaam's *deception* of others (*eplanēthēsan*) is meant to remind the readers of the opponents' deception of others (2:1, 3) and of their own danger (3:17). His *reward* (*misthos*) echoes the earlier remark about the reward of judgment awaiting the opponents; they too will be rewarded, and with a fitting quid-pro-quo retribution (2:13). His legendary love of money resonates with the greed of which the opponents are accused (2:3, 14). Finally, he is a prophet whose words could truly be words of God, if inspired, or false words which lead Israel into debauchery. The author never considers Balaam speaking as an inspired oracle, but he does resemble the "false prophets" spoken of in 2:1. The figure of Balaam was considered a type in Rev 2:14; Jude 11 and here; but the question is, a type of what? The author tailored the figure of Balaam to reflect the vices of his opponents and to serve as another example of a sinner rebuked. Indeed, the biblical Balaam confessed to being shamed by his donkey (Num 22:29), which suggests that the author sees the rebuke (2:16) as an important element of the legend, and as the most fitting riposte where honor is challenged.

POLLUTION AND VICE

The density of terms which depict the corruption of the author's opponents is greatest in 2:12–14. We view this material from the perspective of "purity and pollution," which was discussed in the *introduction to 2 Peter* 6 (h) (1), (3). In general, the opponents are "out of place." They are labeled "blots and blemishes" at the holy meals and meetings of God's holy people (2:13). In terms of explicit terms denoting "uncleanness," three times the author uses the term *phthora* in regard to them; while it means destruction, it connotes putrefaction. In speaking of the effect of leaven in dough, Plutarch uses this term to describe the decomposition which sets in with the leavening process (*Quaes. Rom.* 289F; *Quaes. Conviv.* 659B). This is the effect the author sees his opponents having on others: they corrupt them, deceive them, and cause their ruin. Besides these terms which speak directly of "pollution," the author catalogs a list of vices which serves the same function. The opponents are slaves of "pleasure" (*hēdonē*), one of the four cardinal vices; their eyes are filled with adulteries; they are greedy (*pleonexia*). They practice "dissipation" (*tryphē, entryphōntes*). This term has both a positive and a negative meaning. Philo talks of two kinds of "luxury" or "delight": one is a sense of profound content and joy, which knows no toil or trouble, but the other is weak and wanton, which the vice of pleasure brings (*Cher.* 12). Positively, *tryphē* describes the "paradise of delights" God created for Adam and Eve (Gen 2:15; Philo, *Leg. All.* 1.45, 96; *Cher.* 1; *Post.* 32). Yet normally "luxury" means "dissipation" or excess either of drinking (*Spec. Leg.* 1.99) or sexual immorality (Philo, *Spec. Leg.* 2.240); it is generally linked with the vice "pleasure" (Josephus, *B.J.* 1.462; *Ant.* 5.132; Diodorus of Sicily 19.71.3).

Philo links "dissipation" with "slackness" (*Sac.* 21; *Ebr.* 21; *Spec. Leg.* 2.99), which connotes lack of bodily control. Thus when 2 Peter twice accuses his opponents of "dissipation," his remark implies a range of vices and loss of bodily discipline. "Eyes" are filled with adulteries, and so are undisciplined to exclude evil (see Matt 5:27–29; Mark 9:47). "Mouths" are feasting, but to excess and in dissipation. Since the opponents are accused of "adulteries," the genitals are not controlled. The physical body, then, is completely uncontrolled, which contrasts with the "self-control" which faithful disciples practice (1:6). Finally, instead of being practiced in bodily control, which is the aim of exercise in the gymnasium, they are skilled in wickedness (*gegymnasmenēn*, v 14).

NOTES

GLORIOUS ONES.

The *doxai* mentioned in 2:10 are probably angels, who are called "glorious" because they participate in and embody God's own glory (1 QH 10:8; 2 *Enoch* 22:7; *T. Jud.* 25:2; Philo, *Spec. Leg.* 1.45; Heb 9:5). According to 2:11 angels are engaged in controversy with the opponents. Given the overall polemic of the opponents against the parousia of Jesus and God's great judgment, we suggest that their "insult" to the angels is related to these issues. In regard to Jesus' parousia, New Testament tradition records that the Son of Man will come in glory with his angels to repay every man for what he has done (Matt 16:27). Elsewhere these angels will function in the judgment process itself by separating the good from the wicked (Matt 24:31). In Revelation, God's angels play a direct and active role in punishing the wicked (8:6–9:21; 11:15–19; 14:6–11; 16:21). One of the angels directs the Son of Man to begin the judgment: "Put in your sickle, and reap, for the hour to reap has come, for the harvest of the earth is ripe" (14:15). From the beginning of creation, God's angels guarded the Garden of Delights and kept sinners out of it (Gen 3:24), a role which is presumed here as well. The angels, although insulted, will not give the appropriate riposte to the insult. This does not mean that they cannot do so or that they are thereby shamed. Rather, in this document God alone will reward and punish (2:4–10a).

BEASTS WITHOUT REASON

Aristotle discussed moral states to be avoided and identified three, "vice, incontinence, and brutishness" (*N.E.* 7.1.1 1145a15–b7). Using language reminiscent of purity and pollution, he labeled brutish people as outsiders ("barbarians") or unclean (the result of disease or deformity). People who go beyond all ordinary social and moral standards by reason of vice are especially brutish. Thus by labeling his own opponents as irrational animals, 2 Peter issues a serious honor challenge to them before the group, a challenge backed up by reference to their bodily incontinence and vices.

PLEASURE (HĒDONĒ)

In the popular discussions of morality in the ancient world we read of a tradition of four cardinal vices: pleasure (*hēdonē*), desire (*epithymia*), fear (*phobos*), and grief *(lypē)* (see Diog. Laert. 7.111; Philo, *Dec.* 142–46; *Migr.* 60; Cicero, *De Fin.* 3.10.35; *Tusc. Disp.* 4.6.13–14; see T. Onuki, *Gnosis und Stoa* [Göttingen: Vandenhoeck and Ruprecht, 1989], 30–45). "Pleasure" is said to bring rivalry, boastfulness, and thirst for honor in the soul as well as gluttony and gormandizing in the body (4 Macc 1:25–27; Diog. Laert. 7.114). As one of the four cardinal vices, "pleasure" is a "passion" (*pathos*), which the Stoic Zeno defined as an "irrational [*alogos*] and unnatural movement of the soul" (Diog. Laert. 7.110). In stressing how these vices stand in contradiction to reason, Cicero describes them as "movements of the soul either destitute of reason, or contemptuous of reason, or disobedient to reason" (*Tusc. Disp.* 3.11.24). For Epicurus, "pleasure" first meant the "absence of pain and fear" or *ataraxia* (Diog. Laert. 10.128–29), but it became a caricature of his system. Thus when 2 Peter accuses his opponents of "pleasure and dissipation" (2:13), he evokes this negative understanding of it as a cardinal vice. Furthermore, he labels his opponents as "irrational" beasts (*aloga zōia*), who do not understand, which is an essential part of the definition of "pleasure," as noted above. As Philo noted, "when pleasure [*hēdonē*] is present, reason is in exile" (*Leg. All.* 3.116).

Moreover, in 2:10, 18 and 3:3, 2 Peter accuses his opponents of "desire" (*epithymia*), another of the cardinal vices.

ENTICE (DELEAZONTES)

The basic verb means to bait and catch, as in fishing. It is commonly used in a moral sense as enticement by vice. Philo, for example, regularly speaks of "enticement" by (a) pleasure (*hēdonē*): *Opif.* 166; *Agr.* 102; *Migr.* 29 (see James 1:14); (b) sexual charms: *Ebr.* 50; *Heres* 274; *Congr.* 77; *Virt.* 40; and (c) gluttony: *Spec. Leg.* 4.100. This connotation fits 2 Peter 2:14 and 18, where the author describes his opponents as themselves led by "adultery" (v 14) and dissipation at feasts (v 13). In 2:18 he describes them as enticing with debauchery and desires of the flesh.

Philo also associated "enticement" with deception and delusion (*Heres* 71; *Somn.* 2.101; *Fuga* 189; see Josephus, *B.J.* 5.120). Something which is outwardly pleasing is inwardly corrupt and defiling. Hence, it conveys a sense of "pollution" for the author. Finally, in a suggestive passage, Philo speaks of enticement to a certain kind of freedom: "You entice this multitude with the hope of liberty, and then have saddled it with the greater danger which threatens its life" (*Mos.* 1.171). Philo's usage can enlighten our interpretation of 2:17–18, where first the opponents are said to "entice with debauchery" (v 17) and immediately to "promise freedom," which is really slavery to vice (v 18).

BALAAM SON OF BOSOR

According to Num 22:5 Balaam is "the son of Beor"; we have no other record of his father being "Bosor." It appears that our text intends to give a patronymic identification to Balaam, not a place-name. Most manuscripts read "Bosor," while the occasional scribe appears to have corrected this text to conform to Num 22:5. Although people are known according to their place of origin (Jesus of Nazareth; Paul of Tarsus), the more common identification was in terms of one's father, which seems to be the case here.

MADNESS (PARAPHRONIA)

This is a most unusual word (M-M 461), which occurs only here in the New Testament. Lexicons translate the verb form (*paraphroneō*) as "to conduct oneself in an irrational manner" (Josephus, *Ant.* 19.284; Herodotus 1.109; 3.34; Diodorus of Sicily 16.78.5; 2 Cor 11:23; Zech 12:4). Hence, this "madness" is not the enthusiasm or ecstasy of prophetic inspiration (Philo, *Plant.* 148) but is linked with contentiousness and drunkenness (*Ebr.* 15). Indeed it may have been chosen to deny the Balaam-like false prophets of legitimation and associate them with the irrational beasts described in 2:12, who understand nothing (see

Philo, *Mos.* 1.293; *Mut.* 203). Lack of rationality connotes also ignorance of a rational way of life as well as absence of self-control (Philo, *Leg. All.* 2.69–70).

BIBLIOGRAPHY

Greene, John T., "Balaam as Figure and Type in Ancient Semitic Literature to the First Century B.C.E., with a Survey of Selected Post-Philo Applications of the Balaam Figure and Type," *SBLASP* 1990: 82–147.

———, *Balaam and His Interpreters: A Hermeneutical History of the Balaam Tradition* (Brown Judaic Studies 244. Atlanta: Scholars Press, 1992).

Skehan, P. W., "A Note on 2 Peter 2,13," *Bib* 41 (1960): 69–71.

Vermes, Geza, "The Story of Balaam—the Scriptural Origin of Haggadah," *Scripture and Tradition in Judaism: Haggadic Studies* (SPB 4. Leiden: E. J. Brill, 1961), 127–77.

IX. More Shame on the Opponents: Hypocrisy and Harm (2:17–22)

♦

2 17. These men are springs without water, mists driven by storms;
for them gloomy darkness is kept. 18. They mouth empty
boasts; they entice with debauchery and desires of the flesh those
who but recently fled from the company of those who live in
error. 19. They promise them freedom, but are themselves
slaves of destruction. For people are slaves to that which masters
them. 20. For if they, who fled the pollution of the world by
acknowledging our Lord and Savior Jesus Christ, again are entangled in evil company and are mastered by it, this last state is worse
than the first. 21. Far better for them that they should never
have acknowledged the way of righteousness, than acknowledging
it, to turn away from the holy rule given them. 22. For them
the proverb has proved true: "The dog returns to its vomit" and
"The pig, once washed, wallows in mud."

Rhetoric and Argument

These remarks conclude the riposte to the opponents' challenge. They are less an argument than a verbal attack, a counterchallenge. The riposte found in the rest of ch. 2 continues here with little new material. Both the labels used and the content of the attack have occurred earlier. For example, in terms of the truth of the author's claims, he describes his tradition as "the way of righteousness" (2:21), echoing his earlier claim that he knows "the straight way" (2:15).

And he continues to attack his opponents and their traditions by repeating negative labels. His threat of "gloomy darkness *kept*" (*tetērētai*, 2:17) repeats the same term used in 2:4, 9. He warns of "destruction" (*phthora*) awaiting them (2:19), just as it was threatened in 2:12. Former accusations of sexual immorality (2:12–13), in particular "debauchery" (*aselgeia*, 2:7) and "passion" (*epithymia*, 2:10a), are repeated in 2:18. Deceptive speech (*deleazontes*, 2:14) continues, now with "false promises" (2:19) and "empty boasts" (2:18). New disciples "acknowledged" loyalty to the Lord (2:20) and committed themselves to his Way (2:21); in contrast, the opponents "deny" this Lord and Master (2:1). These same opponents "entice" loyal followers to debauchery (2:18), just as they "enticed" the unstable (2:14). In short, the author repeats and thus deepens his polemic against his opponents by emphasizing the harmful effect which they have on others. Bad enough that they themselves are wicked, but they are causing scandal and harm to the holy followers of the Lord. Paul articulated the principle clearly when he cited the proverb, "Bad company ruins good morals" (1 Cor 15:33). Thus the author seeks to marshal a holy intolerance against this polluting leaven.

Honor and Shame: Continuing Riposte

The author's continuing polemic against his opponents, while perhaps tiresome to modern readers, was both expected and appreciated by readers in a world where honor challenges abounded. Every challenge must be answered with a riposte. It is hardly accidental, then, that the author mocks the empty promises of his opponents. Their scoffing at both the traditional "promises" (3:4, 9) and "prophecies" (1:16–19) of the group is a serious honor challenge both to the author, who vouches for them, and to God, their original author. He responds to this challenge with a fitting riposte, namely, the mocking of their promises. Their words are vain and empty; they lie when they announce "freedom from anxiety and judgment" or "freedom from law." Just as they were likened to "waterless" springs (2:17) and accused of mouthing "empty boasts" (2:18), so their promises are empty, vain, and shameful.

The honor of Jesus is challenged and must be defended. New members of the group once "acknowledged" the Lord; that is, they pledged loyalty to him, acclaimed his sovereignty as Lord and Judge, and swore to follow his Way. The honor of Jesus increased as he was thus publicly acclaimed. But now that honor is challenged and denied, for these same disciples no longer follow his Way, no longer fear his judgment, and no longer expect his triumphal arrival. The teachers of these folk have themselves denied the Master (2:1), thus shaming him; and now recent disciples follow their shameful example. Part of the riposte to this honor challenge is the present public shaming of them. The Lord will deliver the final riposte himself: "Whoever is ashamed of me and of my words in this adulterous generation, of him will the Son of Man also be ashamed when he comes in the glory of his Father with the holy angels" (Mark 8:38). Here, the emphasis is on the shame that these folk have brought upon the Lord, a public reproach of serious import.

Finally, the author resorts to name-calling. Despite the proverb that sticks and stones can hurt our bones but names can never harm us, names and epithets are weapons of great social importance in an honor/shame world. Labels such as "brood of vipers" and "adulterous generation" are hardly innocent; if they succeed in caricaturing someone, they do immense damage to his reputation (see B. J. Malina and J. H. Neyrey, *Calling Jesus Names* [Sonoma, CA: Polebridge, 1988], 35–38). The author effectively calls his opponents "hypocrites," for while they mock his promises, they themselves make false promises. He calls them "waterless" springs and fickle mists (2:17), that is, empty and vain persons. Just as he called the opponents "beasts without reason" (2:12), he likewise calls their disciples names, "dog" and "pig." Both of these convey a strong connotation of impurity, and so function as moral labels with ethical implications. Thus he has sufficiently issued a counterchallenge to those who challenge the traditions of the group.

REDACTION: RELATIONSHIP TO JUDE

Although 2 Peter has followed Jude's material closely up till now, only 2:17–18 appear to be redacted from Jude 12–13 and 16. The author omits the prophecy from Enoch about the coming of the Lord to judge the godless. We can only speculate why so appropriate an oracle would not find its way into a document which explicitly defends this very tradition. The author prides himself on the range of traditions and documents which he knows, so we are puzzled by the omission of *1 Enoch* here as well as *T. Moses* in Jude 9. But let us examine how 2 Peter redacts what he does borrow from Jude.

2 Peter 2:17	*Jude 12–13*
17. These men are springs *without water,* mists driven by storms;	12. They are *rainless* clouds borne by the wind, fruitless trees in autumn, doubly dead and uprooted.

2 Peter 2:17	*Jude 12–13*
	13. They are wild waves of the sea who cast foam over their shames, wandering stars
for them gloomy darkness is kept.	*for whom the gloomy darkness is* forever *kept.*

2 Peter borrows from Jude many ripostes to his opponents, but always tailors them carefully to fit his own context. Instead of Jude's stress on instability (clouds, uprooted trees, foam, and wandering stars), our author calls attention to their emptiness (*anydroi,* waterless springs, 2:17; empty boasts, 2:18). Both authors agree that their instability (2 Peter = mists driven by storms; Jude = clouds borne by the wind) will be eventually reckoned with by being kept in "gloomy darkness."

2 Peter 2:18	*Jude 16*
18. They mouth empty boasts; they entice with debauchery and desires of the flesh those who but recently fled from the company of those who live in error.	16. These men are disgruntled murmurers who go the way of passion. Their mouths speak inflatedly and show partiality for gain.

No specific terms from Jude are borrowed here, but both authors accuse their opponents of dangerous words which entice and seduce others. Jude never mentioned what his grumblers and malcontents specifically said (v 16), but 2 Peter calls attention to their empty boasts (2:18) and false promises (2:19), promises of escape from judgment and punishment. Whereas Jude was content with generic negative labels for his opponents, our author ridicules his adversaries with the same sort of challenge they issued to him, false promises (2:19; see 1:16). Promising freedom, they are slaves. He is, moreover, concerned with the scandal such false speech causes to his group (2:18, 20–22). He interprets their proclamation of freedom as the negation of acknowledgment of Christ (2:21). And he emphasizes how such false doctrines lead to new pollution. The differences lie in the specific way 2 Peter adapts a rather general polemic from Jude into a specific riposte to specific challenges from his opponents.

2 Peter then introduces in 2:20–22 materials of his own. Continuing to challenge his opponents, he describes the harm they cause among the holy disciples of the Lord. Far from leading to purity, self-control, incorruption and

so entry into the world of God (1:4–7), their deviant doctrine creates a situation much worse than the state from which the disciples originally converted. They left a world of corruption when they vowed allegiance to God and Christ and came to follow "the holy rule" and "the way of righteousness." The author likens their apostasy from this new state to the behavior of unclean animals. This recalls the labeling of the opponents earlier as "beasts without reason" (2:12). The observation that the last state is worse than the first is a common reflection in New Testament exhortations (Matt 12:45; Hermas, *Sim.* 9.17.5; Heb 6:4–8).

PURITY AND POLLUTION

These verses contain some of the most vivid language in the document pertaining to "purity" and "pollution." If "purity" has to do with what is "in place," the author clearly describes two different worlds; by use of typical dualistic expressions, he communicates a radical distinction between the pure world of loyal members within the group and the corrupt world of those outside. Once followers lived in error, but fled their evil companions for fellowship with the saints (2:18). Once they too lived corrupt lives, but fled that way of life when they acknowledged the Lord (2:20). Hence, those who "fled" their former lives entered a holy space and became blameless like their Lord and Master. They are now in the right place and so are pure. Those outside are "out of place," and so polluted.

But this holiness is threatened. New disciples of Jesus are being poisoned with false teaching: they are "enticed" and "entangled" in immorality (2:20). The author evaluates these false teachings of his opponents as though they were a type of gangrene (2 Tim 2:17) or leaven (Matt 16:12), that is, a corrupting influence which will pollute what is pure. Then he laments how what is holy becomes profane. Disciples who embraced what is pure and holy ("acknowledge the Lord," 2:20; acknowledge "the way of righteousness," 2:21) are now turning away from this to debauchery and evil. In fact, the author asserts that these new disciples would be better off never having heard of the purity Christ brings, than to embrace it and profane it (see 1 Cor 3:16–17). Something sacred is being polluted. And the last state is worse than the first.

The author uses two similes to describe the pollution of those who lapse from the faith, dogs and pigs. Although the reference to dogs resembles Prov 26:11, it is important to know the cultural meaning attached to dogs and pigs, as well as to vomit (W. S. McCullough, *IDB* 1.862). According to Jewish classification, pigs are inherently "unclean," that is, unfit as sacrifice to God or as food for humans (Lev 11:7; Deut 14:8); they are "unclean" not for biological reasons but because they violate the definition of a "clean" animal according to Jewish notions (Mary Douglas, *Purity and Danger* [London: Routledge and Kegan Paul, 1966], 41–57). Dogs, too, were unclean: they were scavengers, haunting streets and refuse dumps and eating unclean things (Exod 22:31; *m. Bek* 5.6), even human flesh (1 Kgs 14:11; 16:4; 2 Kgs 9:10). Luke tells a parable where dogs lick Lazarus' sores (Luke 16:21). All exuviae which leave the body are dangerous, if not outright polluting: semen, urine, menses, spittle, and vomit (Douglas, *Purity and Danger*, 120–24). Hence, this dog, which is already unclean by virtue of what it eats, returns to its uncleanness to ingest it again. Horace associates unclean dogs with mud-spattered pigs (*Ep.* 1.2.26; 2.2.75). Jesus' remarks about not giving dogs what is holy or putting pearls before swine (Matt 7:6) reflects the same sense of uncleanness attached to these two animals.

The language of purity and pollution is intended to sound a strong moral note, and thus to mobilize the hearers to a sense of intolerance toward the doctrine of the opponents. If they are causing the profanation and pollution of what is holy, they are thus a mortal threat to the group. Such error and the wickedness which follows threaten to corrupt the whole group, and so should be identified, isolated, and expelled.

SPEECH, MOUTH, AND TONGUE

It is a commonplace in ancient literature, Greek as well as Jewish, that the mouth should be guarded and the tongue controlled. James declares "perfect" the man who makes no mistakes in speech (3:2; 1:26; see Martin Dibelius, *James* [Philadelphia: Fortress Press, 1976], 184). A survey of biblical texts indicates the many ways in which an unguarded mouth can err: (a) lies, deceit, crooked speech, deviousness, false witness (Pss 10:7; 36:3; Prov 2:24); (b) anger, attack, challenge (Pss 35:21; 109:2; Prov 21:24; Matt 5:22); (c) smooth words, flattery (Pss 55:21; 78:36); and (d) arrogance, pride, boastfulness (Pss 17:10; 59:12; Sir 20:7). This should sensitize the reader to the data in our document which identifies the false speech of the opponents: (a) verbal challenges to God, the author, and the tradition (1:16; 3:4, 9); (b) reviling speech (*blasphēmeō*, 2:2, 10, 12; *kataphroneō*, 2:10); (c) lying and deceptive speech (false teachers, 2:1; specious arguments, 2:3; empty speech, 2:17; enticement, 2:14, 18; false promises, 2:19; scoffing, 3:3; deceit, 2:15; 3:17).

Why this cultural attention to the mouth? Control of mouth and tongue can profitably be examined under two rubrics: purity and honor and shame. The author and his cultural world greatly valued an orderly way of life, especially one of social and bodily self-control (see *egkrateia*, 1:6; Gal 5:23; Acts 24:25). Social order is replicated by bodily discipline. Speaking praise of God and truth to one's neighbor requires guarding the mouth. Conversely, lack of control of the "little member, the tongue" (James 3:5) can set a forest ablaze. In this document, an evil mouth speaks false doctrines, leading people to further uncontrol of the body, namely, to sexual immorality. False speech leads some to return to uncleanness, like a dog to vomit or a pig to mire.

An evil mouth likewise causes great ruin by disparaging authority in the social game of challenge and riposte. The challenge, moreover, is perceived as a slur on God's honorable word, the divine promises which lead disciples eventually to share the very nature of God (1:4). Not only is God's word put on trial, so is that of Peter (1:16), the early church, and Paul (3:15–16). Such verbal challenges threaten the orderly and honorable structure of the group, shaming the local leaders and the divine Patron who appointed them. James' exhortation about speech likewise discussed the mouth and tongue in terms of purity (e.g., self-control, 3:2; stains, 3:6; poison, 3:8) and shameful disorder (3:4, 7).

NOTES

PROMISE FREEDOM

Commentators interpret this as a libertinistic credo (F. Spitta, *Der zweite Brief des Petrus und der Brief des Judas* [Halle: Verlag der Buchhandlung des Waisenhauses, 1885], 398–400), a gnostic doctrine (J. N. D. Kelly, *The Epistles of Peter and Jude* [London: Adam and Charles Black, 1969], 251), or a type of antinomianism such as Paul faced at Corinth (E. H. Plumptre, *The General Epistles of St. Peter and St. Jude* [Cambridge: Cambridge University Press, 1926], 187). Indeed, the author accuses his opponents of lawlessness (*athesmoi*, 2:7; 3:17; *anomoi*, 2:8) and states that they "turn away from the holy rule given them" (2:21) and "despise authority" (2:10). Yet these opponents, who scoff at the "promise" of the parousia (3:4a), also proclaim a freedom from the destruction of the world at the parousia (3:4b), from rewards and punishments (3:9), and from divine judgment (2:3b, 10).

In response to this challenge, the author mocks them for their empty and fabricated promise, just as they mocked him. Despite their promise of freedom, they are slaves of what they deny: slaves of destruction (2:19; see 2:3b, 12), judgment (2:17; see 2:4–9), and of rewards and punishments (*misthon adikias*, 2:13). And their freedom leads to immorality, sure proof of its error (2:20).

BETTER . . . THAN

G. F. Snyder ("The *Tobspruch* in the NT," 119) identifies the pattern "better . . . than . . ." as a familiar wisdom form commonly found in Hebrew and Christian literature.

Better a dinner of herbs where love is
    than a fatted ox and hatred with it [Prov 15:17].

Better to go to the house of mourning
than to go to the house of feasting [Qoh 7:2].
Better to hear the rebuke of the wise
than to hear the song of fools [Qoh 7:5].
Better to throw oneself into a fiery furnace
than publicly to put a neighbor to shame [*b. Keth.* 67b].
Better to enter life maimed
than with two hands to be thrown into hell [Mark 9:43].
Better to suffer for doing right
than for doing wrong [1 Peter 3:17].

THE WAY OF RIGHTEOUSNESS

The author frequently uses the metaphor of "two ways" ("straight way" versus "way of Balaam," 2:15). The phrase "way of righteousness" is common in the Greek translation of the Bible (Job 24:13; Prov 21:16, 21) as well as in Christian writings (Matt 21:32). Barnabas offers a most suggestive parallel to this passage when he interprets Prov 1:17 to mean: "a man deserves to perish who has knowledge of the way of righteousness, but turns aside into the way of darkness" (5:4). But something more is implied here, for the phrase reflects the tradition of calling the discipleship of Jesus "the Way" (Acts 19:9, 23; 22:4; 24:14). Indeed, these disciples have "acknowledged" "the way of righteousness," that is, given public loyalty to this particular group and its ways.

THE HOLY RULE

Although *entolē* may mean commandment, here it seems to be taken in a more collective sense as "the rule" of the group. It is used in the sense that the loyal son confesses to his father that he has never disobeyed "his rule" (Luke 15:29) or like the charge given Timothy that he "keep the rule" unstained and free from reproach (1 Tim 6:14). Although Christians know specific rules from Jesus (1 Cor 14:37 and 7:10), the usage here suggests that Christ has given a "new law" for his disciples (see Justin, *Dial.* 12.2). In this sense, "the holy rule" is parallel with "the way of righteousness" discussed above.

DOGS AND PIGS

The author, when citing both dogs and pigs, seems to be appealing to commonplaces known to Jews and Greeks. The dog reference, which comes from Prov 26:11, would strike Jewish ears, whereas the reference to the pig would resonate with Greek. For example, a fragment from Heracleitus speaks about pigs preferring mire to clean water (G. S. Kirk, *Heracleitus. The Cosmic Fragments* [Cambridge: Cambridge University Press, 1954], 76–80); Sextus Empiricus quoted a similar remark: "Pigs, too, enjoy wallowing in the most stinking mire rather than in clear and clean water" (*Pyrrh. Hyp.* 1.56; Clem.

Alex. *Protr.* 10.92.4). This is, then, one more example of the multicultural argument of the author.

BIBLIOGRAPHY

Aubineau, Michel, "La thème du 'bourbier' dans la littérature grecque profane et chrétienne," *RSR* 47 (1959): 185–214.

Boismard, M. E., "II Petr. ii, 18," *RB* 64 (1957): 401.

Dunham, D. A., "An Exegetical Study of 2 Peter 2:18–22," *BSac* 140 (1983): 40–54.

Snyder, Graydon F., "The *Tobspruch* in the New Testament," *NTS* 23 (1977): 117–20.

X.
The Fourth Slander: God's Powerful Word Challenged (3:1–4)

♦

3 1. Beloved, I am now writing you this second letter, in both of
which I arouse in your memory a correct understanding,
2. reminding you of the predictions by the holy prophets and the
command of the Lord and Savior through your apostles.
3. Know this first, that in the last days scoffers will come scoffing,
acting according to their peculiar passions, 4. and saying,
"Where is the promise of his coming? For, from the day the
fathers fell asleep, all has remained just as from the beginning of
creation."

Rhetorical Setting

We are always dependent upon the author's version of what his opponents said. Here he appears to be citing their very words, as he quotes them asking a challenging question, "Where is the promise of his coming?" His quotation from the scoffers is critically balanced by a reference to the tradition about "the coming." He appeals to writings which contain the orthodox understanding of the matter, first a previous letter, then the predictions of the prophets, and finally the commands of Jesus handed on by the apostles. This juxtaposition of orthodoxy and heterodoxy serves to label the author's tradition as true and safe, while labeling that of the scoffers as deviant and dangerous.

Redaction: Relationship to Jude

2 Peter 3:1–3	*Jude 17–18*
1. *Beloved,* I am now writing to you this second letter, in both of which I arouse in your memory a correct understanding,	
2. *reminding* you of *the words* of the holy prophets and the command of *the Lord* and Savior through your *apostles.*	17. *Beloved, remember the words* of *the apostles* of *our Lord* Jesus Christ foretold, how they told you:
3. Know this first, that *in the last days scoffers will come* scoffing acting according to their proper *passions*	18. *In the last time scoffers will come* who go the way of godless *passions* . . .

Both authors turn from polemic against their opponents to address of the recipients of their respective letters as "Beloved" (*agapētoi*). 2 Peter begins with an appeal to a constant and widespread tradition. This is his second letter on the topic (3:1), which is intended to remind the addressees not only of the first letter but also of the words of the ancient prophets as well as of the recent apostles. His task of "reminding" them (see 1:12–15) contrasts with the willful forgetting by his opponents (3:5). He claims again to have the correct understanding of the tradition, just as earlier he claimed inspiration for his interpretation (1:20–21). Thus he redacts Jude's modest remarks to fit carefully into his sustained riposte to the opponents' challenge.

Although both authors remind their addressees that "in the last days scoffers will come," the sense of this in 2 Peter is quite specific. Jude reports nothing of the words of his scoffers, whereas 2 Peter indicates the content of the scoffing in v 4, namely, their polemic against "the promise of his coming." Both authors link their opponents' scoffing to one of the cardinal vices, "passion" or *epithymia.* In the case of 2 Peter, this discredits the opponents' challenge to the parousia, for their immoral doctrine could never be from God. Formally, the remarks in 2 Peter are part of the conventions of a farewell address, in which the dying patriarch predicts dire future times for his followers, which is not the case with Jude's remark.

Honor and the Lord's State Visit

We noted in regard to 2:1–3 that the honor of God and Christ was challenged by those who deny their power as judge and their authority as lawgiver and sovereign. The author records another honor challenge to God in the scoffing question, "Where is . . . ?" In the Bible, questions such as "Where is . . . ?" regularly call into question the existence of a person or the truth of something. Such questions are highly insulting and so function as honor challenges. On the occasion of military defeat or failure of justice, Israel's opponents asked "Where is your God?" (Deut 32:37; Judg 6:13; 2 Kgs 18:34; 19:13; Pss 42:3, 10; 79:10; Isa 36:19; 51:13; Jer 2:6; Hos 13:10; Joel 2:17). Scoffers taunted Jeremiah: "Where is the word of the Lord?" (Jer 17:15; see 2 Kgs 2:14; Ps 89:49; Isa 63:11, 15). The same rhetorical form is found in the New Testament as well (see Luke 8:25; 1 Cor 1:20; 15:55).

God's word, the precious or honorable (*timias*) promise (1:4), is being ridiculed. Challenged also is God's power, when the opponents scoff at God's destruction of this world in judgment. As in 2:1, the opponents are not seen as true atheists who deny God's existence, but as people who shame God by rejecting God's purpose and power.

"Scoffers" and "scoffing" should be evaluated in light of honor challenges. In some places *empaizein* is translated as "to insult" (Gen 39:14), but especially as "to make sport of" (Exod 10:2; Num 22:29; Judg 16:25, 27; 1 Sam 6:6; 31:4; Ezek 22:5). Jesus himself is "mocked" (*empaizein*) both by physical and verbal abuse in his passion (Matt 27:29, 31, 41; Luke 23:11). Verbal mockery of this sort is more painful and shameful than physical abuse (Heb 11:36). The people described in 3:3–4 are not simply skeptics, then, but mockers who bring shame on someone or something by challenging questions.

"Promise" is evidently a controversial term in the group of the author. The opponents "promise freedom" (2:19), a promise quite different from God's "precious and greatest promises" (1:4). Thus the scoffers challenge God's promises by offering better ones of their own, which contradict God's promises. God, then, is dishonored. Ironically, God's promise of a cataclysm aids the righteous to escape destruction, whereas the scoffers' promise of freedom from cosmic destruction only assures ruin. Hence, God is dishonored not just by the scoffing at his word, but also by the rejection of his gift which would enable the followers of Jesus to escape ruin and destruction. The honor of God, then, is challenged by the public skepticism of the scoffers; God's word, power, and benefaction are ridiculed.

The author speaks of the Lord's parousia, which has become the technical term for the second coming of the Son of Man (Matt 24:3; 1 Thess 2:19; 4:15), who is the judge of the living and the dead (Acts 10:42; 2 Tim 4:8; James 5:9). This cosmic event was seemingly described in terms of accompanying cosmic phenomena according to Mark 13:24–25/Matt 24:29 and Luke 21:25–26. The gospel scenarios of the parousia are themselves based on earlier prophetic oracles such as Isa 13:10; 34:4; Ezek 32:7–8; Joel 2:10, 31; 3:15. In part such scenarios were elements of the conventional description of the state visit of an honorable sovereign, in particular the God of Israel. The power and honorable status of the sovereign are publicly expressed through symbolic, even cosmic, phenomena. The same is applicable both for the birth of God's Christ (Matt 2:2) and his death (27:45, 51–54). Yet as the document explains later, the parousia of the Lord came to include expectation of new heavens and a new earth, which entails the destruction of the old ones (see Rev 6:12–14; 8:12; 21:1). Thus notions of honor, that is, the cosmic phenomena accompanying the sovereign's visit, are linked with those of purity, the cleansing of the corrupt world and its replacement with a new, pure one.

THE PROMISE

The use of "promise" in regard to the Lord's parousia is unusual in the New Testament. This term tends to refer to phenomena such as (a) the promise of the Holy Spirit (Luke 24:49; Acts 1:4; 2:33, 39; Gal 3:14; Eph 1:13), (b) the promise made to Abraham, Isaac, and Jacob (Acts 7:17; 13:32; 26:6; Rom 4:13; 9:4; 15:8; 2 Cor 7:1; Gal 3:16; Eph 2:12; Heb 6:12; 11:9), (c) the messianic promises already fulfilled in Christ (Acts 13:23; Eph 3:6), and (d) the postmortem reward of life (1 Tim 4:8; Heb 10:36). It is evidently a controversial term in the group of the author, for the opponents "promise freedom" (2:19), a promise quite different from God's "precious and greatest promises" (1:4). Ironically, God's promise of a cataclysm aids the righteous to escape destruction, whereas the scoffers' promise of freedom from cosmic destruction only assures ruin. Hence, God is dishonored not just by the scoffing at his word, but also by the rejection of his gift which would enable the followers of Jesus to escape ruin and destruction.

NOTES

THIS SECOND LETTER

Scholars have suggested four possible referents for the "first letter": (1) 1 Peter (Boobyer, "The Indebtedness"); (2) Jude (T. V. Smith, *Petrine Controversies in Early Christianity* [Tübingen: J. C. B. Mohr, 1985], 74–78); (3) 2 Peter 3 (see M. McNamara, "The Unity of Second Peter: A Reconsideration," *Scr* [1960]: 13–19); and (4) a lost letter. Given the author's wish to be identified as "Simeon Peter," it is easiest to see the reference here to 1 Peter.

CORRECT UNDERSTANDING

The Greek words *eilikrinē dianoia* are commonly translated as "wholesome thinking" or "pure thoughts." In light of the controversy over the interpretation of oracles in 1:20–21 and the correct meaning of certain difficult things in Paul's letters (see 3:17), we render these words as "correct understanding." *Dianoia,* moreover, is not simply the faculty of the mind (C. Spicq, *Les Epîtres de Saint Pierre* [Paris: Gabalda, 1966], 244; K. H. Schelkle, *Die Petrusbriefe, der Judasbrief* [HTKNT 13/2. Freiburg: Herder, 1961], 222) or the process of understanding (R. Knopf, *Die Briefe Petri und Judä* [MeyerK 12. 7th ed.: Göttingen: Vandenhoeck and Ruprecht, 1912], 308), but the very product of the mind, namely, understanding or meaning (J. Behm, "Dianoia," *TDNT* 4.965; LSJ, 405). For example, in the Letter to Aristeas (170–71), the author praises "the natural interpretation" (*physikē dianoia*) of the law, whereby the symbolic meaning of animal sacrifices is explained. In Josephus, *dianoia* refers to both Solomon's "discovery of the meaning" (*dianoian*) of the conundrums of the King of Tyre (*Ant.* 8.143) and his rendering of the difficult sayings of the Queen of Sheba (*Ant.* 8.166). He understands *dianoia* as Daniel's wise interpretation of dreams and visions (*Ant.* 10.217, 234).

The understanding of sacred things must be "correct" (*eilikrinē*); that is, it must be "pure" (i.e., not mixed with heresy), and "correct" (i.e., not wrong), and "true" (i.e., not false). This qualification is more an epistemological than a moral note (F. Büchsel, "Eilikrinēs," *TDNT* 2.398); Philo uses it repeatedly to describe true knowledge versus sense perception (*Leg. All.* 1.88–89; 3.111; *Ebr.* 101, 189, 190; *Mig.* 222; *Her.* 98, 308; *Somn.* 2.20, 74, 134; *Mos.* 2.40). It refers to foreseeing as well as remembering (*Spec. Leg.* 1.99), and describes a type of insight which prophesies the future (*Spec. Leg.* 1.219).

REMINDING AND REMEMBERING

The author contrasts himself with his opponents in terms of reminding and remembering versus forgetting. In 1:12–13 he states that his aim is to leave a lasting remembrance of the tradition. And in fact he reminds the church first by repetition of his eyewitness experience (1:16), then by recitation of scriptural examples (2:4–9, 15–16), and finally by recollection of a previous letter (3:1) and the words of the prophets and the Lord (3:2). Specifically, he reminds them about the traditions concerning the parousia and God's judgment (3:5–7, 8, 9, 10, 13, 15). He contrasts his reminding with the opponents' forgetting (*lanthanei*, 3:5, 8), which he interprets as a willful rejection of the truth of the tradition. He styles himself, then, according to gospel commands: leaders are commanded to "watch" and "be prepared" in regard to the parousia (Mark 13:33–37) and disciples are commanded to "remember" and "watch" (1 Thess 5:6; Acts 20:31; 1 Cor 16:13).

LAST DAYS

It is typical of farewell addresses to contain predictions of future crises for the clan or group. Jesus is credited with predicting future harassment of his followers

(Mark 14:27; John 16:1–4, 32) and future false teachers in their midst (Mark 13:22–23). Paul likewise predicted wolves attacking the flock after his death (Acts 20:29–30). The author has already indicated that false teachers will come to disturb the group (2:1–2).

ALL HAS REMAINED THE SAME

Some ancient thinkers acclaimed the world "eternal in the past" (*agenētos*) and "imperishable in the future" (*aphthartos*). For example, Plutarch attributes to Epicurus this sense of the complete eternity of the world: "the universe is infinite, ungenerated [*agenēton*] and imperishable [*aphtharton*]" (*Adv. Colotem* 1114 A). This may be found frequently in the writings of Aristotle (*de Caelo* 1.12 282 a 25) and Philo (*Aet.* 7, 10, 12, 20, 69, 93; *Somn.* 2.283). Although formal discussions of cosmology abound among ancient thinkers, the issue here is no mere debate over abstract philosophical ideas, but a challenge to the traditional doctrine of God as well. Thinkers such as Epicurus denied divine providence, saying that God is not moved in any way, either to create the world or to judge it. The opponents of 2 Peter mock certain doctrines about God: (a) the Lord's coming, (b) the slowness of God's judgment, and in fact, (c) the very idea of divine judgment (2:1, 3). Hence, God's honor is challenged once more by the mockery of divine power to act in the physical world as well as the world of human affairs.

BIBLIOGRAPHY

Allmen, Daniel von, "L'apocalyptique juive et le retard de la parousie en II Pierre 3:1–13," *RTP* 16 (1966): 256–58.

Boobyer, G. H., "The Indebtedness of 2 Peter to 1 Peter," in *New Testament Essays: Studies in Memory of T. W. Manson* (A. J. B. Higgins, ed.; University of Manchester Press, 1959), 34–53.

Cavallin, H. C. C., "The False Teachers of 2 Pt as Pseudo-prophets," *NovT* 21 (1979): 263–70.

Vögtle, Anton, "Die Parousie- und Gerichtsapologetik 2 P 3," *Das Neue Testament und die Zukunft des Kosmos* (Düsseldorf: Patmos Verlag, 1979), 121–32.

Zmijewski, J., "Apostolische Paradosis und Pseudepigraphie im Neuen Testament," *BZ* 23 (1979): 161–71.

XI. REPLY TO THE FOURTH SLANDER: DIVINE WORD OF JUDGMENT DEFENDED (3:5–7)

♦

3 5. For in holding this, they forget that from of old by the word of
God the heavens were created and earth was put together out of
and through water. 6. Then by these the world was flooded with
water and destroyed. 7. By the same word the heavens and earth
are now stored up for fire, kept for the day of judgment and
destruction of the ungodly.

HONOR DEFENDED

The author delivers his riposte in 3:5–7 to the challenge to God's honor in 3:3–4. In mockery of the promise of the great state visit of the King, the scoffers shame God by rejecting his divine power over creation, especially power to destroy the world in a purifying fire. In response, the author defends the honorable word of God, noting that as the heavens and earth were created by God's powerful and reliable word, so that same word proclaims the world's end. Whereas the power of God was impugned, our author acclaims God's power, both to create and to judge (see 2:9–10). And as God has defended his honor through a judgment of the ungodly by water in Noah's time (see 2:5), so God will vindicate his power with a fiery judgment of the ungodly in the future. The mockers are labeled "ungodly," highlighting their perceived role as casting shame on God's authority and power. Thus God's honor is defended by the celebration of divine power, reliable word, and judgment. Every challenge must be answered.

TWO POWERS

The author, who has always championed the orthodox doctrine about God, now alludes to God's basic actions of creation and judgment. This reflects the theology found in Philo and rabbinic tradition that God's actions in the world are summarized and known in two basic powers, creative power (*dynamis poiētikē*) and executive power (*dynamis basilikē*). Philo reflects this tradition about God when he describes the ark of the covenant; on top of the ark are the two cherubim and above them God rests. In an allegorical mode, Philo likens the two cherubim to the two basic powers of God. Because the passage has direct bearing on how we understand God's power in 3:5–7, we cite it in full:

> I should myself say that they [the Cherubim] are allegorically representations of the two most august and highest potencies [*dynameis*] of Him that is, the creative and the kingly. His creative potency is called God [*theos*], because through it He placed and made and ordered this universe, and the kingly is called Lord [*kyrios*], being that with which He governs what has come into being and rules it steadfastly with justice [*Mos.* 2.99; see also *Plant.* 85–89; *Fuga* 101; *Abr.* 121–22].

God, then, has two basic powers, creative and kingly; each power represents a fundamental name of the Deity, either "God" or "Lord." In the beginning God created the world by his creative power and maintains it by his providence. At the end of time, by his kingly power God will judge the world, raising the dead and apportioning rewards and punishments. Thus when 2 Peter defends God's power and action at the world's creation and its conclusion, he is again expounding the orthodox doctrine about the Deity.

Moreover, this doctrine of God was a commonplace in the ancient world of Israel. Paul explicitly cites it in his remarks about Abraham's faith in God in Rom 4:17: he believed that God could raise the dead (executive or eschatological power) as well as create something from nothing (creative power). Likewise, John 5:18–29 claims that now Jesus shares these basic powers (J. H. Neyrey, *An Ideology of Revolt* [Philadelphia: Fortress Press, 1988], 21–29). Thus, not only is 2 Peter concerned to defend the tradition of theodicy, the judgmental actions of God, but at stake is a broader defense of God's very powers, creative and executive. Ernst Käsemann ("An Apologia for Primitive Christian Eschatology," 178) once complained that the true theological problem with this document "lies in the fact that its eschatology lacks any vestige of Christological orientation." This remark totally ignores the fact that the conflict in 2 Peter is over theodicy and theology, the doctrine of God professed by the early church. Käsemann did not see that the author is ever concerned to defend the honor of God.

WORD OF GOD

Bauckham (*Jude, 2 Peter*, 296–97) notes how unusual is the expression that the world was both created and destroyed by the word of God. The issue probably depends less on cosmological theory than the immediate crisis surrounding the various words of God in the document. On the one hand, scoffers mock the prophetic word (3:3), but speak empty and seductive words themselves (2:18). They themselves promise freedom from judgment (2:19), but seduce others with false words (2:3). In response, the author defends the prophetic word of God (1:17–21) and the promises of God (1:4; 3:4, 9, 13). This word of God is found in the Scriptures (2:4–8, 15–16, 22), the words of the prophets and apostles (3:2), and the inspired words of Paul (3:15–16). The author's own allusion to a "first letter" (3:1) indicates another appeal to a traditional word about God's promises. As noted above, attacks on and defense of God's word are best seen in the light of God's honor. The defense of God's prophetic word, of course, is ever the concern of biblical prophets (see Isa 40:8; 45:23; 55:11).

NOTES

FORGET

The scoffers ignore or forget (3:5), whereas the author remembers and reminds (1:13–15; 3:1–3). The former do not simply suffer lapses of memory but challenge what the author holds sacred and defends. The constant remembering of examples from biblical history illustrates an important aspect of the parenetic role of the author.

OUT OF AND THROUGH WATER

The prepositions here are somewhat confusing. The creation account in Genesis 1 describes how the dry land was separated "out of" the waters above and below, which explains the first phrase here. But it is less clear from Scripture how the earth was made "through" water. The subsequent destruction of the world "through water" (*hydati*, v 6) balances the creative action and thus probably serves as the rhetorical parallel for interpreting the first phrase. On "the metaphysics of prepositions," see Thomas Tobin, "The Prologue of John and Hellenistic Jewish Speculation," *CBQ* 52 (1990): 259.

STORED UP

This translation contains the note that God has a "treasury" of judgment. Philo offered a valuable clue to this expression when he joined two passages from Deuteronomy whose common bond was God's "treasuries." On the one hand, God is said to "open his good treasury, the heavens" (Deut 28:12) to dispense rain and fertility. But God has another treasury in which evils are stored. About these two treasuries Philo writes: "For there are with God treasuries [*thēsauroi*] as of good things so also of evil things. As He saith in the Great Song, 'Are not these laid up in store with me, sealed up in My treasuries in the day of vengeance' . . . You see that there are treasuries of evil things" (*Leg. All.* 3.105–6). *Tg. Yer. II* of Deut 32:34–35 likewise speaks of God's treasuries: "Is not this the cup of punishment, mixed and ordained for the wicked, sealed in my treasuries for the day of great judgment?"

DAY OF JUDGMENT AND DESTRUCTION

The coming of God to judge will eventually be described both in terms of the destruction of the old world and the creation of new heavens and a new earth. Here judgment and destruction are highlighted, probably as part of the riposte to the scoffers' denial of God's judgment and their assertion that "all remains the same."

BIBLIOGRAPHY

Allmen, Daniel von, "L'apocalyptique juive et le retard de la parousie en II Pierre 3:1–13," *RTP* 16 (1966): 260–62.

Barnard, L. W., "The Judgment in II Peter iii," *ExpT* 68 (1957): 302.

Chaine, J., "Cosmogonie aquatique et conflagration finale d'après la *secunda Petri*," *RB* 46 (1937): 207–16.

Käsemann, Ernst, "An Apologia for Primitive Christian Eschatology," *Essays on New Testament Themes* (Philadelphia: Fortress Press, 1982), 169–95.

Meier, S., "2 Peter 3:3–7—an Early Jewish and Christian Response to Eschatological Skepticism," *BZ* 32 (1988): 255–57.

Segal, Alan, and Dahl, Nils, "Philo and the Rabbis on the Names of God," *JSJ* 9 (1978): 1–28.

Testa, P. E., "La distruzione del mondo per il fuoco nella seconda epistola de san Pietro," *RivB* 10 (1962): 252–81.

Vögtle, Anton, "Die Parousie- und Gerichtsapologetik 2 P 3," *Das Neue Testament und die Zukunft des Kosmos* (Düsseldorf: Patmos Verlag, 1979), 132–37.

XII.
The Fifth Slander and Reply: Delay of Divine Judgment Defended (3:8–13)

◆

3 8. Beloved, do not let this one fact escape your notice, that with
the Lord, one day is as a thousand years and a thousand years are
as one day. 9. The Lord does not delay about the promise, as
some reckon "delay," but is forbearing toward you. For he does
not wish any to be destroyed, but all to reach repentance.
10. For the day of the Lord will come like a thief. Then the
heavens will pass away with a roar; the elements will be burned up
and dissolved; and the earth and all its works will be found out.
11. Since all these will be dissolved in this way, what sort of
people ought you be, in holy and pious lives. 12. You await and
hasten the coming of the Day of God, when the heavens will be
set on fire and dissolved and the elements burned and melted.
13. According to his promise, we await "new heavens and a new
earth," where righteousness will dwell.

Once More in Defense of the Honor of the Lord

The current passage continues the riposte to the honor of the Lord begun in 3:5–7. Both passages are linked by the phrase "escape your notice": in v 5 the scoffers deliberately ignore the powerful word of God which creates the heavens and earth, and in v 8 the author exhorts his group not to ignore God's sure promise to destroy the heavens and earth, despite the human difficulty of reckoning time. The latest challenge to the Lord is found in the way the scoffers reckon the slowness of the Lord to come and judge. Because God is slow to come, this means that he will not come to exercise power and judgment. The Lord's honor, then, is challenged on two fronts, as impotence in regard to judgment and as the failure of the Lord's promise or word of honor.

In defense of God's honor, the author affirms the quality of time which belongs to the realm of God. Bruce Malina ("Christ and Time: Swiss or Mediterranean?" *CBQ* 51 [1989]: 1–31) presented a model of how first-century Mediterranean peoples understood time. Basically ancient people concern themselves with what happens "today"; they appropriately pray for today's bread (Matt 6:11) or find today's evils sufficient (Matt 6:34). The future belongs to God alone, and it is shameful to delve into it or speculate about it (Malina, 15). The scoffers here are not so much encroaching on the prerogatives of divine time but simply rejecting anything but what can be experienced today, namely, the stability of the world, the nonfulfillment of the promise of the parousia, and the delay of divine judgment. In short, they are concerned only with "today," not the future. Part of the "freedom" which they promise (2:19) consists in present rejection of the future, the realm of God's providence and just judgment. In their concern for "today," they reject God's future time.

As well as God's time is challenged, so is the word of honor of the Lord. According to them, the "promise" of the Lord is an unfaithful word, for it has not come to pass. We recall from the notes to 3:5–7 how the author strove to defend the word of the Lord. One's honor requires that one be faithful to oaths and promises. God's faithful word was a staple affirmation in Paul's letters (Rom 9:6; 1 Cor 1:8; 2 Cor 1:18; 1 Thess 5:24); and God's various oaths were celebrated in Heb 3:11; 4:1–3; 7:20–24. On "word of honor," see Bruce Malina, *The New Testament World: Insights from Cultural Anthropology* (Atlanta: John Knox Press, 1981), 37–38.

In substance, the contempt shown for the Lord's word and for heavenly time effectively challenges the Lord's power, the most salient feature of honor in the ancient world. The scoffers' reckoning of the Lord's "delay" constitutes a rejection of power to come and judge. This mockery in turn calls into question the Lord's role as lawmaker and enforcer of laws. As the author interprets his opponents, they reject the traditional understanding of God as sovereign; they call into question God's providential powers to create and to judge. The honor of God has been impugned. This cannot stand.

In defense of the Lord's honor, the author affirms basically what the scoffers shamed. He reaffirms the incalculable nature of divine time (v 8), the providential nature of the delay of judgment as a gift of time for repentance (v 9), and the power of God to end the world and bring it to judgment (v 10).

INSCRUTABILITY OF DIVINE TIME AND PSALM 90:4

In defense of the incalculable character of divine time, the author cites Ps 90:4; although in an adapted mode. The psalm itself proclaims the complete eternity of God, without beginning or ending, in contrast to the brief existence of mortals. This author does not engage in a contrast between eternal and mortal beings, but stresses that human reckoning of time does not apply to God; for, concerning the Deity, one day is as a thousand years and a thousand years are as one day. Put simply, mortals cannot understand divine chronometry. As we stated above, it is shameful for mortals to encroach on divine prerogatives; to attempt such is a form of idolatry (Deut 18:10–13).

2 Peter, moreover, is not the first person to use Ps 90:4. In general the psalm was cited apropos of the beginning of the world and its end. It was used specifically: (1) to define the length of one of the days of creation (*Gen. R.* VIII.2; *b. Ros. Has.* 31a; *Lev. R.* XIX.1; *Song of Songs R.* V.11; *Num. R.* 4; *Midr. Psalms* 25.8; *Barn.* 15.4); (2) to explain why Adam lived for a thousand years after his sin (*Jub* 4:29–30; *Gen. R.* XIX.8; *Num. R.* V.4 and XXIII.13; Irenaeus, *Adv. Haer.* V.xxiii.2 and xxviii.3); (3) to calculate the length of the Messiah's day (*Midr. Psalms* 90.7; *Yalkut Shimeoni* to Ps 72; *B. Sanh.* 99a); and (4) to explain the length of the world (*Barn.* 15.4; Irenaeus, *Adv. Haer.* V.xxiii; *2 Enoch* 33:1–2; *Pesikta R.* 40.2).

The mysterious indeterminacy of divine time, of course, seems to be the use of Ps 90:4 in 2 Peter. And the second use of the psalm stated above (i.e., the length of Adam's day) also seems appropriate. God declared to Adam concerning the prohibition of eating the fruit that "on the day that you eat it you shall die" (Gen 2:17). Yet Scripture records that Adam did not die immediately, but lived almost a thousand years, which was explained by this midrash:

> "Remember, O Lord, Thy compassions and Thy mercies for they have been from of old" (Ps 25:6). R. Joshua b. Nehemiah interpreted it: [show Thy mercies] wherewith Thou didst treat Adam, for thus saidst Thou to him: "For in the day that thou eatest thereof thou shalt surely die" (Gen 2:17) and hadst Thou not given him one day of Thine, which is a thousand years? [*Gen. R.* XXII.1].

This use, while it is not the source for 3:8, contains structural similarities. God's word will surely come true: Adam will die; but God's mercy delayed punishment. In 2 Peter, God's word will prove true, after God grants mercy to sinners for repentance. Nevertheless, God's time remains mysterious and inscrutable to mortals. Thus God's honor is defended, even as divine mercy is praised.

DELAY

Evidently "delay" (*bradynei, bradytēta*) can be interpreted in many ways. The scoffers apparently reckon the delay of the Lord's promise as evidence of its falseness (3:9a); God will not come (and judge). "Delay" thus functions as a challenge to the group's claim concerning God's word and sovereignty. As we stated in the introduction to 2 Peter 5 (b), Epicureans used the delay of divine judgment as a formal argument against the doctrine of God's providence in the world. In Plutarch's *The Delay of Divine Judgment*, the characters cite the slowness of retribution as the most telling argument against the traditional doctrine: "The delay [*bradytēs*] and procrastination of the Deity in punishing the wicked appears to me the most telling argument by far" (548C); ". . . his slowness [*bradytēs*] destroys belief in providence" (549B). Matthew's gospel offers a comparable example; a wicked servant says "My master is delayed" (*chronizei*, 24:48; see 25:5), which means that he does not expect ever to be held to account for his deeds. And so he acts wickedly on the premise that the master will never judge him (24:49). Watson (*Invention, Arrangement, and Style*, 131) argued that Hab 2:3 stands behind the discussion on "delay"; it was cited and commented upon frequently in the first century (1QHab 7:5–12; 2 *Apoc. Bar.* 20:6; Heb 10:37). But this does not take into account the common use of "delay" as a formal argument against divine judgment. Nevertheless, "delay" functions in here as an argument against the traditional doctrine of God's judgment.

WHAT SORT OF PEOPLE?

People in the ancient world were very unlike modern Westerners who prize a kind of individualism, who celebrate freedom from the past, and who enshrine their individualism in a penumbra of rights. As we described this in the general introduction ("Group-Oriented Person"), ancient peoples might be described as non- and even anti-individualists, whose identity rests in their family membership and whose basic self-knowledge is what is told to them by others. Males are known as sons of their fathers (e.g., James and John are "sons of Zebedee" in Mark 1:19; 3:17) and females in terms of their fathers or husbands (Luke 1:5, 27; 8:3). They are socialized from birth to know their place in the family (first or second son) and in the village (carpenter, farmer, fisherman). They depend on the ascription of honor by others and its acknowledgment. In short, they are socialized to be part of a family or guild, to think of the common good rather than personal wishes, and to let their conscience be formed by others (after all, "conscience" basically means "knowledge with [another]": *syn-eidēsis* or *conscientia;* see B. J. Malina and J. H. Neyrey, "First-Century Personality: Dyadic, Not Individual," *The Social World of Luke-Acts* [Peabody, MA: Hendrickson, 1991], 76–80).

From the very beginning of this document, its addressees were instructed how to think about themselves. They are clients of a great benefactor (1:1, 3–4) and owe their patron honor, respect, and obedience. They are "brothers and sisters" (1:10) in a new kinship group. Even Jesus depends on God's ascription of his identity and honor, as he is told by God that he is "my beloved Son in whom I am well pleased" (1:17). And the author strives to keep the identity of his addressees shaped by his orthodox teaching, rather than by the scoffing and false promises of other teachers. Even prophets and interpreters are themselves dependent on the inspiration of God's spirit, not their individual whims or thoughts (1:20–21).

What sort of lives ought such dyadic people to live? The classical ethical distinction between indicative and imperative may fit here. Since the "indicative" of the lives of the addressees is socialized by God's call and benefaction, then the "imperative" of that identity is to live up to the social expectations of it. Since the identity of these disciples of Jesus is that of people whom God has saved from corruption and to whom God has promised eternal life, then the honorable course of action is to live up to the expectations of such benefaction and to strive to live a life worthy of such a calling.

What sort of lives? First, they should believe God's promises about the parousia (v 12), accepting God's word. Then their lives ought to be lives of holiness and piety, that is, lives of faithfulness to God's call of virtue and purity (1:5–7) and lives of loyalty to the honorable patron, God (1:3–4). But above all, they are lives of obedience and faithfulness, certainly to God and Christ, but also to the prophets and teachers sent them, including the author. Such lives are characterized by "remembrance" of the tradition (not willful forgetting) and by "correct" thinking about difficult or controversial matters, such as the "day" of the parousia (3:8) or its "delay" (3:9, 15). Moreover, given this socialization or "indicative," such lives are spent in waiting and preparation (3:12, 13, 14) or in holding fast (3:17).

MULTICULTURAL ARGUMENT

Certain Jewish traditions concerning the coming judgment of God described it in terms of a failure of the heavenly bodies (Matt 24:29; Mark 13:24–25). Sometimes it is likened to an oven which will burn up all evil (Mal 4:1). But clearly the old heavens and earth will be rolled up and discarded (Isa 34:4; Heb

1:11). In the synoptic gospels, Jesus is credited with saying that "the heavens and earth will pass away" before his words fail (Matt 5:18; 24:35; Luke 16:17; 21:33; *Did.* 10:6), although this remark does not formally predict their passing away. Since judgment is often associated with God's purifying wrath, fire is a common element (Matt 3:10, 12). After God's judgment, new heavens and a new earth are predicted (Isa 65:17; 66:22; Rev 21:1). Elements of this tradition are known throughout the New Testament, but 2 Peter 3:10–13 is one of the clearest summary descriptions of it.

Greek ears would hear this material in terms of the Stoic doctrine of "conflagration" (*ekpyrōsis*) and "regeneration" (*paliggenesia*; *SVF* II.183–91). On the one hand, the world was finite, for it will be consumed in fire ("conflagration"; see Lucretius, *R.N.* 5.381–410; Philo, *Heres* 228; Cicero, *Nat. Deor.* 2.46.118). But it is also immortal, for it is always reconstituted ("regeneration") in a ceaseless cycle (see Philo, *Spec. Leg.* 1.208; *Mos.* 2.65; Seneca, *Ad Marciam* 26.6–7; Arius Didymus in Eusebius, *Prep. Evan.* 15.18; Philo, *Aet.* 9, 47, 76, 107). Philo notes that after the "conflagration," a "new world" is created (*Aet.* 89). According to Justin, Christians quickly noted the similarity between the Greek theory of a fiery end of the world and its reconstitution and their own tradition of a similar kind (*Apol.* 1.20). The argument here seems phrased precisely to appeal to Jewish-Christian and Greek ears alike (see G. Delling, "Stoicheion," *TDNT* 7.673–74, 686).

NOTES

FORBEARANCE

The correct interpretation of the Lord's "delay" is not his failure to judge, but his long-suffering or forbearance of sinners to allow them time to repent before judgment. There were several traditions in antiquity concerning the attributes of God; in one stream, God had thirteen attributes, but other branches focused on two pivotal ones, mercy and justice. When God is described as merciful, kind, forbearing, and the like, such predication goes back to the revelation made to Moses in Exod 34:6–7 in which God's two pivotal attributes were proclaimed:

(a) *mercy:* "The Lord, the Lord, a God merciful and gracious, slow to anger . . ."

(b) *judgment:* ". . . who will by no means clear the guilty, visiting the iniquity of the fathers upon the children"

This revelation, then, became a traditional way of describing God (Num 14:18; Neh 9:17; Ps 86:15; 103:14; 145:8; Joel 2:18; Jonah 4:2; Nah 1:3; Wis 15:1). This text from Exodus, moreover, became the privileged locus for Jewish assertions about God's two attributes:

> Woe to the wicked who turn the Attribute of Mercy into the Attribute of Judgment. Wherever the Tetragrammaton is employed it connotes the Attribute of Mercy, as in the verse, The Lord, the Lord God, merciful and gracious" [*Gen. R.* 33.3; 73.3; *Exod. R.* III.3; *Midr. Ps* 56.10].

In the LXX God's first attribute, mercy, was translated as *makrothymos*. God's slowness to punish allowed time for repentance, and so should not be interpreted as divine impotence, but as one more benefaction. In this the author alludes to the same sort of tradition found in Paul's remarks in Rom 2:4, where "the riches of God's kindness and forbearance and patience . . . should lead you to repentance." This very interpretation seems to be the sense of 3:15 and its equation of forbearance with salvation. As such, then, the author defends God's providence by interpreting delay as a gift to prevent judgment, which is sure to come.

THIEF

Prohibition of theft is one of the Ten Commandments (Exod 20:15; Mark 10:19; Matt 19:18; Rom 13:9), and theft is listed as one of the vices which keep Christians from inheriting God's kingdom (1 Cor 6:10). It is always viewed negatively in the New Testament (Matt 6:19–20; John 10:1, 8, 10; 1 Peter 4:15; Rom 2:21). Theft is an honor challenge, the attempt by the thief to gain advantage by another's loss. Yet thief serves as a metaphor for Jesus and his judgment. According to Matt 24:43, Jesus compares the desired readiness for the parousia of the Son of Man to the vigilance the head of a household should have to forestall a thief's breaking into his house. Yet Paul's use of this tradition actually likens the day of the Lord to a thief (1 Thess 5:2, 4); and Rev 3:3 and 16:15 go so far as to record the prophetic voice of Jesus describing his coming as that of a thief (GThom 21; *Did.* 16.1). Our phrase in 3:10 is identical with that in 1 Thess 5:2, and possibly dependent upon it, since the author claims to know "all Paul's letters" (3:16). In general, there seems to be a tradition dating back to Jesus which compares the parousia to the coming of a thief, a parabolic remark which shocks peasants and artisans to vigilance and defense of their honor.

HEAVENS, ELEMENTS, EARTH

The author operates out of a cosmology typical of his age. He organizes his world according to the basic categories of "heaven and earth," with the occasional mention of "the elements":

3:5–7	heavens, earth, *kosmos*
3:10	heavens, elements, earth

3:12 heavens, elements
3:13 heavens and earth

In 3:5–7 he speaks of the creation of the heavens and the earth, noting that the earth's basic "element" is "water" (3:5); the *kosmos*, presumably the earth, has been judged by a watery destruction (3:6), and both heavens and earth are destined for a future fiery destruction and judgment (3:7). It is this future conflagration which is developed in 3:10, where the heavens are predicted as "passing away," while "the elements" are burned and dissolved.

Exactly how should we understand "the elements"? Bauckham (*Jude, 2 Peter*, 315–17) lists three scholarly options: (a) earth, air, fire, and water; (b) the heavenly bodies; and (c) hostile spiritual powers. Scholarly opinion favors the middle option, citing in support Isa 34:4 LXX, Justin, 2 *Apol.* 5.2; *Dial.* 23.3 (G. Delling, "Stoicheion," *TDNT* 7, 681–82). Yet the first option (four basic elements) has much to recommend it, especially in 2 Peter 3. First, the basic "element" of the earth was "water" (3:5; Delling, "Stoicheion," 672–75). Second, tradition attributed to Jesus a remark that although "the heavens and the earth would pass away," Jesus' word would remain (Mark 13:31; Matt 24:25; Luke 16:17; 21:33; see Matt 5:18). In 3:10, the author says that only "the heavens" will pass away. What about earth? We know from 3:7 that heavens and earth are preserved for a fiery judgment. But what is burned and melted are "the elements," which would seem at least to include earth. Again in 3:12 the heavens will be set on fire and dissolved and the elements burned and dissolved; since the total world is imagined, it would seem that "the elements" here refer to earth as well as heavens. Finally, in 3:13 the author predicts "new heavens and a new earth." The point is that in 3:5–13 the total world—heavens and earth—is envisioned, either as created, judged by water, judged by fire, or re-created. And so the two references to "the elements" in 3:10 and 12 seem to refer to heavens and earth, or at least to include earth.

FOUND OUT

The manuscripts here offer a bewildering variety of alternative readings, attesting to the difficulty of interpreting this term. Although Bruce Metzger and team allow "found out" to stand, they give it a low probability rating and declare it "devoid of meaning in the context" (*A Textual Commentary on the Greek New Testament* [New York: United Bible Societies, 1971], 706). Yet in light of forensic procedure, "being found" is a plausible and contextually appropriate term. Evidently it implies that something will be revealed, uncovered, and brought to light, which might be goodness to be rewarded or evil to be requited. For example, evil may be found (Gal 2:17) or people found to be opposing God (Acts 5:39) or accusations made after a finding is held (Acts 24:5). Good may be revealed (Phil 3:9), or faith be found praiseworthy (1 Peter 1:7). Paul speaks of being found as either a trustworthy steward (1 Cor 4:2) or a false prophet (1 Cor 15:15). Upon scrutiny no evil may be found (Acts 13:28; 23:9; 24:20). In this very document, the author exhorts his hearers "to be found by the Lord without spot or blemish" at the parousia (3:14). In the context of judgment, rewards, and punishments, then, "being found" suggests forensic investigation of the heart, a quality regularly credited to God. F. W. Danker ("II Peter 3:10 and Psalms of Solomon 17:10," ZNW 53 [1962]: 82–86) offered parallels for this very meaning from Ps. Sol 17:10 and 1 Sam 26:18.

AWAIT

Although disciples should generally "watch" or be morally vigilant (1 Cor 16:13; Col 4:2; 1 Peter 5:8), watching (*grēgorein*) is the specific activity of those expecting the master's return on the day of the Lord (Matt 24:42, 43; Mark 13:34–37; 1 Thess 5:6; Rev 16:15). This author does not use "watch" but "await" (*prosdokaō*), but in the same context and in the same sense. Disciples "await" the day of the Lord (v 12) and new heavens and a new earth (v 13). Thus they are prepared in righteousness for it (v 14; see "prepared" in Matt 24:44; 25:10; Luke 12:40; 14:10).

BIBLIOGRAPHY

Allmen, David von, "L'Apocalyptique juive et le retard de la parousie en II Pierre 3:1–13," *RTP* 99 (1966): 255–74.

Bauckham, R. J., "The Delay of the Parousia," *TynB* 31 (1980): 3–36.

Bonus, A., "2 Peter III. 10," *ExpT* 32 (1920–21): 280–81.

Chaine, J., "Cosmogonie aquatique et conflagration finale d'après la *secunda Petri*," *RB* 46 (1937): 207–16.

Delling, Gerhard, "Stoicheion," *TDNT* 7.670–87.

Jacono, V., "La *PALIGGENESIA* in S. Paolo e nell' ambiente pagano," *Bib* 15 (1934): 369–98.

Lenhard, H., "Ein Beitrag zur Ubersetzung von II Ptr. 3.10d," ZNW 52 (1961): 128–29.

Milligan, G., "2 Peter III. 10," *ExpT* 32 (1920–21): 331.

Neyrey, Jerome, "The Form and Background of the Polemic in 2 Peter," *JBL* 99 (1980): 423–30.

Olivier, F., "Une correction au texte de Nouveau Testament: II Pierre 3,10," *Essai dans le domaine du monde Gréco-Romain Antique et dans celui de Nouveau Testament* (Geneva: Librairie Droz, 1963), 129–52.

Otto, J. K. T. von, "Haben Barnabas, Justinus und Irenäus den zweiten Petrusbrief (3,8) benutzt?" *Zeitschrift für wissenschaftliche Theologie* 20 (1877): 525–29.

Riesner, R., "Der zweite Petrus-Brief und die Eschatologie," *Zukunftserwartung in biblischer Sicht. Beiträge zur Eschatologie* (G. Maier, ed.; Wuppertal: R. Brockhaus, 1984), 124–43.

Roberts, J. W., "A Note on the Meaning of II Peter 3:10d," *ResQ* 6 (1962): 32–33.

Smitmans, Adolf, "Das Gleichnis vom Dieb," *Wort Gottes in der Zeit: Festschrift Karl Hermann Schelkle* (Helmut Feld and Josef Nolte, eds.; Düsseldorf: Patmos-Verlag, 1973), 43–68.

Testa, P. E., "La distruzione del mondo per il fuoco nella 2 ep. di Pietro 3:7, 10, 13," *RivB* 10 (1962): 252–81.

Thiede, C. P., "A Pagan Reader of 2 Peter: Cosmic Conflagration in 2 Peter 3 and the *Octavius* of Minucius Felix," *JSNT* 26 (1986): 79–96.

Vögtle, Anton, "Die Parousie- und Gerichtsapologetik 2 P 3," *Das Neue Testament und die Zukunft des Kosmos* (Düsseldorf: Patmos Verlag, 1979): 138–39.

Wenham, D., "Being 'Found' on the Last Day: New Light on 2 Peter 3.10 and 2 Corinthians 5.3," *NTS* 33 (1989): 477–79.

Wilson, W. E., "*Heurethesetai* in 2 Pet. iii. 10," *ExpT* 32 (1920–21): 44–45.

Wolters, A., "Worldview and Textual Criticism in 2 Peter 3:10," *WTJ* 49 (1987): 405–13.

XIII. Final Exhortation and Letter Closing: Stand Firm in the Tradition (3:14–18)

◆

3 14. Therefore, beloved, as you look forward to this, strive to be
found by him spotless, unblemished, and at peace. 15. Reckon
the forbearance of the Lord as salvation, even as our beloved
brother Paul wrote to you according to the wisdom given him.
16. He speaks about these matters in all his letters, in which there
are things hard to interpret, and which the untutored and unstable
distort to their own ruin, as they do also with the other Scriptures.
17. But you, beloved, know this beforehand; guard lest you be led
astray by the deceit of the lawless and fall away from your proper
constancy. 18. Grow in the favor and knowledge of our lord and
savior Jesus Christ. To him be glory both now and on the day of
eternity.

Epistolary Form

Typical New Testament letters end with greetings to and from specific persons of the church, as well as postscripts and doxologies.

Greetings	*Postscripts*	*Doxologies*
Rom 16:3–16, 21–23	———	Rom 16:25–27
1 Cor 16:19–20	1 Cor 16:21–22	1 Cor 16:23–24

Greetings	*Postscripts*	*Doxologies*
2 Cor 13:12–13	———	2 Cor 13:14
———	Gal 6:18	Gal 6:16, 18
———	Eph 6:21–22	Eph 6:23–24
Phil 4:21–22	Phil 4:14–19	Phil 4:20, 23
1 Thess 5:26	1 Thess 5:27	1 Thess 25:24–24
———	2 Thess 3:17	2 Thess 3:16, 18
2 Tim 4:19	2 Tim 4:20–21	2 Tim 4:22
Titus 3:15a	———	Titus 3:15b
Philemon 23–24	———	Philemon 25
1 Peter 5:13–14	1 Peter 5:12	1 Peter 5:11, 14b

This letter ends with a simple doxology, in this case praise to Jesus, not to God. Commentators take the document's perfunctory closing with a simple doxology as further evidence of its pseudepigraphical character as a letter.

Occasionally a letter's ending may reflect themes and issues raised at its beginning (e.g., Rom 1:1–6; 16:25–27), not just forming an inclusion, but highlighting major themes. 2 Peter began with acknowledgment of heavenly benefaction ("grace and peace multiplied," 1:2; "knowledge," 1:2, 3, 5) by Jesus, who is both "Savior" (1:1) and "Lord" (1:2). It ends with an exhortation to grow in that benefaction, both "grace/favor" and "knowledge" from Jesus Christ who is again both "Lord" and "Savior" (3:17). The letter's doxology, moreover, speaks of Jesus' glory both now and on the day of eternity; the mention of that future day seems to summarize the recent discussion about the day of his coming. These are not bland formulas, for the letter was concerned with acknowledging the debt of honor due Jesus, both as benefactor and as judge at the parousia. And part of his benefaction was the very promises and prophecies of his coming.

Typically "glory" is given to God alone (Rom 16:27; 1 Cor 10:31; Phil 1:11), and to give glory to other gods diminishes God's glory. Only in 2 Corinthians do we find passing mention of the "glory of Christ" (3:18; 4:4; 8:23). Yet here, glory is formally ascribed to Jesus Christ. Earlier the author noted that God ascribed "honor and glory" to him on the mountain when he was transfigured (1:17), thus authorizing the church to honor Jesus even as God honors him (see John 5:23).

THE IDEA OF PURITY: SPOTLESS AND UNBLEMISHED

We have noted that "purity" is a general abstract term used by anthropologists to describe what a given culture applies to persons, things, and places which completely fill their definition. In terms of the cultural background of the author, the specific notions of "purity" derive from Jewish and scriptural traditions. For example, Leviticus describes something as blameless which is "perfect, without blemish" (22:19); that is, the object must be bodily complete, perfect in form, and without defect. To be pure it must be as completely itself as possible, with no admixture of something else and with no deficiencies. According to Septuagintal usage, the Pentateuch exclusively uses the term "unblemished" to describe the purity or perfection of animals sacrificed to God, whether bulls (Exod 29:1), goats (Lev 4:23), lambs (Lev 4:32), rams (Lev 5:15, 18), calves (Lev 9:2–3), or red heifers (Num 19:2). These sacrifices, moreover, must be offered by an unblemished priest (1 Macc 4:42; see Josephus *B.J.* 1.269–70; *Ant.* 14.366; 15.17). When Christians describe Jesus either as priest or sacrificial victim, he too is "unblemished" (Heb 9:14; 1 Peter 1:19). According to Lev 21:16–21, only those who enjoy unblemished perfection of the body may come into the temple and offer sacrifice (see also 1QSa 2:3–10; 1QM 7:4–7).

The same term and understanding extend from the objects offered in sacrifice to the persons who made the offerings. According to Lev 11:44–45, God commands his followers to be like God: "Be ye holy as I am holy." God's holiness consists in perfection and even "blamelessness" (Ps 17:30 LXX); his way is "blameless" (2 Sam 22:31 LXX). Since nothing evil, unjust, imperfect, or corrupt is found in God, those who worship this God must likewise be perfect in holiness. The Scriptures use "unblemished" more generally to describe observant persons (Pss 36:18; 118:1 LXX) and their blameless way (Pss 100:1; 118:1; Ezek 28:15). "All unblemished hearts are acceptable" to God (Prov 22:11).

Although *amōmos* generally suggests something beyond reproach or shame (F. Hauck, "Amōmos," *TDNT* 4.829–30), we should understand it in terms of the Jewish association with purity and perfection. First, it appears here in conjunction with a purity-related term, "spotless." Moreover, the author has shamed his opponents for being "spots and blemishes" on the holy gathering (2:13), even as he constantly links them with corruption (2:12, 19). Finally, our author has already exhorted the church members to live "holy and pious lives" (3:11), and to flee from all corruption (1:4). Now he calls on them to be found "spotless and blameless."

This language may be considered a parenetic commonplace in the New Testament. Paul's letters regularly speak of the Christian moral ideal as "holy and blameless" (Eph 1:4; 5:27; Col 1:22), "blameless, innocent and without blemish" (Phil 2:15); disciples must be "unstained and without reproach" as they await the return of the Lord (1 Tim 6:13). Thus, the followers of the holy and perfect God must themselves also be completely free from evil and perfectly obedient to the ways of God.

To ensure this kind of perfection, lines are carefully drawn and fences erected to distinguish and keep separate the sacred and the profane, the perfect and the blemished, the spotless and the sinful. Dualistic contrasts tend to be a preferred mode of definition and distinction in New Testament documents. In this passage the true disciples are those who know and accept the correct interpretation of Paul and the tradition, as opposed to those who distort his letters and the tradition. They reckon "forbearance" correctly as "salvation," not as "delay of judgment" (3:9). Hence, they are stable in their loyalty (*stērigmou*, 3:17) as opposed to the untutored and unstable heretics (3:16). Their end is salvation (3:14), not ruin (3:16).

Group-Oriented Personality, Honor and Authority

We have noted that honor and authority may be either ascribed to someone by a higher-ranking person or claimed by a person on the basis of some achievement. Our author credits Paul with God's ascribed authority, using a formula similar to that found in Paul's own claims to legitimate authority:

- entrusted with a commission: 1 Cor 9:17; Gal 2:7; 1 Thess 2:4
- a gift given to me: 1 Cor 3:10; 15:10
- authority the Lord has given me: 2 Cor 10:8; 13:10

Thus Paul does not promote himself, but reflects what God says about him and wants acknowledged by others about Paul. Our author too claims the same dependence on Jesus' authorization (1:14) and God's prophetic inspiration (1:20–21). Thus group-oriented persons take their cue from God and honor those whom God honors.

In contrast, the opponents are "untutored," that is, they are completely self-made, and lack the legitimacy that comes from studying with an honorable master (Acts 22:3; see John 7:15). They speak on their own authority, which the author challenges when he labels them "untutored and unstable." They stand outside of the ancient tradition, denying elements of the group's confession (2:3; 3:4, 9) and distorting Paul's writings and other Scriptures. Such independence would be considered highly suspect and quite dishonorable.

Paul, in All His Letters

It is generally agreed among scholars that Paul's letters in some form were collected at the end of the first century (Jack Finegan, "The Original Form of the Pauline Collection," *HTR* 49 [1956]: 85–86). One or another letter even seems to have circulated independently (Gamble, "The Redaction of the Pauline Letters," 417). And although we are not clear about the extent of the earliest collection of Paul's letters, the Apostolic Fathers Clement, Ignatius, and Polycarp know the letters to Rome, Corinth, and Thessalonika (see Karl Donfried, *The Setting of Second Clement in Early Christianity* [NovTSup 38. Leiden: E. J. Brill, 1974], 93–95).

If we could be certain just what letters our author knows, this would aid in our historical reconstruction of the collection of Paul's letters as well as of the formation of the canon. But this proves quite difficult. A conservative viewpoint argues that 2 Peter seems to know Romans (2 Peter 3:9, 15 = Rom 2:4), and perhaps 1 Thessalonians (2 Peter 3:10 = 1 Thess 5:2). But many more allusions and echoes from Paul's letters can be found in this document. Readers are reminded of the extensive list of possible parallels between Paul's letters and 2 Peter presented in the introduction to 2 Peter 6 (f) (3).

A number of historical questions arise here. Why mention Paul at all, especially if his letters contain things "hard to interpret" and easily "distorted"? Moreover, is our author strategically ignoring the differences between Peter and Paul (see Gal 2:11–14)? Might the opponents be claiming Paul as their authority in challenging the traditions our author defends? Our author seems to be presenting himself as fully orthodox, faithful to traditions found in the gospels (1:16–18) and in the general tradition (3:1). This might profitably be understood as a claim of legitimacy in virtue of a tradition which is held always by all peoples everywhere. There is only one tradition of teaching on God's judgment and Jesus' parousia; the "false teachers and prophets" who scoff at it are automatically discredited. Hence, the particularities of Paul's letters are ignored in favor of his acceptance as a representative of the tradition; and any historical disagreement between Peter and Paul is either ignored for this reason or simply not known. It is best, then, to read 3:15–16 in terms of a harmonizing tendency which is calculated to present the impression of a fixed tradition of early Christian theology.

NOTES

PEACE

The context of 3:14 suggests that we understand "peace" in terms of its semitic root *šlm*, meaning "complete" or "whole." Linked as it is with being "spotless and unblemished," it connotes a state of purity or holiness. This meaning is found in Isa 32:17, where peace is linked with righteousness (see Pss 72:7; 85:10); occasionally it is juxtaposed with wickedness (Ps 34:14). The closest New Testament parallel is Paul's concluding remark in 1 Thess 5:23, "May the

God of peace sanctify you wholly; may your spirit . . . be kept sound and blameless at the coming of our Lord." Paul noted a "false peace" which scoffed at the parousia and any concern to be ready for it. Here our author exhorts to peace in eagerness for it.

FORBEARANCE

The author repeats the correction he gave in 3:9 to the scoffers' derision of the delay of judgment. Divine forbearance is a benefaction to us, a grant of time to repent and be found spotless. Again, 2 Peter is concerned to give a "correct interpretation" of all things (3:1), whether the correct meaning of the "day" of the Lord (3:8) or of God's "delay" (3:9).

KNOW THIS BEFOREHAND

Forewarned is forearmed. A characteristic element of testaments and farewell discourses is a prediction of wolves tearing the community and false teachers spreading their poison (Acts 20:29–30; see 3:3–4). Knowing the authentic tradition, the church can then spot these wolves and be on its guard.

BIBLIOGRAPHY

Conti, M., "La Sophia di 2 Petr. 3.15," *RivB* 17 (1969): 121–38.

Gamble, Harry, "The Redaction of the Pauline Letters and the Formation of the Pauline Corpus," *JBL* 94 (1975): 403–18.

Hiebert, D. E., "Selected Studies from 2 Peter. Part 4: Directives for Living in Dangerous Days: An Exposition of 2 Peter 3:14–18a," *BSac* 141 (1984): 330–40.

Neyrey, Jerome H., "Unclean, Common, Polluted, and Taboo," *Forum* 4/4 (1988): 72–82.

Ring, R., *The Meaning and Significance of II Peter 3:15b–17* (Unpublished dissertation: University of Chicago, 1955).

Schmitals, W., "On the Composition and Earliest Collection of the Major Epistles of Paul," *ZNW* 51 (1960): 225–45.

2 Peter: Bibliography

♦

Abbott, E. A., "The Second Epistle of St. Peter," *Exp* 2 (1882): 49–63, 139–53, 204–19.

Alexander, T. D., "Lot's Hospitality: A Clue to His Righteousness," *JBL* 104 (1985): 289–91.

Allmen, D. von, "L'apocalyptique juive et le retard de la parousie en II Pierre 3:1–13," *RTP* 99 (1966): 255–74.

Baasland, E., "2 Peters brev og urkristelig profeti. Eksegese av 2, Pet. 1,12–21," *Tidsskrift for Teologi og Kirke* 53 (1982): 19–35.

Barnard, L. W., "The Judgment in II Peter iii," *ExpT* 68 (1958): 302.

Barnett, A. E., "The Second Epistle of Peter," *The Interpreter's Bible* (Nashville: Abingdon Press, 1957), 12.163–206.

Bauckham, Richard J., "The Delay of the Parousia." *TynB* 31 (1981): 3–36.

———, "2 Peter: A Supplementary Bibliography," *JETS* 25 (1982): 91–93.

———, *Jude, 2 Peter* (Word Biblical Commentary 50. Waco, TX: Word Books, 1983).

———, "James, 1 and 2 Peter," *It Is Written: Scripture Citing Scripture. Essays in Honour of Barnabas Lindars* (D. A. Carson and H. G. M. Williamson, eds.; Cambridge: Cambridge University Press, 1988), 303–17.

———, "2 Peter: An Account of Research," *ANRW* 2.25.2 (1988): 3713–52.

———, "Pseudo-Apostolic Letters," *JBL* 107 (1988): 469–94.

Beker, J. C., "Second Letter of Peter," *IDB* 3.767–71.

Berger, Klaus, "Streit um Gottes Vorsehung. Zur Position der Gegner im 2. Petrusbrief," *Tradition and Re-Interpretation in Jewish and Early Christian Literature: Essays in Honour of Jürgen C. H. Lebram* (J. W. van Henten, ed.; Leiden: E. J. Brill, 1986), 136–49.

Bigg, Charles, *A Critical and Exegetical Commentary on the Epistles of St. Peter and St. Jude* (Edinburgh: T. & T. Clark, 1902).

Blakely, W. A., *Manuscript Relationships as Indicated by the Epistles of Jude and II Peter* (Unpublished dissertation: Emory University, 1964).

Blank, J., "The Person and Office of Peter in the New Testament," *Concilium* 3 (1973): 42–55.

Böhmer, J., "Tag und Morgenstern? zu II Petr. 1.19," ZNW 22 (1923): 228–33.

Boismard, M. E., "II Petr. ii, 18," *RB* 64 (1957): 401.

Bonus, A., "2 Peter III. 10." *ExpT* 32 (1920–21): 280–81.

Boobyer, G. H., *St. Mark and the Transfiguration Story* (Edinburgh: T. & T. Clark, 1942).

———, "The Indebtedness of 2 Peter to 1 Peter," *New Testament Essays: Studies in Memory of T. W. Manson* (A. J. B. Higgins, ed.; University of Manchester Press, 1959), 34–53.

———, "II Peter," *Peake's Commentary on the Bible* (M. Black and H. H. Rowley, eds.; London: Thomas Nelson, 1962), 1031–34.

Bornhäuser, K., "Vom Morgenstern," *Monatsschrift für Pastoraltheologie* (1922): 147–48.

Bowman, John W., *The Letter to the Hebrews, the Letter of James, the First and Second Letters of Peter* (Richmond, VA: John Knox Press, 1963).

Boys-Smith, E. P., " 'Interpretation' or 'Revealment': 2 Pet. i. 20. II," *ExpT* 8 (1896–97): 331–32.

Bratcher, Robert G., A *Translator's Guide to the Letters from James, Peter and Jude* (New York: United Bible Societies, 1984).

Bretscher, P. G., "Exodus 4:22–23 and the Voice from Heaven," *JBL* 87 (1968): 301–11.

Brown, Raymond E., "Peter," *IDBSup* 654–57.

Brown, Raymond E., Donfried, Karl, and Reumann, John (eds.), *Peter in the New Testament* (Minneapolis: Augsburg Publishing House, 1973).

Caulley, T. S., *The Idea of Inspiration in 2 Peter 1:16–21*. (Unpublished dissertation: Tübingen, 1983).

Cavallin, H. C. C., "The False Teachers of 2 Pt as Pseudo-prophets," *NovT* 21 (1979): 263–70.

Chaine, J., "Cosmogonie aquatique et conflagration finale d'après la *secunda Petri*," *RB* 46 (1937): 207–16.

———, *Les Epîtres catholique: La seconde Epître de saint Pierre, les Epîtres de saint Jean, l'Epître de saint Jude* (EBib. 2d ed. Paris: Gabalda, 1939).

Chang, A. D., "Second Peter 2:1 and the Extent of the Atonement," *BSac* 142 (1985): 52–63.

Chase, F. H., "Second Epistle of Peter," A *Dictionary of the Bible* (J. Hastings, ed.; New York: Scribners, 1900), 3.796–818.

Cothenet, E., "La tradition selon Jude et 2 Pierre," *NTS* 35 (1989): 407–20.

Conti, M., "La Sophia di 2 Petr. 3.15," *RivB* 17 (1969): 121–38.

Cooper, W. H., "The Objective Nature of Prophecy According to II Peter," *Lutheran Church Quarterly* 13 (1940): 190–95.

Cox, S., "From Starlight to Sunlight. 2 Peter i.16–20," *Exp* 1/1 (1875), 169–85.

———, "Lot. 2 Peter II. 7, 8," *Exp* 2/8 (1884): 270–80.

Cranfield, C. E. W., *I & II Peter and Jude: Introduction and Commentary* (London: SCM Press, 1960).

Crehan, J., "New Light on 2 Peter from the Bodmer Papyrus," *Studia Evangelica*, vol. 7 (Berlin: Akademie-Verlag, 1982), 145–49.

Curran, J. T., "The Teaching of II Peter 1:20," *TS* 4 (1943): 347–68.

Dalton, W. J., "The Interpretation of 1 Peter 3,19 and 4,6, Light from 2 Peter," *Bib* 60 (1979): 547–55.

Danker, F. W., "II Peter 3:10 and Psalm of Solomon 17:10," ZNW 53 (1962): 82–86.

———, "The Second Letter of Peter," *Hebrews, James, 1 and 2 Peter, Jude, Revelation* (G. Krodel, ed.; Philadelphia: Fortress Press, 1977), 81–91.

———, "2 Peter 1: A Solemn Decree," *CBQ* 40 (1978): 64–82. Reprinted in his *Benefactor* (St. Louis: Clayton Publishing House, 1982), 453–67.

Davey, G. R., "Old Testament Quotations in the Syriac Version of I and II Peter," *Parole de l'orient* 3/2 (1972): 353–64.

Desjardins, M., "The Portrayal of the Dissidents in 2 Peter and Jude: Does It Tell Us More About the 'Godly' than the 'Ungodly'?" *JSNT* 30 (1987): 89–102.

Dillenseger, P. J., "L'authenticite de la II[a] Petri," *Melanges de la Faculté orientale de l'Université Saint-Joseph, Beyrouth* 2 (1907): 173–212.

Donfried, Karl P., *The Setting of Second Clement in Early Christianity* (NovTSup 38. Leiden: E. J. Brill, 1974).

Dschulnigg, P., "Der theologische Ort des Zweiten Petrusbrief," BZ 33 (1989): 161–77.

Dunham, D. A., "An Exegetical Study of 2 Peter 2:18–22," *BSac* 140 (1983): 40–54.

Dunnett, W. M., "The Hermeneutics of Jude and 2 Peter: The Use of Ancient Jewish Traditions," *JETS* 31 (1988): 287–92.

Durand, A., "Le Sens de II Petri, 1,20," *RSR* 2 (1911): 187–89.

Elliott, John H., "A Catholic Gospel. Reflections on 'Early Catholicism' in the New Testament," *CBQ* 31 (1969): 213–23.

———, *I-II Peter/Jude* (Augsburg Commentary on the New Testament. Minneapolis: Augsburg Publishing House, 1982), 119–58.

———, "Peter, Silvanus and Mark in 1 Peter and Acts. Sociological-Exegetical Perspectives on a Petrine Group in Rome," *Wort in der Zeit. Festgabe für K. H. Rengstorf* (W. Haubeck and M. Bachmann, eds.; Leiden: E. J. Brill, 1980), 250–67.

Ernst, C., "The Date of II Peter and the Deposit of Faith," *The Clergy Review* 47 (1962): 686–89.

Falconer, R. A., "Is Second Peter a Genuine Epistle to the Churches of Samaria?" *Exp* 6/5 (1902): 459–72; 6/6 (1902): 47–56, 117–27, 218–27.

Farkasfalvy, D., "The Ecclesial Setting of Pseudepigraphy in Second Peter and Its Role in the Formation of the Canon," *Second Century* 5 (1985): 3–29.

Farmer, William R., "Some Critical Reflections on Second Peter," *Second Century* 5 (1985): 30–46.

Farrar, F. W., "Dr. Abbott on the Second Epistle of St. Peter," *Exp* 2/3 (1882): 401–23.

———, "The Second Epistle of St. Peter and Josephus," *Exp* 3/8 (1888): 58–69.

Flanders, Helmut J., *The Relation of Jude to II Peter* (Unpublished dissertation: Southern Baptist Theological Seminary, 1951).

Foerster, W., "Peter, Second Epistle of," *Dictionary of the Bible* (J. Hastings, ed.; rev. ed. F. C. Grant and H. H. Rowley; New York: Scribners' Sons, 1961), 757–59.

Fornberg, Tord, *An Early Church in a Pluralistic Society: A Study of 2 Peter* (ConBNT 9. Lund: C. W. K. Gleerup, 1977).

Fransen, I., "Le Feu de la Gloire (2 Pierre)," *BVC* 33 (1960): 26–33.

Fuchs, Eric, and Reymond, Pierre, *La Deuxième Epître de Saint Pierre, L'Epître de Saint Jude* (Geneva: Labor et Fides, 1988).

Glasson, T. F., *Greek Influence in Jewish Eschatology* (London: SPCK, 1961).

Green, Michael, *2 Peter Reconsidered* (London: Tyndale, 1961).

———, *The Second Epistle General of Peter and the General Epistle of Jude* (2d ed. Leicester: Inter-Varsity Press, 1987).

Grispino, J. A., and Dilanni, A., "The Date of II Peter and the Deposit of Faith," *The Clergy Review* 46 (1961): 601–10.

Gross, J., "*La divinisation du chrétien d'après grecs* (Paris: Gabalda, 1939).

Grundmann, W., *Der Brief des Judas und der zweite Brief des Petrus* (THKNT 15. Berlin: Evangelische Verlagsanstalt, 1974).

Harrington, Daniel J., "The 'Early Catholic' Writings of the New Testament. The Church Adjusting to World-History," *The Word and the World* (R. J. Clifford and G. W. MacRae, eds.; Cambridge, MA: Weston College Press, 1973), 97–113.

Harvey, A. E., "The Testament of Simeon Peter," *A Tribute to Geza Vermes. Essays on Jewish and Christian Literature and History*. (P. R. Davies and R. T. White, eds.; Sheffield: JSOT Press, 1990), 339–54.

Hauck, F., *Die katholischen Briefe* (NTD 10. 8th ed. Göttingen: Vandenhoeck and Ruprecht, 1957).

Hiebert, D. E., "Selected Studies from 2 Peter. Part 1: The Necessary Growth in the Christian Life: An Exposition of 2 Peter 1:5–11," *BSac* 141 (1984): 43–54.

———, "Selected Studies from 2 Peter. Part 2: The Prophetic Foundation for the Christian Life: An Exposition of 2 Peter 1:19–21," *BSac* 141 (1984): 158–68.

———, "Selected Studies from 2 Peter. Part 3: A Portrayal of False Teachers: An Exposition of 2 Peter 2:1–3," *BSac* 141 (1984): 255–65.

———, "Selected Studies from 2 Peter. Part 4: Directives for Living in Dangerous Days: An Exposition of 2 Peter 3:14–18a," *BSac* 141 (1984): 330–40.

Holzmeister, H., "Vocabularium Secundae Epistolae S. Petri Erroresque Quidam de eo Divulgati," *Bib* 30 (1949): 339–55.

Hupper, William G., "Additions to 'A 2 Peter Bibliography,' " *JETS* 23 (1980): 65–66.

James, M. R., *The Second Epistle General of Peter and the General Epistle of Jude* (Cambridge: Cambridge University Press, 1912).

Johnson, Luke T., "Conflict and Christian Self-Definition," *BibT* 25 (1987): 215–19.

Käsemann, Ernst, "An Apologia for Primitive Christian Eschatology," *Essays on New Testament Themes* (Philadelphia: Fortress Press, 1982), 169–95.

Kelly, J. N. D., *The Epistles of Peter and Jude* (London: Adam and Charles Black, 1969).

King, M. A., "Jude and 1 and 2 Peter: Notes on the Bodmer Manuscript," *BSac* 121 (1964): 54–57.

Klein, G., *Die zwölf Apostel: Ursprung und Gehalt einer Idee* (FRLANT 59. Göttingen: Vandenhoeck and Ruprecht, 1961).

———, "Der zweite Petrusbrief und das neutestamentliche Kanon," *Ärgernisse: Konfrontationen mit dem Neuen Testament* (Munich: C. Kaiser, 1970), 109–14.

Klinger, J., "The Second Epistle of Peter: An Essay in Understanding," *St. Vladimir's Theological Quarterly* 17/1–2 (1973): 152–69.

Knoch, O., "Das Vermächtnis des Petrus: Der 2. Petrusbrief," *Wort Gottes in der Zeit. Festschrift für K. H. Schelkle* (H. Feld and J. Nolte, eds.; Düsseldorf: Patmos-Verlag, 1973), 149–65.

Knopf, R., *Die Briefe Petri und Judä* (MeyerK 12. 7th ed. Göttingen: Vandenhoeck and Ruprecht, 1912).

Kugelman, Richard, *James and Jude* (New Testament Message 19. Wilmington, DE: Michael Glazier, 1980).

Kühl, Ernst, *Die Briefe Petri und Judae* (MeyerK 12. 6th ed. Göttingen: Vandenhoeck and Ruprecht, 1897).

Leaney, A. R. C., *The Letters of Peter and Jude* (Cambridge: Cambridge University Press, 1967).

Lenhard, H., "Ein Beitrag zur Übersetzung von II Ptr. 3.10d," *ZNW* 52 (1961): 128–29.

———, "Noch einmal zu 2 Petr 3 10d." *ZNW* 69 (1978): 136.

Lenski, R. C. H., *The Interpretation of the Epistles of St. Peter, St. John and St. Jude* (Columbus, OH: Wartburg, 1945).

Lias, J. J., "The Genuineness of the Second Epistle of St. Peter," *BSac* 70 (1913): 599–606.

Lindemann, A., *Paulus im altesten Christentum: Das Bild des Apostels und die Rezeption der paulinischen Theologie in der frühchristlichen Literatur bis Marcion* (BHT 58. Tübingen: J. C. B. Mohr, 1979).

Lonning, I., "Tradisjon og skrift. Eksegese av 2 Petr 1,19–21," *NorTT* 72 (1971): 129–54.

Louw, J., "Wat Wordt in II Petrus 1:20 Gesteldt?" *NedTTs* 19 (1965): 202–12.

Lövestam, E., "Eschatologie und Tradition im 2. Petrusbrief," *The New Testament Age: Essays in Honor of B. Reicke* (W. C. Weinrich, ed.; Macon, GA: Mercer University Press, 1984), 287–300.

McNamara, M., "The Unity of Second Peter. A Reconsideration," *Scr* 12 (1960): 13–19.

Maier, F., "Ein Beitrag zur Priorität des Judasbriefs," *TQ* 87 (1905): 547–80.

———, "Die Echtheit des Judas- und 2. Petrusbriefes: Eine Antikritik, vornemlich gegen H. I. Holtzmann," *ZTK* 30 (1906): 693–729.

Marshall, I. H., *Kept by the Power of God: A Study of Perseverance and Falling Away* (London: Epworth, 1969).

———, " 'Early Catholicism' in the New Testament," *New Dimensions and New Testament Studies* (R. N. Longenecker and M. C. Tenney, eds.; Grand Rapids, MI: Zondervan Publishing House, 1974), 217–31.

Mayor, Joseph B., "Notes on the Text of the Second Epistle of Peter," *Exp* 6/10 (1904): 284–93.

———, *The Epistle of St. Jude and the Second Epistle of St. Peter* (New York: Macmillan and Company, 1907).

Meier, S., "2 Peter 3:3–7—an Early Jewish and Christian Response to Eschatological Skepticism," *BZ* 32 (1988): 255–57.

Michaels, J. Ramsey, "Second Peter and Jude—Royal Promises," *The New Testament Speaks* (G. W. Barker, W. L. Lane, and J. R. Michaels, eds.; New York: Harper and Row, 1969), 346–61.

Michl, J., *Die katholischen Briefe* (RNT 8. 2d ed. Regensburg: Frederich Pustet, 1968).

Milligan, G., "2 Peter III. 10," *ExpT* 32 (1920–21): 331.

Moffatt, J., *The General Epistles: James, Peter and Judas* (MNTC. London: Hodder and Stoughton, 1928).

Molland, E., "La thèse 'La prophétie n'est jamais venue de la volonté de l'homme' (2 Pierre 1,21) et les Peseudo-Clementines," *ST* 9 (1955): 67–85.

Neyrey, Jerome H., *The Form and Background of the Polemic in 2 Peter* (Unpublished dissertation: Yale University, 1977).

———, "The Apologetic Use of the Transfiguration in 2 Peter 1:16–21," *CBQ* 42 (1980): 504–19.

———, "The Form and Background of the Polemic in 2 Peter," *JBL* 99 (1980): 407–31.

———, "The Second Epistle of Peter," *NJBC* 64.1017–22 (1990).

Olivier, F., "Une correction au texte du Nouveau Testament: II Pierre 3,10," *RPT* 8 (1920): 237–78. Reprinted in *Essais dans le domaine du monde greco-romain antique et dans celui du Nouveau Testament* (Geneva: Librairie Droz, 1963), 129–52.

Otto, J. K. T. von, "Haben Barnabas, Justinus und Irenäus den zweiten Petrusbrief (3,8) benutzt?" *Zeitschrift für wissenschaftliche Theologie* 20 (1877): 525–29.

Overstreet, R. L., "A Study of 2 Peter 3:10–13," *BSac* 137 (1980): 354–71.

Pearson, Birger A., "A Reminiscence of Classical Myth at II Peter 2.4," *GRBS* 10 (1969): 71–80.

———, "James, 1–2 Peter, Jude," *The New Testament and Its Modern Interpreters* (E. J. Epp and G. W. MacRae, eds.; Philadelphia: Fortress Press, 1987), 371–406.

Picirilli, Robert E., *An Exegesis of the Greek Text of Second Peter: Chapters One and Two* (Unpublished dissertation: Bob Jones University, 1964).

———, "The Meaning of 'Epignosis,' " *EvQ* 47 (1975): 85–93.

———, "Allusions to 2 Peter in the Apostolic Fathers," *JSNT* 33 (1988): 57–83.

Plumptre, E. H., *The General Epistles of St. Peter and St. Jude* (Cambridge: Cambridge University Press, 1926).

Quacquarelli, A., "Similitudini sentenze e proverbi in S. Pietro," *San Pietro: Atti della XIX Settimana Biblica* (Associazione Biblica Italiana: Brescia: Paideia, 1967), 425–42.

Rappaport, S., "Der Gerechte Lot. Bemerkung zu II Ptr. 2,7.8." ZNW 29 (1930): 299–304.

Reicke, B., *The Epistles of James, Peter and Jude* (AnB 37. Garden City, NY: Doubleday, 1964).

Richards, W. L., "Textual Criticism on the Greek Text of the Catholic Epistles: A Bibliography," *AUSS* 12 (1974): 103–11.

Riesner, R., "Der zweite Petrus-Brief und die Eschatologie," *Zukunftserwartung in biblischer Sicht. Beiträge zur Eschatologie* (G. Maier, ed.; Giessen: Brunnen, 1984), 124–43.

Rinaldi, G., "La 'sapienza data' a Paolo (2 Petr. 3:15)," *San Pietro: Atti della XIX Settimana Biblica* (Associazione Biblica Italiana. Brescia: Paideia, 1967), 395–441.

Ring, R., *The Meaning and Significance of II Peter 3:15b–17* (Unpublished dissertation: University of Chicago, 1955).

Roberts, J. W., "A Note on the Meaning of II Peter 3:10d." *ResQ* 6 (1962): 32–33.

Robson, E. I., *Studies in the Second Epistle of St. Peter* (Cambridge: Cambridge University Press, 1915).

Ru, G. de, "De Authenticiteit van II Petrus," *NedTTs* 24 (1969/70): 2–12.

Scheidacker, W., "Der erste und der zweite Petrusbrief," *Die Zeichen der Zeit* 27 (1973): 271–78.

Schelkle, K. H., *Die Petrusbriefe, der Judasbrief* (HTKNT 13/2. Freiburg: Herder, 1961).

———, "Spätapostolisches Briefe als frühkatholisches Zeugnis," *Neutestamentliche Aufsatze* (J. Blinzler, O. Kuss, and F. Mussner, eds.; Regensburg: F. Pustet, 1963), 225–32.

Schlatter, A., *Die Briefe des Petrus, Judas, Jakobus, der Brief an die Hebräer* (Stuttgart: Calwer Verlag, 1964).

Schmidt, D., *The Peter Writings: Their Redactors and Their Relationships* (Unpublished dissertation: Northwestern University, 1972).

Schneider, J., *Die Briefe des Jakobus, Petrus, Judas und Johannes: Die katholischen Briefe* (NTD 10. 9th ed. Göttingen: Vandenhoeck and Ruprecht, 1961).

Schrage, W., *Die "katholischen" Briefe: Die Briefe des Jakobus, Petrus, Johannes, und Judas* (NTD 10. 11th ed. Göttingen: Vandenhoeck and Ruprecht, 1973).

Schutter, William L., "1 Peter 4.17, Ezekiel 9.6, and Apocalyptic Hermeneutics," *SBLASP* 1987: 276–84.

Senior, Donald, *1 and 2 Peter* (New Testament Message 20. Wilmington, DE: Michael Glazier, 1980).

———, "The Letters of Jude and 2 Peter," *BibT* 25 (1987): 209–14.

Sibinga, J. S., "Une Citation du Cantique dans la Secunda Petri," *RB* 73 (1966): 107–18.

Sickenberger, J., "Engels-oder Teufelslasterer im Judasbriefe (8–10) und im 2 Petrusbriefe (2,10–12)?" *Mitteilungen der schlesischen Gesellschaft für Volkskunde* 13–14 (1911–12): 621–39.

Sidebottom, E. M., *James, Jude and 2 Peter* (NCB. London: Thomas Nelson, 1967).

Simms, A. E., "Second Peter and the Apocalypse of Peter," *Exp* 5/8 (1898): 460–71.

Skehan, Patrick W., "A Note on 2 Peter 2,13," *Bib* 41 (1960): 69–71.

Smith, Terence V., *Petrine Controversies in Early Christianity: Attitudes Towards Peter in Christian Writings of the First Two Centuries* (Tübingen: J. C. B. Mohr, 1985).

Smitmans, A., "Das Gleichnis vom Dieb," *Wort Gottes in der Zeit* (H. Feld and J. Nolte, eds.; Düsseldorf: Patmos-Verlag, 1973), 43–68.

Snyder, John, *The Promise of His Coming: The Eschatology of 2 Peter* (Unpublished dissertation: University of Basel, 1978).

———, "A 2 Peter Bibliography," *JETS* 22 (1979): 265–67.

Soards, Marion L., "1 Peter, 2 Peter, and Jude as Evidence for a Petrine School," *ANRW* 2.25.5 (1988): 3828–49.

Soden, H. von, *Hebräerbrief, Briefe des Petrus, Jakobus, Judas* (HKNT 3/2. Freiburg: J. C. B. Mohr, 1899).

Spence, R. M., "Private Interpretation," *ExpT* 8 (1896–97): 285–86.

Spicq, Ceslas, *Les Epîtres de Saint Pierre* (Paris: Gabalda, 1966).

Spitta, F., *Der zweite Brief des Petrus und der Brief des Judas* (Halle: Verlag der Buchhandlung des Waisenhauses, 1885).

———, "Die Petrusapokalypse und der zweite Petrusbrief," ZNW 12 (1911): 237–42.

Stein, Robert H., "Is the Transfiguration (Mark 9:2–8) a Misplaced Resurrection-Account?" *JBL* 95 (1976): 79–95.

Talbert, C. H., "II Peter and the Delay of the Parousia," VC 20 (1966): 137–45.

Testa, P. E., "La distruzione del mondo per il fuoco nella 2 ep. di Pietro 3:7, 10, 13," *RivB* 10 (1962): 252–81.

Thiede, Carsten P., "A Pagan Reader of 2 Peter: Cosmic Conflagration in 2 Peter 3 and the *Octavius* of Minucius Felix," *JSNT* 26 (1986): 79–96.

Vögtle, Anton, "Die Parousie- und Gerichtsapologetik 2 P 3," *Das Neue Testament und die Zukunft des Kosmos* (Düsseldorf: Patmos-Verlag, 1970), 121–42.

———, "Die Schriftwerdung der apostolischen Paradosis nach 2 Petr. 1,12–15," *Neues Testament und Geschichte* (H. Baltensweiler and B. Reicke, eds.; Zürich: Theologischer Verlag, 1972), 297–305.

Wand, J. W. C., *The General Epistles of St. Peter and St. Jude* (London: Methuen, 1934).

Watson, Duane F., *Invention, Arrangement, and Style: Rhetorical Criticism of Jude and 2 Peter* (SBLDS 104. Atlanta: Scholars Press, 1988).

Wenham, D., "Being 'Found' on the Last Day: New Light on 2 Peter 3.10 and 2 Corinthians 5.3," *NTS* 33 (1989): 477–79.

Werdermann, Hermann, *Die Irrlehrer des Judas- und 2 Petrusbriefes* (Gütersloh: C. Bertelsmann, 1913).

Wifstrand, A., "Stylistic Problems in the Epistles of James and Peter," *ST* 1 (1948): 170–82.

Wilson, W. E., "*Heurethesetai* in 2 Pet. iii.10," *ExpT* 32 (1920–21): 44–45.

Windisch, Hans, *Die katholischen Briefe* (HNT 15. 3d ed. Tübingen: J. C. B. Mohr, 1951).

Witherington, Ben, "A Petrine Source in 2 Peter," *SBLASP* 1985: 187–92.

Wolters, A., " 'Partners of the Deity': A Covenantal Reading of 2 Peter 1:4," *CTJ* 25 (1990): 28–44.

———, "Worldview and Textual Criticism in 2 Peter 3:10," *WTJ* 49 (1987): 405–13.

Zmijewski, J., "Apostolische Paradosis und Pseudepigraphie im Neuen Testament: 'Durch Erinnerung wachhalten' (2 Petr 1, 13; 3,1)," *BZ* 23 (1979): 161–71.

Index of Biblical Texts

♦

HEBREW BIBLE AND APOCRYPHA

OLD TESTAMENT APOCRYPHA

Sirach

1 Maccabees

2 Maccabees

3 Maccabees

4 Maccabees

NEW TESTAMENT

Matthew

Ephesians

Philippians

Colossians

1 Thessalonians

INDEX OF ANCIENT AUTHORS AND WORKS

◆

Index of Topics

◆